Interdisciplinary Research on Close Relationships

Interdisciplinary Research on Close Relationships

The Case for Integration

Edited by

Lorne Campbell and Timothy J. Loving

American Psychological Association • Washington, DC

Published by
American Psychological Association
750 First Street, NE
Washington, DC 20002
www.apa.org

To order
APA Order Department
P.O. Box 92984
Washington, DC 20090-2984
Tel: (800) 374-2721; Direct: (202) 336-5510
Fax: (202) 336-5502; TDD/TTY: (202) 336-6123
Online: www.apa.org/pubs/books
E-mail: order@apa.org

In the U.K., Europe, Africa, and the Middle East, copies may be ordered from
American Psychological Association
3 Henrietta Street
Covent Garden, London
WC2E 8LU England

Typeset in Goudy by Circle Graphics, Inc., Columbia, MD

Printer: Edwards Brothers, Inc., Ann Arbor, MI
Cover Designer: Mercury Publishing Services, Rockville, MD

The opinions and statements published are the responsibility of the authors, and such opinions and statements do not necessarily represent the policies of the American Psychological Association.

Library of Congress Cataloging-in-Publication Data

Interdisciplinary research on close relationships : the case for integration / edited by Lorne Campbell and Timothy J. Loving.
     p. cm.
  Includes index.
  ISBN-13: 978-1-4338-1072-5
  ISBN-10: 1-4338-1072-7
  1. Interpersonal relations. 2. Social psychology—Research. I. Campbell, Lorne, 1973-
II. Loving, Timothy J.
  BF636.I57 2012
  155.9'2—dc23

                         2011033529

British Library Cataloguing-in-Publication Data

A CIP record is available from the British Library.

Printed in the United States of America
First Edition

DOI: 10.1037/13486-000

CONTENTS

CONTRIBUTORS

Katharine Ann Buck, PhD, Department of Human Development and Family Sciences, The University of Texas at Austin

Lorne Campbell, PhD, Department of Psychology, University of Western Ontario, London, Ontario, Canada

W. Andrew Collins, PhD, Institute of Child Development, University of Minnesota, Minneapolis

Lisa M. Diamond, PhD, Department of Psychology, University of Utah, Salt Lake City

Theodore Dix, PhD, Department of Human Development and Family Sciences, The University of Texas at Austin

Robert E. Emery, PhD, Psychology Department, University of Virginia, Charlottesville

Christopher P. Fagundes, PhD, Department of Psychology, University of Utah, Salt Lake City

Steven W. Gangestad, PhD, Department of Psychology, University of New Mexico, Albuquerque

Joanna Herres, PhD, Department of Psychology, University of Delaware, Newark

Nancy E. Hill, PhD, Graduate School of Education, Harvard University, Cambridge, MA

Erin Horn, PhD, Psychology Department, University of Virginia, Charlottesville

Aletha C. Huston, PhD, Department of Human Development and Family Sciences, The University of Texas at Austin

Ted L. Huston, PhD, Department of Human Development and Family Sciences, The University of Texas at Austin

Roger Kobak, PhD, Department of Psychology, University of Delaware, Newark

Timothy J. Loving, PhD, Department of Human Development and Family Sciences, The University of Texas at Austin

Lisa A. Neff, PhD, Department of Human Development and Family Sciences, The University of Texas at Austin

Harry T. Reis, PhD, Department of Clinical and Social Sciences in Psychology, University of Rochester, Rochester, NY

Jessica E. Salvatore, PhD, Institute of Child Development, University of Minnesota, Minneapolis

Huyn Joo Shim, PhD, Psychology Department, University of Virginia, Charlottesville

Jeffry A. Simpson, PhD, Department of Psychology, University of Minnesota, Minneapolis

Catherine Surra, PhD, Director, Behavioral Sciences and Education, Penn State Harrisburg, Middletown, PA

PREFACE

In September 2008, the first editor of this volume, Lorne Campbell, was on sabbatical from the Department of Psychology at the University of Western Ontario and was fortunate to be supported by a Donald D. Harrington Faculty Fellowship at the University of Texas at Austin that enabled him to spend a year in the Department of Human Development and Family Sciences (HDFS). The HDFS department at Texas is distinctive in that scholars representing different disciplines and using myriad methodological approaches are housed in the same department. The common thread among these scholars is a focus on close relationships. Of course, close relationships come in many forms, including parent–child, friendship, extended family networks, social networks, and romantic relationships (to name a few). Shortly after Campbell settled into his new office, his conversations with his new colleagues—including the second editor of this volume, Timothy J. Loving—began to reflect the department's diversity in terms of the types of relationships under study (both in the HDFS and in the field of relationship science more generally), the disciplines involved in studying these relationships, and the methodologies used both within and across disciplines.

These discussions were very illuminating and highlighted for us the challenges faced by the field of relationship science as well as the opportunities afforded when a given broad topic is approached from multiple viewpoints. In terms of the former, one major challenge is directly related to the growth of the field of relationship science: Namely, as the field continues to grow, it has become increasingly difficult for scholars who are scattered across multiple disciplines and study different types of close relationships to conduct truly integrative and interdisciplinary research. This challenge is emphasized in Chapters 1, 11, and 12 of this volume. At the same time, however, we felt strongly that an excellent opportunity comes with this challenge. Relationship scholars, particularly younger scholars looking to find a research niche, can benefit greatly by filling in the gaps exposed by the increasing divergence between disciplines. The field as a whole, of course, will benefit tremendously as well.

Motivated by our discussions, we collectively decided to utilize the resources offered by the Harrington Fellowship program, as well as the University of Texas at Austin's School of Human Ecology, the HDFS, and Margaret Dunlap Thompson Excellence Endowment in Child and Family Studies to host a symposium that would bring together the diverse expertise that exists in our field. The primary objective of this symposium was to provide a comprehensive, interdisciplinary perspective on close relationship processes. We invited the following six scholars, who study different types of relationships and relationship processes using varied methodological approaches, to speak at the Texas Symposium on Close Relationships: Robert E. Emery, Steven W. Gangestad, Nancy E. Hill, Roger Kobak, Harry T. Reis, and Jeffry A. Simpson. The symposium, hosted at the University of Texas at Austin on May 8–9, 2009, drew a large number of attendees and generated a lively discussion of ideas. Given the success of the symposium, we believed that an edited volume that shared the same goal of the symposium was timely for the field of relationship science. We were fortunate to be able to work with the American Psychological Association (APA) to develop and publish such an edited volume. With the support and guidance of APA, we invited additional scholars to contribute chapters to this edited volume and are thankful that they accepted our invitation. The topic area of each chapter, and how the chapters contribute to the goal of the volume, are discussed in Chapter 1.

It is our hope that this volume cogently presents the case that the field of relationship science will benefit tremendously if and when it takes a more concerted effort to integrate findings and ideas across disciplines. Additionally, we believe that the chapters in this volume demonstrate the overall diversity of the field of relationship science and highlight how interdisciplinary approaches offer novel insights into old and new problems alike.

Interdisciplinary
Research on
Close
Relationships

1

RESEARCH ON CLOSE RELATIONSHIPS: CALL FOR AN INTERDISCIPLINARY INTEGRATION

LORNE CAMPBELL AND CATHERINE SURRA

What is a close relationship? How do we know when people are in a close relationship? On the surface, these questions may seem simple. In reality, however, defining a close relationship is almost like trying to catch a fish with your bare hands—the concept of a close relationship is slippery, and just when you think you have a firm grip, it shoots out of your hands. Part of the difficulty, as observed by Ellen Berscheid (1999), is that relationships are akin to great forces of nature such as gravity, electricity, and the four winds; they are powerful, but ultimately invisible. We do not see the wind, but we do see the blades of the windmill continually spinning to produce electricity. Similarly, we do not see a close relationship when we observe two individuals standing together, but we are able to see how these individuals influence each other over time. Echoing this sentiment, a well-established definition of a close relationship is eloquent in its simplicity: "The close relationship is one of strong, frequent, and diverse interdependence that lasts over a considerable period of time" (Kelley et al., 1983, p. 38). The quintessential feature of a close relationship, therefore, is that the thoughts, feelings, and behaviors of at least two people across time are causally connected.

This straightforward definition easily lends itself to relationships formed at all stages of life. The first important relationship common to all human infants is the one with their caregivers, as babies are completely dependent on them for their survival for an extended period of time. Forming an emotional bond with caregivers is therefore essential for survival, and the quality of the relationship between infant and caregiver has a profound effect on all subsequent close relationships the infant will form over his or her life (Bowlby, 1969, 1973, 1980; Mikulincer & Shaver, 2007; see also Chapters 3, 6, and 7, this volume). As children age, they also develop friendships with nonfamilial peers, and they form close emotional bonds with some friends that have important implications for future development (see Chapter 6). And generally beginning in adolescence, individuals develop romantic attractions (see Chapter 9) and enter into romantic relationships. Romantic relationships play an important role throughout most of our lives (see Chapters 2, 4, 7, and 8), and interestingly, over 90% of people in the world will marry at least once before they die (Buss, 1985). Marital unions, however, do not always last forever, and relationship dissolution can have pernicious effects on spouses as well as children (see Chapter 10). Many other meaningful relationships play a central role in our lives as well, with the result being that close relationship scholars have a lot of ground to cover in trying to understand relationship processes in many different types of relationships across the life span.

It has been suggested that the fundamental motivation for humans to enter into and maintain close relationships is a universal and intense need to belong—to feel connected to others in enduring relationships (Baumeister & Leary, 1995; Kirkpatrick & Ellis, 2001). Indeed, when asked what factors make life most meaningful, the majority of people first mention satisfying close relationships, particularly their romantic relationships (Berscheid, 1985). In addition to greater life satisfaction, individuals who have more positive close relationships also experience more positive psychological and physical well-being (e.g., Clark & Lemay, 2010; Kiecolt-Glaser & Newton, 2001; Suls & Wallston, 2003). The existence of significant close relationships across the life span, and the quality of these relationships, are arguably the most important factors for understanding individuals' health and happiness throughout their lives (see Chapter 4). The study of close relationship processes is therefore essential in order to identify sources of mental and physical well-being as well as to inform micro- and macrolevel interventions designed to improve mental and physical health.

It is somewhat surprising, then, that our understanding of close relationships up until around the 1960s was largely informed by poets, fiction writers, and musicians rather than academic scholars. This began to change in the 1960s and 1970s as social scientists began to seriously investigate close relationship processes, and a strong theoretical approach to the study of close relationships was called for by Harold Kelley and his colleagues a relatively short time ago in 1983. The field of relationship science is therefore relatively young, but it has made great gains as a field of scientific study, with two journals dedicated solely to the study of close relationships (the *Journal of Social and Personal Relationships* began in 1984 and *Personal Relationships* began in 1994) and relationship research appearing routinely in numerous well-respected, peer-reviewed academic journals.

Reflecting on the rise of research on close relationship processes and the importance of close relationships in all facets of human life, Berscheid (1999) proposed that relationship science has the potential to unite scholars across disciplines, to help integrate the many subdisciplines addressing close relationships, and to inform the development of governmental policy addressing issues of great importance to families. These sentiments were recently echoed by Reis (2007; see also Chapter 2, this volume), who further suggested that one important way to achieve these goals is to develop central organizing themes for the diverse phenomena relationship scientists study (see also Kruglanski, 2006). Whereas Berscheid viewed the field of relationship science as greening, 8 years later Reis suggested that relationship science was beginning to ripen. Against this backdrop, the future for relationship science looks very bright indeed.

At present, however, relationship science is at a crossroads. One implication of the existence, and importance, of the different types of close relationships that humans form across the life span is that close relationships are investigated across many diverse disciplines. For example, psychologists of many stripes (e.g., social, clinical, cognitive, developmental, industrial/organizational, counseling), sociologists, anthropologists, communication scholars, economists, marital and family therapists, and health scientists (e.g., doctors, nurses, pharmacologists) conduct research on close relationship processes. And this list is not exhaustive. The field of relationship science is also diverse regarding the types of investigative methods used within each of these disciplines (e.g., interviews, case studies, survey samples, experiments, psychophysiological approaches, longitudinal designs). Such diversity should allow for a more detailed understanding of close relationship processes, but for many reasons researchers from different disciplines, and those who focus on different levels of explanation, rarely have the opportunity to integrate their findings to provide a deeper, holistic model of close relationship functioning (see Chapter 11 for a more thorough discussion of the difficulties inherent in interdisciplinary research). For relationship science to realize its full potential, we argue that its expansion into numerous disciplines needs to be coupled with the development of strong and meaningful interdisciplinary connections. Without these connections, the field of relationship science has the potential to fragment into a number of smaller research endeavors that do not share a common theoretical or empirical nomenclature, severely limiting the cross-fertilization of ideas needed to address important problems (see Chapter 11).

The call for relationship science to evolve from a multidisciplinary enterprise to a truly interdisciplinary one is not new (see Chapter 12), and it follows a long history of similar suggestions for the integration of knowledge in theory and in practice in a variety of domains. This historical debate is germane to the integration of relationship science as it highlights the benefits of interdisciplinary integration and the perils of increased specialization, particularly when seemingly insurmountable barriers between these specialties exist. We briefly summarize this ongoing debate, and we then attempt to demonstrate the benefits of adopting an interdisciplinary approach for understanding one well-studied sphere of close relationship research: mate attraction and selection.

DIFFERENT CULTURES: THE BENEFITS OF INTERDISCIPLINARY PERSPECTIVES

In an essay published in the obscure Romanian journal *Revista de Psihologie* in 1938, Gordon Allport asked if the study of personality was a problem for the sciences or the arts (see also Allport, 1942). At that time, the study of personality under the aegis of psychological theory was in its infancy, whereas the development of character in literature had a long and illustrious history (as it still does). For example, who can forget J. D. Salinger's Holden Caulfield in *The Catcher in the Rye*, Margaret Mitchell's Scarlet O'Hara in *Gone With the Wind*, or William Shakespeare's star-crossed lovers, Romeo and Juliet? Authors in literature and the humanities devote a lot of time and ink to developing complex characters forced to make important behavioral decisions across many contexts, whereas in 1938 psychologists were primarily concerned with correlating scores assessed at one sitting on various scales tapping different facets of personality across large samples of study participants. In essence, the literary authors were the ones concerned with the study of the person and the complexities of personality, whereas the psychologists were concerned with impersonal correlations between abstract constructs.

Perhaps unsurprisingly, Allport concluded that both psychologists and authors should continue with the study of personality but that each discipline could learn from the other. He recommended that the field of personality psychology look to literature to learn about the nature of personality traits or inner dispositions that can be identified and defined. Traits imply consistency of behavior and, thus, predictability. When Rhett Butler said to Scarlet O'Hara, "Frankly, my dear, I don't give a damn," in response to her pleas not to leave her, it was completely consistent with his brash and decisive personality. Additionally, Allport advised personality psychologists to heed the complexity in the style and the coherence of the personalities authors create, which often develop through a process of self-confrontation. Last, literary authors focus on individuals over time and across contexts, not simply on generalities observed in large samples at one period of time, as in the research on personality being published by psychologists.

Overall, Allport advised that the psychological investigation of personality should move away from making broad generalizations about the nonexistent "average" human mind. He suggested that an interdisciplinary study of personality, with the scientists paying close attention to the work of artists, would lead to the development of a more powerful nomological network of laws defining human personality. The strengths psychologists brought to the study of personality were its disciplined scientific character (e.g., the scientific method and the need for agreement of results, not ideas) and the reality that scientists must heed facts and are expected to secure facts from controlled and verifiable sources. Allport believed that the study of personality could flourish by adopting an interdisciplinary perspective, and indeed it has. Allport's argument is not limited, of course, to the study of personality. Instead, his message was that any discipline that fails to take into account the developments in other fields focusing on the same or similar topics will simply not be able to generate a thorough understanding of the subject matter under study.

A few years later, C. P. Snow made an argument very similar to that of Allport, but his focus was much broader in scope. In the Rede lecture of 1959, Snow shared his views that the intellectual life of Western society was represented by two polar opposite groups, or cultures. On the one hand were literary intellectuals, or the arts and humanities, and on the other were the scientists. In between these two groups existed

> a gulf of mutual incomprehension—sometimes (particularly among the young) hostility and dislike, but most of all lack of understanding. They have a curious distorted image of each other. Their attitudes are so different that, even on the level of emotion, they can't find much common ground. (Snow, 1998, p. 4)

After attending several international conferences addressing close relationship processes this past decade, we (the authors) have also observed, at times, some "mutual incomprehension" between scholars of different disciplines.

Snow (1998) noted that a major problem with the lack of communication between these two cultures was that significant policy decisions that affected the lives of millions of people were being made by one group (the literary intellectuals) with minimal, or no, reference to the empirical research of the other (the scientists). Examples germane to relationship science include the fact that governments often make public policy on issues relating to marriage (e.g., who should be allowed to marry, incentives for enrolling in premarital courses), family policy (e.g., adoption, poverty and homelessness, violence prevention), cohabitation (e.g., common-law marriage, division of property following nonmarital dissolution), and marital dissolution (how divorce can be prevented, and how the effects of divorce on children can be minimized; see Chapter 10). According to Berscheid (1999), "It is not only the promise but the obligation of relationship science to inform such debates" (p. 263). An equally important limitation of the divide between the two cultures is that creative ideas often develop at the intersection of disciplines, and a lack of interdisciplinary explorations jeopardizes innovation.

Kagan (2009) expanded Snow's two cultures to three cultures: natural scientists, social scientists, and humanists. At the heart of Kagan's argument is that each culture has different vocabularies, describing a target from unique angles. Translation of theoretical meaning and conclusions is therefore not always straightforward (see also Chapter 12). For example, consider what it means to say that someone has a "big heart." A natural scientist may be suggesting that the person has a medical problem (e.g., cardiomegaly, or an enlarged heart) that requires immediate intervention (e.g., medication to reduce high blood pressure). A social scientist may be describing a person with a secure attachment orientation who is comfortable providing support and assistance to a romantic partner. A humanist, however, may be describing a heightened state of morality, leading people to engage in humanitarian efforts in troubled regions of the world. Unique perspectives developed within each culture generate valuable yet insufficient information for the understanding of the phenomena under study. The field of relationship science is represented by scholars in the broad disciplinary categories identified by Kagan, and as we highlight later in our discussion on mate selection processes, there are often unique vocabularies within different disciplines to describe similar phenomena. It is the integration of these three cultures that promises to exponentially enhance our understanding of interpersonal behavior.

Echoing the arguments of Snow and Kagan, Slingerland (2008) discussed the deep divide that currently exists between the sciences and the humanities. The humanities, according to Slingerland, believe in a mind–body dualism—that understanding the essence of human existence is not accessible via the natural sciences. For example, to understand how humans think of the world around them, it is not necessary to consider the role of the eye, the ear, or the brain in perception. Similarly, when trying to comprehend the love a mother feels for her newborn baby, it is not necessary to consider the role of oxytocin or reference reproductive success. Slingerland argued that ignoring human biology or the evolutionary journey responsible for the development of modern human biology is a serious mistake in our endeavour to more fully understand human existence, and he believes that as a field the humanities will eventually cease to be relevant if it continues to adhere to a mind–body dualism. According to Slingerland, an interdisciplinary approach not only results in a more complete understanding of human behavior but also provides room for traditional disciplines to grow and evolve. The field of relationship science should heed this advice and make efforts to integrate across disciplines as it continues to expand into more and more (potentially isolated) specialties.

Using arguments similar to those presented above, E. O. Wilson (1998) argued that the boundaries between scientific specialties need to disappear; that is, he argued for *consilience*, or the unity of knowledge. As more specialities have appeared, more boundaries have appeared, and relatively less communication between the specialities has resulted. These boundaries are not abstract lines drawn between groups of scientists; they are very real indeed. The natural sciences, social sciences, and humanities are often physically separated on university campuses. Even within the social sciences, for example, there are barriers that effectively limit the ability of scholars from different departments to come into physical contact and discuss mutual interests. Most often these specialities are located in separate buildings, sometimes at opposite ends of campus. Structurally, the faculties are often organized each with its own department, and departments are often located in different sections of a building (if they actually share a building). Specialities also often have their own professional societies, host their own conferences, and have different funding agencies with review panels consisting of members from a particular speciality. A number of different search engines for locating research also exist (e.g., Google Scholar, PsycINFO, PubMed, Science Citation Index, to name a few; see also Chapter 12), and in many instances they do not access the same corpus of publications. In much the same way that geographic isolation ultimately leads to the evolution of unique physiological traits in members of the same species, the isolation of specialties also leads to the evolution of unique vocabularies, methods, and theories across disciplines (see Chapter 11). According to Wilson, increased specialization without a concurrent interdisciplinary integration will ultimately limit the growth of scientific knowledge (see Giacomini, 2004; Hall et al., 2006).

A common theme in the work of Allport, Snow, Kagan, Slingerland, and Wilson is that the growth of scientific knowledge in any field of study is curbed when boundaries between disciplines investigating similar phenomena are allowed to crystallize and thus stifle interdisciplinary research endeavors. This argument is particularly relevant for the field of relationship science given that close relationship processes are the focus of study across a diverse array of disciplines, making it difficult to traverse the increasing number of barriers that exist between disciplines. If efforts are not made to break down the barriers between disciplines in the study of relationship processes, the growth of specialties will prosper, whereas the field of relationships as a whole will contract.

In the next section, we attempt to illustrate how adopting an interdisciplinary approach to the study of close relationships facilitates understanding them and generates novel research hypotheses. Specifically, we focus on mate selection in heterosexual relationships, one of the most widely studied topics in the field of relationship science. We draw from the literature of three different disciplines that presently study mate selection and highlight the unique perspective of each. Our goal is to provide one concrete example of the benefits that can accrue from breaking down the barriers between different disciplines that address similar topics.

MATE SELECTION: AN INTERDISCIPLINARY APPROACH

The description and explanation of contemporary patterns of mate selection and marital behavior is arguably the greatest challenge confronting relationship scholars. What was once a fairly orderly and predictable pathway, from casual dating to serious dating, engagement, and marriage, has become more unpredictable. This unpredictability, however, varies by social class, race, and ethnicity. Whether marriage occurs at all, for example, is increasingly varied by subpopulation. For example, the rate of marriage for Black people is considerably lower than the rate for White people (Brown, 2000), and whether cohabitation substitutes for marriage in the short or long term also varies greatly by subpopulation.

Social scientists from different disciplines have responded in unique ways to the study of fragmented mate selection behaviors. For instance, sociologists have responded with an unprecedented focus on explaining why mate selection behaviors are different in different subpopulations. Sociologists therefore concentrate on questions that involve changes in relationship status, such as the change from cohabitation to marriage, dating to cohabitation, or cohabitation to dissolution and how these changes vary by social class, race, and ethnicity. Social psychologists and communication scholars, in contrast, typically do not address differences across subpopulations but instead search for properties that are universal in close relationships. For example, communication scholars have emphasized the role of messages that are hurtful or deceptive in different types of relationships, whereas social psychologists have focused on such constructs as positive regard or responsiveness (see Chapter 2) in romantic heterosexual and other relationships.

Support for these conclusions about how different disciplines have responded to the way mate selection is studied comes from an investigation examining trends in articles published in eight major journals from 1990–2001 (Surra, Boettcher-Burke, Cottle, West, & Gray, 2007; Surra, Gray, Boettcher, Cottle, & West, 2006). The authors sampled 791 empirical studies on dating and mate selection that were published in 577 articles. Analyses showed that sociology journals published the highest percentage of articles on mate choice (70%), whereas communication journals published 80% of their papers on universal relationship properties. Psychology and interdisciplinary journals published about 43% of their papers on relationship properties. In addition, researchers, primarily sociologists, who studied mate choice (homogamy, changes in status, marital timing, cohabitation, the courtship continuum) were more likely to report and preserve in statistical analyses distinctions among individuals or relationships that held different statuses, such as daters, marrieds, or cohabitants. Those who studied universal properties were more likely to collapse different statuses (e.g., daters with marrieds) or to not report status when describing their samples. Over time, research on universal properties became more common and research on mate selection less common.

These results suggest that researchers from the different disciplines are studying mate selection from unique vantage points and, more important, that the separation among these disciplines is increasing over time. As we have argued up to this point, such a trend toward monodisciplinarity and away from interdisciplinarity limits scholars' ability to fully understand and explain mate selection behaviors. In the next section, we examine one subpopulation, the economically disadvantaged in the United States, to show how a more interdisciplinary approach would benefit scholars' ability to explain current trends in mate selection for this group.

Changes in Mate Selection Among the Economically Disadvantaged

Three interconnected trends characterize the mate selection behaviors of the poor and near poor: a movement away from marriage, a preference for cohabitation, and childbearing outside of marriage (see Surra & Boelter, in press, for a more thorough review). Research has shown consistently declining rates of marriage and lower marriage rates among those who live in unfavorable economic conditions. In one study, for example, women's own poverty decreased their likelihood of marriage within a given year such that women who were poor were about 72% as likely to wed as were women who were not poor (McLaughlin & Lichter, 1997). In addition, men's having no income reduced the likelihood of marriage, particularly in younger cohorts (Sweeney, 2002). The Fragile Families study investigated a nationally representative sample of unmarried couples who were parents in 20 U.S. cities; 73% of mothers and 56% of fathers in the study were poor or near poor (Edin, Kefalas, & Reed, 2004). For mothers who were dating their partners at the time of the child's birth, the odds of marrying over a 1-year period were 10 times less if they had no earnings than the odds for mothers who earned over $25,000 (Osborne, 2005). Similar results have been found for poor men.

The lower rates of union formation among the economically disadvantaged cannot be attributed to a weaker desire for marriage or a lesser value placed on marriage. Qualitative research on poor women has shown that they have a high regard for marriage but often believe they cannot meet standards for economic stability or relational quality (Edin & Kefalas, 2005). Although most respondents in the Fragile Families study were optimistic about marriage (Gibson-Davis, Edin, & McLanahan, 2005), financial considerations and a lack of financial stability were cited as considerations for nonmarriage in 75% of the cases. Such factors as consistently making ends meet, using money wisely, accumulating savings, and paying for a wedding figured into decisions about marriage.

The economically disadvantaged are also more likely to experience non-marital childbearing (Edin & Kefalas, 2005; Ellwood & Jencks, 2002). An analysis of survey data from the U.S. Department of Labor of about 10,000 men and women showed that 78% of women who were high school dropouts had a birth by age 25, whereas the comparable figure for those who graduated from college was 20% (Ellwood, Wilde, & Batchelder, 2009). By age 40, the figures were 86% and 74%, respectively. Although marriage may seem out of reach for those with fewer economic resources, childbearing is not (Gibson-Davis et al., 2005). Poor or near-poor women see little reason to delay having children because of the high value they place on children and confidence in their ability to mother well. Marriage seems more out of reach than childbearing because of the difficulty finding men who are suitable for marriage, beliefs about economic supports that should be in place for marriage to occur (e.g., home ownership), and high ideals for what constitutes a good marriage partner and a good marriage.

The poor and near poor are also much more likely to cohabit than they are to wed. The increase in cohabitation from 1987 to 1995 was dominated by increases among the less educated (Bumpass & Lu, 2001). By 1995, the proportion of women who had ever cohabited was 59% of high school dropouts and 37% of college graduates. Cohabitation may be an adaptive response to poor and uncertain employment prospects. Studies of employment instability, measured by such variables as number of different jobs held, number of months employed, and less than full-time, full-year employment have indicated that it is associated with greater movement into cohabitation and lesser movement into marriage (Clarkberg, 1999; Oppenheimer, 2003). Transitions out of cohabitation via marriage were also less common for the poor and near poor even if they were parents. Among unmarried parents who were cohabiting, the likelihood of marriage from the time the child was born to the time the child was 3 years old declined by 37% if they fell below the poverty threshold (Gibson-Davis, 2009). Poor women who were mothers saw cohabitation as a short-term transition to marriage that placed fewer demands on relational and economic standards they believed should be in place for marriage to occur (Edin & Kefalas, 2005; Edin et al., 2004).

Economic Explanations for Changes in Mate Selection Among the Economically Disadvantaged

Sociological research has focused on explaining the mate selection behaviors of the poor and near poor in terms of their economic characteristics and experiences. A preferred theory is Becker's (1991) gender specialization or gains-to-marriage theory. The central tenet of the theory is that the benefits of marrying are greater when the division of labor is specialized such that the female partner works at home while the male partner works outside the home. Gender specialization enables spouses to distribute energies in the most productive way, particularly given the higher wages available to men in the labor market. Even if specialization does not occur along gender lines, Becker maintained that economic and other benefits are greater if one partner concentrates on household work and the other on market labor.

A competing theory focuses on women's economic independence. Recent economic changes, particularly the decline in manufacturing jobs for men and the increase in service sector jobs for women, have altered the way in which men and women view their marriage market opportunities, and these changes have had an especially hard impact on the poor (Cherlin, 2005). The basic tenet of this theory is that opportunities for women to earn wages have reduced the gains of marriage for women and their reliance on men in the marriage bargain, thereby eroding the influence of the traditional marital exchange in mate selection decisions (e.g., Gaughan, 2002; Oppenheimer, 1997; Xie, Raymo, Goyette, & Thornton, 2003). Women now have more freedom in their mate choice decisions; they may delay marriage, reject it altogether, or replace it permanently or temporarily with cohabitation. The hypothesis derived from this theory is that women's economic independence will have negative effects on marriage.

Results from the Fragile Families study and other national surveys generally support gender specialization theory as it pertains to marriage decisions and the stability of dating relationships. For unmarried parents who were dating at the start of the study, the odds of breaking up increased significantly when the male partner's earnings were in the lowest income category (between $10,000 and $24,999), and the odds of marriage doubled if men's earnings were $25,000 or more (Carlson, McLanahan, & England, 2004). Hourly wages also had a positive effect on the stability of dating relationships, and marriage was less likely for Black and White men who had no earnings and for White men who were high school dropouts (Sweeney, 2002).

Changes in economic prospects are linked to the likelihood of marriage in ways that gender specialization theory would predict. Among all unmarried parents, increases in fathers' earnings from the time the child was born to the time the child reached 3 years of age predicted increases in the likelihood of marriage, whereas changes in mothers' earnings had no effect on marriage (Gibson-Davis, 2009). For cohabiting couples who became poor over the 3-year study period, the odds of marriage declined by 37%. Oppenheimer (2003) found that employment instability, measured as a change from full-time, full-year employment to less than full-time, full-year employment, was associated with a decline in marriage. White men whose employment situation deteriorated were 139% more likely to cohabit, and Black men were 78% more likely to cohabit.

Studies of the characteristics of local marriage markets also sometimes support the idea that the availability of men with good economic prospects affects marriage decisions. Within local marriage markets, the proportion of men who were unemployed predicted declines in marriage (Lichter, LeClere, & McGlaughlin, 1991), and the availability of men with earnings above the poverty level increased the likelihood of marrying for the first time for poor and nonpoor women alike (McLaughlin & Lichter, 1997).

Among the poor and near poor, the theory of women's economic independence has received inconsistent support, depending on whether the theory is tested at the individual level or the marriage-market level. Market-level measures of female employment, earnings, and public assistance predicted declines in proportions of those currently married (Lichter et al., 1991), and among poor African Americans in metropolitan marriage markets, the higher was the average economic status of women and the average level of public aid, the lower was the prevalence of marriage (Fossett & Kiecolt, 1993). When individual-level characteristics were measured, findings usually contradicted the theory of women's economic independence. In a number of studies, all types of unions—marriages, cohabitation, and dating—were more likely to form and be maintained when women were better off economically with respect to employment, time in the labor force, income, or education (Carlson et al., 2004; Franklin, Smith, & McMiller, 1995; Lichter & Qian, 2008; McLaughlin & Lichter, 1997).

Considering Economics and Relationships Together to Explain Mate Selection Among the Disadvantaged

Few studies in the sociological tradition have juxtaposed economic characteristics with qualities of relationships in order to explain union formation among the disadvantaged. Those studies that have, however, have shown the powerful ways in which qualities of relationships alter the influence of economic conditions on mate selection. Investigations that relied on data from the Fragile Families study, for example, have shown that relational quality mediated the connection between economic characteristics and marriage. In one case, the odds of marriage more than doubled when men earned more than

$25,000, but this effect was nonsignificant once attitudinal and relational quality variables were considered (Carlson et al., 2004). The effects of other economic variables, such as fathers' education, poverty threshold, and income-to-needs ratio, on the likelihood of marriage were reduced when individuals' estimates of the chance of marriage were included in models (Gibson-Davis, 2009; Waller & McLanahan, 2005).

The fact that the negative impact of economic hardship on relationships is ameliorated when relationships are of good quality was well established during the 1990s in a program of research by Rand Conger and his colleagues. In one study, they assessed economic hardship in rural farm families (Conger et al., 1990). Results showed that the income-to-needs ratio, unstable work, and economic pressure increased the subjective experience of economic strain. However, the effects of husbands' economic strain on wives' marital quality were mediated by husbands' expressions of warmth and hostility during interactions. Husbands' hostility had both direct effects on wives' perceptions of marital instability and indirect effects on wives' perceptions of marital instability through wives' marital quality. Similar findings, though less strong, were obtained for wives. Results from another study showed that, for both husbands and wives, conflict between work and family increased psychological distress and that psychological distress influenced marital quality and stability directly and indirectly through its impact on the warmth and hostility of marital interactions (Matthews, Conger, & Wickrama, 1996).

Results from the few studies that have examined relational and economic characteristics in tandem have underscored the additional explanatory power that comes from pairing the interpersonal with the economic. In the next section, we explore more deeply how drawing simultaneously from social psychology, interpersonal communication, and sociology might further enrich the explanatory power of economic approaches. We use the concept of relational uncertainty—a construct studied in different ways in all three disciplines—to illustrate the potential added value of an interdisciplinary approach.

Relational Uncertainty and Mate Selection Among the Economically Disadvantaged

Both qualitative and quantitative research in the sociological tradition suggest that the hesitancy to wed among the poor goes beyond economic factors. Hesitation to wed among disadvantaged mothers was fueled by doubts about the partner's readiness for marriage, questions about the quality of the relationship, and fears of divorce (Waller, 2002). However, another study of women in low-income neighborhoods found no support for the idea that they fear divorce (Cherlin, Cross-Barnet, Burton, & Garrett-Peters, 2008). About 75% of the women disagreed with statements such as "Getting divorced is embarrassing for a woman" and "It's best to avoid marriage because is usually doesn't work out." The authors concluded that, instead of a generalized fear of divorce, what may be driving hesitancy about marriage is "apprehension about the difficulty of successfully managing an intimate relationship" (Cherlin et al., 2008, p. 932). From the viewpoint of social psychology and interpersonal communication, what may have appeared to be a generalized fear of divorce may be specific to doubts about whether a particular relationship should lead to marriage.

Distrust of the opposite sex may also fuel a lack of confidence in relationships in this subpopulation. In qualitative research, unmarried poor mothers in three cities discussed two sources of distrust of the opposite sex: fears that they would lose control over household decisions and activities if they were to wed and doubts that men would remain faithful (Edin, 2000). Quantitative assessments of gender distrust (e.g., beliefs about whether the opposite sex could be trusted to be faithful and not to take advantage of the other) have shown that a one-unit increase in gender distrust decreased the odds of marriage 43% and the odds of cohabitation 13% over a 1-year period (Carlson et al., 2004). Unmarried parents reported lower estimates of the chance of marriage when both partners distrusted the opposite gender and when mothers distrusted more than fathers (Waller & McLanahan, 2005).

Thus, sociological studies have uncovered evidence suggesting that a set of doubtful beliefs might add up to a lack of confidence that one's relationship is marriageable. Those who study properties of relationships, including scholars in social psychology and interpersonal communication, are apt to observe that one problem with the way these fearful beliefs have been studied within sociology is that measures have confounded generalized beliefs with relationship-specific beliefs, thereby mixing beliefs from two different levels of analysis. Fears of divorce and distrust in the opposite sex reflect generalized beliefs about relationships, whereas beliefs about whether one's relationship is viable for marriage are relationship specific. Although generalized beliefs may affect relationship-specific beliefs, the latter is a more proximal, and probably a more powerful, predictor of commitment decisions.

Scholars from social psychology and interpersonal communication have devoted considerable attention to the study of hesitations and lack of confidence in one's relationship. Relational uncertainty, or the degree of confidence that individuals have in their perceptions of involvement in a particular relationship, is one such construct (Solomon & Theiss, 2008). A concept closely related to uncertainty is ambivalence about serious involvement, which centers on fears of losing one's independence, confusion about one's feelings, and the like (Braiker & Kelley, 1979). Relationship uncertainty and ambivalence are thought to occur most strongly when relationships are moving from casual to more serious levels of involvement, when turbulence over the decision about whether to commit more seriously is strongest (Braiker & Kelley, 1979; Solomon & Knobloch, 2001; Solomon & Theiss, 2008). Both longitudinal (Solomon & Theiss, 2008) and retrospective studies support this notion (Braiker & Kelley, 1979; Huston, Surra, Fitzgerald, & Cate, 1981), and longitudinal research supports the idea that partners whose commitment is increasing over time are more sensitive to fluctuations in commitment (Arriaga, Reed, Goodfriend, & Agnew, 2006).

One strategy for reducing uncertainty and navigating the turmoil associated with it is for partners to talk about their problems and doubts. A study of self-reported events that increased uncertainty (i.e., resulted in a questioning of basic beliefs about the relationship) showed that some individuals responded to events by discussing them, but others responded by avoiding discussion of the events. Not talking about events was associated with more negative relationship outcomes, including ending the relationship or becoming less close (Planalp & Honeycutt, 1985).

Yet, talking about events when relationships are uncertain may be difficult, resulting in a tendency to avoid discussion of topics that, ironically, might resolve uncertainties. Knobloch and Carpenter-Theune (2004) found that relationship uncertainty was positively associated with the number of topics avoided, with the importance of the topic to the relationship, and with assessments of the threat to self and relationship of discussing the topic. In marriages, relational uncertainty increased assessments that partners' messages were less affiliative, more dominant, more threatening, and less involved, even when outside observers interpreted such messages as neutral (Knobloch, Miller, Bond, & Mannone, 2007). Despite the fact that partners may be aware of the benefits of talking about difficult topics, they may find it too threatening to do so.

Sources of Relational Uncertainty in the Nonmarital Relationships of the Economically Disadvantaged: An Interdisciplinary Approach

There exist a number of sources of uncertainty in the relationships of romantic partners who are economically disadvantaged, but perhaps the most important one is the instability of employment and earnings described previously, which, in turn, is likely to introduce uncertainty about future economic prospects that are central to the selection of a mate (Oppenheimer, 2003). Chronic infidelity is another source of confusion about commitment for these partners, especially when relationships are newly developing or changing (Hill, 2007). Multipartner fertility, or having a child with an alternative partner, often introduces an ongoing threat to a target relationship. In the Fragile Families study, more than 40% of fathers and mothers had a child with an alternative partner (Harknett, 2008). As a result, fathers and mothers in a romantic relationship frequently must deal with the presence of alternative partners with whom they share parenting responsibilities. These alternative partners become a constant source of doubt and sexual jealousy for those who are trying to form a committed relationship (Hill, 2007).

Summary

The study of ambivalence and uncertainty about relationships, when paired with the study of the economic characteristics of partners, helps to paint a more complete and detailed picture of why mate selection patterns occur as they do among the economically disadvantaged. The economic uncertainties experienced by the poor and the near poor are sufficient to introduce partly committed partners to a flood of questions about whether a particular relationship is economically viable. Add to this flood of economic uncertainties the doubts imposed on relationships by conditions that surround the lives of poor unmarried partners, including threats from alternative partners, questions about intimacy and degree of involvement, and the willingness to discuss difficult topics. Under these circumstances, partners' ability to navigate the transition to a committed relationship is likely to be overwhelmed by uncertainty. It is no wonder that the conviction of commitment becomes an even more distant and seemingly unattainable goal.

The goal of this section on mate selection was to show the benefits that can be accrued when adopting an interdisciplinary approach. Sociologists tend to focus on differences among subpopulations, whereas social psychologists and communication scholars tend to focus on universal properties across subpopulations. Each approach has shed light on human mate choice, but we believe that combining a focus on the differences among subpopulations (e.g., economic factors) with a focus on the universal properties of romantic relationships (e.g., uncertainty in relationships) will ultimately shed more explanatory light on the process of mate selection. Similar conclusions can be drawn regarding any area of research relevant to relationship science.

PURPOSE AND ORGANIZATION OF THIS VOLUME

The chapters in this volume discuss the benefits of interdisciplinary research and how such research can be achieved. Interdisciplinary theoretical frameworks regarding human relations are also highlighted. The remaining 11 chapters are grouped into four main parts.

Part I contains three chapters addressing the concept of interpersonal responsiveness and emotion regulation in close relationships. In Chapter 2, Harry T. Reis argues that the field of relationship science needs more consistent theoretical approaches to the study of similar relationships processes.

Specifically, he suggests that "perceived partner responsiveness," or how accepted, cared for, and understood people feel they are by their close partners, is the common thread linking a large number of empirical investigations that use different labels for the same psychological process. In Chapter 3, Theodore Dix and Katharine Ann Buck use a theoretical framework similar to Reis's to investigate social approach and avoidance motivation in early parent–child relationships. The concept of perceived partner responsiveness, therefore, is not limited to one class of close relationships. In Chapter 4, Lisa M. Diamond and Christopher P. Fagundes discuss how individuals respond to social threat and social rejection. They explore individuals' emotional responses as well as physiological responses indicative of poor coping and health.

Part II focuses more attention on relationships in early life. In Chapter 5, Nancy E. Hill discusses parental influences on peer relations, highlighting the strong role that cultural context plays in this process. In Chapter 6, Roger Kobak and Joanna Herres investigate the relative influence of parents and peers on adolescents' lives and their relationships with others, over time.

Part III focuses on adult close relationships. In Chapter 7, Jessica E. Salvatore, W. Andrew Collins, and Jeffry A. Simpson demonstrate how early life experiences can shape individual's experiences in their relationships in adulthood. In Chapter 8, Lisa A. Neff presents data from a large sample of newlyweds and emphasizes the role of external stress on relationship functioning. She argues that researchers need to take into account the context in which marital interactions unfold. In Chapter 9, Steven W. Gangestad argues that relationship science can benefit by incorporating evolutionary approaches to the study of human behavior. He presents a program of research showing that women's mate preferences and relationship-focused behaviors shift across the menstrual cycle, a shift that would not be predicted by standard cultural accounts of human behavior. In Chapter 10, Robert E. Emery, Hyun Joo Shim, and Erin Horn discuss the consequences of divorce for spouses as well as children. They also consider divorce policies across different cultures and challenge relationship scholars to think about the effect of different divorce policies on the consequences of divorce for those involved and society at large.

Part IV contains two concluding chapters. In Chapter 11, Aletha C. Huston discusses her journey through her academic career and her interdisciplinary research endeavours. She points out the hurdles that exist for true interdisciplinary research to bloom and thrive, and she offers some suggestions for how to achieve this elusive goal. Last, Chapter 12 by Timothy J. Loving and Ted L. Huston correctly points out that scholars have called for an interdisciplinary integration of the relationship sciences for as long as the field has existed, but that such an integration has not yet been achieved. They discuss some possible reasons for this lack of interdisciplinary integration to date and suggest a path to true interdisciplinary scholarship for relationship science.

The scholars contributing to this volume were primarily trained in psychology departments, but as we just discussed, and as a quick glance at the chapter titles shows, the types of close relationships assessed in this volume are diverse. Additionally, it is evident from these chapters that a number of different methodological approaches were used in the research projects discussed. It is also the case that many of the authors adopted an interdisciplinary approach when carrying out their own program of research. We feel that this edited volume represents an important collection of ideas and research from people adopting different research perspectives that will serve to generate new research ideas and collaborations, and define a research agenda for the study of close relationship processes in the future.

REFERENCES

Allport, G. (1938). Personality: A problem for science or a problem for art? *Revista de Psihologie, 1,* 488–502.

Allport, G. (1942). *The use of personal documents in psychological science.* New York, NY: Social Science Research Council.

Arriaga, X. B., Reed, J. T., Goodfriend, W., & Agnew, C. R. (2006). Relationship perceptions and persistence: Do fluctuations in perceived partner commitment undermine dating relationships? *Journal of Personality and Social Psychology, 91,* 1045–1065. doi:10.1037/0022-3514.91.6.1045

Baumeister, R. F., & Leary, M. R. (1995). The need to belong: Desire for interpersonal attachments as a fundamental human motivation. *Psychological Bulletin, 117,* 497–529. doi:10.1037/0033-2909.117.3.497

Becker, G. S. (1991). *A treatise on the family* (enlarged edition). Cambridge, MA: Harvard University Press.

Berscheid, E. (1985). Interpersonal attraction. In G. Lindzey & E. Aronson (Eds.), *The handbook of social psychology* (pp. 413–484). New York, NY: Random House.

Berscheid, E. (1999). The greening of relationship science. *American Psychologist, 54,* 260–266. doi:10.1037/0003-066X.54.4.260

Bowlby, J. (1969). *Attachment and loss: Vol. 1. Attachment.* New York, NY: Basic Books.

Bowlby, J. (1973). *Attachment and loss: Vol. 2. Separation: Anxiety and anger.* New York, NY: Basic Books.

Bowlby, J. (1980). *Attachment and loss: Vol. 3. Loss: Sadness and depression.* New York, NY: Basic Books.

Braiker, H. B., & Kelley, H. H. (1979). Conflict in the development of close relationships. In R. L. Burgess & T. L. Huston (Eds.), *Social exchange in developing relationships* (pp. 135–168). San Diego, CA: Academic Press.

Brown, S. L. (2000). Union transitions among cohabitors: The significance of relationship assessments and expectations. *Journal of Marriage and Family, 62*, 833–846. doi:10.1111/j.1741-3737.2000.00833.x

Bumpass, L., & Lu, H. (2001). Trends in cohabitation and implications for children's family context in the United States. *Population Studies, 54*, 29–41. doi:10.1080/713779060

Buss, D. M. (1985). Human mate selection. *American Scientist, 73*, 47–51.

Carlson, M., McLanahan, S., & England, P. (2004). Union formation in fragile families. *Demography, 41*, 237–261. doi:10.1353/dem.2004.0012

Cherlin, A. J. (2005). American marriage in the early twenty-first century. *The Future of Children, 15*, 33–55. doi:10.1353/foc.2005.0015

Cherlin, A., Cross-Barnet, C., Burton, L. M., & Garrett-Peters, R. (2008). Promises they can keep: Low-income women's attitudes toward motherhood, marriage, and divorce. *Journal of Marriage and Family, 70*, 919–933. doi:10.1111/j.1741-3737.2008.00536.x

Clark, M. S., & Lemay, E. P. (2010). Close relationships. In S. T. Fiske, D. T. Gilbert, & G. Lindzey (Eds.), *Handbook of social psychology* (Vol. 2, pp. 898–940). Hoboken, NJ: Wiley.

Clarkberg, M. (1999). The price of partnering: The role of economic well-being in young adults' first union experiences. *Social Forces, 77*, 945–968. doi:10.2307/3005967

Conger, R. D., Elder, G. H., Jr., Lorenz, F. O., Conger, K. J., Simons, R. L., Whitbeck, L. B., . . . Melby, J. N. (1990). Linking economic hardship to marital quality and stability. *Journal of Marriage and Family, 52*, 643–656. doi:10.2307/352931

Edin, K. (2000). What do low-income single mothers say about marriage? *Social Problems, 47*, 112–133. doi:10.1525/sp.2000.47.1.03x0282v

Edin, K., & Kefalas, M. (2005). *Promises I can keep: Why poor women put motherhood before marriage*. Berkley, CA: University of California Press.

Edin, K., Kefalas, M. J., & Reed, J. M. (2004). A peek inside the black box: What marriage means for poor unmarried parents. *Journal of Marriage and Family, 66*, 1007–1014. doi:10.1111/j.0022-2445.2004.00072.x

Ellwood, D. T., & Jencks, C. (2002). *The spread of single-parent families in the United States since 1960*. Cambridge, MA: Harvard University, John F. Kennedy School of Government.

Ellwood, D. T., Wilde, E. T., & Batchelder, L. (2009). *The mommy track divides: The impact of childbearing on wages of women of differing skill levels*. Cambridge, MA: Harvard University, John F. Kennedy School of Government.

Fossett, M. A., & Kiecolt, K. J. (1993). Mate availability and family structure among African Americans in U.S. metropolitan areas. *Journal of Marriage and Family, 55*, 288–302. doi:10.2307/352802

Franklin, D. L., Smith, S. E., & McMiller, W. E. P. (1995). Correlates of marital status among African American mothers in Chicago neighborhoods of concentrated poverty. *Journal of Marriage and Family, 57*, 141–152. doi:10.2307/353823

Gaughan, M. (2002). The substitution hypothesis: The impact of premarital liaisons and human capital on marital timing. *Journal of Marriage and Family, 64*, 407–419. doi:10.1111/j.1741-3737.2002.00407.x

Giacomini, M. (2004). Interdisciplinarity in health services research: Dreams and nightmares, maladies and remedies. *Journal of Health Services Research & Policy, 9*, 177–183. doi:10.1258/1355819041403222

Gibson-Davis, C. M. (2009). Money, marriage, and children: Testing the financial expectations and family formation theory. *Journal of Marriage and Family, 71*, 146–160. doi:10.1111/j.1741-3737.2008.00586.x

Gibson-Davis, C. M., Edin, K., & McLanahan, S. (2005). High hopes but even higher expectations: The retreat from marriage among low-income couples. *Journal of Marriage and Family, 67*, 1301–1312. doi:10.1111/j.1741-3737.2005. 00218.x

Hall, J. G., Bainbridge, L., Buchan, A., Cribb, A., Drummond, J., Gyles, C., . . . Solomon, P. (2006). A meeting of minds: Interdisciplinary research in the health sciences in Canada. *Canadian Medical Association Journal, 175*, 763–771. doi:10.1503/cmaj.060783

Harknett, K. (2008). Mate availability and unmarried parent relationships. *Demography, 45*, 555–571. doi:10.1353/dem.0.0012

Hill, H. D. (2007). Steppin' out: Infidelity and sexual jealousy among unmarried parents. In P. England & K. Edin (Eds.), *Unmarried couples with children* (pp. 104–132). New York, NY: Russell Sage Foundation.

Huston, T. L., Surra, C. A., Fitzgerald, N. M., & Cate, R. M. (1981). From courtship to marriage: Mate selection as an interpersonal process. In S. Duck & R. Gilmour (Eds.), *Personal relationships 2: Developing personal relationships* (pp. 53–88). London, England: Academic Press.

Kagan, J. (2009). *The three cultures: Natural sciences, social sciences, and the humanities in the 21st century.* New York, NY: Cambridge University Press. doi:10.1017/CBO9 780511576638

Kelley, H. H., Berscheid, E., Christensen, A., Harvey, J. H., Huston, T. L., Levinger, G., . . . Peterson, D. R. (1983). *Close relationships.* New York, NY: Freeman.

Kiecolt-Glaser, J. K., & Newton, T. (2001). Marriage and health: His and hers. *Psychological Bulletin, 127*, 472–503. doi:10.1037/0033-2909.127.4.472

Kirkpatrick, L. A., & Ellis, B. J. (2001). An evolutionary-psychological approach to self-esteem: Multiple domains and multiple functions. In G. J. O. Fletcher & M. S. Clark (Eds.), *Blackwell handbook of social psychology: Interpersonal processes* (pp. 411–436). Malden, MA: Blackwell.

Knobloch, L. K., & Carpenter-Theune, K. E. (2004). Topic avoidance in developing relationships: Associations with intimacy and relational uncertainty. *Communication Research, 31*, 173–205. doi:10.1177/0093650203261516

Knobloch, L. K., Miller, L. E., Bond, B. J., & Mannone, S. E. (2007). Relational uncertainty and message processing in marriage. *Communication Monographs, 74,* 154–180. doi:10.1080/03637750701390069

Kruglanski, A. W. (2006). Theories as bridges. In P. A. M. Van Lange (Ed.), *Bridging social psychology: Benefits of transdisciplinary approaches* (pp. 21–32). Mahwah, NJ: Erlbaum.

Lichter, D. T., LeClere, F. B., & McGlaughlin, D. K. (1991). Local marriage markets and the marital behavior of Black and White women. *American Journal of Sociology, 96,* 843–867. doi:10.1086/229610

Lichter, D. T., & Qian, Z. (2008). Serial cohabitation and the marital life course. *Journal of Marriage and Family, 70,* 861–878. doi:10.1111/j.1741-3737.2008.00532.x

Matthews, L. S., Conger, R. D., & Wickrama, K. A. S. (1996). Work-family conflict and marital quality: Mediating processes. *Social Psychology Quarterly, 59,* 62–79. doi:10.2307/2787119

McLaughlin, D. K., & Lichter, D. T. (1997). Poverty and the marital behaviour of young women. *Journal of Marriage and Family, 59,* 582–594. doi:10.2307/353947

Mikulincer, M., & Shaver, P. R. (2007). *Attachment in adulthood: Structure, dynamics, and change.* New York, NY: Guilford Press.

Oppenheimer, V. K. (1997). Women's employment and the gain to marriage: The specialization and trading model. *Annual Review of Sociology, 23,* 431–453. doi:10.1146/annurev.soc.23.1.431

Oppenheimer, V. K. (2003). Cohabiting and marriage during young men's career-development process. *Demography, 40,* 127–149.

Osborne, C. (2005). Marriage following the birth of a child among cohabiting and visiting parents. *Journal of Marriage and Family, 67,* 14–26. doi:10.1111/j.0022-2445.2005.00002.x

Planalp, S., & Honeycutt, J. M. (1985). Events that increase uncertainty in personal relationships. *Human Communication Research, 11,* 593–604. doi:10.1111/j.1468-2958.1985.tb00062.x

Reis, H. T. (2007). Steps toward the ripening of relationship science. *Personal Relationships, 14,* 1–23. doi:10.1111/j.1475-6811.2006.00139.x

Slingerland, E. (2008). *What science offers the humanities: Integrating body and culture.* New York, NY: Cambridge University Press.

Snow, C. P. (1998). *The two cultures.* Cambridge, England: Cambridge University Press.

Solomon, D. H., & Knobloch, L. K. (2001). Relational uncertainty, partner interference, and intimacy within dating relationships. *Journal of Social and Personal Relationships, 18,* 804–820. doi:10.1177/0265407501186004

Solomon, D. H., & Theiss, J. A. (2008). A longitudinal test of the relational turbulence model of romantic relationship development. *Personal Relationships, 15,* 339–357. doi:10.1111/j.1475-6811.2008.00202.x

Suls, J., & Wallston, K. A. (2003). (Eds). *Social psychological foundations of health and illness.* Malden, MA: Blackwell.

Surra, C. A., & Boelter, J. M. (in press). Mate selection. In G. W. Peterson & K. R. Bush (Eds.), *Handbook of marriage and family* (3rd ed.). New York, NY: Springer.

Surra, C. A., Boettcher-Burke, T. M. J., Cottle, N. R., West, A., & Gray, C. R. (2007). The treatment of relationship status in research on dating and mate selection. *Journal of Marriage and Family, 69,* 207–221. doi:10.1111/j.1741-3737.2006.00354.x

Surra, C. A., Gray, C. R., Boettcher, T. M. J., Cottle, N. R., & West, A. (2006). From courtship to universal properties: Research on dating and mate selection, 1950–2003. In D. Perlman & A. Vangelisti (Eds.), *Cambridge handbook of personal relationships* (pp. 113–130). New York, NY: Cambridge University Press. doi:10.1017/CBO9780511606632.008

Sweeney, M. M. (2002). Two decades of family change: The shifting economic foundations of marriage. *American Sociological Review, 67,* 132–147. doi:10.2307/3088937

Waller, M. R. (2002). *My baby's father: Unmarried parents and paternal responsibility.* Ithaca, NY: Cornell University Press.

Waller, M. R., & McLanahan, S. S. (2005). "His" and "her" marriage expectations: Determinants and consequences. *Journal of Marriage and Family, 67,* 53–67. doi: 10.1111/j.0022-2445.2005.00005.x

Wilson, E. O. (1998). *Consilience: The unity of knowledge.* New York, NY: Vintage Books.

Xie, Y., Raymo, J. M., Goyette, K., & Thornton, A. (2003). Economic potential and entry into marriage and cohabitation. *Demography, 40,* 351–367. doi:10.1353/dem.2003.0019

I

INTERPERSONAL RESPONSIVENESS IN CLOSE RELATIONSHIPS

2

PERCEIVED PARTNER RESPONSIVENESS AS AN ORGANIZING THEME FOR THE STUDY OF RELATIONSHIPS AND WELL-BEING

HARRY T. REIS

As we humans go through life, we are involved in many different goals and activities. We go to school or work; we pursue hobbies, pastimes, and other recreational interests; we socialize with friends, relatives, coworkers, and acquaintances; we care for children, aging parents, and others; and we engage in subsistence activities like preparing meals, managing finances, maintaining our living spaces and vehicles, and sleeping. Traversing all of these is the impact of relationships. Virtually all day-to-day activity requires coordination of our actions with those of other people on whom we depend and who depend on us. In other words, for most people most of the time, successfully accomplishing most life tasks and goals is intrinsically interwoven with how they interact with others.

The fact of interdependence with others reflects the importance of social relations in human evolution. Humans are a social species. Mechanisms for relating to and coordinating with others are deeply wired into our neural architecture, as described by numerous theorists (e.g., Buss & Kenrick, 1998; Reis, Collins, & Berscheid, 2000). Reflecting this complexity, a vast and growing literature has emerged describing the nature of social relations and the myriad processes that regulate them. This literature provides compelling evidence about the role of relationships in life activity and personal well-being.

The strength of this evidence notwithstanding, there exists as yet no general set of unifying principles for understanding how the many and diverse manifestations of relationships influence well-being (see also Chapters 1 and 12, this volume). In this chapter, I argue that perceived partner responsiveness represents one possible unifying principle for linking and making theoretical sense of the numerous constructs that researchers across various disciplines have used to study relationships and well-being. My argument rests on the premise that for relationship science to become a cumulative science, it will be necessary to articulate how the field's various constructs, hypotheses, and findings relate to one another. That articulation is likely to facilitate the development of integrative theories, simultaneously including biological substrates, cognitive and affective mechanisms, and interpersonal manifestations, and will also make possible the design and implementation of effective interventions. Thus, the goal of this chapter is to suggest how perceived partner responsiveness may provide movement forward from the promising early stages of our field—the "greening of relationship science" that Berscheid (1999) so aptly described.

The chapter begins with a brief overview of evidence about the importance of relationships to human health and psychological well-being. I then discuss the idea of core organizing principles—principles that can help link the diverse constructs that the relationship science literature comprises. This is followed by a description of perceived partner responsiveness, a construct that I believe has significant potential to serve as a core organizing principle for relationship science. Next, to illustrate how this might work, I briefly review three research programs from our laboratory that show how, by identifying common core principles, a single unifying theme may encompass seemingly disparate phenomena and thereby foster theoretical coherence among them. These three programs concern benefits of perceived partner responsiveness for personal well-being, the role of partners in capitalizing on positive events, and the impact of perceived regard in mediating the benefits of partner esteem for relationship well-being.

RELATIONSHIPS MATTER FOR HEALTH AND WELL-BEING

Dozens of studies have documented an association between interpersonal circumstances and health. Some of these studies approached health and interpersonal circumstances in the broadest possible way. For example, House, Landis, and Umberson (1988) reviewed several large epidemiological studies of the effects of social integration on "all-cause" mortality across the life span. Their analyses concluded that low social integration (defined in terms of neighborhood, social, and family involvement) was a strong risk factor for premature mortality, with a relative risk ratio comparable to that associated with more traditional risk factors such as tobacco use, obesity, and high blood pressure. More recent reviews of similar data sets have confirmed this association (Berkman, Glass, Brissette, & Seeman, 2000).

Studies of specific illnesses also support this conclusion. For example, Coyne et al. (2001) examined the impact of marital quality on survival following the diagnosis of congestive heart failure. Four years later, individuals in high-quality marriages were about twice as likely to still be alive as individuals in low-quality marriages. King and Reis (2009) corroborated these findings in a sample of coronary artery bypass surgery patients initially studied by King, Reis, Porter, and Norsen (1993). We sorted our sample into the following three groups: married persons who were above the median in self-reported marital satisfaction shortly after their surgery, married persons who were below the median in marital satisfaction after their surgery, and unmarried persons. Fifteen years later, these groupings were significantly related to survival. Almost 80% of the high-satisfaction group was still alive, compared with 62% of the low-satisfaction group and 37% of the unmarried group. These two studies are consistent with the findings of Uchino, Cacioppo, and Kiecolt-Glaser's (1996) extensive review, which concluded that relationship stresses and strains had direct and deleterious effects on the functioning of the endocrine, cardiovascular, and immune systems (see also Chapter 4).

Turning to psychological well-being, extensive evidence shows that relationships affect mental health. For example, beginning with the seminal work of Brown and Harris in the 1970s, research has consistently shown that relationship problems are a potent proximal cause of clinical depression (Brown & Harris, 1978; Weissman, 1987). Similarly, severe isolation or otherwise inadequate social involvement can trigger pathological loneliness, which is itself associated with various other mental and health disorders (Cacioppo & Patrick, 2008). Family dysfunction, particularly hostile conflict, is associated with poorer recovery and relapse in many major mental disorders (Hooley & Hiller, 1997). It should not be surprising, then, that at least one study has found that relationship problems are the primary referring problem among psychotherapy patients (Pinsker, Nepps, Redfield, & Winston, 1985).

Psychological well-being goes well beyond the absence of major mental disorders. When it comes to what might be called everyday well-being, relationships play a significant role. Typical of this literature is a finding from Veroff, Douvan, and Kulka's (1981) survey of a representative sample of approximately 2,200 Americans. Among various questions, they asked their respondents, "What was the last bad thing to happen to you?" About half spontaneously mentioned an interpersonal problem or conflict, or the death of a significant other. Similarly, but on the bright side, a 2005 *Time* magazine poll asked, "What are your major sources of happiness?" Of their respondents, 77% mentioned relationships with children, 76% mentioned friends, 75% mentioned contributing to the lives of others, and 73% cited spouses and other romantic partners. It may even be the case that simply highly valuing close relationships and a sense of community, relative to noninterpersonal goals such as money, fame, and beauty, is sufficient to foster happiness and personal well-being (Kasser & Ryan, 1993).

Extensive research has confirmed the results of these polls, as indicated by the conclusions of reviews of this vast literature. For example, approaching this topic from the relationships side, Berscheid and Reis (1998) concluded that "relationships are people's most frequent source of both happiness and distress" (p. 243). Diener et al. (1999), following their review of 3 decades' worth of research on subjective well-being, drew a similar conclusion: "The happy person . . . has social confidants" (p. 295). The evidence supporting these conclusions is sufficiently compelling that it led David Myers (1992) to assert, "The importance of social relations to human happiness is a 'deep truth'" (p. 154). Deep truths are something that psychological science could use more of.

Evolutionary psychology has suggested one broad reason why relationships are so closely associated with health and well-being. Many contemporary models are founded on the idea that interactions with other people, and particularly ongoing relationships with them, represented one of the key adaptations in human evolution. Buss and Kenrick (1998) summarized these models in proposing the following:

> Evolutionary psychology places social interaction and social relationships squarely within the center of the action. In particular, social interactions and relationships surrounding mating, kinship, reciprocal alliances, coalitions, and hierarchies are especially critical, because all appear to have strong consequences for successful survival and reproduction. From an evolutionary perspective, the functions served by social relationships have been central to the design of the human mind. (p. 994)

In other words, because well-functioning groups had significant adaptive advantages over individuals and less well-coordinated groups, attributes that facilitated social relations became part of the human genome (e.g., Bugental, 2000; Caporael, 1997; Wilson, Van Vugt, & O'Gorman, 2008; see also Chapter 9, this volume). Successful relationships indicate that the relevant biologically based systems are functioning effectively, supporting the organism's well-being. Long-term problematic relationships, on the other hand, suggest dysregulation of these systems.

Ontogeny may in certain respects recapitulate phylogeny (Gould, 1977), and in this regard extensive evidence has demonstrated that relationships exert pervasive influences on human behavior and development throughout life (Reis, Collins, et al., 2000). Hartup and Stevens (1997) reviewed this evidence, drawing the following conclusion:

Friendships are developmentally significant throughout the life course. First, friends are cognitive and affective resources from childhood through old age, fostering self-esteem and a sense of well-being. Second, friends socialize one another, especially with respect to age-related tasks that must be mastered for individuals to achieve good outcomes. Third, supportive and intimate relationships between socially skilled individuals seem to be developmental advantages, whereas conflict-ridden relationships between troubled individuals seem to be disadvantages. (p. 366)

Consistent with the evolutionary account, then, the ability to initiate, foster, mend, and sustain relationships is critical for navigating nearly all domains of activity throughout life.

IN SEARCH OF CENTRAL ORGANIZING PRINCIPLES

If the association between relationships and well-being is considered an established fact, as I believe it should be, then the next question that needs to be asked is, "What is it about relationships that contributes to well-being?" Relationship science has no shortage of entrants into this derby. Consider, for example, the following selective and admittedly idiosyncratic list of constructs that have been proposed as definitions or exemplars of the types of high-quality relationships that contribute to psychological health and effective activity: secure attachment (Mikulincer & Shaver, 2007), social support (Cohen, Underwood, & Gottlieb, 2000), intimacy (Reis & Shaver, 1988), belongingness (Baumeister & Leary, 1995), communal need satisfaction (Clark & Mills, 1993), perceived partner responsiveness (Reis, Clark, & Holmes, 2004), trust (Simpson, 2007), constructive risk regulation (Murray, Holmes, & Collins, 2006), autonomy support (Deci & Ryan, 1987), self-verification (Swann, 1990), self-expansion (Aron & Aron, 1997), commitment (Rusbult, Coolsen, Kirchner, & Clarke, 2006), partner affirmation (Rusbult, Finkel, & Kumashiro, 2009), emotional acceptance (Jacobson & Christensen, 1998), friendship-based marriage (Gottman, 1999), social network integration (House, Landis, & Umberson, 1988), rapport (Tickle-Degnen & Rosenthal, 1990), and well-regulated communication about conflict (Gottman, 1994).

An interventionist wishing to devise a plan for enhancing human welfare by improving relationships would be hard pressed to identify the most prominent target among these (and numerous other) alternatives. This, to me, highlights in a somewhat embarrassing manner the absence of consensus about the field's central phenomena. To be sure, we often (and appropriately) celebrate the desirable diversity of our methods and theories, but at the same time we often fail to take the next and equally important step: considering how these multiple and diverse elements might be integrated into a systematic, coherent account of the phenomena we strive to understand. As I have argued in more detail elsewhere (Reis, 2007), for relationship science to become a mature, cumulative science, it will be necessary to place less emphasis on how various phenomena and findings differ from one another and to instead pay more attention to developing collective theoretical models of how the parts relate to the whole (see also Chapter 1).

It might be argued, with some legitimacy, that relationship science is still too young a discipline (Berscheid, 1999) to expect much progress at such a lofty goal. With no disrespect to our youth, I nevertheless propose that the field's forward motion, both as a basic science and as a foundation for interventions, might benefit from attention to questions about "core organizing principles." The search for core organizing principles would ask us to consider questions like the following:

> What are the fundamental problems that we intend to solve? What do we know about the natural history and social ecology of these core problems? Which relationship problems have what known consequences? What common knowledge do we possess about these phenomena? Which major theories would most scholars agree represent dominant approaches to the core phenomena of relationship science? (Reis, 2007, p. 7)

What would having a set of core organizing principles buy the field? For one thing, it would simplify the currently challenging task of weaving together theories and findings from different research programs into a broad-based, cohesive account. It would draw attention to commonalities and connections among seemingly differentiated constructs, while at the same time bringing to light gaps in the network of constructs (see also Chapter 12). It would also push investigators to consider before embarking on a program of research how their work relates to these broader principles and fits into general models. It would facilitate generalization across research programs and topics. And it would ground interventions and applications in a well-defined set of theories and findings whose outcomes and potential side effects might be better anticipated than is now the case (Bradbury, 2002; Reis, 2002). If nothing else, core organizing principles would make relationship science textbooks look more like a spiderweb of interconnected theories and findings and less like a lengthy list of freestanding topics and studies.

Let me be clear about one thing: I do not suggest that relationship science needs a singular vision, nor that the field should abandon specialization and attention to detail—features that are essential to progress in all cumulative sciences. Nevertheless, I believe we would benefit from a better understanding of the core principles that make our ideas cohere, our findings connect, and our relationships work. Were such principles available, I believe they would promote research on the ways in which relationships help and harm human well-being.

PERCEIVED PARTNER RESPONSIVENESS: A CANDIDATE CORE ORGANIZING PRINCIPLE

Previously, I listed a series of relationship constructs that have been linked to well-being in theory and research. These constructs can be distinguished from one another in various ways, but an element common to all of them is perceived partner responsiveness to the self. Reis et al. (2004) defined *perceived partner responsiveness* "as a process by which individuals come to believe that relationship partners both attend to and react supportively to central, core defining features of the self" (p. 203). This general definition encompasses several more specific themes, all of which appear repeatedly in relationships research, as follows:

- *A sense of being valued, understood, and cared for.* Validation—believing that partners value the self—is often conceptualized as a basic goal in social interaction (e.g., Goethals & Darley, 1977; Reis & Shaver, 1988; Sullivan, 1953). Perceived understanding—believing that partners "get the facts right" about oneself—underlies validation in the sense that expressions of value, no matter how flattering or self-enhancing, are likely to feel irrelevant, inauthentic, hollow, or even hostile when they are not linked to self-conceptions (Swann, 1990). Feeling cared for refers to nurturance, as well as the perception of partners' availability and willingness to provide support when the need arises (Bowlby, 1988).
- *Interactions that foster warmth, acceptance, and belongingness.* Interactions that promote warmth, affection, and liking contribute to feelings of acceptance and belongingness (e.g., Tickle-Degnen & Rosenthal, 1990; see also Chapter 3, this volume). Acceptance meets basic, and likely innate, needs for belonging (Baumeister & Leary, 1995), as well as fostering a sense of assurance that the investment and sacrifice necessary to maintain a committed relationship will not end up in rejection or other undesirable outcomes (Murray et al., 2006). Reflecting this reasoning, several marital-relationship therapies stress the importance of communicating acceptance of one's partner as a person as a foundation for problem solving and conflict resolution (Jacobson & Christensen, 1998).

- *Feeling that during interaction, partners are attentive and caring with respect to important personal needs, goals, values, and aspirations.* Although perceived partner responsiveness emphasizes perceptions, these perceptions are unlikely to arise or endure solely in the mind (unless, perhaps, the individual is delusional). Instead, as Reis et al. (2004) reviewed, perceptions of a partner's responsiveness typically reflect interactions in which the reality of responsive interaction can be objectively verified. To be sure, motivated processes may distort perceptions of a partner's behavior in one way or another; however, because most people have tolerably accurate perceptions of social reality, over time perceptions of partner responsiveness tend to reflect what transpires during actual interaction. Traditionally, responsiveness is studied through partner responses to personal needs—that is, to support given (or not given) when problems occur. Responsiveness also pertains to more proactive sorts of support—that is, to active support for the attainment of personal goals and other features of the wished-for ideal self (Rusbult, Reis, & Kumashiro, 2009).

- *Trusting that the partner will "be there" when needs arise.* Trust entails the expectation that a partner will support one's best interests, even when they conflict with the partner's own personal interests. In relationships, trust tends to be inferred from this type of "diagnostic situation"—that is, situations in which the partner has had to choose between self-interest and sacrificing for the good of the other (Holmes & Rempel, 1989). When conflicts or significant needs arise, trust promotes openness and a willingness to rely on the partner for support (Simpson, 2007), which creates an opportunity for responsiveness to be offered and perceived. Furthermore, perceived trust engenders offered trust, following norms of reciprocity. This occurs because perceived responsiveness in trust-diagnostic situations fosters commitment to the relationship, which in turn engenders subsequent responsive behavior toward the partner (Rusbult, Reis, et al., 2009).

In summary, all of these processes characterize perceived partner responsiveness—the belief that a relationship partner is attentive to and behaviorally supportive of core, defining features of the self. Although it may seem from this account that perceived partner responsiveness is conceptually similar to better known constructs such as intimacy, closeness, social support, or attachment security, I reiterate that perceived partner responsiveness is intended as a broader construct, highlighting commonalities among these and other important relationship processes. In other words, although perceived partner responsiveness is an important (and in some instances key) element of these better known processes, it casts a wider conceptual net, encompassing more diverse phenomena than each of them does individually. Thus, it might reasonably be assumed that perceived partner responsiveness is a reasonable candidate for a core organizing principle of relationship science.

THREE EMPIRICAL EXAMPLES OF PERCEIVED PARTNER RESPONSIVENESS

To serve as a core organizing principle, beyond describing and summarizing important relationship processes, a construct should span diverse phenomena. That is, the theory and research included under this (or any other candidate) core principle should provide an umbrella for reasonably broad and varied constructs, so that the identification of commonalities—the act of providing links in the aforementioned spiderweb of ideas—is genuinely insight-producing rather than simply restating similar ideas and findings. In that spirit, in the remainder of this chapter, I describe research from three different programs conducted in our laboratory. Although each program addresses nominally distinct research questions, each speaks to the significance of perceived partner responsiveness. As such, then, these lines of research can be considered complementary components of the general principle.

Perceived Partner Responsiveness and Personal Well-Being

Because relational success is associated with positive outcomes across diverse indicators of psychological, affective, and physical well-being (see Lyubomirsky, King, & Diener, 2005; Reis, Collins, et al., 2000, for reviews), and because perceived partner responsiveness contributes to relational success (e.g., Canavello & Crocker, 2010; Laurenceau, Barrett, & Pietromonaco, 1998; Laurenceau, Barrett, & Rovine, 2005; Reis & Patrick, 1996), it follows that perceived partner responsiveness ought to be associated broadly and unambiguously with personal well-being. Existing evidence supports this proposition. For example, perceived partner responsiveness contributes to personal evaluations of self-worth (Leary & Baumeister, 2000; Mikulincer & Shaver, 2007) and is correlated with a broad constellation of indicators of psychological health, emotional well-being, and life satisfaction (e.g., Dozier, Stovall-McClough, & Diener et al., 1999; Albus, 2008). Studies in our and related labs have shown that perceived partner responsiveness is even associated with better sleep quality (Carmichael & Reis, 2005) and healthier, more positive attitudes toward sex, especially among women (Birnbaum, 2007).

What types of social encounters are most likely to foster these benefits? This is a complex question that no single method or study can resolve. Reis, Sheldon, Gable, Roscoe, and Ryan (2000) adopted a then-novel approach to this question by using a daily diary method to determine what sorts of everyday interactions were most likely to coincide with days in which basic relatedness needs were satisfied. Their study considered seven different types of social interactions: talking about personally meaningful subjects, doing activities together, just hanging out, pleasantness and fun, feeling understood and appreciated during interactions, quarrels and arguments, and interactions in which one felt self-consciousness or judged. Multilevel modeling was used to control for individual differences, so that the results represented daily variations around an individual's mean levels of relatedness-need satisfaction. Not surprisingly, all seven forms of interaction were related to need fulfillment. However, when directly contrasted with one another, the strongest effects were obtained for feeling understood and appreciated. A replication of this study (Reis, 2009) obtained the same result: Relatedness needs are most likely to be satisfied on days in which people feel understood and appreciated in their social interaction.

In the achievement domain, perceived partner responsiveness also has been shown to predict better outcomes. For example, children who describe their teachers as responsive to their needs tend to do better in school (e.g., Murray & Greenberg, 2000). College students who feel that attachment figures are responsive and supportive display higher achievement motivation, lower fear of failure, and more approach-oriented (as opposed to avoidance-oriented) motives toward their school work, and view their college courses as relatively more challenging than threatening (Elliot & Reis, 2003). Caprariello and Reis (2006) found a similar pattern in college athletes' reports about participation in competitive athletics.

Although perceived partner responsiveness is typically studied in the context of intimate relationships, it also applies in less personal relationships. In one such study, Reis et al. (2008) surveyed 819 individuals in the United States, Canada, and the United Kingdom about the extent to which they felt that their primary care physicians were responsive to their needs and concerns and were interested in their thoughts and feelings. A notable aspect of this research is that although linguistically and culturally similar, these three countries have dissimilar medical systems in which the relationship between patients and primary care physicians differs markedly. Nonetheless, in all three countries, there was a clear association between perceived physician responsiveness and subjective health status, even after controlling for the impact of gender, age, marital status, years as patient, and general satisfaction with medical care received from that physician. This finding dovetails with other research showing that patient-centered communication (that is, a communication process between physician and patient that emphasizes responsiveness, openness, and active participation by the patient in all decisions) yields significantly greater patient satisfaction (Epstein & Street, 2007) and, in one study, an 11% reduction in health care costs (Epstein, Alper, & Quill, 2004).[1]

A final example showing how perceived partner responsiveness may contribute to individual well-being comes from self-regulation research. It is well-known that interaction with relationship partners provides an important vehicle for adaptive self-regulation (see Carmichael, Smith, Caprariello, Tsai, & Reis, 2007, for a review; see also Chapter 4, this volume). But can even thinking about responsive partners serve as an adaptive resource under threatening circumstances? Caprariello and Reis (2009) conducted two experiments to examine this possibility. In the first experiment, while performing a very difficult remote-associates task that had been described as a predictor of academic performance, participants were subliminally primed with the name of someone whom they had nominated as a responsive relationship partner. In control conditions, the subliminal prime was the name of an acquaintance or a random string of letters. After a distractor task, participants took a memory test to see how well they remembered the items they had not solved. (We considered better memory as a sign of ongoing curiosity about the missed items; forgetting, in contrast, was considered a reflection of the desire to dismiss memory of the failed task.) As expected, relative to the control conditions, participants primed with the name of a responsive partner had significantly better memory for the failed items.

A second, conceptually similar experiment examined self-handicapping as a defensive response to the prospect of failure. We introduced participants to the Trier Social Stress Task (Kirschbaum, Pirke, & Hellhammer, 1993) by leading them to expect that they were to be videotaped in a subtraction race— counting backwards as quickly as possible from 1,978 by a randomly selected two-digit number. Prior to the subtraction race, participants were asked to write a brief essay about someone who they felt was a responsive partner, or in three different control conditions, a friend who was not particularly responsive but who they had fun with, an acquaintance, or a neutral object (something that helps organize their daily activities). They were then asked to check which of 14 external circumstances might hamper their performance in the subtraction race. These reasons were selected from self-handicapping research (Strube, 1986) as potential rationalizations for failure (e.g., "insufficient rest"). The more reasons checked off, the greater the defensive response—that is, the greater the desire to externalize responsibility for the possibility of poor performance on this stressful task. As expected, in the three control conditions,

---

[1]Presumably because, among several reasons, fewer unnecessary diagnostic tests are ordered (Epstein et al., 2004).

threat fostered increased tendencies to self-handicap. In the responsiveness-priming condition, however, consistent with the earlier study, perceiving the task as threatening led to lesser self-handicapping. These two experiments mesh well with other studies showing that priming with the name of positively valenced, close others lessens defensive responses to failure on a significant academic task (Kumashiro & Sedikides, 2005) and that priming with secure attachment representations can increase intergroup tolerance, prosocial behavior, and personal well-being (Mikulincer & Shaver, 2007).

In summary, the methodological diversity of the research described in this section (correlational studies, meta-analytical reviews, large surveys, daily diary studies, and laboratory experiments) and the range of domains covered (emotional well-being, daily need satisfaction, academic achievement, health care, and social cognition) suggest that the construct of perceived partner responsiveness has broad applicability to the study of relationships and human well-being. This is exactly what a central organizing principle should do.

Perceived Partner Responsiveness and Capitalizing on Positive Events

Perceived partner responsiveness is commonly studied in the context of negative events. Three types of situations dominate the literature. First, social support researchers study the nature and extent of partner responses to reports of personal problems or stressful events (e.g., Burleson, 2009). A second avenue of research examines partner responses when conflicts of interest occur—for example, when partners' personal preferences differ (e.g., Rusbult et al., 2001). The assumption here is that partners demonstrate responsiveness by prioritizing the other's needs and wishes over their own. The third context examines situations in which the individual's basic sense of personal or relational security has been threatened (Mikulincer & Shaver, 2007; Murray et al., 2006). Responsive partners are those who provide sensitive, situationally appropriate support.

Undoubtedly, these types of negative situations are critical for establishing and maintaining responsiveness in relationships. Nevertheless, the field's seemingly near-exclusive focus on problems, conflicts, and threat has obscured the complementary importance of more positive situations. Relationships, after all, are not just about fixing problems and responding to stressors. Perceived partner responsiveness is influential in at least two general types of positive situations. The first pertains to supporting a partner's personal growth and goal attainment (Feeney, 2004; Rusbult, Finkel, et al., 2009), and the second concerns responses to a partner's personal success or other good fortune. Our capitalization research examines this latter process, which I now discuss.

Capitalization refers to the process of reflecting on personal good fortune and thereby deriving additional benefit from it. One such method, proposed originally by Langston (1994), involves sharing the news with other persons. That friends can help a person savor good news is not surprising. When Argyle and Henderson (1984) studied the relative value of different friendship rules or norms, "sharing news of success" came out as the most highly ranked rule. ("Showing emotional support" and "volunteering help in time of need" were ranked second and third, respectively.) Nonetheless, personal success may create mixed feelings for partners. For example, in response to a partner's accomplishment, a person may experience pride or envy, depending on several factors, including closeness and the accomplishment's self-relevance (Scinta & Gable, 2005; Tesser, 1986). Personal positive events may threaten stable patterns of interaction within a relationship, such as when a new job entails relocation or added time commitment at work, or when one partner suddenly has more income or status than the other. Reporting news of such good fortune to a partner represents a capitalization attempt: It provides an opportunity for the partner to respond enthusiastically, signaling concern for the other's well-being and vicarious pleasure, or to respond ambivalently or indifferently, indicating disinterest in the other's welfare and distance in the relationship.

Our capitalization research has examined two outcomes of capitalization interactions, event-related affect and relationship resources (see Gable & Reis, 2010, for a review). In both cases, the capitalization attempt is theorized to create an opportunity for partners to demonstrate understanding, valuing, and caring for the other, through the vehicle of supportive responses to a personal accomplishment. In this way, empathic partners may express admiration for, and engagement with, the self's accomplishments, a process similar to what Kohut (1971) called *mirroring*. Mirroring, he theorized, triggers mental representations of self as positively valued by the other (e.g., Fonagy, Gergely, Jurist, & Target, 2002), leading people to develop positive metaperceptions (or "perceptions of what others think of the self"; Kenny, 1994). Research shows that both event-related affect and feelings about a relationship depend on the nature of the partners' response to capitalization attempts.

We have examined event-related affect in two ways. First, in one of a series of laboratory experiments (Reis et al., 2010), participants were provided a list and asked to rate the three things that had made them happiest during the past 2 years. They were then asked to describe one of these events (randomly selected) to an interviewer who had been trained to respond in either an active-enthusiastic or a passive-disengaged manner. Active responses included copious amounts of eye contact, smiling, and other engaging nonverbal expressions, as well as statements such as, "Your friends must be really proud of you." Passive responses consisted of slouching, fidgeting, avoiding eye contact, and using monotone speech, accompanied by statements such as "Oh yeah, that's nice." Conversations lasted for about 8 minutes, after which participants were asked to rerate their three happiest events. When the confederate had been active and enthusiastic, results revealed a boost in ratings of the event that had been discussed, whereas the other two events were rated about the same as in the prediscussion ratings. In contrast, in the passive condition, none of the event ratings improved. Other experiments in this series have shown similar benefits from talking to active-enthusiastic interviewers in comparison to positive-mood inductions (e.g., a humorous film) and written descriptions of positive events.

We also looked at event-related affect in a diary study. Every day for 14 days, college students described and rated their "best positive" and "worst negative" event of the day. They were also asked if they had told another person and, if so, how enthusiastically (for the positive event) and comfortingly (for the negative event) that person had replied. Two or 3 days after the final diary, without forewarning, participants were given a list of the events from all 14 diaries and asked to evaluate those events "now." As predicted, ratings of positive events were significantly more likely to increase if those events had been told to another person. Also as predicted, follow-up ratings of positive events increased if partners' responses had been perceived as enthusiastic. (These analyses controlled for the positivity of that event, as rated on the day of occurrence.) Thus, sharing news about daily positive events with an enthusiastic listener was associated with subsequent increases in positive feelings about those events.

As for negative events, relating those events to others did not yield significant change in later ratings of those events. However, listeners' perceived comfortingness was significantly and positively associated with later ratings. (Again, both results control for the negativity of the event, rated on its day of occurrence.) The positive correlation indicates that when partners' responses were perceived as helpful and comforting, later event ratings were more negative, suggesting that partners' responses validated participants' views of how bad those events had been, thereby magnifying them.

Capitalization also helps build social resources in relationships, the second outcome our research has examined. Our theorizing here is similar to that previously discussed. Capitalization attempts present partners with an opportunity to demonstrate support for self-relevant accomplishments and goals, which can foster recognition of concern and regard for the self and, more generally, intimacy (Reis et al., 2004). Disinterested or deprecating responses, in contrast, create distance between self and partner. Our early studies utilized the Perceived Responses to Capitalization Attempts scale, which assesses perceptions of how a partner generally responds to being told of one's good news (Gable, Reis, Impett, & Asher, 2004). Studies of both college-student and middle-age community samples have revealed that the perception of enthusiastic, engaged responses is associated with higher relationship satisfaction and intimacy, and, in daily diary data, higher frequencies of everyday positive interactions. Passive or destructive responses are, in contrast, associated with lower satisfaction and intimacy, and fewer positive interactions. It is unlikely that these results are attributable entirely to perceptions. In a laboratory-observation study, Gable, Gonzaga, and Strachman (2006) found that coding of partner responsiveness to capitalization attempts by independent observers predicted relationship well-being and stability 2 months later.

Because our theorizing highlights the intimacy-building potential of responses to capitalization attempts, it is important to show that the capitalization process does more than generate positive affect. Reis et al. (2010) replicated the experimental protocol described earlier, adding two new control conditions. In one, the participant and interviewer engaged in a highly enjoyable and engaging interaction developed by Fraley and Aron (2004), in which participants described a series of Dr. Seuss pictures that the interviewer had to draw (without seeing the picture directly). A second condition was similar to the capitalization condition, but here the interviewer simply took notes on the participant's account, with minimal commentary. Both the capitalization and fun conditions produced greater liking for the interviewer and more positive affect than the notes condition did. But when asked about trust, responsiveness, or the willingness to disclose sensitive personal information, participants in the capitalization condition rated the interviewer more favorably than did participants in the other two conditions (which did not differ significantly from each other). Thus, this experiment demonstrates that capitalization interactions build intimacy and not just liking.

The daily diary study described previously yielded a conceptually related finding (Reis et al., 2010). In that study, participants nominated a target person—someone they were likely to interact with every day of the 14-day diary period. In addition to describing their best event of each day, participants also reported whether they had informed their target person about those events and, if they had, how the target had responded. In a different portion of the diary, participants reported on their relationship with the target on that day—specifically, how nice, accommodating, and willing to sacrifice they had been toward the target. (These dimensions were chosen as indicators of the willingness to enact "prorelationship transformations," a key indicator of relationship well-being in interdependence theory; Rusbult, Verette, Whitney, Slovik, & Lipkus, 1991.) As expected, both telling partners about good news and perceiving their responses as enthusiastic led to significantly enhanced propartner orientations. Because these analyses controlled for the prior-day's orientation, capitalization can be understood to foster relationship change from one day to the next, rather than implicating general dispositions toward a partner.

Finally, although perceived partner responsiveness is usually thought of as a quality that pertains to close, communal relationships, it may also apply in more superficial relationships. Even limited social contacts present an opportunity for interacting partners to acknowledge and reflect the personal significance of what is being discussed. To test this idea, Reis et al. (2010) approached young adults at several locations, asking if they would participate in a brief survey for $1. If they agreed, participants were then asked to describe, in an audio recording, "the best thing that had happened to them during the past week." The female experimenter took notes and responded in one of four ways: with enthusiasm (e.g., by stating, "Wow, that's fantastic . . . the best one I've heard today"), with neutral feedback (e.g., "OK, thanks, now let's go on"), with disparaging feedback (e.g., "Are you sure that's the best thing?"), or after neutral feedback, by offering participants a piece of candy from a box that the interviewer had supposedly just received from her grandparents. (This condition controls for positive affect. Prior research has shown that an unexpected gift of a small treat can increase positive affect and prosocial behavior; Isen & Levin, 1972.) Participants were then given an envelope containing $2—$1 more than had been promised. The dependent variable was whether the participant spontaneously returned the seemingly accidental overpayment to the experimenter. We considered such a return as an indication of a prosocial orientation toward the experimenter. As expected, participants were significantly more likely to return the overpayment in the enthusiastic-feedback condition (68%) than in the candy (51%), neutral (48%), and disparaging (36%) conditions. Men and women did not differ significantly.

In summary, our research shows that the act of sharing good news with an engaged, enthusiastic listener may play a valuable role in helping partners capitalize on personal good fortune. Thus, although perceived responsiveness is usually conceptualized in terms of responses to conflicts of interest, disagreement, problems, and stressors—so-called diagnostic situations (Rusbult & Van Lange, 1996)—its relevance is also apparent when good things happen. The common thread between these two types of situations suggests the viability of perceived partner responsiveness as a core organizing principle.

Perceived Partner Responsiveness and Relationship Maintenance

When a relationship becomes close, partners learn to depend on each other to carry out everyday activities and to work toward long-term goals. This fact of interdependence requires that partners enact strategies for regulating the risks inherent in relying on, and thereby making oneself vulnerable to, another person (Murray et al., 2006). Researchers refer to these relationship maintenance strategies as behavioral, cognitive, and affective mechanisms designed to promote relationship well-being and foster persistence. There are many such mechanisms (see Canary & Stafford, 1992; Rusbult, Olsen, Davis,

& Hannon, 2001, for reviews); here, I focus on a particularly influential process—positive illusions.

Positive illusions refer to the tendency to regard partners in an idealized light, viewing them more favorably than they view themselves. Positive illusions have been linked to a variety of positive outcomes for both partners in close relationships, such as increased love, satisfaction, and trust, and decreased risk of breakup (Murray, Holmes, & Griffin, 1996a, 1996b). This occurs, presumably, because the tendency to interpret partners' attributes and behavior in the best possible light facilitates dealing with the inevitable conflicts, ambiguities, and uncertainties that all close relationships entail. Existing research has focused on the role of one partner having positive illusions about the other partner. Theorizing about perceived partner responsiveness leads us to ask about the recipient of this idealized attention: To what extent do the benefits of positive illusions depend on being aware of a partner's regard for oneself? Note that this is akin to asking about the impact of reflected appraisals, which research has suggested plays a key role in belongingness and self-esteem (Leary & Baumeister, 2000) and in feeling secure in particular relationships (Holmes & Cameron, 2005).

We investigated this question in a sample of 88 married couples ranging in age from 21 to 73 years. They had been married for an average of 10.2 years. Each spouse provided three sets of ratings using Murray et al.'s (1996a, 1996b) 24 trait adjectives: how they saw themselves (self-ratings), how they saw their partners (partner ratings), and how they believed their partners saw them (reflected appraisals). These various ratings were then used to predict daily relationship satisfaction in a 2-week, daily diary study. An important methodological note is that the trait ratings and daily satisfaction measures were collected on different days with distinct methods, thereby minimizing the impact of certain artifacts (e.g., mood, contemporaneity; Reis & Gable, 2000).

Four sets of analyses are relevant here. First, consistent with the idea of positive illusions, there are benefits to having a partner who values oneself. Both men and women whose partners rated them highly reported significantly greater daily relationship satisfaction (controlling for self-ratings). Second, again consistent with prior work, positive reflected appraisals—how participants believed that their partners saw them—were significantly related to greater daily satisfaction (again controlling for self-ratings). Third, each partner's reflected appraisals were significantly predicted by the other's actual partner ratings. Because this analysis controlled for self-ratings, it indicates that reflected appraisals are not simply projections of self-ratings, but rather are based in the reality of the other partner's perceptions. Fourth, and most important, reflected appraisals (feeling valued) mediate the benefits of favorable ratings by a partner on daily satisfaction. That is, as shown in Figure 2.1, the cross-partner benefits of one's partner's positive illusions on the other's

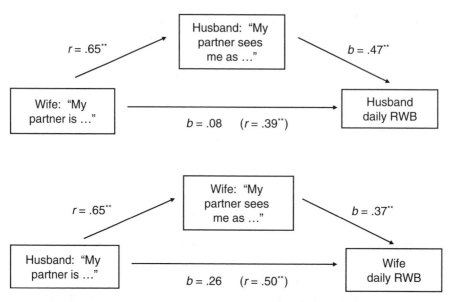

Figure 2.1. Feeling valued mediates the effect of actually being valued on relationship outcomes. The figure presents standardized regression coefficients for simplicity. Analyses control for self-ratings. Structural equation models using the couple as the unit of analysis yielded the same findings. Each partner's relationship satisfaction score was the average of all daily ratings across 2 weeks. RWB = relationship well-being. **$p < .01$.

relationship satisfaction were mediated (nearly fully for husbands, partially for wives) by reflected appraisals. These analyses show, in short, that the benefits of positive illusions, one of the more influential relationship maintenance mechanisms, largely depend on perceived partner responsiveness.

In more general terms, many forms of relationship maintenance are associated with self-regulatory processes, inasmuch as interaction with close relationship partners contributes to the pursuit of self-relevant goals. Extensive research documents the impact of interaction with, and feedback from, partners on the operation of such well-known self-regulatory processes as self-enhancement, self-verification, and self-affirmation (Carmichael et al., 2007). Interaction, especially with intimates, provides a context for partners to demonstrate responsiveness by showing awareness of a partner's goals and behavioral support of efforts to meet them. Because interdependent partners are instrumental in fulfilling many important life goals (Fitzsimons & Finkel, 2010), responsiveness often facilitates, and nonresponsiveness often hampers, effective self-regulation. We therefore see perceived partner responsiveness providing a potentially fruitful theoretical link between the currently disparate literatures on self-regulation and relationship maintenance.

CONCLUSION

Relationship science, like most of the social sciences, but unlike the physical and natural sciences, is often accused of being a horizontal discipline. That is, knowledge accumulates in more or less parallel bits, each finding or theory standing more or less independently, adding novel contributions that have approximately the same level of depth or complexity. In a vertical discipline, in contrast, new knowledge builds directly on what was known before, so that over time insights become deeper, precision grows, and the object of scrutiny is understood better and better. To comprehend phenomena in a vertical discipline, one must appreciate all of the building blocks that contribute to it. Phenomena can be understood by themselves in horizontal disciplines, without reference to related or underlying processes.

What will it take for relationship science to become a vertical discipline? A key requirement is the identification of core organizing principles that bind together into a coherent framework the field's various theories and empirical findings. Core organizing principles provide a conceptual umbrella for related constructs, thereby making it possible to specify how the parts (individual theories and phenomena) contribute to the whole (behavior in relationships). In some respects, core organizing principles are similar to what Cronbach and Meehl (1955), in a landmark paper about construct validity, called a *nomological network*—a theoretical framework for constructs and an empirical framework for measurement, along with linkages between them. Core organizing principles for the field take this idea one step further: linking networks for various constructs into a single framework for understanding how relationships function, how they affect the individuals who participate in them, and how they relate to larger social networks.

It may be apparent to readers of this volume that the field is not yet ready to choose its core organizing principles and set about the task of putting relationship theories and findings into place. Although scholars have been interested in relationships for as long as there have been scholars (Reis, in press), relationship science is a young discipline whose greening (Berscheid, 1999) still stands primarily as a call to action rather than as a notice of accomplishment. Nonetheless, realizing the value of core organizing principles and beginning the search for them are likely to help move the field in a vertical rather than a horizontal direction. To me, this seems an essential step toward crafting a sophisticated, accurate, and useful relationship science.

REFERENCES

Argyle, M., & Henderson, M. (1984). The rules of friendship. *Journal of Social and Personal Relationships, 1*, 211–237. doi:10.1177/0265407584012005

Aron, A., & Aron, E. N. (1997). Self-expansion motivation and including other in the self. In S. Duck (Ed.), *Handbook of personal relationships: Theory, research, and interventions* (2nd ed., pp. 251–270). Chichester, England: Wiley.

Baumeister, R. F., & Leary, M. R. (1995). The need to belong: Desire for interpersonal attachment as a fundamental human motivation. *Psychological Bulletin, 117,* 497–529. doi:10.1037/0033-2909.117.3.497

Berkman, L. F., Glass, T., Brissette, I., & Seeman, T. E. (2000). From social integration to health: Durkheim in the new millennium. *Social Science & Medicine, 51,* 843–857. doi:10.1016/S0277-9536(00)00065-4

Berscheid, E. (1999). The greening of relationship science. *American Psychologist, 54,* 260–266. doi:10.1037/0003-066X.54.4.260

Berscheid, E., & Reis, H. T. (1998). Attraction and close relationships. In D. T. Gilbert, S. Fiske, & G. Lindzey (Eds.), *The handbook of social psychology* (4th ed., Vol. 2, pp. 193–281). Boston, MA: McGraw-Hill.

Birnbaum, G. E. (2007). Attachment orientations, sexual functioning, and relationship satisfaction in a community sample of women. *Journal of Social and Personal Relationships, 24,* 21–35. doi:10.1177/0265407507072576

Bowlby, J. (1988). *A secure base.* New York, NY: Basic Books.

Bradbury, T. N. (2002). Research on relationships as a prelude to action. *Journal of Social and Personal Relationships, 19,* 629–638. doi:10.1177/0265407502195005

Brown, G. W., & Harris, T. O. (1978). *Social origins of depression: A study of psychiatric disorder in women.* London, England: Tavistock.

Bugental, D. B. (2000). Acquisition of the algorithms of social life: A domain-based approach. *Psychological Bulletin, 126,* 187–219. doi:10.1037/0033-2909.126.2.187

Burleson, B. R. (2009). Understanding the outcomes of supportive communication: A dual-process approach. *Journal of Social and Personal Relationships, 26,* 21–38. doi:10.1177/0265407509105519

Buss, D. M., & Kenrick, D. T. (1998). Evolutionary social psychology. In D. Gilbert & S. Fiske (Eds.), *The handbook of social psychology* (4th ed., Vol. 2, pp. 982–1026). Boston, MA: McGraw-Hill.

Cacioppo, J. T., & Patrick, W. (2008). *Loneliness.* New York, NY: Norton.

Canary, D. J., & Stafford, L. (1992). Relational maintenance strategies and equity in marriage. *Communication Monographs, 59,* 243–267. doi:10.1080/03637759209 376268

Canavello, A., & Crocker, J. (2010). Creating good relationships: Responsiveness, relationship quality, and interpersonal goals. *Journal of Personality and Social Psychology.*

Caporael, L. R. (1997). The evolution of truly social cognition: The core configurations model. *Personality and Social Psychology Review, 1,* 276–298. doi:10.1207/s153279 57pspr0104_1

Caprariello, P. A., & Reis, H. T. (2006, January). *Attachment and exploration in the domain of sports achievement.* Poster session presented at the annual meeting of the Society for Personality and Social Psychology conference, Palm Springs, CA.

Caprariello, P. A., & Reis, H. T. (2009). *The role of perceived partner responsiveness in minimizing defensive reactions to failure.* Unpublished manuscript, University of Rochester.

Carmichael, C. L., & Reis, H. T. (2005). Attachment, sleep quality, and depressed affect. *Health Psychology, 24,* 526–531. doi:10.1037/0278-6133.24.5.526

Carmichael, C. L., Tsai, F. F., Smith, S. M., Caprariello, P. A., & Reis, H. T. (2007). The self and intimate relationships. In C. Sedikides & S. Spencer (Eds.), *The self in social psychology* (pp. 285–309). New York, NY: Psychology Press.

Clark, M. S., & Mills, J. (1993). The difference between communal and exchange relationships: What it is and is not. *Personality and Social Psychology Bulletin, 19,* 684–691. doi:10.1177/0146167293196003

Cohen, S., Underwood, L. G., & Gottlieb, B. H. (2000). *Social support measurement and intervention.* New York, NY: Oxford University Press.

Coyne, J. C., Rohrbaugh, M. J., Shoham, V., Sonnega, J. S., Nicklas, J. M., & Cranford, J. A. (2001). Prognostic importance of marital quality for survival of congestive heart failure. *The American Journal of Cardiology, 88,* 526–529. doi:10.1016/S0002-9149(01)01731-3

Cronbach, L. J., & Meehl, P. (1955). Construct validity in psychological tests. *Psychological Bulletin, 52,* 281–302. doi:10.1037/h0040957

Deci, E. L., & Ryan, R. M. (1987). The support of autonomy and the control of behavior. *Journal of Personality and Social Psychology, 53,* 1024–1037. doi:10.1037/0022-3514.53.6.1024

Diener, E., Suh, E. M., Lucas, R. E., & Smith, H. L. (1999). Subjective well-being: Three decades of progress. *Psychological Bulletin, 125,* 276–302. doi:10.1037/0033-2909.125.2.276

Dozier, M., Stovall-McClough, K. C., & Albus, K. E. (2008). Attachment and psychopathology in adulthood. In J. Cassidy & P. R. Shaver (Eds.), *Handbook of attachment* (2nd ed., pp. 718–744). New York, NY: Guilford Press.

Elliot, A. J., & Reis, H. T. (2003). Attachment and exploration in adulthood. *Journal of Personality and Social Psychology, 85,* 317–331. doi:10.1037/0022-3514.85.2.317

Epstein, R. M., Alper, B., & Quill, T. (2004). Communicating evidence for participatory decision making. *JAMA, 291,* 2359–2366.

Epstein, R. M., & Street, R. L., Jr. (2007). *Patient-centered communication in cancer care: Promoting healing and reducing suffering* (NIH Publication No. 07-6225). Bethesda, MD: National Cancer Institute.

Feeney, B. C. (2004). A secure base: Responsive support of goal strivings and exploration in adult intimate relationships. *Journal of Personality and Social Psychology, 87,* 631–648. doi:10.1037/0022-3514.87.5.631

Fitzsimons, G. M., & Finkel, E. J. (2010). Interpersonal influences on self-regulation. *Current Directions in Psychological Science, 19,* 101–105. doi:10.1177/0963721410364499

Fonagy, P., Gergely, G., Jurist, E., & Target, M. (2002). *Affect regulation, mentalization, and the development of the self*. New York, NY: Other Press.

Fraley, B., & Aron, A. (2004). The effect of a shared humorous experience on closeness in initial encounters. *Personal Relationships, 11*, 61–78. doi:10.1111/j.1475-6811.2004.00071.x

Gable, S. L., Gonzaga, G., & Strachman, A. (2006). Will you be there for me when things go right? Supportive responses to positive event disclosures. *Journal of Personality and Social Psychology, 91*, 904–917. doi:10.1037/0022-3514.91.5.904

Gable, S. L., & Reis, H. T. (2010). Good news! Capitalizing on positive events in an interpersonal context. In M. P. Zanna (Ed.), *Advances in experimental social psychology* (pp. 195–257). San Diego, CA: Academic Press.

Gable, S. L., Reis, H. T., Impett, E., & Asher, E. R. (2004). What do you do when things go right? The intrapersonal and interpersonal benefits of sharing positive events. *Journal of Personality and Social Psychology, 87*, 228–245. doi:10.1037/0022-3514.87.2.228

Goethals, G. R., & Darley, J. (1977). Social comparison theory: An attributional perspective. In J. Suls & R. Miller (Eds.), *Social comparison processes: Theoretical and empirical perspectives* (pp. 259–278). Washington, DC: Hemisphere.

Gottman, J. M. (1994). *What predicts divorce? The relationship between marital processes and marital outcomes*. Hillsdale, NJ: Erlbaum.

Gottman, J. M. (1999). *The seven principles for making marriage work*. New York, NY: Random House.

Gould, S. J. (1977). *Ontogeny and phylogeny*. Cambridge, MA: Harvard University Press.

Hartup, W. W., & Stevens, N. (1997). Friendships and adaptation in the life course. *Psychological Bulletin, 121*, 355–370. doi:10.1037/0033-2909.121.3.355

Holmes, J. G., & Cameron, J. (2005). An integrative review of theories of interpersonal cognition: An interdependence theory perspective. In M. W. Baldwin (Ed.), *Interpersonal cognition* (pp. 415–447). New York, NY: Guilford Press.

Holmes, J. G., & Rempel, J. K. (1989). Trust in close relationships. In C. Hendrick (Ed.), *Review of personality and social psychology, Vol. 10: Close relationships* (pp. 187–220). London, England: Sage.

Hooley, J. M., & Hiller, J. B. (1997). Family relationships and major mental disorder: Risk factors and preventive strategies. In S. Duck (Ed.), *Handbook of personal relationships* (2nd ed., pp. 621–648). Chichester, England: Wiley.

House, J. S., Landis, K. R., & Umberson, D. (1988, July 29). Social relationships and health. *Science, 241*, 540–545. doi:10.1126/science.3399889

Isen, A. M., & Levin, P. F. (1972). Effect of feeling good on helping: Cookies and kindness. *Journal of Personality and Social Psychology, 21,* 384–388. doi:10.1037/h0032317

Jacobson, N. S., & Christensen, A. (1998). *Acceptance and change in couple therapy: A therapist's guide to transforming relationships.* New York, NY: Norton.

Kasser, T., & Ryan, R. M. (1993). A dark side of the American dream: Correlates of financial success as a central life aspiration. *Journal of Personality and Social Psychology, 65,* 410–422. doi:10.1037/0022-3514.65.2.410

Kenny, D. A. (1994). *Interpersonal perception: A social relations analysis.* New York, NY: Guilford Press.

King, K., & Reis, H. T. (2009). *Marriage and long-term survival of coronary artery bypass surgery.* Unpublished manuscript, University of Rochester.

King, K. B., Reis, H. T., Porter, L. A., & Norsen, L. H. (1993). Social support and long-term recovery from coronary artery surgery: Effects on patients and spouses. *Health Psychology, 12,* 56–63. doi:10.1037/0278-6133.12.1.56

Kirschbaum, C., Pirke, K., & Hellhammer, D. (1993). The Trier Social Stress Test: A tool for investigating psychobiological stress responses in a laboratory setting. *Neuropsychobiology, 28,* 76–81. doi:10.1159/000119004

Kohut, H. (1971). *The analysis of the self.* New York, NY: International Universities Press.

Kumashiro, M., & Sedikides, C. (2005). Taking on board liability-focused information: Close positive relationships as a self-bolstering resource. *Psychological Science, 16,* 732–739. doi:10.1111/j.1467-9280.2005.01603.x

Langston, C. A. (1994). Capitalizing on and coping with daily-life events: Expressive responses to positive events. *Journal of Personality and Social Psychology, 67,* 1112–1125. doi:10.1037/0022-3514.67.6.1112

Laurenceau, J. P., Barrett, L. F., & Pietromonaco, P. (1998). Intimacy as an interpersonal process: The importance of self-disclosure, partner disclosure, and perceived partner responsiveness in interpersonal exchanges. *Journal of Personality and Social Psychology, 74,* 1238–1251. doi:10.1037/0022-3514.74.5.1238

Laurenceau, J. P., Barrett, L. F., & Rovine, M. J. (2005). The interpersonal process model of intimacy in marriage: A daily-diary and multilevel modeling approach. *Journal of Family Psychology, 19,* 314–323. doi:10.1037/0893-3200.19.2.314

Leary, M. R., & Baumeister, R. F. (2000). The nature and function of self-esteem: Sociometer theory. In M. P. Zanna (Ed.), *Advances in experimental social psychology* (Vol. 32, pp. 1–62). San Diego, CA: Academic Press.

Lyubomirsky, S., King, L., & Diener, E. (2005). The benefits of frequent positive affect: Does happiness lead to success? *Psychological Bulletin, 131,* 803–855. doi:10.1037/0033-2909.131.6.803

Mikulincer, M., & Shaver, P. R. (2007). *Attachment in adulthood.* New York, NY: Guilford Press.

Murray, C., & Greenberg, M. T. (2000). Children's relationship with teachers and bonds with school: An investigation of patterns and correlates in middle childhood. *Journal of School Psychology, 38,* 423–445. doi:10.1016/S0022-4405 (00)00034-0

Murray, S. L., Holmes, J. G., & Collins, N. L. (2006). Optimizing assurance: The risk regulation system in relationships. *Psychological Bulletin, 132,* 641–666. doi:10. 1037/0033-2909.132.5.641

Murray, S. L., Holmes, J. G., & Griffin, D. (1996a). The benefits of positive illusions: Idealization and the construction of satisfaction in close relationships. *Journal of Personality and Social Psychology, 70,* 79–98. doi:10.1037/0022-3514.70.1.79

Murray, S. L., Holmes, J. G., & Griffin, D. (1996b). The self-fulfilling nature of positive illusions in romantic relationships: Love is not blind, but prescient. *Journal of Personality and Social Psychology, 71,* 1155–1180. doi:10.1037/0022-3514.71. 6.1155

Myers, D. G. (1992). *The pursuit of happiness: Who is happy—and why.* New York, NY: William Morrow.

Pinsker, H., Nepps, P., Redfield, J., & Winston, A. (1985). Applicants for short-term dynamic psychotherapy. In A. Winston (Ed.), *Clinical and research issues in short-term dynamic psychotherapy* (pp. 104–116). Washington, DC: American Psychiatric Association.

Reis, H. T. (2002). Action matters, but relationship science is basic. *Journal of Social and Personal Relationships, 19,* 601–611. doi:10.1177/0265407502195002

Reis, H. T. (2007). Steps toward the ripening of relationship science. *Personal Relationships, 14,* 1–23. doi:10.1111/j.1475-6811.2006.00139.x

Reis, H. T. (2009). *Interactions that make for need satisfaction.* Unpublished analyses, University of Rochester.

Reis, H. T. (in press). A brief history of relationships research in social psychology. In A. Kruglanski & W. Stroebe (Eds.), *The history of social psychology.* New York, NY: Psychology Press.

Reis, H. T., Clark, M. S., & Holmes, J. G. (2004). Perceived partner responsiveness as an organizing construct in the study of intimacy and closeness. In D. J. Mashek & A. Aron (Eds.), *Handbook of closeness and intimacy* (pp. 201–225). Mahwah, NJ: Erlbaum.

Reis, H. T., Clark, M. S., Pereira Gray, D. J., Tsai, F. F., Brown, J. B., Stewart, M., & Underwood, L. G. (2008). Measuring responsiveness in the therapeutic relationship: A patient perspective. *Basic and Applied Social Psychology, 30,* 339–348. doi: 10.1080/01973530802502275

Reis, H. T., Collins, W. A., & Berscheid, E. (2000). The relationship context of human behavior and development. *Psychological Bulletin, 126,* 844–872. doi:10.1037/ 0033-2909.126.6.844

Reis, H. T., & Gable, S. L. (2000). Event sampling and other methods for assessing everyday experience. In H. T. Reis & C. Judd (Eds.), *Handbook of research methods in social psychology* (pp. 190–222). New York, NY: Cambridge University Press.

Reis, H. T., & Patrick, B. C. (1996). Attachment and intimacy: Component processes. In A. Kruglanski & E. T. Higgins (Eds.), *Social psychology: Handbook of basic principles* (pp. 523–563). New York, NY: Guilford Press.

Reis, H. T., & Shaver, P. (1988). Intimacy as an interpersonal process. In S. W. Duck (Ed.), *Handbook of personal relationships* (pp. 367–389). Chichester, England: Wiley.

Reis, H. T., Sheldon, K., Gable, S. L., Roscoe, J., & Ryan, R. M. (2000). Daily well-being: The role of autonomy, competence, and relatedness. *Personality and Social Psychology Bulletin, 26,* 419–435. doi:10.1177/0146167200266002

Reis, H. T., Smith, S. M., Carmichael, C. L., Caprariello, P. A., Tsai, F. F., Rodrigues, A., & Maniaci, M. R. (2010). Are you happy for me? How sharing positive events with others provides personal and interpersonal benefits. *Journal of Personality and Social Psychology, 99,* 311–329.

Rusbult, C. E., Coolsen, M. K., Kirchner, J. L., & Clarke, J. (2006). Commitment. In A. Vangelisti & D. Perlman (Eds.), *Cambridge handbook of personal relationships* (pp. 615–635). New York, NY: Cambridge University Press.

Rusbult, C. E., Finkel, E. J., & Kumashiro, M. (2009). The Michelangelo phenomenon. *Current Directions in Psychological Science, 18,* 305–309. doi:10.1111/j.1467-8721.2009.01657.x

Rusbult, C. E., Olsen, N., Davis, J. L., & Hannon, P. A. (2001). Commitment and relationship maintenance mechanisms. In J. H. Harvey & A. Wenzel (Eds.), *Close romantic relationships: Maintenance and enhancement* (pp. 87–113). Mahwah, NJ: Erlbaum.

Rusbult, C. E., Reis, H. T., & Kumashiro, M. (2009). *Perceived responsiveness and the Michelangelo phenomenon.* Unpublished manuscript, Vrije Universiteit, Amsterdam.

Rusbult, C. E., & Van Lange, P. A. M. (1996). Interdependence processes. In E. T. Higgins & A. Kruglanski (Eds.), *Social psychology: Handbook of basic principles* (pp. 564–596). New York, NY: Guilford Press.

Rusbult, C. E., Verette, J., Whitney, G. A., Slovik, L. F., & Lipkus, I. (1991). Accommodation processes in close relationships: Theory and preliminary empirical evidence. *Journal of Personality and Social Psychology, 60,* 53–78. doi:10.1037/0022-3514.60.1.53

Scinta, A., & Gable, S. L. (2005). Performance comparisons and attachment: An investigation of competitive responses in close relationship. *Personal Relationships, 12,* 357–372. doi:10.1111/j.1475-6811.2005.00120.x

Simpson, J. A. (2007). Foundations of interpersonal trust. In A. W. Kruglanski & E. T. Higgins (Eds.), *Social psychology: Handbook of basic principles* (2nd ed., pp. 587–607). New York, NY: Guilford Press.

Strube, M. (1986). An analysis of the self-handicapping scale. *Basic and Applied Social Psychology, 7,* 211–224. doi:10.1207/s15324834basp0703_4

Sullivan, H. S. (1953). *The interpersonal theory of psychiatry*. New York, NY: Norton.

Swann, W. B., Jr. (1990). To be adored or to be known: The interplay of self-enhancement and self-verification. In R. Sorrentino & E. T. Higgins (Eds.), *Handbook of motivation and cognition* (Vol. 2, pp. 408–448). New York, NY: Guilford Press.

Tesser, A. (1986). Some effects of self-evaluation maintenance on cognition and action. In R. M. Sorrentino & E. T. Higgins (Eds.), *Handbook of motivation and cognition: Foundations of social behavior* (pp. 435–464). New York, NY: Guilford Press.

Tickle-Degnen, L., & Rosenthal, R. (1990). The nature of rapport and its nonverbal correlates. *Psychological Inquiry, 1*, 285–293. doi:10.1207/s15327965pli0104_1

Uchino, B. N., Cacioppo, J. T., & Kiecolt-Glaser, J. K. (1996). The relationship between social support and physiological processes: A review with emphasis on underlying mechanisms and implications for health. *Psychological Bulletin, 119*, 488–531. doi:10.1037/0033-2909.119.3.488

Veroff, J., Douvan, E., & Kulka, R. A. (1981). *Mental health in America: Patterns of help-seeking from 1957 to 1976*. New York, NY: Basic Books.

Weissman, M. M. (1987). Advances in psychiatric epidemiology: Rates and risks for major depression. *American Journal of Public Health, 77*, 445–451. doi:10.2105/AJPH.77.4.445

Wilson, D. S., Van Vugt, M., & O'Gorman, R. (2008). Multilevel selection theory and major evolutionary transitions: Implications for psychological science. *Current Directions in Psychological Science, 17*, 6–9. doi:10.1111/j.1467-8721.2008.00538.x

3

THE EMERGENCE OF SOCIAL APPROACH AND AVOIDANCE MOTIVATION IN EARLY PARENT–CHILD RELATIONSHIPS

THEODORE DIX AND KATHARINE ANN BUCK

Individuals differ in their tendencies to approach or avoid social interaction and social relationships. Some seek social contact. They take social initiative, communicate easily and openly, experience pleasure during social interaction, and form close personal ties. Others shy away from social contact. They can be withdrawn and passive, communicate less, experience anxiety in social situations, and fail to maintain close personal ties. These differences have important consequences. As a general rule, happiness and adjustment are better when people are motivated to approach social interaction, worse when they are motivated to avoid it (Baumeister & Leary, 1995; Gable, 2006). Where do these differences come from? In this chapter, we argue that parent–child interaction in the first 2 to 3 years of life may play an initial formative role. We evaluate the interactions that may be critical and the processes that may stabilize children's early approach and avoidance tendencies. Our analysis emphasizes the complex interplay between genes and environments as very young children begin to construct representations of their affective experiences with others, particularly parents.

SOCIAL APPROACH AND AVOIDANCE MOTIVATION: AN OVERVIEW

As a rule, humans are motivated to develop close interpersonal ties and to avoid rejection and ostracism. Social motivation evolved because group living and close social bonds enabled humans to survive in diverse environments (Baumeister & Leary, 1995; Fiske, 2005). Closely related to the brain's pleasure and pain systems, two motive systems are at the center of most analyses of social motivation: social approach and social avoidance (Gable, Reis, & Elliot, 2000). Approach motivation leads individuals to seek and enjoy social contact; avoidance motivation leads individuals to minimize it and to compromise, comply, and avoid friction with others (Chen, Chen, Li, & Wang, 2009). Individuals high in approach motivation tend to be active, assertive, self-confident, and relaxed (McAdams, 1992); individuals high in avoidance motivation tend to be timid, passive, and withdrawn (Coplan, Prakash, O'Neil, & Armer, 2004). To some extent, virtually everyone is motivated to obtain positive, and avoid negative, social contact. Individual differences in the strength of these motives are well documented, however, and appear to be relatively stable from early childhood to adulthood (Asendorpf, Denissen, & van Aken, 2008; Caspi, Harrington, et al., 2003).

Approach–avoidance tendencies are regulated by cognitive and affective processes that distinguish approach from avoidant individuals. Individuals high in approach motivation attend selectively to positive social cues, evaluate ambiguous cues positively, and remember positive information more than do individuals low in approach motivation. They experience positive emotions during social interaction and disappointment when desired social outcomes are not achieved (Förster, Grant, Idson, & Higgins, 2001; Higgins, Roney, Crowe, & Hymes, 1994). In contrast, individuals high in avoidance motivation attend selectively to negative or threat cues, evaluate ambiguous cues negatively, and tend to remember negative information (Derryberry & Reed, 1994; Nikitin & Freund, 2008). They tend to make internal self-blaming attributions (Caspi, Elder, & Bem, 1988; Rubin, Coplan, & Bowker, 2009) and experience shame, guilt, anxiety, and irritation in social encounters (Förster et al., 2001; Higgins et al., 1994). Relative to individuals low in avoidance motivation, individuals high in avoidance motivation communicate less often, less directly, and less openly (Coplan & Evans, 2009; Daly & McCroskey, 1984).

Individual differences linked to approach and avoidance are evident soon after birth. Early research on children's temperaments emphasized individual differences in withdrawal in 2- to 3-month-olds (Thomas, Chess, Birch, Hertzig, & Korn, 1963). More recent work has demonstrated that even newborns differ in variables related to approach and avoidance, specifically soothability, negative emotionality, and stress reactivity (Gunnar, Porter, Wolf,

Rigatuso, & Larson, 1995; Stifter & Fox, 1990). Across the first half-year, stable individual differences are present in negative affect and gazing away (Moore, Cohn, & Campbell, 2001). Negative reactivity in the early months predicts avoidance tendencies at 9 months; positive affectivity predicts approach tendencies at 9 months (Hane, Fox, Henderson, & Marshall, 2008). Differences in vagal tone and reactivity measured as early as 2 days predict infant reactivity at 5 months (Stifter & Fox, 1990). By 6 to 9 months, children separated from mothers in the Strange Situation procedure show consistent tendencies to approach or avoid mothers on reunion (e.g., Waters, 1978).

Such differences appear to be critical to adjustment in both children and adults. Children high in avoidance motivation are likely to be rejected by peers (Coplan, Findlay, & Nelson, 2004; Gazelle & Rudolph, 2004; Harrist, Zaia, Bates, Dodge, & Pettit, 1997) and to develop depressive and anxiety disorders (Findlay, Coplan, & Bowker, 2009; Rubin, Chen, Bowker, & McKinnon, 1995). These relations emerge early. Infants who show approach tendencies with mothers at 6 months show fewer externalizing problems at 18 months (Moore et al., 2001). Research on adults is consistent with this pattern. Avoidance motivation predicts anxiety and negative attitudes toward social bonds; approach motivation predicts satisfaction with social life and positive attitudes toward social bonds (Gable, 2006). Withdrawal is linked to social anxiety, major depressive disorders, and poor physical health (Hirshfeld-Becker et al., 2008; Shipley, Weiss, Der, Taylor, & Deary, 2007). In general, absence of close social bonds is associated with unhappiness, depression, and other health problems (Argyle, 1987; Myers, 1992).

ORIGINS OF APPROACH AND AVOIDANCE MOTIVATION IN EARLY CHILDHOOD

The origins of differences in approach and avoidance tendencies are not well understood, but there is reasonable consensus that they result from biological factors, environmental factors, and their interaction (e.g., Caspi, Snugden, et al., 2003; Fox, Henderson, Marshall, Nichols, & Ghera, 2005; Rubin et al., 2009). Evidence for biological underpinnings is plentiful. Studies have demonstrated that genetic markers predict approach and avoidance tendencies (Hariri et al., 2002; Munafò et al., 2003); twin studies have shown significant concordance as genetic similarity increases (Boomsma, van Beijsterveldt, & Hudziak, 2005; Eaves et al., 1997; Goldsmith & Lemery-Chalfant, 2008; Haberstick, Schmitz, Young, & Hewitt, 2005; Topolski et al., 1997), and neurophysiological studies have demonstrated distinct physiological substrates (Fox, Nichols, et al., 2005).

Yet, the degree to which genetic predispositions are expressed appears to depend on the environment. Research links familial, cultural, and other environmental factors to variability in social motivation. This work shows, first, that education and training can reduce withdrawn behavior in children by enhancing their social skills and reducing their social anxiety (e.g., Bienert & Schneider, 1995; Furman, Rahe, & Hartup, 1979; Rapee, Kennedy, Ingram, Edwards, & Sweeney, 2005). In random assignment studies, infants whose mothers are trained to sooth and play with them are more sociable than infants in matched control groups (van den Boom, 1994). Similarly, withdrawn children assigned to one-on-one interaction with younger peers reduce their withdrawal more than do peers in the control group (Furman, Rahe, & Hartup, 1979). Second, widely observed cultural variation in social motivation also indicates the potential importance of social environments (see also Chapter 5, this volume). In Asian cultures, for example, children display more shyness and withdrawal than in Western cultures. These differences correspond with the extent to which withdrawal is valued and adaptive in these cultures (Chen et al., 2009; Rubin et al., 2009). Third, studies link differences in parenting, particularly parents' responsiveness and control, to differences in children's approach and avoidance tendencies (e.g., Rubin et al., 2009).

Such research has led to proposals that approach and avoidance motivation result from specific combinations of genes and environments, that is, from gene–environment interactions (Caspi, Snugden, et al., 2003; Gazelle & Ladd, 2003; Rubin et al., 2009). Genetic predispositions are thought to lead children to choose or elicit environments that promote approach or avoidance tendencies. Fearful children, for example, elicit rejection from peers and attempts by parents to manage children and environments to minimize children's fear. These in turn appear to promote inhibition and withdrawal (Rubin et al., 2009). Children's genetic predispositions may also lead the same environment to affect children differently. Harsh rejecting parenting may lead genetically fearful children to become anxious and over time to develop stable avoidance tendencies, a result that may be far less likely if children instead are relatively fearless.

A MODEL OF THE EARLY DEVELOPMENT OF APPROACH AND AVOIDANCE MOTIVATION

How do successive interchanges between particular children in particular environments lead to differences in approach–avoidance tendencies? Figure 3.1 displays a model that addresses this question. In brief, the model implies that in the early years children accumulate social experiences that depend on

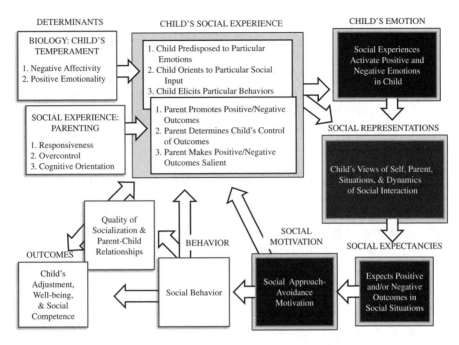

DETERMINANTS   CHILD'S SOCIAL EXPERIENCE   CHILD'S EMOTION

BIOLOGY: CHILD'S
TEMPERAMENT

1. Negative Affectivity
2. Positive Emotionality

1. Child Predisposed to Particular
   Emotions
2. Child Orients to Particular Social
   Input
3. Child Elicits Particular Behaviors

Social Experiences
Activate Positive and
Negative Emotions
in Child

SOCIAL EXPERIENCE:
PARENTING

1. Responsiveness
2. Overcontrol
3. Cognitive Orientation

1. Parent Promotes Positive/Negative
   Outcomes
2. Parent Determines Child's Control
   of Outcomes
3. Parent Makes Positive/Negative
   Outcomes Salient

SOCIAL REPRESENTATIONS

Child's Views of Self, Parent,
Situations, & Dynamics
of Social Interaction

Quality of
Socialization &
Parent-Child
Relationships

OUTCOMES   BEHAVIOR   SOCIAL MOTIVATION   SOCIAL EXPECTANCIES

Child's
Adjustment,
Well-being,
& Social
Competence

Social Behavior

Social Approach-
Avoidance
Motivation

Expects Positive
and/or Negative
Outcomes in
Social Situations

Figure 3.1. Model of the early development of social approach and avoidance motivation.

their temperaments and the behaviors of their parents. Because parents often control whether children's needs are promoted, they influence whether children have joyful, fulfilling social interactions or problematic distressing ones. Because children's temperaments influence children's emotional reactions to these interactions, temperaments also determine whether children experience joy, anxiety, and other emotions when interacting with parents. From these affect-laden exchanges with parents, children come to form representations of their earliest social experiences. They begin to understand why social events transpire as they do and to anticipate whether particular interactions will yield positive or negative emotions and outcomes. They then use these representations to form social expectancies; they come to anticipate that positive or negative outcomes will occur in particular social interactions and, thus, are motivated either to approach or avoid these interactions. The resulting approach–avoidance tendencies then affect their relationships and social experiences, which in turn influence their happiness and adjustment over time. For some children, initial approach–avoidance tendencies may change as they encounter new and different social experiences. For others, early tendencies may persist.

Six propositions central to the model are our focus. First, children's temperaments influence early approach and avoidance motivation because they regulate children's emotional responses to interactions with parents. Second, parents influence children's approach–avoidance tendencies by creating interactions that children experience as positive or negative. Third, early approach–avoidance tendencies also reflect the conjoint effects of children's characteristics and particular kinds of parenting on children's experience of emotion. Fourth, children's emotional reactions with parents are the basis for cognitive-affective representations that regulate their social expectancies, that is, whether they expect positive or negative outcomes from social interaction. These expectancies are the basis of children's approach–avoidance tendencies. Fifth, approach–avoidance tendencies with parents influence the quality of parents' teaching and socialization and, thereby, significant aspects of children's development. Sixth, approach–avoidance tendencies with parents generalize to interactions with nonparents and affect children's social experiences outside of the family. We now review each of these in turn.

THE BIOLOGICAL COMPONENT

Biologically based temperaments may predispose children to experience particular emotions during interactions with parents. Models of temperament stress individual differences in emotional reactivity and the ability to regulate this reactivity (Sanson & Rothbart, 1995). Our model's first emphasis is that biological factors that influence when, how often, and how strongly children activate particular emotions with parents may be critical to children's early approach–avoidance tendencies.

Conceptualization

Two dimensions of child temperament that recur across studies have direct links to social approach and avoidance (Sanson & Rothbart, 1995). *Negative affectivity* is the tendency to become anxious, angry, distressed, or discouraged. It is related to neuroticism, anxiety, shyness, fearfulness, and irritability. *Positive affectivity* is the tendency to experience joy, pleasure, and positive emotion. It is related to extroversion, sociability, surgency, and social responsiveness (Bell & Chapman, 1986; Sanson & Rothbart, 1995). Research has demonstrated that positive affectivity predicts approach tendencies and negative affectivity, avoidance tendencies (Elliot & Thrash, 2002; Larsen & Augustine, 2009; Zelenski & Larsen, 1999).

Emotion-related temperaments may influence children's social motivation in two ways. First, they lead children to experience emotions that motivate them to seek or avoid similar interactions in the future. Avoidance motivation is linked to ready activation of the amygdale and to low thresholds for anxiety and arousal (Fox, Henderson, et al., 2005; Kagan, Snidman, & Arcus, 1993; Rubin et al., 2009). Children high in negative affectivity often experience distress during social interaction and should try to reduce interactions in which distress is anticipated. Children high in positive affectivity often experience pleasure during social interaction and should try to increase interactions in which pleasure is anticipated. Second, children's positive and negative affectivity influence the behaviors they elicit from others (Caspi et al., 1988; Rubin et al., 2009). Children high in negative affectivity, for example, may elicit negative reactions from parents that fail to address children's ongoing interests. Children's resulting distress should then lead them to anticipate, and avoid, such interaction in the future.

Empirical Support

Research has documented a biological-temperamental basis for approach and avoidance motivation (Rubin et al., 2009; Fox, Henderson, et al., 2005). A polymorphism in a promoter of the serotonin transporter gene on chromosome 17q is associated with avoidant tendencies; individuals with the short allele of this promoter have increased serotonergic function, high neuroticism, and avoidant traits (Battaglia et al., 2005; Caspi, Snugden, et al., 2003; Hariri et al., 2002; Munafò et al., 2003). Evidence also links the dopamine receptor D4 (*DRD4*) gene to approach-related behavior (Benjamin, Patterson, Greenberg, Murphy, & Hamer, 1996; Ebstein, Novick, Umansky, Priel, & Osher, 1996). *DRD4* is associated, for example, with brain regions linked to the behavioral activation system (Plomin & Caspi, 1999). Genetic variants in noradrenergic receptors have also been found in individuals with strong approach tendencies (Comings et al., 2000).

A role for genetics is evident as well in twin studies. Eaves et al. (1997) reported that heritability for anxiety avoidance accounts for 60% of the variance in avoidance tendencies, although estimates decrease over time (Haberstick et al., 2005). Boomsma et al. (2005) reported, for example, that heritability accounted for 76% of the variance in avoidance at age 3 years but only 48% at age 12 years. Somewhat lower estimates have emerged in other studies (e.g., .24–.47, Topolski et al., 1997). In addition, approach and avoidance tendencies have distinct physiological substrates. Individuals high in social approach exhibit high left prefrontal activation, whereas those high in social avoidance exhibit high right prefrontal activation (Sutton & Davidson, 1997). Shyness, withdrawal, and related tendencies have also been linked to reactivity in the amygdala, to low cardiac vagal tone, and to high cortisol activity (Fox, Henderson, et al., 2005; Schwartz & Rauch, 2004). These studies suggest that biological predispositions are probably critical to children's emerging social motivation, particularly dispositions related to anxiety.

THE ENVIRONMENTAL COMPONENT: PARENT–CHILD INTERACTION

Environments too, and specifically parents, may influence children's early approach–avoidance tendencies. Our model's second emphasis is three variables that have been stressed in parenting research: parents' overcontrol, their emphasis on seeking positive or avoiding negative outcomes, and their responsiveness to the child.

Overly Controlling Parenting

Control is an important dimension of parenting. Although some parental control is necessary, parents who are highly controlling may overregulate children's behavior, preempt children's self-regulation, and interfere with children's ongoing interests and agendas. Such parenting may be one environmental factor influencing children's early approach and avoidance motivation.

Conceptualization

Parents' levels of control are thought to influence children's approach–avoidance tendencies for several reasons (Rubin et al., 2009). Controlling parents are thought to undermine children's autonomy, reduce their sense of control, and inhibit their development of self-regulation skills. Rubin et al. (2009) proposed that parents high in control promote children's withdrawal because they "over manage situations for their children, restrict their children's behaviors, discourage independence, and control their children's activities. As a result [these children] . . . may not develop necessary coping and problem solving strategies" (p. 150).

Empirical Support

Rubin et al. (2009) reviewed numerous studies that support these ideas. For example, 1- and 2-year-olds are more likely to be fearful and inhibited if their mothers are oversolicitous and controlling (Rubin et al., 1997). Associations between overprotective parenting and inhibition are evident, as well, in 4- to 5-year-olds (Coplan, Prakash, et al., 2004; see also Lieb et al., 2000; Rubin, Cheah, & Fox, 2001). These and other studies have demonstrated consistently that the children of highly protective and controlling parents tend to be inhibited or withdrawn.

Promoting Self- and Ought-Regulatory Foci

Based on self-discrepancy theory, Higgins and his colleagues proposed that parents influence the development of approach–avoidance tendencies by sensitizing children to positive or negative outcomes (Higgins, 1996; Higgins et al., 1994). Parents who regulate children with threats and punishments lead them to an ought-self regulatory focus: They become sensitive to what is expected of them and to negative consequences that occur when these expectations are violated. These children ought to be high in avoidance motivation. In contrast, parents who regulate children by stressing positive outcomes to be attained lead children to an ideal-self regulatory focus: Children become sensitive to ideal outcomes for which they can strive and the parental affection, respect, and other positive consequences that occur when ideals are realized. These children ought to be high in approach motivation. Higgins specified that children with different regulatory foci should develop different representations of potential outcomes, differential accessibility of these representations in memory, and different affective reactions to events. As yet, research has not examined these developmental hypotheses.

Responsive Parenting

Responsive parents are sensitive to children. They read children's affective signals; attend to children's behavior and communications; and generally are positive, supportive, and effective at handling children's needs and interests.

Conceptualization

Researchers have proposed that responsive parenting leads to high approach and low avoidance motivation. Theories related to attachment (Ainsworth, Blehar, Waters, & Wall, 1978), effectance (Dix, Stewart, Gershoff, & Day, 2007; Lamb & Easterbrooks, 1981), mutual regulation (Tronick & Gianino, 1986), and social learning (Bandura, 1977) all imply that children acquire social motivation in part by learning to approach parents who are reinforcing and responsive and to avoid parents who are aversive and unresponsive. Approaching responsive parents tends to reduce children's distress and produce positive outcomes; approaching unresponsive parents often increases children's distress and can produce negative outcomes. Although different theories propose somewhat different mechanisms, generally responsiveness is thought to promote approach and reduce avoidance motivation because it (a) enables social experiences to be rewarding and therefore attractive; (b) links positive outcomes to individuals, thereby promoting positive relationships; and (c) facilitates children's self-efficacy by increasing their control over the outcomes of social interaction.

Empirical Support

Few studies have examined how parents' responsiveness relates to early inhibition specifically with parents. There is evidence, however, that mothers with depressive symptoms are consistently unresponsive and have children who are withdrawn in situations other than parent–child interaction (Cummings & Davies, 1994; Dix & Meunier, 2009; Downey & Coyne, 1990). Associated with unresponsive parenting, avoidant attachment has also been linked to children's withdrawal from peers (Rubin et al., 2009). Studies of somewhat older children are consistent with these findings. Hane, Cheah, Rubin, and Fox (2008) reported that shyness was stable from ages 4 to 7 if mothers were unresponsive (low positive, high negative), but not if mothers were responsive (high positive, low negative). With 4- to 5-year-olds, Coplan, Prakash, et al. (2004) found that low child inhibition was associated with responsive, authoritative parenting.

Some evidence has suggested that children's withdrawal specifically from parents may begin early in development and result in part from unresponsive parenting. Studies that track gaze and gaze aversion in the first months of life have shown that infants are attracted to, and maintain focus on, positive yet restrained parental input, but turn away from excessive unresponsive input (Brazelton, Koslowski, & Main, 1974; Field, 1977). The inherent aversiveness to infants of unresponsive social contact is evident, as well, in results of still-face studies. Although mixed, these studies have suggested that instructing parents to stop responding leads infants to reduce approach to and increase withdrawal from parents (Mesman, van Ijzendoorn, & Bakersman-Kranenburg, 2009). Meta-analysis of these studies shows that positive maternal behavior, critical to maternal responsiveness, predicts high social interest in infants (Mesman et al., 2009). Furthermore, if mothers are depressed and therefore likely to be unresponsive, infants turn away more often and attempt less often to reestablish contact (Field et al., 2007; Moore et al., 2001).

Research in our laboratory has examined relations between maternal responsiveness and the initiative and communication of young children with their mothers. We expected that as mothers' depressive symptoms increased, their responsiveness would decline and, as a result, their children would withdraw from mother–child interaction. To test this, we observed mothers interacting with 1- and young 2-year-olds (M = 20 months) during waiting, play, and cleanup interactions. We coded three sets of child behaviors related to approach and avoidance tendencies: (a) children's initiation of positive interaction with mothers, (b) their passive versus active reactions to maternal control, and (c) their open versus inhibited expression of emotion.

We predicted, first, that as mothers' depressive symptoms and unresponsive behavior increased, children would expect mothers to respond unfavorably to their approach behavior and, therefore, would initiate fewer positive contacts. In both sequential analyses and global assessments, this was observed (Dix, Cheng, & Day, 2009). Sequential analyses showed that maternal responsiveness led to an immediate 30% increase in children's taking the initiative to approach mothers and involve them in play. Similarly, global analyses demonstrated that children who initiated few positive interactions had mothers who were high in depressive symptoms and low in responsiveness. For example, only 21% of children whose mothers were low in responsiveness were high in positive initiation, whereas 50% of children whose mothers were high in responsiveness were high in positive initiation. Only 28% of children whose mothers were high in depressive symptoms were high in positive initiation, whereas 49% of children whose mothers were low in depressive symptoms were high in positive initiation. The data also show that older children initiated more positive contact with mothers than younger children did when depressive symptoms were low, but not when depressive symptoms were high. In low-depressed dyads, children appeared to be learning to take initiative across early development, but not in high-depressed dyads. Thus, research has suggested that depressive symptoms and unresponsive parenting predict low approach and engagement specifically with mothers.

We expected comparable findings for children's passivity in the face of maternal control. As mothers' depressive symptoms and unresponsive behavior increase, children should infer that active engagement with and resistance to mothers are unlikely to elicit favorable reactions. When mothers made requests that children help clean up or avoid "forbidden" toys, we coded whether children who failed to comply did so actively or passively. As predicted, when mothers were low in responsiveness, children responded passively (Dix et al., 2007). When mothers were unresponsive (i.e., asynchronous), for example, 54% of children were highly passive; when mothers were responsive, only 21% were. Similar results were found for depressive symptoms. When mothers were low in depressive symptoms, 49% of children often resisted actively; when mothers were high in depressive symptoms, only 16% of children did so. Furthermore, the tendency for older children to be less passive than younger children was absent if mothers were high in depressive symptoms. Thus, with 1- and 2-year-olds, mothers' depressive symptoms and low responsiveness predicted a passive, withdrawn response to maternal control.

We expected that mothers' depressive symptoms and unresponsive behavior might also undermine young children's attempts to approach and engage mothers with emotion. In early development, when verbal skills are limited, children use expressions of emotion to elicit maternal attention and support (Buss & Kiel, 2004; Gianino & Tronick, 1988). Yet, because depressed or unresponsive mothers fail to react positively to children's emotional signals, we expected their children to inhibit displays of emotion. By coding children's facial displays, we supported these predictions (Dix, Meunier, Lusk, & Perfect, in press). As mothers' depressive symptoms increased and their responsive behavior declined, children displayed fewer facial emotions, both positive and negative. Furthermore, mothers' low responsive behavior mediated the relation of their depressive symptoms to children's low rates of facial emotion. Thus, in a sample of 1- and 2-year-olds, mothers' depressive symptoms and low responsiveness predicted inhibition of children's facial affect.

Conclusions From Parenting Studies

Collectively, these studies demonstrate links between parent behavior and the development of children's early approach and avoidance motivation. In relations with peers (Rubin et al., 2009) and parents (e.g., Dix et al., 2009), children's approach–avoidance tendencies are associated with parental responsiveness and parents' levels of control and intrusiveness (see also Chapter 2, this volume).

INTERACTION OF CHILDREN'S PREDISPOSITIONS AND EXPERIENCE WITH PARENTS

Not only do biological and environmental factors individually affect children's approach–avoidance motivation, but their conjoint effects may be critical as well. Our model's third emphasis is that the affective experiences children have with parents depend on the characteristics of particular parent–child dyads. Understanding early approach–avoidance motivation may require knowledge of how child and parent characteristics moderate the impact of the other.

Conceptualization

Parents' unresponsiveness and excessive control may not have the same effect on all children (Rubin et al., 2009). We expect that children high in negative affectivity and low in positive affectivity may be vulnerable to these parental inputs. They may develop high avoidance motivation, for example, even when parents are only moderately unresponsive. In contrast, children low in negative affectivity and high in positive affectivity may be less vulnerable and might show average avoidance even with parents who are controlling and unresponsive. Furthermore, when either temperament or parenting is extreme, the impact of the other may be attenuated. Extremely harsh, unresponsive parenting may promote problematic anxiety and avoidance in most children, for example, even in children with relatively low negative affectivity or high positive affectivity. Thus, to predict approach or avoidance tendencies well, researchers may need to examine interactions between predispositions and environmental factors.

Empirical Support

Studies that assess gene–environment interactions in the prediction of children's social motivation are rare. There is evidence, however, that children with the short allele of the gene for the serotonin transporter (*5-HTT*) may be at risk for behavioral inhibition only if their mothers are low in social support (Fox, Nichols, et al., 2005). Similarly, the short allele of the *5-HTT* gene appears to moderate the impact of stressful events on internalizing disorders (Caspi, Snugden, et al., 2003). Although not measuring genetic markers directly, other research has demonstrated interactions between environmental factors and preexisting tendencies that may have a genetic basis. More than that of nonfearful children, for example, the compliance and moral development of fearful children are undermined by forceful parenting (Kochanska, 1995); inhibited 18-month-olds are at high risk for elevated cortisol only if their mothers are intrusive and overcontrolling (Nachmias, Gunnar, Mangelsdorf, Parritz, & Buss, 1996); children's withdrawal is likely to become stable only if they are in environments in which they are excluded by their peers (Gazelle & Ladd, 2003). Given evidence that fearfulness and related dispositions have a genetic component, a reasonable interpretation of such findings is that environments selectively promote or reduce genetically linked approach and avoidance tendencies.

COGNITIVE–AFFECTIVE REPRESENTATIONS: CAUSAL SCHEMATA AND SOCIAL EXPECTANCIES

It is an inherent tendency of the brain to construct representations that enable humans to predict the outcomes of behavior. This enables them to control outcomes and, thus, promote their survival and well-being. The model's fourth emphasis is that the emergence of these cognitive–affective representations in the first years of life may form the basis of early approach–avoidance motivation.

Conceptualization

Children's approach and avoidance tendencies may emerge in part as children come to represent and predict the outcomes of social encounters. This occurs, we suggest, as children construct representations of the patterns of affect they have experienced in the interactions their predispositions and parenting contexts have yielded (see Figure 3.1). On the one hand, these representations are models of the past; they are associative, and later causal, models of persons, events, and social processes that account for the affective outcomes children have already experienced. On the other hand, they are models of the future; they enable children to control events by anticipating when positive and negative affect is likely to occur. When representations yield positive predictions in diverse settings, approach motivation should be high; when they yield negative predictions, avoidance motivation should be high.

Social expectancies are central to theories of motivation and behavior. Kuhl (1985) wrote the following:

> Most theories of motivation suggest that individuals are continuously processing motivationally relevant information, that is, information regarding the subjective value of anticipated consequences of various action alternatives and the probability of securing these consequences by performing various actions in question. (p. 101; e.g., Bandura, 1997; Fishbein & Ajzen, 1975; Mischel & Shoda, 1995; Rotter, 1982)

Clinical researchers have emphasized that negative expectancies are a hallmark of social anxiety and avoidance-related disorders (for a review, see Hirsch & Clark, 2004). Learning researchers have stressed that negative expectancies maintain conditioned avoidance behavior (e.g., Lovibond, Saunders, Weidemann, & Mitchell, 2008; Ly & Roelofs, 2009). The centrality of affect to social expectancies is also consistent with prior analyses. Tronick and Gianino (1986; Gianino & Tronick, 1988) argued, for example, that it is infants' recurrent experience of unregulated negative emotion with parents that leads them to expect interaction to be aversive and to regulate their negative emotion by turning away.

Social representations are developing even in infancy. Attachment, mutual responsiveness, and learning approaches each emphasize that from contingent responses to their behavior, infants learn to recognize patterns that connect particular actions with particular outcomes (Ainsworth et al., 1978; Gewirtz & Pelaez-Nogueras, 1992; Lamb & Easterbrooks, 1981; Terabulsy, Tessier, & Kappas, 1996; Tronick & Gianino, 1986). From these patterns they learn to expect that their actions will elicit parent behavior that was elicited reliably in the past. Initially, social representation should be dominated by the child's model specifically of interactions with parents. In early development, parents are the child's principal interaction partner. They control many of the child's outcomes and emotional experiences. As proposed in numerous developmental and clinical theories, expectancies acquired from parents may then generalize to other relationships (e.g., Ainsworth et al., 1978; Tronick & Gianino, 1986; see also Chapter 7, this volume). As children interact increasingly with siblings and other children, parental influence no doubt declines, but initially, parent–child interaction is likely to be the principal determinant of children's social expectancies.

Developmentally, these representations probably begin as simple expectancies. Infants may link a small set of concretely conceptualized action-event units to a small set of outcomes (e.g., "If I cry, things get better," or "If I cry, someone comes and things get better"). Over time associations become causal schemata. They incorporate multiple, abstract factors and the processes that connect them. They may incorporate, for example, the partner's intentions, thoughts, and feelings; the child's own dispositions and likely reactions; complex aspects of situations; multiple possible outcomes; and implicit theories of the dynamics of behavior and human functioning. In 6-year-olds, schemata might look like this: "If I cry because I'm hurt, mother will come and help," and "If I cry to demand something, mother will get mad and tell me to stop."

For approach and avoidance tendencies, the heart of these representations is the connection between patterns of input from parents and the affectively tinged outcomes the child comes to expect. As have others (Gianino & Tronick, 1988; Tronick & Gianino, 1986), we assume that children's regular experience of positive or negative affect undergirds the approach and avoidance component to these social representations. Accurate representations should enable children to anticipate, quickly and automatically, whether they will experience pleasure or discomfort and whether they can control the outcomes that cause these emotions.

We expect that these early social representations are malleable. As children gain social experience, they add data to be understood; the representations that model their experiences should change. Yet, several forces also press for continuity in these representations and, therefore, in children's approach and avoidance tendencies. First, children's affective reactions in part reflect genetic dispositions that are unlikely to change. Second, if consistent over time, parenting that shapes children's approach–avoidance tendencies may stabilize children's initial social representations. Third, social representations summarize significant amounts of experience. Thus, they may be altered little by conflicting evidence from a modest set of new interactions. Fourth, social representations often lead children to display emotions and behaviors that elicit reactions from partners that confirm these representations (Caspi et al., 1988; Rubin et al., 2009). Fifth, by avoiding social interaction, avoidant individuals fail to develop the social skills needed to increase positive outcomes and fail to participate in interactions that might contradict unrealistically negative expectancies. For many children, these stabilizing processes may lead early approach or avoidant tendencies to persist. For other children, diversity of social experiences may change approach and avoidance tendencies as children age.

Empirical Support

Research has linked expectancies to approach–avoidance tendencies. Research on social anxiety disorders, for example, has shown that individuals high in avoidance motivation rate the potential negative outcomes of social events as more negative and more likely to occur (Hirsch & Clark, 2004). Cognitively oriented research has demonstrated the role of expectancies in explaining the conditioning of simple avoidance responses (e.g., Declercq, de Houwer, & Baeyens, 2008; Lovibond et al., 2008). In social psychology, research has shown that expectancies predict behavioral intentions and social behavior (Ames, 2008). Negative expectancies in turn are linked to high cortisol secretion, demonstrating their relation to social anxiety.

Even infants formulate simple social expectancies. Consider that newborns can be operantly conditioned (Gewirtz & Pelaez-Nogueras, 1992); even newborns can initiate simple behavior in anticipation of outcomes they received in the past. Within the first half-year, infants regulate vocal approach behavior with implicit positive outcomes expectancies; they initiate bursts of nonverbal vocalizing when mothers become unresponsive (Goldstein, Schwade, & Bornstein, 2009). By 6 months they also regulate their behavior using parents' facial emotion as a guide: They avoid what parents react to with fear and approach what parents react to with pleasure (Saarni, Campos, & Camras, 2006). These simple expectancies involve little of the abstract elaboration they will have in a few years, but inherent in these behavioral adjustments appears to be the regulation of approach and avoidance by implicit expectancies: "Given my mothers' fear, approach will yield negative outcomes"; "given her joy, approach will yield positive outcomes."

Within the first half-year, infants also develop expectancies about the behavior of animate versus inanimate objects (Wynn, 2008). By this time, they recognize that persons and other animate objects act to actualize their goals and intentions. Infants use this knowledge to evaluate persons and regulate their approach–avoidance behavior (Meltzoff, 1995; Wynn, 2008). When observing puppets or other animate objects, for example, infants interpret observed movements as though controlled by the object's intentions. They expect that actors will persist to produce intended outcomes and infer the valence of their intentions from whether intended outcomes are good or bad. By 12 months, infants interpret others' current behavior in terms of that person's prior behavior in a different context (Kuhlmeier, Wynn, & Bloom, 2003). That infants prefer puppets that have previously displayed good intentions over those that have displayed bad intentions demonstrates that they have formed expectancies and approach tendencies on the basis of the puppet's prior behavior (Hamlin, Wynn, & Bloom, 2007; Wynn, 2008).

Most clearly relevant to our analysis, research has linked the approach-related behavior of infants and young children with their mothers to the likelihood that they will elicit positive support from mothers. When infants are only 4 to 6 months old, their tendencies to initiate bids with their mothers are related to secure mother–child attachment and mothers' displaying contingent smiling during preceding interactions (Cohn, Campbell, & Ross, 1991; Mcquaid, Bibok, & Carpendale, 2009). In the second year, children are particularly likely to initiate interaction with mothers immediately following responsive maternal behavior and with mothers who are warm, responsive, and low in depressive symptoms (Dix et al., 2009; Landry, Smith, Miller-Loncar, & Swank, 1998). Collectively, these studies suggest that, even in the first year of life, infants (a) engage in an implicit social–cognitive analysis that anticipates positive and negative outcomes and (b) initiate approach and avoidance behavior on the basis of this analysis.

DEVELOPMENTAL CONSEQUENCES: IMPACT OF INITIAL APPROACH AND AVOIDANCE TENDENCIES ON PARENT–CHILD RELATIONSHIPS

Experimental research has demonstrated that children's behavior elicits particular kinds of parenting (Bell & Chapman, 1986). Our fifth emphasis is that understanding the role of approach–avoidance tendencies in child development requires understanding how these tendencies shape the early parenting environments in which children are reared.

Conceptualization

Because they influence parent–child relationships, children's tendencies to approach or avoid parents may profoundly influence early development. Early parent–child interaction has been linked to innumerable aspects of child development, from acquisition of language, self-control, and a sense of security to autonomy, executive control over behavior, and the ability to coordinate behavior with the interests of others (Brownell & Kopp, 2007). To a considerable degree, these developments appear to emerge from full engagement with sensitive, responsive parents, that is, from active, ongoing coregulation of joint parent–child interactions in which children and parents act in frequent, extended, and predominantly positive and supportive exchanges.

Children motivated to avoid such exchanges should be at a developmental disadvantage. When avoidance is strong, it may lead to parent–child interactions that are shorter, less frequent, more poorly coordinated, and less likely to elicit children's sustained attention (Dix et al., 2009). In some families, withdrawn children often may be ignored or overlooked. As Caspi et al. (1988) suggested, they may not "experience many of the role and rule negotiations important to the growth of social knowledge and social skills" (p. 825). When parent–child interaction does occur, high avoidance may lead children to attend to and process interactions less effectively. More than other children, they may focus on potentially problematic outcomes or seek ways to exit interactions, rather than process parental input. As a result, they may develop representations of social interaction that differ from those of other children. Hoffman (1983) stressed that children's negative emotion reduces their attention to parental input and results in less effective storage of sociomoral information.

Avoidance motivation may also tax parents' ability to understand and engage children. With fewer affective signals, less direct communication, and less attention and responsiveness to parents, children high in avoidance motivation may require advanced parenting skills if interactions are to be frequent and well-coordinated. Approach motivation may also be critical to the trusting and mutually responsive relationships that enable children to explore the world confidently and that motivate them to attend to and comply with parents' socialization efforts. Research has suggested that motives to please parents and maintain positive parent–child relationships may enable children to resist their egoistic impulses for the sake of integrating into cooperative partnerships with others (Hoffman, 1983). Positive approach motivation should also enable parents to use less forceful methods to elicit compliance (Kochanska, 1995), a quality of discipline linked to the development of morality and social skill (e.g., Hoffman, 1983).

Empirical Support

Research has not examined directly how children's approach or avoidant behaviors specifically with parents relate to parental socialization and parent–child relationships. Several lines of work, however, are consistent with relations proposed here. First, experimental studies have demonstrated that children high in sociability or person orientation elicit more positive, responsive behavior from adults than do children low on these variables (Bell & Chapman, 1986). Second, children's full positive engagement with sensitive parents promotes receptiveness to parental influence; they develop greater empathy, willing compliance, and responsiveness to parents' socialization efforts (e.g., Kochanska, 1997; Kochanska, Aksan, & Carlson, 2005). Third, children high in interest in, and initiative with, mothers are less likely to come from at-risk dyads (Dix et al., 2007; Landry, Smith, Miller-Loncar, & Swank, 1997) and more likely to be cooperative (Biringen et al., 2005; Lehman, Steier, Guidash, & Wanna, 2002), to have mothers who are sensitive (Dix et al.,

2007; Zimmerman & McDonald, 1995), and to be securely attached (Aviezer, Sagi, Joels, & Ziv, 1999; Biringen, 2000; we should note that attachment research has linked avoidant behavior in the Strange Situation procedure to various parent–child variables but has not isolated inhibition and examined its effects on parents or socialization).

DEVELOPMENTAL CONSEQUENCES: IMPACT OF INITIAL APPROACH AND AVOIDANCE TENDENCIES ON RELATIONSHIPS WITH PERSONS OTHER THAN PARENTS

Theories of early development stress that social skills and mental models of social relationships emerge first in parent–child interaction and subsequently affect children's relations with persons other than parents. Our model's sixth emphasis is that early approach–avoidance tendencies with parents influence development because they affect children's early relationships with peers, siblings, grandparents, and other adults.

Conceptualization

As children extend their social sphere beyond parents, they have to rely initially on representations and behaviors acquired from parents. If they have developed strong avoidance motivation with parents, initially they are likely to orient toward other partners with reticence and low positive initiative. These behaviors tend to elicit aversive reactions from peers and others, stabilizing representations and making change unlikely (Caspi et al., 1988; Coplan, Prakash, et al., 2004; Rubin et al., 2009). Initial avoidance tendencies with parents are unlikely to be overcome easily with either strangers, who tend to be threatening, or young peers, who are unskilled, unpredictable, and inflexible. Thus, for some children, strong avoidance tendencies acquired initially with parents may undermine early peer, sibling, and other relationships, thereby stabilizing the affective–cognitive structures and withdrawn behaviors that support these tendencies (see also Chapter 6, this volume).

Empirical Support

Researchers have rarely isolated children's early approach–avoidance tendencies with parents and used them to predict children's behavior with peers and others. At a general level, connections between parent and peer behavior are well documented. In early development, for example, secure parent–child relationships predict peer competence and relationship quality (Schneider, Atkinson, & Tardif, 2001). Characterized in part by avoidant behavior with parents in the Strange Situation procedure ambivalent attachment in particular predicts withdrawal from peers (Rubin et al., 2009). Other research has demonstrated connections between low-competent peer relations and behaviors with mothers that are related to children's inhibition. High negative reactivity at 4 months, for example, predicts withdrawal from peers at 30 months (Glöggler & Pauli-Pott, 2008). Toddlers' proximity seeking and time spent with mothers, when coupled with tendencies to interact with strangers, predicts social reticence in 4-year-olds (Rubin, Burgess, & Hastings, 2002). Indirect evidence is also present in studies that link mothers' perceptions of children's shyness, inhibition, and negative emotionality to subsequent withdrawal from peers (Broberg et al., 1990; Coplan, Findlay, et al., 2004; Coplan, Prakash, et al. 2004). To the extent that these perceptions reflect children's behavior with mothers themselves, these associations may reflect relations between inhibition with mothers and withdrawal from peers. Yet, for the most part research has yet to demonstrate directly that approach–avoidance tendencies with mothers generalize to interactions with peers and others outside the family.

CONCLUSION

Few aspects of human social relationships are more central than whether individuals seek or avoid social contact. The origins of this motivation are evident in infant social reactivity and responsiveness and appear central to adjustment and well-being throughout life. Although genetic and environmental factors are consistently linked with these motives, little is known about how these factors interact and how approach–avoidance tendencies may emerge, and then stabilize or change, across development. We argue that children's early relationships with parents are the medium in which social motivation initially emerges. It is with parents that infants and young children first experience patterns of positive or negative emotions during social interaction. It is these patterns, we propose, that lead children initially to expect that social interaction is likely to be positive (approach) or negative (avoidance). For some children, social experiences across persons and contexts may be relatively consistent and thus may reinforce the early emotional patterns and expectancies children learn from parents. For others, diverse or changing inputs may lead to experiences that are contrary to those obtained with parents and thus may alter social motivation across age or contexts. In either case, we have suggested that it is the construction of social expectancies from the experience of emotions with parents that sets children on an initial approach or avoidance trajectory. Understanding how genetic and experiential processes lead children to construct these expectancies and how they stabilize or change over time is a central task for researchers trying to understand social withdrawal and social competence.

REFERENCES

Ainsworth, M. S., Blehar, M. C., Waters, E., & Wall, S. (1978). *Patterns of attachment: A psychological study of the Strange Situation*. Hillsdale, NJ: Erlbaum.

Ames, D. R. (2008). Assertiveness expectancies: How hard people push depends on the consequences they predict. *Journal of Personality and Social Psychology, 95*, 1541–1557. doi:10.1037/a0013334

Argyle, M. (1987). *The psychology of happiness*. London, England: Methuen.

Asendorpf, J. B., Denissen, J. J. A., & van Aken, M. A. G. (2008). Inhibited and aggressive preschool children at 23 years of age: Personality and social transitions into adulthood. *Developmental Psychology, 44*, 997–1011. doi:10.1037/0012-1649.44.4.997

Aviezer, O., Sagi, A., Joels, T., & Ziv, Y. (1999). Emotional availability and attachment represents in kibbutz infants and their mothers. *Developmental Psychology, 35*, 811–821. doi:10.1037/0012-1649.35.3.811

Bandura, A. (1977). *Social learning theory*. Englewood Cliffs, NJ: Prentice Hall.

Bandura, A. (1997). *Self-efficacy: The exercise of control*. New York, NY: Freeman.

Battaglia, M., Ogliari, A., Zanoni, A., Citterio, A., Pozzoli, U., Giorda, R., . . . Marino, C. (2005). Influence of the serotonin transporter promoter gene and shyness on children's cerebral responses to facial expressions. *Archives of General Psychiatry, 62*, 85–94. doi:10.1001/archpsyc.62.1.85

Baumeister, R. F., & Leary, M. R. (1995). The need to belong: Desire for interpersonal attachments as a fundamental human motivation. *Psychological Bulletin, 117*, 497–529. doi:10.1037/0033-2909.117.3.497

Bell, R. Q., & Chapman, M. (1986). Child effect in studies using experimental or brief longitudinal approaches to socialization. *Developmental Psychology, 22*, 595–603. doi:10.1037/0012-1649.22.5.595

Benjamin, J., Li, L., Patterson, C., Greenberg, B. D., Murphy, D. L., & Hamer, D. H. (1996). Population and familial association between the D3 dopamine receptor gene and measures of novelty seeking. *Nature Genetics, 12*, 81–84. doi:10.1038/ng0196-81

Bienert, H., & Schneider, B. H. (1995). Deficit-specific social skills training with peer-nominated aggressive-disruptive and sensitive-isolated preadolescents. *Journal of Clinical Child Psychology, 24*, 287–299.

Biringen, Z. (2000). Emotional availability: Conceptualization and research findings. *American Journal of Orthopsychiatry, 70*, 104–114. doi:10.1037/h0087711

Biringen, Z., Damon, J., Grigg, W., Mone, J., Pipp-Siegel, S., Skillern, S., & Stratton, J. (2005). Emotional availability: Differential predictions to infant attachment and kindergarten adjustment based on observation time and context. *Infant Mental Health Journal, 26*, 295–308. doi:10.1002/imhj.20054

Boomsma, D. I., van Beijsterveldt, C. E. M., & Hudziak, J. J. (2005). Genetic and environmental influences on anxious/depression during childhood: A study from the

Netherlands Twin Register. *Genes, Brain and Behavior, 4,* 466–481. doi:10.1111/j.1601-183X.2005.00141.x

Brazelton, T. B., Koslowski, B., & Main, M. (1974). The origin of reciprocity: The early mother-infant interaction. In M. Lewis & L. Rosenblum (Eds.), *The effect of the infant on its caregiver* (pp. 49–79). New York, NY: Wiley.

Broberg, A., Lamb, M. E., & Hwang, P. (1990). Inhibition: Its stability and correlates in sixteen- to forty-month-old children. *Child Development, 61,* 1153–1163. doi:10.2307/1130883

Brownell, C. A., & Kopp, C. B. (2007). Transitions in toddler socioemotional development: Behavior, understanding, relationships. In C. A. Brownell & C. B. Kopp (Eds.), *Socioemotional development in the toddler years* (pp. 1–39). New York, NY: Guilford Press.

Buss, K. A., & Kiel, E. J. (2004). Comparison of sadness, anger, and fear facial expressions when toddlers look at their mothers. *Child Development, 75,* 1761–1773. doi:10.1111/j.1467-8624.2004.00815.x

Caspi, A., Elder, G. H., Jr., & Bem, D. J. (1988). Moving away from the world: Life-course patterns of shy children. *Developmental Psychology, 24,* 824–831. doi:10.1037/0012-1649.24.6.824

Caspi, A., Harrington, H., Milne, B., Amell, J. W., Theodore, R. F., & Moffitt, T. E. (2003). Children's behavioral styles at age 3 are linked to their adult personality traits at age 26. *Journal of Personality, 71,* 495–514. doi:10.1111/1467-6494.7104001

Caspi, A., Snugden, K., Moffitt, T. E., Taylor, A., Craig, I. W., Harrington, H., . . . Poulton, R. (2003, July 18). Influence of life stress on depression: Moderation by a polymorphism in the 5-HTT gene. *Science, 301,* 386–389. doi:10.1126/science.1083968

Chen, X., Chen, H., Li, D., & Wang, L. (2009). Early childhood behavioral inhibition and social and school adjustment in Chinese children: A five-year longitudinal study. *Child Development, 80,* 1692–1704. doi:10.1111/j.1467-8624.2009.01362.x

Cohn, J. F., Campbell, S. B., & Ross, S. (1991). Infant response to the still-face paradigm at 6 months predicts avoidant and secure attachment at 12 months. *Development and Psychopathology, 3,* 367–376. doi:10.1017/S0954579400007574

Comings, D. E., Johnson, J. P., Gonzalez, N. S., Huss, M., Saucier, G., McGue, M., . . . MacMurray, J. (2000). Association between the adrenergic alpha 2A receptor gene (ADRA2A) and measures of irritability, hostility, impulsivity and memory in normal subjects. *Psychiatric Genetics, 10,* 39–42. doi:10.1097/00041444-200010010-00007

Coplan, R. J., & Evans, M. A. (2009). At a loss for words? Introduction to the special issue on shyness and language development. *Infant and Child Development, 18,* 211–215. doi:10.1002/icd.620

Coplan, R. J., Findlay, L. C., & Nelson, L. J. (2004). Characteristics of preschoolers with lower perceived competence. *Journal of Abnormal Child Psychology, 32,* 399–408. doi:10.1023/B:JACP.0000030293.81429.49

Coplan, R. J., Prakash, K., O'Neil, K., & Armer, M. (2004). Do you "want" to play? Distinguishing between conflicted shyness and social disinterest in early childhood. *Developmental Psychology, 40*, 244–258. doi:10.1037/0012-1649.40.2.244

Cummings, E. M., & Davies, P. T. (1994). Maternal depression and child development. *Journal of Child Psychology and Psychiatry, 35*, 73–112. doi:10.1111/j.1469-7610.1994.tb01133.x

Daly, J., & McCroskey, J. C. (1984). *Avoiding communication: Shyness, reticence, and communication apprehension.* Beverly Hills, CA: Sage.

Declercq, M., de Houwer, J., & Baeyens, F. (2008). Evidence for an expectancy-based theory of avoidance behavior. *Quarterly Journal of Experimental Psychology: Human Experimental Psychology, 61*, 1803–1812. doi:10.1080/17470210701851214

Derryberry, D., & Reed, M. A. (1994). Temperament and attention: Orienting toward and away from positive and negative signals. *Journal of Personality and Social Psychology, 66*, 1128–1139. doi:10.1037/0022-3514.66.6.1128

Dix, T., Cheng, N., & Day, W. H. (2009). Connecting with parents: Mothers' depressive symptoms and responsive behaviors in the regulation of social contact by one- and young two-year-olds. *Social Development, 18*, 24–50. doi:10.1111/j.1467-9507.2008.00488.x

Dix, T., & Meunier, L. N. (2009). Depressive symptoms and parenting competence: An analysis of 13 regulatory processes. *Developmental Review, 29*, 45–68. doi:10.1016/j.dr.2008.11.002

Dix, T., Meunier, L. N., Lusk, K., & Perfect, M. (in press). Mothers' depressive symptoms and children's facial emotion: Examining the depression-inhibition hypothesis. *Development and Psychopathology.*

Dix, T., Stewart, A., Gershoff, E. T., & Day, W. (2007). Autonomy and children's reactions to being controlled: Evidence that both compliance and defiance may be positive markers in early development. *Child Development, 78*, 1204–1221. doi:10.1111/j.1467-8624.2007.01061.x

Downey, G., & Coyne, J. C. (1990). Children of depressed parents: An integrative review. *Psychological Bulletin, 108*, 50–76. doi:10.1037/0033-2909.108.1.50

Eaves, L. J., Silberg, J. L., Meyer, J. M., Maes, H. H., Siminoff, E., Pickles, A., . . . Hewitt, J. K. (1997). Genetics and developmental psychopathology: 2. The main effects of genes and environment on behavioral problems in the Virginia Twin Study of Adolescent Behavioral Development. *Journal of Child Psychology and Psychiatry, 38*, 965–980. doi:10.1111/j.1469-7610.1997.tb01614.x

Ebstein, R. P., Novick, O., Umansky, R., Priel, B., & Osher, Y. (1996). Dopamine D4 receptor (D4DR) exon III polymorphism associated with the human personality trait of novelty seeking. *Nature Genetics, 12*, 78–80. doi:10.1038/ng0196-78

Elliot, A. J., & Thrash, T. M. (2002). Approach-avoidance motivation in personality: Approach and avoidance temperament goals. *Journal of Personality and Social Psychology, 82*, 804–818. doi:10.1037/0022-3514.82.5.804

Field, T. (1977). Effects of early separation, interactive deficits, and experimental manipulations on infant-mother face-to-face interaction. *Child Development, 48*, 763–771. doi:10.2307/1128325

Field, T., Hernandez-Reif, M., Diego, M., Feijo, L., Vera,Y., Gil, K., & Sanders, C. (2007). Still-face and separation effects on depressed mother-infant interactions. *Infant Mental Health Journal, 28*, 314–323. doi:10.1002/imhj.20138

Findlay, L. C., Coplan, R. J., & Bowker, A. (2009). Keeping it all inside: Shyness, internalizing coping strategies, and socio-emotional adjustment in middle childhood. *International Journal of Behavioral Development, 33*, 47–54. doi:10.1177/0165025408098017

Fishbein, M., & Ajzen, I. (1975). *Belief, attitude, intention, and behavior: An introduction to theory and research*. Reading, MA: Addison-Wesley.

Fiske, S. T. (2005). Coping with rejections: Core social motives across cultures. In K. D. Williams, J. P. Forgus, & von Hippel, W. (Eds.), *The social outcast: Ostracism, social exclusions, rejection, and bullying* (pp. 185–198). New York, NY: Psychology Press.

Förster, J., Grant, H., Idson, L. C., & Higgins, E. T. (2001). Success/failure feedback, expectancies, and approach/avoidance motivation: How regulatory focus moderates classic relations. *Journal of Experimental Social Psychology, 37*, 253–260. doi:10.1006/jesp.2000.1455

Fox, N. A., Henderson, H. A., Marshall, P. J., Nichols, K. E., & Ghera, M. (2005). Behavioral inhibition: Linking biology and behavior within a developmental framework. *Annual Review of Psychology, 56*, 235–262. doi:10.1146/annurev.psych.55.090902.141532

Fox, N. A., Nichols, K. E., Henderson, H. A., Rubin, K., Schmidt, L., Hamer, D., . . . Pine, D. S. (2005). Evidence for a gene-environment interaction in predicting behavioral inhibition in middle childhood. *Psychological Science, 16*, 921–926. doi:10.1111/j.1467-9280.2005.01637.x

Furman, W., Rahe, D. F., & Hartup, W. W. (1979). Rehabilitation of socially withdrawn preschool children through mixed-age and same-age socialization. *Child Development, 50*, 915–922. doi:10.2307/1129315

Gable, S. L. (2006). Approach and avoidance social motives and goals. *Journal of Personality, 74*, 175–222. doi:10.1111/j.1467-6494.2005.00373.x

Gable, S. L., Reis, H. T., & Elliot, A. J. (2000). Behavioral activation and inhibition in everyday life. *Journal of Personality and Social Psychology, 78*, 1135–1149. doi:10.1037/0022-3514.78.6.1135

Gazelle, H., & Ladd, G. W. (2003). Anxious solitude and peer exclusion: A diathesis-stress model of internalizing trajectories in childhood. *Child Development, 74*, 257–278. doi:10.1111/1467-8624.00534

Gazelle, H., & Rudolph, K. D. (2004). Moving toward and away from the world: Social approach and avoidance motivation trajectories in anxious solitary youth. *Child Development, 75*, 829–849. doi:10.1111/j.1467-8624.2004.00709.x

Gewirtz, J. L., & Pelaez-Nogueras, M. (1992). B. F. Skinner's legacy to human infant behavior and development. *American Psychologist, 47*, 1411–1422. doi:10.1037/0003-066X.47.11.1411

Gianino, A., & Tronick, E. Z. (1988). The mutual regulation model: The infant's self and interactive regulation and coping and defensive capacities. In T. M. Field, P. M. McCabe, & N. Schneiderman (Eds.), *Stress and coping across development* (pp. 47–68). Hillsdale, NJ: Erlbaum.

Glöggler, B., & Pauli-Pott, U. (2008). Different fear-regulation behaviors in toddler-hood: Relations to preceding infant negative emotionality, maternal depression, and sensitivity. *Merrill-Palmer Quarterly, 54*, 86–101. doi:10.1353/mpq.2008.0013

Goldsmith, H. H., & Lemery-Chalfant, K. (2008). Behavioral genetics: Genetic influences on individual differences in approach and avoidance. In A. J. Elliot (Ed.), *Handbook of approach and avoidance motivation* (pp. 187–202). New York, NY: Taylor & Francis.

Goldstein, M. H., Schwade, J. A., & Bornstein, M. H. (2009). The value of vocalizing: Five-month-old infants associate their own non-cry vocalizations with responses from caregivers. *Child Development, 80*, 636–644. doi:10.1111/j.1467-8624.2009.01287.x

Gunnar, M. R., Porter, F. L., Wolf, C. M., Rigatuso, J., & Larson, M. C. (1995). Neonatal stress reactivity: Predictions to later emotional temperament. *Child Development, 66*, 1–13. doi:10.2307/1131186

Haberstick, B. C., Schmitz, S., Young, S. E., & Hewitt, J. K. (2005). Contributions of genes and environments to stability and change in externalizing and internalizing problems during elementary and middle school. *Behavior Genetics, 35*, 381–396. doi:10.1007/s10519-004-1747-5

Hamlin, J. K., Wynn, K., & Bloom, P. (2007, November 22). Social evaluation in pre-verbal infants. *Nature, 450*, 557–559. doi:10.1038/nature06288

Hane, A. A., Cheah, C., Rubin, K. H., & Fox, N. A. (2008). The role of maternal behavior in the relation between shyness and social reticence in early childhood and social withdrawal in middle childhood. *Social Development, 17*, 795–811. doi:10.1111/j.1467-9507.2008.00481.x

Hane, A. A., Fox, N. A., Henderson, H. A., & Marshall, P. J. (2008). Behavioral reactivity and approach-withdrawal bias in infancy. *Developmental Psychology, 44*, 1491–1496. doi:10.1037/a0012855

Hariri, A. R., Mattay, V. S., Tessitore, A., Kolachana, B., Fera, F., Goldman, D., . . . Weinberger, D. R. (2002, July 19). Serotonin transporter genetic variation and the response of the human amygdala. *Science, 297*, 400–403. doi:10.1126/science.1071829

Harrist, A. W., Zaia, A. F., Bates, J. E., Dodge, K. A., & Pettit, G. S. (1997). Subtypes of social withdrawal in early childhood: Sociometric status and social-cognitive differences across four years. *Child Development, 68*, 278–294. doi:10.2307/1131850

Higgins, E. T. (1996). Ideals, oughts, and regulatory focus. In P. M. Gollwitzer & J. A. Bargh (Eds.), *The psychology of action* (pp. 91–114). New York, NY: Guilford Press.

Higgins, E. T., Roney, C., Crowe, E., & Hymes, C. (1994). Ideal versus ought predilections for approach and avoidance: Distinct self-regulatory systems. *Journal of Personality and Social Psychology, 66,* 276–286. doi:10.1037/0022-3514.66.2.276

Hirsch, C. R., & Clark, D. M. (2004). Information processing bias in social phobia. *Clinical Psychology Review, 24,* 799–825. doi:10.1016/j.cpr.2004.07.005

Hirshfeld-Becker, D. R., Micco, J., Henin, A., Bloomfield, A., Biederman, J., & Rosenbaum, J. (2008). Behavioral inhibition. *Depression and Anxiety, 25,* 357–367. doi:10.1002/da.20490

Hoffman, M. (1983). Affective and cognitive processes in moral internalization. In E. T. Higgins, D. N. Ruble, & W. W. Hartup (Eds.), *Social cognition and social development* (pp. 236–274). New York, NY: Cambridge University Press.

Kagan, J., Snidman, N., & Arcus, D. (1993). On the temperamental categories of inhibited and uninhibited children. In K. H. Rubin & J. B. Asendorpf (Eds.), *Social withdrawal, inhibition, and shyness in childhood* (pp. 19–28). Hillsdale, NJ: Erlbaum.

Kochanska, G. (1995). Children's temperament, mothers' discipline, and security of attachment: Multiple pathways to emerging internalization. *Child Development, 66,* 597–615. doi:10.2307/1131937

Kochanska, G. (1997). Mutually responsive orientation between mothers and their young children: Implications for early socialization. *Child Development, 68,* 94–112. doi:10.2307/1131928

Kochanska, G., Aksan, N., & Carlson, J. J. (2005). Temperament, relationships, and young children's receptive cooperation with their parents. *Developmental Psychology, 41,* 648–660. doi:10.1037/0012-1649.41.4.648

Kuhl, J. (1985). Volitional mediators of cognitive-behavior consistency: Self-regulatory processes and action versus state orientation. In J. Kuhl & J. Beckmann (Eds.), *Action control: From cognition to behavior* (pp. 101–125). New York, NY: Springer-Verlag.

Kuhlmeier, V., Wynn, K., & Bloom, P. (2003). Attribution of dispositional states by 12-month-olds. *Psychological Science, 14,* 402–408. doi:10.1111/1467-9280.01454

Lamb, M. E., & Easterbrooks, M. A. (1981). Individual differences in parental sensitivity: Origins, components, and consequences. In M. E. Lamb & L. R. Sherrod (Eds.), *Infant social cognition* (pp. 127–153). Hillsdale, NJ: Erlbaum.

Landry, S. H., Smith, K. E., Miller-Loncar, C. L., & Swank, P. R. (1997). Responsiveness and initiative: Two aspects of social competence. *Infant Behavior and Development, 20,* 259–262. doi:10.1016/S0163-6383(97)90027-8

Landry, S. H., Smith, K. E., Miller-Loncar, C. L., & Swank, P. R. (1998). The relation of change in maternal interactive styles to the developing social competence of full-term and preterm infants. *Child Development, 69,* 105–123.

Larsen, R. J., & Augustine, A. A. (2009). Basic personality dispositions related to approach and avoidance: Extraversion/neuroticism, BAS/BIS, and positive/negative affectivity. In A. J. Elliot (Ed.), *Handbook of approach and avoidance motivation* (pp. 151–164). New York, NY: Taylor & Francis.

Lehman, E. B., Steier, A. J., Guidash, K. M., & Wanna, S. Y. (2002). Predictors of compliance in toddlers: Child temperament, maternal personality, and emotional availability. *Early Child Development and Care, 172,* 301–310. doi:10.1080/030 04430212124

Lieb, R., Wittchen, H., Hofer, M., Feutsch, M., Stein, M., & Merikangas, K. (2000). Parental psychopathology, parenting styles, and the risk of social phobia in off-spring: A prospective-longitudinal community study. *Archives of General Psychiatry, 57,* 859–866. doi:10.1001/archpsyc.57.9.859

Lovibond, P. F., Saunders, J. C., Weidemann, G., & Mitchell, C. J. (2008). Evidence for expectancy as a mediator of avoidance and anxiety in a laboratory model of human avoidance learning. *Quarterly Journal of Experimental Psychology: Human Experimental Psychology, 61,* 1199–1216. doi:10.1080/17470210701503229

Ly, V., & Roelofs, K. (2009). Social anxiety and cognitive expectancy of aversive outcomes in avoidance conditioning. *Behaviour Research and Therapy, 47,* 840–847. doi:10.1016/j.brat.2009.06.015

McAdams, D. P. (1992). The intimacy motive. In C. P. Smith, J. W. Atkinson, D. C. McClelland, & J. Veroff (Eds.), *Motivation and personality: Handbook of thematic content analysis* (pp. 224–228). New York, NY: Cambridge University Press. doi:10.1017/CBO9780511527937.016

Mcquaid, N. E., Bibok, M. B., & Carpendale, J. I. M. (2009). Relation between maternal contingent responsiveness and infant social expectations. *Infancy, 14,* 390–401. doi:10.1080/15250000902839955

Meltzoff, A. N. (1995). Understanding the intentions of others: Re-enactment of intended acts by 18-month-old children. *Developmental Psychology, 31,* 838–850. doi:10.1037/0012-1649.31.5.838

Mesman, J., van Ijzendoorn, M. H., & Bakersman-Kranenburg, M. J. (2009). The many faces of the still-face paradigm: A review and meta-analysis. *Developmental Review, 29,* 120–162. doi:10.1016/j.dr.2009.02.001

Mischel, W., & Shoda, Y. (1995). A cognitive-affective system theory of personality: Reconceptualizing situations, dispositions, dynamics, and invariance in personality structure. *Psychological Review, 102,* 246–268. doi:10.1037/0033-295X.102.2.246

Moore, G. A., Cohn, J. F., & Campbell, S. B. (2001). Infant affective responses to mother's still face at 6 months differentially predict externalizing and internalizing behaviors at 18 months. *Developmental Psychology, 37,* 706–714. doi:10.1037/0012-1649.37.5.706

Munafò, M. R., Clark, T. G., Moore, L. R., Payne, E., Walton, R., & Flint, J. (2003). Genetic polymorphisms and personality in healthy adults: A systematic review and meta-analysis. *Molecular Psychiatry, 8,* 471–484. doi:10.1038/sj.mp.4001326

Myers, D. (1992). *The pursuit of happiness*. New York, NY: Morrow.

Nachmias, M., Gunnar, M., Mangelsdorf, S., Parritz, R. H., & Buss, K. (1996). Behavioral inhibition and stress reactivity: The moderating role of attachment security. *Child Development, 67,* 508–522. doi:10.2307/1131829

Nikitin, J., & Freund, A. M. (2008). The role of social approach and avoidance motives for subjective well-being and the successful transition to adulthood. *Applied Psychology, 57,* 90–111. doi:10.1111/j.1464-0597.2008.00356.x

Plomin, R., & Caspi, A. (1999). Behavioral genetics and personality. In L. A. Pervin & O. P. John (Eds.), *Handbook of personality: Theory and research* (2nd ed., pp. 251–276). New York, NY: Guilford Press.

Rapee, R. M., Kennedy, S., Ingram, M., Edwards, S., & Sweeney, L. (2005). Prevention and early intervention of anxiety disorders in inhibited preschool children. *Journal of Consulting and Clinical Psychology, 73,* 488–497. doi:10.1037/0022-006X.73.3.488

Rotter, J. B. (1982). *The development and application of social learning theory*. New York, NY: Praeger.

Rubin, K. H., Burgess, K. B., & Hastings, P. D. (2002). Stability and social-behavioral consequences of toddlers' inhibited temperament and parenting behaviors. *Child Development, 73,* 483–495.

Rubin, K. H., Cheah, C. S. L., & Fox, N. (2001). Emotion regulation, parenting, and display of social reticence in preschoolers. *Early Education and Development, 12,* 97–115. doi:10.1207/s15566935eed1201_6

Rubin, K. H., Chen, X., Bowker, A., & McKinnon, J. (1995). The Waterloo Longitudinal Project: Predicting adolescent internalizing and externalizing from early and mid-childhood. *Development and Psychopathology, 7,* 751–764. doi:10.1017/S0954579400006829

Rubin, K. H., Coplan, R. J., & Bowker, J. (2009). Social withdrawal in childhood. *Annual Review of Psychology, 60,* 141–171. doi:10.1146/annurev.psych.60.110707.163642

Rubin K. H., Hastings, P. D., Stewart, S. L., Henderson, H. A., & Chen, X. (1997). The consistent and concomitants of inhibition: Some of the children, all the time. *Child Development, 68,* 467–483.

Saarni, C., Campos, J. J., & Camras, L. (2006). Emotional development. In W. Damon & R. M. Lerner (Series Eds.) & N. Eisenberg (Vol. Ed.), *Handbook of child psychology: Vol. 3. Social, emotional, and personality development* (6th ed., pp. 226–299). New York, NY: Wiley.

Sanson, A. V., & Rothbart, M. K. (1995). Child temperament and parenting. In M. H. Bornstein (Ed.), *Handbook of parenting: Vol. 4. Applied and practical parenting* (lst ed., pp. 299–321). Hillsdale, NJ, Erlbaum.

Schneider, B. H., Atkinson, L., & Tardif, C. (2001). Child-parent attachment and children's peer relations: A quantitative review. *Developmental Psychology, 37,* 86–100. doi:10.1037/0012-1649.37.1.86

Schwartz, C. E., & Rauch, S. L. (2004). Temperament and its implications for neuroimaging of anxiety disorders. *CNS Spectrums, 9*, 284–291.

Shipley, B. A., Weiss, A., Der, G., Taylor, M. D., & Deary, I. J. (2007). Neuroticism, extraversion, and mortality in the UK Health and Lifestyle Survey: A 21-year prospective cohort study. *Psychosomatic Medicine, 69*, 923–931.

Stifter, C., & Fox, N. E. (1990). Infant reactivity: Physiological correlates of newborn and 5-month temperament. *Developmental Psychology, 26*, 582–588. doi:10.1037/0012-1649.26.4.582

Sutton, S. K., & Davidson, R. J. (1997). Prefrontal brain asymmetry: A biological substrate of the behavioral approach and inhibition systems. *Psychological Science, 8*, 204–210. doi:10.1111/j.1467-9280.1997.tb00413.x

Terabulsy, G. M., Tessier, R., & Kappas, A. (1996). Contingency detection and the contingent organization of behavior in interactions: Implications for socioemotional development in infancy. *Psychological Bulletin, 120*, 25–41. doi:10.1037/0033-2909.120.1.25

Thomas, A., Chess, S., Birch, H. G., Hertzig, M. E., & Korn, S. (1963). *Behavioral individuality in early childhood.* New York, NY: New York University Press.

Topolski, T. D., Hewitt, J. K., Eaves, L. J., Silberg, J. L., Meyer, J. M., Rutter, M., . . . Simonoff, E. (1997). Genetic and environmental influences on child reports of manifest anxiety, and symptoms of separation anxiety and overanxious disorders: A community-based twin study. *Behavior Genetics, 27*, 15–28. doi:10.1023/A:1025607107566

Tronick, E. Z., & Gianino, A. F., Jr. (1986). The transmission of maternal disturbance to the infant. *New Directions in Child Development, 34*, 5–11.

van den Boom, D. C. (1994). The influence of temperament and mothering on attachment and exploration: An experimental manipulation of sensitive responsiveness among lower-class mothers with irritable infants. *Child Development, 65*, 1457–1477. doi:10.2307/1131511

Waters, E. (1978). The reliability and stability of individual differences in infant-mother attachment. *Child Development, 49*, 483–494. doi:10.2307/1128714

Wynn, K. (2008). Some innate foundations of social cognition. In S. Stich (Ed.), *The innate mind* (Vol. 3, pp. 330–347). New York, NY: Oxford University Press. doi:10.1093/acprof:oso/9780195332834.003.0017

Zelenski, J. M., & Larsen, R. J. (1999). Susceptibility to affect: A comparison of three personality taxonomies. *Journal of Personality, 67*, 761–791. doi:10.1111/1467-6494.00072

Zimmerman, L., & McDonald, L. (1995). Emotional availability in infants' relationships with multiple caregivers. *American Journal of Orthopsychiatry, 65*, 147–152. doi:10.1037/h0079586

4

EMOTION REGULATION IN CLOSE RELATIONSHIPS: IMPLICATIONS FOR SOCIAL THREAT AND ITS EFFECTS ON IMMUNOLOGICAL FUNCTIONING

LISA M. DIAMOND AND CHRISTOPHER P. FAGUNDES

One of the most robust findings to emerge from health psychology over the past 30 years is that individuals in enduring, committed romantic relationships have longer, healthier, and happier lives than unmarried individuals (Cheung, 1998; Horwitz, McLaughlin, & White, 1998; Mastekaasa, 1994; Murphy, Glaser, & Grundy, 1997; Ross, 1995; Ryff, Singer, Wing, & Love, 2001; Stack, 1998; Stack & Eshleman, 1998). This effect cannot be attributed to overall social integration, given that individuals' most intimate relationships appear to promote health and well-being above and beyond generalized social support (Ross, 1995; Ryff et al., 2001). Hence, the maintenance of an enduring, well-functioning, emotionally intimate affectional bond makes a unique contribution to mental and physical well-being over the life course.

What are the psychobiological mechanisms underlying this effect? Previous research has indicated that emotional experience and regulation within close relationships play critical roles. On an everyday basis, our closest social partners influence how we feel and how we manage these feelings, and these processes directly influence multiple physiological systems underlying health and disease (Kiecolt-Glaser, McGuire, Robles, & Glaser, 2002a; Repetti, Taylor, & Seeman, 2002; Ryff et al., 2001). In the present chapter, we focus on the immunological consequences of these processes within close relationships, specifically highlighting the growing evidence that emotions elicited by social threat (e.g., interpersonal rejection, denigration, criticism, hostility, bullying) have the strongest effects on immunological functioning. We argue that a key reason for the unique health relevance of close relationships is that these relationships represent primary sites for the experience and regulation of emotions associated with social threat, and hence their associated physiological effects.

Furthermore, the specific emotion-regulation strategies that have proven most effective in moderating the immunological effects of social threat (rumination, suppression, disclosure, and reframing) are in fact most commonly undertaken during interactions with close social others. Hence, although these cognitive and behavioral strategies are typically investigated as individual-level processes, we contend that a greater focus on the interpersonal regulation of social threat within close relationships offers particular promise for revealing the mechanisms through which these relationships influence long-term health.

We begin by reviewing the role of emotional experience in explaining links between close relationships and health outcomes, focusing particular attention on research suggesting the specific importance of emotions associated with social threat. We then turn our attention to psychoneuroimmunological research on emotions and relationships, highlighting findings that support our view that individuals' closest relationships provide the most common and important contexts for the experience and the regulation of immunologically relevant emotions related to social threat. We conclude by identifying some of the most promising directions for future research on the interpersonal "coregulation" of immunologically relevant emotions within individuals' closest relationships.

EMOTIONS, RELATIONSHIPS, AND HEALTH: MOVING TOWARD GREATER SPECIFICITY

Results of numerous studies converge to indicate that emotions represent a critical pathway through which close relationships influence health outcomes (reviewed in Diamond & Hicks, 2004; Kiecolt-Glaser, McGuire, Robles, & Glaser, 2002b; Repetti et al., 2002; Ryff & Singer, 2001). Specifically, close relationships represent primary sites for the day-to-day elicitation of powerful negative and positive emotions, which are known to have direct relevance for disease-relevant autonomic, neuroendocrine, and immunological processes. In the most general terms, poorly functioning relationships involve high levels of stress, high negative affect, low social support, and low positive affect, each of which has been associated with detrimental patterns of physiological functioning (for reviews, see Cohen, 2004; Graham, Christian, & Kiecolt-Glaser, 2006b; Kiecolt-Glaser, Glaser, Cacioppo, & Malarkey, 1998; Kiecolt-Glaser, Gouin, & Hantsoo, 2009; Loving, Heffner, & Kiecolt-Glaser, 2006; Taylor, Dickerson, & Klein, 2002; Uchino, 2006). These patterns include parasympathetic and sympathetic nervous system functioning, cardiovascular parameters such as cardiac output and vascular resistance, neuroendocrine activation in the hypothalamic–pituitary–adrenocortical and sympathetic–adrenal–medullary axes, release of pituitary hormones such as prolactin and growth hormone, neurohormones such as oxytocin, neuropeptides such as corticotropin-releasing hormone and adrenocorticotropic hormone, and multiple immunological parameters, which are discussed later in more detail.

Yet this impressive specificity in parsing the multidimensional effects of psychological distress (and the types of close relationships that elicit or attenuate that distress) has not historically been matched by specificity in parsing different types of negative emotions (and, again, the types of close relationships that elicit or attenuate these emotions). Rather, negative emotional states (most commonly, stress) have often been presumed relatively interchangeable with respect to their physiological consequences, the notable exception being that greater emotional intensity is uniformly expected to elicit correspondingly greater physiological effects (reviewed and critiqued by Kemeny, 2003).

In recent years, however, an increasing number of researchers have critiqued this investigative approach, noting that it basically hearkens back to Seyle's outmoded generality model of the physiological consequences of stress (Seyle, 1956). The alternative model is an *integrated specificity* model that considers the distinct adaptive behavioral–motivational goals (and distinct adaptive significance) of different classes of emotions and affective states (Brosschot, Gerin, & Thayer, 2006; Dickerson & Kemeny, 2004; Weiner, 1992; see also Chapter 3, this volume). In short, the integrated specificity model maintains that different emotional states do not converge to a common pathway of physiological function (and dysfunction), but instead have distinct physiological correlates corresponding to their motivational and adaptive context. This model has received increasing empirical support in recent years (reviewed in Kemeny & Shestyuk, 2008) and has also yielded conceptually meaningful interpretations of otherwise conflicting findings on the physiological correlates of stress (Denson, Spanovic, & Miller, 2009; Dickerson & Kemeny, 2004).

The most consistent and robust evidence for the integrated specificity model comes from research documenting the distinct health-related consequences of social threats to the self, including feelings of shame, ostracism, social rejection, interpersonal hostility, and isolation (Dickerson, Gable, Irwin, Aziz, & Kemeny, 2009; Dickerson, Gruenewald, & Kemeny, 2004, 2009;

Kemeny, 2009; Kemeny & Shestyuk, 2008). As we review in the next section, emotions associated with social threat appear to have particular relevance for immunological functioning and hence play a potentially powerful role in long-term health outcomes. Notably, research on the immunological consequences of social threat has generally focused on threats perceived from the larger social group and has not devoted much attention to the context of individuals' closest relationships. Yet experiences of rejection, intimidation, and shame are frequently experienced and/or alleviated during day-to-day interactions with our closest relationship partners. Furthermore, given that day-to-day interaction patterns with close relationship partners typically become stable over time, the emotions that individuals experience in this context arguably have the strongest effects on immunological functioning because these effects compound over time (reviewed in Repetti et al., 2002; Ryff et al., 2001; Seeman, 2003). For example, studies have found that sustained histories of negative interpersonal interactions are associated with cumulative "wear and tear" on multiple stress-regulatory systems, which in turn has long-term detrimental effects on health (Lupien et al., 2006; Marin, Martin, Blackwell, Stetler, & Miller, 2007; Miller, Chen, & Zhou, 2007; Seeman & Gruenewald, 2006; Seeman, Singer, Ryff, Dienberg Love, & Levy-Storms, 2002).

Of course, such processes are typically set in motion long before individuals settle into enduring romantic and marital ties, and some would argue that individuals' earliest intimate relationships (with primary caregivers) have particularly influential roles on long-term physiological functioning (Cicchetti, 2002; Halfon & Hochstein, 2002; McEwen, 2008; Repetti et al., 2002). Also, early relationships with primary caregivers are known to have enduring influences on the patterns of interpersonal and emotional functioning that individuals develop and maintain over the life span (reviewed in Diamond & Fagundes, 2008; see also Chapters 3 and 7, this volume). Hence, although in this chapter we focus on adult romantic relationships, the interpersonal and emotional processes that we discuss should be understood to have their origins in early, formative family relationships.

With this developmental context in mind, we begin with a brief review of emotion regulation and its interpersonal context; then, we turn to research on the psychoneuroimmunological implications of emotions that are enacted and regulated within adults' closest social ties.

EMOTION REGULATION AND COREGULATION

The constructs of affect and emotion regulation have been defined and operationalized in diverse ways. Generally, *emotion regulation* refers to internal and transactional processes through which individuals consciously or unconsciously modulate the experience or expression of emotions elicited by environmental events (Eisenberg, Fabes, Guthrie, & Reiser, 2000; Gross, 1999; Thompson, 1994). *Affect regulation* typically refers to similar processes of modulation, but the regulated "output" includes broader, ongoing affective states and mood, and not just discrete, situationally triggered emotions (Larsen, 2000). Most of the research that we review concerns the experience and management of discrete emotions rather than general affective states, and so we generally refer to emotion regulation. Also, although we distinguish between emotional experience and emotion regulation, we acknowledge that the distinction between these constructs is notoriously difficult to pin down (Gross, 1999). Some have argued, for example, that there is no such thing as an "unregulated" emotion and that self-regulatory processes are fundamentally interbraided with all emotional experience (Fridja, 1986; Tomkins, 1984).

We generally agree with this perspective but continue to find the construct of emotion regulation useful for delineating the specific, cognitive, behavioral, and interpersonal mechanisms through which emotional states are consciously or unconsciously modulated across both short and long time scales. In the present chapter, we focus on four such mechanisms that have been shown to have specific effects on immunological functioning: rumination, suppression, disclosure, and reframing (for more extensive discussion of these strategies, see Band & Weisz, 1988; Belsky, Friedman, & Hsieh, 2001; Broderick, 1998; Glynn, Christenfeld, & Gerin, 2002; Gross, 1998; Gross & Levenson, 1993; Rottenberg, Salomon, Gross, & Gotlib, 2005; Scheier, Weintraub, & Carver, 1986). Although most prior studies of these strategies have examined how individuals deploy them (or fail to do so), we maintain that each of these strategies can be (and quite frequently is) enacted at a dyadic level and particularly within romantic ties. Across the entire life span, individuals seek (or simply accept) assistance from social partners with managing emotions and affective states (Gross & Munoz, 1995; Thompson, 1994), but individuals' most intimate and important social ties play a particularly central role in this regard (Cassidy, 1994; Hazan & Zeifman, 1994; Thompson, 1994; Trinke & Bartholomew, 1997). In infancy and childhood, caregivers assist infants with emotion regulation through the provision of soothing, comfort, and physical contact; in adolescence and adulthood, social partners assist with emotion regulation through increasingly diverse cognitive and behavioral strategies, such as communicating empathy, assisting with problem solving, providing alternative interpretations of problems, eliciting laughter, or providing distractions (Magai, Cohen, Gomberg, Malatesta, & Culver, 1996; Thompson, 1994).

A potent example of these processes is provided by Pasupathi (2001), who demonstrated how memories for personal events and experiences are coconstructed through the simple process of recounting them to others; the implicit and explicit feedback provided by the listener (both verbally and nonverbally) influences the "teller's" emotional experience while recounting the memory as well as the emotional character of the memory itself. Similarly, research on coping with both major and minor stressors has suggested that a fundamental (but often uninvestigated and invisible) aspect of this process is the extent to which a problem is appraised as shared with important social others (Berg, Johnson, Meegan, & Strough, 2003; Berg, Meegan, & Deviney, 1998). This has demonstrated that although "coping" is often conceptualized as a process that resides in the individual, in actuality it is frequently enacted dyadically.

A key characteristic of such dyadic emotion-regulation processes within adult couple relationships (as opposed to parent–child relationships) is that they are fundamentally bidirectional. Whereas parents provide emotion regulation for their children but do not seek it in return, long-standing romantic partners have reciprocal influences on one another's emotional states through a series of intentional and unintentional processes that some have denoted *coregulation* (reviewed in Sbarra & Hazan, 2008). Research has provided consistent evidence for emotion coregulation in cohabiting couples, most typically in the form of one partner's negative emotions, experiences, and events "spilling over" to influence the other partner's emotional states (Bolger, DeLongis, Kessler, & Wethington, 1989; Crouter, Bumpus, Maguire, & McHale, 1999; Larson & Almeida, 1999; Saxbe & Repetti, 2010; Story & Repetti, 2006), either through specific disclosures or through simple time spent together in close proximity (Butner, Diamond, & Hicks, 2007; Hicks & Diamond, 2008; Schoebi, 2008). Given that the majority of individuals in the United States live with a spouse or romantic partner (Krieder, 2005), a cohabiting partner's day-to-day emotions, behaviors, and cognitions may therefore represent the most potent and enduring emotion "regulators" in an individual's life.

Key questions, then, are how these coregulatory processes manifest themselves physiologically and how they influence long-term health. Although links between interpersonal experiences and health-related physiological processes have been documented across a wide range of physiological systems (Gardner, Gabriel, & Diekman, 2000), we focus our discussion on the immune system, given its well-documented implications for clinically relevant health outcomes (reviewed in Kemeny & Gruenewald, 1999; Kemeny & Shestyuk, 2008; Kiecolt-Glaser et al., 2002b; Ridker, Hennekens, Buring, & Rifai, 2000) and given its similarly well-documented links to interpersonal experiences and their emotional contexts (Graham, Christian, & Kiecolt-Glaser, 2006a; Graham et al., 2006b; Kiecolt-Glaser, Bane, Glaser,

& Malarkey, 2003; Kiecolt-Glaser, Fisher, Ogrocki, & Stout, 1987; Kiecolt-Glaser et al., 2009).

THE IMMUNE SYSTEM: A BRIEF OVERVIEW

The immune system involves both *natural* (innate) and *specific* (adaptive) immunity. Natural immunity provides an immediate (and general) response to foreign invaders such as bacteria and certain viruses. In contrast, specific immunity provides a slower developing response that is tailored for the specific threat at hand. In many cases, natural immunity is sufficiently protective on its own; because specific immunity typically takes several days to fully emerge, it is usually only engaged for threats that are somewhat enduring. For example, transient psychological stressors typically provoke increases in numerous markers of natural immunity, but not specific immunity (Segerstrom & Miller, 2004).

The key markers for natural immune responses are granulocytes (specifically, neutrophils and macrophages) and natural killer (NK) cells. Granulocytes can be conceptualized as "first responders," immediately congregating to the site of an injury or infection to counteract detrimental effects. For example, macrophages release "communication" molecules called cytokines, which facilitate fever and inflammation (and are thereby denoted *proinflammatory* cytokines). Although we often think of fever and inflammation as signs of illness, they are actually powerful signs of healing, as they are necessary for destroying viral and bacterial pathogens. However, too much cytokine-induced inflammation does more harm than good: Individuals with chronic low-grade inflammation show progressive declines in physical functioning and greater disease risk, and researchers have linked these processes to specific proinflammatory cytokines such as interleukin-1 (IL-1), IL-6, and tumor necrosis factor-alpha (TNF-α). Excessive levels of these cytokines predict greater overall morbidity and mortality among older adults and have been specifically linked to cardiovascular disease, arthritis, Type 2 diabetes, and numerous cancers (Ershler & Keller, 2000; Mills, Parker, Dimsdale, Sadler, & Ancoli-Israel, 2005).

NK cells also play a key role in effective immune functioning. They work by "recognizing" the presence of foreign invaders on the surfaces of cells and immediately releasing toxic substances to kill the affected cell. Thus, they are particularly important for stopping viral infections early on, before specific immunity is engaged. Effective NK functioning (which includes not only the total proliferation of NK cells but also their level of activity and their degree of toxicity to the infected cells) is associated with lower risks for numerous physical health problems, particularly viral illnesses and cancers (reviewed in Kiecolt-Glaser et al., 2002b).

EMOTIONS AND IMMUNE FUNCTION

There is substantial evidence that both transient and chronic emotional states are associated with numerous markers of immune functioning, including total numbers of immune lymphocytes; the ratio of different types of lymphocytes; secretion of proinflammatory cytokines and subsequent inflammatory response; cellular response to inoculations; likelihood and duration of illness in responses to infection exposure; and healing speed for minor, controlled wounds (reviewed in Cohen & Herbert, 1996; Kiecolt-Glaser et al., 2002a, 2002b). Although effects for one marker do not necessarily extend to others, and although the duration and clinical relevance of detected effects are sometimes unclear (with notable exceptions such as Cohen, 2001), the overall link between emotional functioning and immune functioning is robust.

Many studies of this link have focused on the negative immunological implications of immediate and/or anticipated stress (reviewed in Benschop et al., 1998; Cohen, Miller, & Rabin, 2001; Kemeny, 2003; Kemeny & Shestyuk, 2008; O'Leary, 1990), whether naturally occurring or laboratory induced (Bachen et al., 1992; Benschop et al., 1998; Cacioppo et al., 1995; Lacey et al., 2000; Sgoutas-Emch et al., 1994). Conversely, studies have also found that positive experiences and emotions are associated with more adaptive patterns of immune functioning, independent of personality traits such as extraversion and agreeableness (Cohen, Alper, Doyle, Treanor, & Turner, 2006; Cohen, Doyle, Turner, Alper, & Skoner, 2003; Marsland, Cohen, Rabin, & Manuck, 2006).

Notably, however, the strength of empirical evidence for these linkages varies considerably from study to study (Denson et al., 2009; Dickerson & Kemeny, 2004). This is a key reason that researchers have increasingly argued that tests for general associations between immune functioning and "bad versus good emotions" should be supplanted by a more specific investigative approach that takes into account the motivational context and adaptive significance of different types of emotions (Dickerson & Kemeny, 2004; Kemeny & Shestyuk, 2008; Weiner, 1992). Research in this vein has reliably found that emotions associated with social threats to the self (i.e., shame, embarrassment, anger, or depression elicited by social evaluation, hostile provocation, or interpersonal rejection) have the most pronounced and consistent immunological consequences, particularly on the production of proinflammatory cytokines (Ackerman, Martino, Heyman, Moyna, & Rabin, 1998; Altemus, Rao, Dhabhar, Ding, & Granstein, 2001; Dickerson, Kemeny, Aziz, Kim, & Fahey, 2004; Goebel, Mills, Irwin, & Ziegler, 2000; Quan et al., 2001; Stark et al., 2001). Dickerson, Gruenewald, and Kemeny (2004, 2009) argued that this is because the release of proinflammatory cytokines in response to social threat is an evolved adaptive response that served to prepare the organism for social antagonism or to facilitate a functional self-protective response of submission or disengagement (Dickerson, Gruenewald, et al., 2004, 2009). It is only when these short-term immunological responses persist over time that they become maladaptive.

IMPLICATIONS FOR RELATIONSHIP FUNCTIONING

We envision two main pathways through which close relationship partners might influence the experience and regulation of emotions associated with social threat. First, one's partner might be the threat. This would be the case for relationships characterized by high levels of hostility, criticism, or interpersonal aggression. Second, one's partner might modulate feelings of social threat that are experienced at the hands of others. Of course, distinctions between relationships that provoke versus avoid hostility, and that provide mutual support versus denigration, have long been a staple of research on relationship stability and satisfaction (reviewed in Diamond, Fagundes, & Butterworth, 2010). Our contention is that these distinctions have just as much relevance for individuals' immunological functioning and hence their long-term health.

Evidence for the first pathway (i.e., romantic partners as social threats) comes from extensive psychoneuroimmunological research on married couples demonstrating that interpersonal hostility (typically assessed through laboratory-based conflict interactions) provides a potent risk factor for compromised immune functioning. For example, in a study of healthy newlywed couples with high overall marital satisfaction, participants who exhibited more negative and hostile behaviors during a 30-min marital problem discussion showed poorer immune functioning over the next 24 hr across four functional immune essays (i.e., NK cell lysis and the blastogenic response to Con A, PHA, and a monoclonal antibody to the T3 receptor; Kiecolt-Glaser, Malarkey, Chee, & Newton, 1993). In an experimental study examining how quickly each member of 42 married dyads recovered from a wound following both a conflict and supportive interaction with his or her partner, couples' blister wounds healed more slowly and local cytokine production of IL-6, TNF-α, and IL-1 was lower at wound sites following marital conflicts than after social support interactions (Kiecolt-Glaser et al., 2005). Furthermore, couples who demonstrated consistently higher levels of hostile behaviors across both interactions healed at a rate of 60% less than low-hostile couples. Similar findings have been replicated in older populations. For example, in a study of 31 older couples who had been married an average of 42 years, both men and women who displayed more negative behaviors during a marital disagreement exhibited poorer (or weaker) immune responses across three different immune function indices (Kiecolt-Glaser et al., 1997).

Collectively, these findings suggest that the immunologically detrimental features of poorly functioning relationships derive from partners' propensities to attack one another's "social selves" through criticism, denigration, contempt, and hostility. Notably, these are precisely the same interpersonal behaviors that Gottman (1991, 1994; Gottman, Coan, Carrère, & Swanson, 1998; Gottman & Levenson, 1992) has found to be most detrimental to relationship quality and most predictive of divorce. On this point, it bears noting that although any social partner can launch such an attack, intimate partners arguably have the most effective "ammunition" for doing so by virtue of their intimate knowledge of one another (e.g., giving them particular power to provoke shame) and by virtue of the emotional importance of these relationships (see, e.g., the model of "risk regulation" in close relationships by Murray, Holmes, & Collins, 2006, which emphasizes the degree to which the benefits of intimacy are necessarily accompanied by risks stemming from dependency and the potential for rejection). Hence, the emotions associated with social threat are likely to be particularly intense and to have particularly strong immunological consequences when triggered by intimate partners.

RELATIONSHIPS AS REGULATORS: DETRIMENTAL EFFECTS

Whereas the first pathway conceptualizes intimate partners as sources of social threat, the second pathway conceptualizes intimate partners as moderators of social threat. In poorly functioning relationships, partners might actually exacerbate threats to the self by facilitating emotion-regulation strategies such as rumination and suppression. Studies have reliably detected pronounced negative immunological consequences of rumination and perseverative worrying, including production of both leukocytes and lymphocytes (Thomsen et al., 2004), NK cell production (Segerstrom, Solomon, Kemeny, & Fahey, 1998), and antibody production in response to influenza vaccines (Segerstrom, Glover, Craske, & Fahey, 1999; Segerstrom, Schipper, & Greenberg, 2008). Although rumination and worry are typically conceptualized and measured as individual-level processes, they obviously occur within interpersonal contexts. Every time that an individual discloses worries and concerns to a close relationship partner, that partner's response has the potential to magnify and extend the ruminative process ("You did what? No wonder you're worried, you'll probably get fired") or to interrupt it ("You're overreacting, I bet nobody even remembers what you said during that meeting"). Hence, although tendencies for rumination are often viewed as person-level traits, we might also consider the degree to which different types of relationships provide contexts that either support or interrupt rumination. Therefore, one provocative direction for future psychoneuroimmunological research might be to assess whether individuals' whose partners regularly interrupt ruminative worry are less susceptible to the negative immunological effects of negative emotions.

Another maladaptive emotion-regulation strategy with immunological implications is emotional suppression. Although negative emotions such as shame and hostility are associated with detrimental patterns of immunological functioning, attempts to suppress such emotions only compound the damage (reviewed in Kemeny & Gruenewald, 1999; Pennebaker, 1993). This may explain why individuals with an avoidant attachment style (characterized by tendencies to protect the social self through emotional distancing, inhibition, and suppression) show detrimental patterns of cellular immune function and inflammation. For example, one recent study found that highly avoidant women exhibited lower NK cell cytotoxicity (Picardi et al., 2007), and a study of married couples found that avoidant partners showed elevated IL-6 production during marital conflict (Gouin et al., 2009). In an interpersonal context, some partners may develop "habits" of emotional inhibition and suppression if they perceive that their partners are unwilling or unable to support them in times of distress. This is a particularly intriguing possibility given that low perceived support is a reliable predictor of poor immunological functioning (Esterling, Kiecolt-Glaser, & Glaser, 1996). For example, in a study of healthy men, those who perceived lower support exhibited lower NK cell numbers (Miyazaki et al., 2003). Lower levels of perceived support have also been shown to be associated with lower NK cell activity among cancer patients and chronically stressed caregivers of spouses with dementia (Baron, Cutrona, Hicklin, Russell, & Lubaroff, 1990; Chen, Li, & Li, 2005; Esterling, Kiecolt-Glaser, Bodnar, & Glaser, 1994; Esterling et al., 1996). Hence, one possibility is that the worst immunological outcomes might be evident in individuals who adopt emotion-regulation strategies of inhibition and suppression specifically in response to perceptions of low support from their romantic partners.

RELATIONSHIPS AS REGULATORS: BENEFICIAL EFFECTS

In direct contrast to the examples provided above, partners in well-functioning relationships might be uniquely capable of repairing threats to the social self and attenuating emotions such as shame and anger. It bears noting that such beneficial effects of well-functioning relationships have long been conceptualized and investigated as "stress buffering" effects; we might just as well think of them as "shame buffering" effects, given the relevance of social threat for immunological functioning.

Research has found that the emotion-regulation strategies of emotional disclosure and positive reframing (which are often described in terms of "benefit finding" or "self-enhancement") have well-documented immunological benefits, and both of these strategies are likely to be enhanced and facilitated by supportive romantic partners. For example, emotional disclosure has been associated with lower antibody titers to the Epstein-Barr virus (Esterling, Antoni, Kumar, & Schneiderman, 1990) and appears to be particularly effective when it facilitates cognitive processing and "meaning making" in the context of stressful events (Bower, Kemeny, Taylor, & Fahey, 2003; O'Cleirigh, Ironson, Fletcher, & Schneiderman, 2008). Hence, particularly immunologically relevant features of relationship quality may be the extent to which partners regularly disclose stressors and other meaningful events and feelings to one another, and the degree to which such disclosures are met with empathy, sensitivity, and attention versus disengagement and avoidance.

Such disclosures provide potent opportunities for positive reframing and self-enhancement, which in many ways represents the direct opposite of social threat. Whereas social threats involve feelings of denigration, rejection, self-blame, and heightened awareness of one's faults and shortcomings, positive reframing replaces these negative cognitions and negative self-views with an emphasis on one's own positive traits, motives, and characteristics and with the potential benefits that derive even from stressful experiences (Bower et al., 2003; Bower & Segerstrom, 2004). An increasing body of research has suggested that cognitive self-enhancement and positive reframing of stressors has direct physiological benefits for immunological and other health-related physiological processes (reviewed in Segerstrom, Roach, & Chang, 2008; Taylor, Kemeny, Reed, Bower, & Gruenewald, 2000; Taylor, Lerner, Sherman, Sage, & McDowell, 2003). For example, Segerstrom, Taylor, Kemeny, Reed, and Visscher (1996) found that HIV-positive individuals who attributed negative life events to negative aspects of their own selves showed significantly faster declines in CD4 (helper T cell) levels over an 18-month period, controlling for potential confounds such as depression and health behaviors. Other research has found similar effects, demonstrating that attributions of self-blame are associated with decreased T-helper cell/T-suppressor cell ratios and also reduced lymphocyte responses to mitogens (Kamen-Siegel, Rodin, Seligman, & Dwyer, 1991). Particularly strong evidence for the importance of self-views comes from research showing that experimental manipulations designed to increase negative self-evaluations lead to declines in NK cell activity (Strauman, Lemieux, & Coe, 1993), whereas interventions designed to reduce self-blame and other negative self-evaluations produced increased NK cell activity and other immune parameters (Antoni et al., 1991).

Notably, studies documenting the beneficial health effects of self-enhancing beliefs and positive attributions do not typically ask their participants where they got these positive cognitions, but it is highly likely that close relationship partners play a significant role in establishing and maintaining these perceptions. In fact, studies of relationship functioning have reliably found that individuals who regularly enhance one another's self-concepts, maintaining even overly generous perceptions of a partner's traits and motives, have happier and longer lasting relationships (Murray, Holmes, & Griffin, 1996, 2004). Clearly, these interpersonal processes have beneficial effects on health as well. In fact, one reason that emotional disclosure is associated with immunological benefits is that when an individual reveals fears and insecurities to his or her partner, the partner has an immediate opportunity to counteract negative self-concepts and attributions and replace them with self-enhancing cognitions and attributions.

CONCLUSION

Research on the health implications of close relationships would profit from a greater emphasis on close relationships as primary sites for the experience and regulation of emotions related to social threat, which are known to have pronounced immunological consequences. Whereas most prior research has conceptualized the experience and regulation of such emotions as intra-individual processes, we emphasize instead their embeddedness in day-to-day dyadic interchanges with our most intimate and important social partners (see also Chapter 2, this volume). During such interchanges, partners can elicit a partner's shame and denigration through hostility and criticism, or instead counteract it, actively repairing negative self-views that individuals may have "brought home" from aversive experiences with other members of their social network. In the course of routine conversations about the events of the day, partners can permit and even magnify one another's tendencies for ruminative worry, or they can interrupt it with counterexamples, reappraisals, and alternative interpretations. During disclosures of emotionally relevant experiences, partners can support one another's processes of cognitive analysis, positive reappraisal, and meaning making, or they can shut down such disclosures through emotional disengagement and withdrawal.

The fact that such interpersonal processes have direct implications for relationship satisfaction and stability should not be surprising and, in fact, has generated a voluminous body of research over the past 30 years (reviewed in Diamond et al., 2010). Yet the possibility that these exact processes also have specific, demonstrable effects on immunological functioning and other health-related physiological processes would provide some of the most powerful evidence to date of the health implications of well-functioning intimate relationships. Whereas previous research has ably demonstrated links between global features of relationship functioning and health-related physiological processes, the next step is to document these associations at the level of specific interpersonal processes. We anticipate that the next generation of interdisciplinary research on close relationships will take up this challenge, using multiple methods and measures to pinpoint the specific types of words, gestures, behaviors, and cognitions exchanged between romantic partners that have the most beneficial (or detrimental) effects on both mental and physical functioning over the life course.

REFERENCES

Ackerman, K. D., Martino, M., Heyman, R., Moyna, N. M., & Rabin, B. S. (1998). Stressor-induced alteration of cytokine production in multiple sclerosis patients and controls. *Psychosomatic Medicine, 60,* 484–491.

Altemus, M., Rao, B., Dhabhar, F. S., Ding, W., & Granstein, R. D. (2001). Stress-induced changes in skin barrier function in healthy women. *The Journal of Investigative Dermatology, 117,* 309–317. doi:10.1046/j.1523-1747.2001.01373.x

Antoni, M. H., Baggett, L., Ironson, G., LaPerriere, A., August, S., Klimas, N., . . . Fletcher, M. A. (1991). Cognitive-behavioral stress management intervention buffers distress responses and immunologic changes following notification of HIV-1 seropositivity. *Journal of Consulting and Clinical Psychology, 59,* 906–915. doi:10.1037/0022-006X.59.6.906

Bachen, E. A., Manuck, S. B., Marsland, A. L., Cohen, S., Malkoff, S. B., Muldoon, M. F., & Rabin, B. S. (1992). Lymphocyte subset and cellular immune responses to a brief experimental stressor. *Psychosomatic Medicine, 54,* 673–679.

Band, E. B., & Weisz, J. R. (1988). How to feel better when it feels bad: Children's perspectives on coping with everyday stress. *Developmental Psychology, 24,* 247–253. doi:10.1037/0012-1649.24.2.247

Baron, R. S., Cutrona, C. E., Hicklin, D., Russell, D. W., & Lubaroff, D. M. (1990). Social support and immune function among spouses of cancer patients. *Journal of Personality and Social Psychology, 59,* 344–352. doi:10.1037/0022-3514.59.2.344

Belsky, J., Friedman, S. L., & Hsieh, K. H. (2001). Testing a core emotion-regulation prediction: Does early attentional persistence moderate the effect of infant negative emotionality on later development? *Child Development, 72,* 123–133. doi:10.1111/1467-8624.00269

Benschop, R. J., Geenen, R., Mills, P. J., Naliboff, B. D., Kiecolt-Glaser, J. K., Herbert, T. B., . . . Cacioppo, J. T. (1998). Cardiovascular and immune responses to acute psychological stress in young and old women: A meta-analysis. *Psychosomatic Medicine, 60,* 290–296.

Berg, C. A., Johnson, M. M. S., Meegan, S. P., & Strough, J. (2003). Collaborative problem-solving interactions in young and old married couples. *Discourse Processes, 35,* 33–58. doi:10.1207/S15326950DP3501_2

Berg, C. A., Meegan, S. P., & Deviney, F. P. (1998). A social-contextual model of coping with everyday problems across the lifespan. *International Journal of Behavioral Development, 22,* 239–261. doi:10.1080/016502598384360

Bolger, N., DeLongis, A., Kessler, R. C., & Wethington, E. (1989). The contagion of stress across multiple roles. *Journal of Marriage and Family, 51,* 175–183. doi:10.2307/352378

Bower, J. E., Kemeny, M. E., Taylor, S. E., & Fahey, J. L. (2003). Finding positive meaning and its association with natural killer cell cytotoxicity among participants in a bereavement-related disclosure intervention. *Annals of Behavioral Medicine, 25,* 146–155. doi:10.1207/S15324796ABM2502_11

Bower, J. E., & Segerstrom, S. C. (2004). Stress management, finding benefit, and immune function: Positive mechanisms for intervention effects on physiology. *Journal of Psychosomatic Research, 56,* 9–11. doi:10.1016/S0022-3999(03)00120-X

Broderick, P. C. (1998). Early adolescent gender differences in the use of ruminative and distracting coping strategies. *The Journal of Early Adolescence, 18,* 173–191. doi:10.1177/0272431698018002003

Brosschot, J. F., Gerin, W., & Thayer, J. F. (2006). The perseverative cognition hypothesis: A review of worry, prolonged stress-related physiological activation, and health. *Journal of Psychosomatic Research, 60,* 113–124. doi:10.1016/j.jpsychores.2005.06.074

Butner, J., Diamond, L. M., & Hicks, A. M. (2007). Attachment style and two forms of affect coregulation between romantic partners. *Personal Relationships, 14,* 431–455. doi:10.1111/j.1475-6811.2007.00164.x

Cacioppo, J. T., Malarkey, W. B., Kiecolt-Glaser, J. K., Uchino, B. N., Sgoutas-Emch, S. A., Sheridan, J. F., . . . Glaser, R. (1995). Heterogeneity in neuroendocrine and immune responses to brief psychological stressors as a function of autonomic cardiac activation. *Psychosomatic Medicine, 57,* 154–164.

Cassidy, J. (1994). Emotion regulation: Influences of attachment relationships. *Monographs of the Society for Research in Child Development, 59*(2–3, Serial No. 240), 228–249.

Chen, H., Li, X.-Y., & Li, Z.-H. (2005). Psychosocial factor and immune function of patients with breast cancer before operation. *Chinese Mental Health Journal, 19,* 557–560.

Cheung, Y. B. (1998). Accidents, assaults, and marital status. *Social Science & Medicine, 47,* 1325–1329. doi:10.1016/S0277-9536(98)00210-X

Cicchetti, D. (2002). The impact of social experience on neurobiological systems: Illustration from a constructivist view of child maltreatment. *Cognitive Development, 17,* 1407–1428.

Cohen, S. (2001). Social relationships and susceptibility to the common cold. In C. D. Ryff & B. H. Singer (Eds.), *Emotion, social relationships, and health* (pp. 221–232). New York, NY: Oxford University Press.

Cohen, S. (2004). Social relationships and health. *American Psychologist, 59,* 676–684. doi:10.1037/0003-066X.59.8.676

Cohen, S., Alper, C. M., Doyle, W. J., Treanor, J. J., & Turner, R. B. (2006). Positive emotional style predicts resistance to illness after experimental exposure to rhinovirus or influenza A virus. *Psychosomatic Medicine, 68*, 809–815. doi:10.1097/01.psy.0000245867.92364.3c

Cohen, S., Doyle, W. J., Turner, R. B., Alper, C. M., & Skoner, D. P. (2003). Emotional style and susceptibility to the common cold. *Psychosomatic Medicine, 65*, 652–657. doi:10.1097/01.PSY.0000077508.57784.DA

Cohen, S., & Herbert, T. B. (1996). Health psychology: Psychological factors and physical disease from the perspective of human psychoneuroimmunology. *Annual Review of Psychology, 47*, 113–142. doi:10.1146/annurev.psych.47.1.113

Cohen, S., Miller, G. E., & Rabin, B. S. (2001). Psychological stress and antibody response to immunization: A critical review of the human literature. *Psychosomatic Medicine, 63*, 7–18.

Crouter, A. C., Bumpus, M. F., Maguire, M. C., & McHale, S. M. (1999). Linking parents' work pressure and adolescents' well-being: Insights into dynamics in dual earner families. *Developmental Psychology, 35*, 1453–1461. doi:10.1037/0012-1649.35.6.1453

Denson, T. F., Spanovic, M., & Miller, N. (2009). Cognitive appraisals and emotions predict cortisol and immune responses: A meta-analysis of acute laboratory social stressors and emotion inductions. *Psychological Bulletin, 135*, 823–853. doi:10.1037/a0016909

Diamond, L. M., & Fagundes, C. P. (2008). Developmental perspectives on links between attachment and affect regulation over the lifespan. *Advances in Child Development and Behavior, 36*, 83–134. doi:10.1016/S0065-2407(08)00003-7

Diamond, L. M., Fagundes, C. P., & Butterworth, M. R. (2010). Intimate relationships across the lifespan. In M. E. Lamb, L. White, & A. Freund (Eds.), *Handbook of lifespan development* (Vol. 2, pp. 379–433). New York, NY: Wiley.

Diamond, L. M., & Hicks, A. M. (2004). Psychobiological perspectives on attachment: Implications for health over the lifespan. In J. A. Simpson & W. S. Rholes (Eds.), *Adult attachment: New directions and emerging issues* (pp. 240–263). New York, NY: Guilford Press.

Dickerson, S. S., Gable, S. L., Irwin, M. R., Aziz, N., & Kemeny, M. E. (2009). Social-evaluative threat and proinflammatory cytokine regulation: An experimental laboratory investigation. *Psychological Science, 20*, 1237–1244. doi:10.1111/j.1467-9280.2009.02437.x

Dickerson, S. S., Gruenewald, T. L., & Kemeny, M. E. (2004). When the social self is threatened: Shame, physiology, and health. *Journal of Personality, 72*, 1191–1216. doi:10.1111/j.1467-6494.2004.00295.x

Dickerson, S. S., Gruenewald, T. L., & Kemeny, M. E. (2009). Psychobiological responses to social self threat: Functional or detrimental? *Self and Identity, 8*, 270–285. doi:10.1080/15298860802505186

Dickerson, S. S., & Kemeny, M. E. (2004). Acute stressors and cortisol responses: A theoretical integration and synthesis of laboratory research. *Psychological Bulletin, 130*, 355–391. doi:10.1037/0033-2909.130.3.355

Dickerson, S. S., Kemeny, M. E., Aziz, N., Kim, K. H., & Fahey, J. L. (2004). Immunological effects of induced shame and guilt. *Psychosomatic Medicine, 66*, 124–131. doi:10.1097/01.PSY.0000097338.75454.29

Eisenberg, N., Fabes, R. A., Guthrie, I. K., & Reiser, M. (2000). Dispositional emotionality and regulation: Their role in predicting quality of social functioning. *Journal of Personality and Social Psychology, 78*, 136–157. doi:10.1037/0022-3514.78.1.136

Ershler, W. B., & Keller, E. T. (2000). Age-associated increased interleukin-6 gene expression, late-life diseases, and frailty. *Annual Review of Medicine, 51*, 245–270. doi:10.1146/annurev.med.51.1.245

Esterling, B. A., Antoni, M. H., Kumar, M., & Schneiderman, N. (1990). Emotional repression, stress disclosure responses, and Epstein-Barr viral capsid antigen titers. *Psychosomatic Medicine, 52*, 397–410.

Esterling, B. A., Kiecolt-Glaser, J. K., Bodnar, J. C., & Glaser, R. (1994). Chronic stress, social support, and persistent alterations in the natural killer cell response to cytokines in older adults. *Health Psychology, 13*, 291–298. doi:10.1037/0278-6133.13.4.291

Esterling, B. A., Kiecolt-Glaser, J. K., & Glaser, R (1996). Psychosocial modulation of cytokine-induced natural killer cell activity in older adults. *Psychosomatic Medicine, 58*, 264–272.

Fridja, N. H. (1986). *The emotions*. Cambridge, England: Cambridge University Press.

Gardner, W. L., Gabriel, S., & Diekman, A. B. (2000). Interpersonal processes. In J. T. Cacioppo, L. G. Tassinary, & G. G. Berntson (Eds.), *Handbook of psychophysiology* (2nd ed., pp. 643–664). New York, NY: Cambridge University Press.

Glynn, L. M., Christenfeld, N., & Gerin, W. (2002). The role of rumination in recovery from reactivity: Cardiovascular consequences of emotional states. *Psychosomatic Medicine, 64*, 714–726. doi:10.1097/01.PSY.0000031574.42041.23

Goebel, M. U., Mills, P. J., Irwin, M. R., & Ziegler, M. G. (2000). Interleukin-6 and tumor necrosis factor-α production after acute psychological stress, exercise, infused isoproterenol: Differential effects and pathways. *Psychosomatic Medicine, 62*, 591–598.

Gottman, J. M. (1991). Predicting the longitudinal course of marriages. *Journal of Marital and Family Therapy, 17*, 3–7. doi:10.1111/j.1752-0606.1991.tb00856.x

Gottman, J. M. (1994). *What predicts divorce?* Hillsdale, NJ: Erlbaum.

Gottman, J. M., Coan, J., Carrère, S., & Swanson, C. (1998). Predicting marital happiness and stability from newlywed interactions. *Journal of Marriage and Family, 60*, 5–22. doi:10.2307/353438

Gottman, J. M., & Levenson, R. W. (1992). Marital processes predictive of later dissolution: Behavior, physiology, and health. *Journal of Personality and Social Psychology, 63*, 221–233. doi:10.1037/0022-3514.63.2.221

Gouin, J.-P., Glaser, R., Loving, T. J., Malarkey, W. B., Stowell, J., Houts, C., & Kiecolt-Glaser, J. K. (2009). Attachment avoidance predicts inflammatory responses to marital conflict. *Brain, Behavior, and Immunity, 23*, 898–904. doi:10.1016/j.bbi.2008.09.016

Graham, J. E., Christian, L. M., & Kiecolt-Glaser, J. K. (2006a). Marriage, health, and immune function. In S. R. H. Beach, M. Z. Wamboldt, N. J. Kaslow, R. E. Heyman, M. B. First, L. G. Underwood, & D. Reiss (Eds.), *Relational processes and DSM-V: Neuroscience, assessment, prevention, and treatment* (pp. 61–76). Washington, DC: American Psychiatric Association.

Graham, J. E., Christian, L. M., & Kiecolt-Glaser, J. K. (2006b). Close relationships and immunity. In R. Ader (Ed.), *Psychoneuroimmunology* (Vol. 2, pp. 781–798). Burlington, MA: Elsevier Academic Press.

Gross, J. J. (1998). Antecedent- and response-focused emotion regulation: Divergent consequences for experience, expression, and physiology. *Journal of Personality and Social Psychology, 74*, 224–237. doi:10.1037/0022-3514.74.1.224

Gross, J. J. (1999). Emotion regulation: Past, present, future. *Cognition and Emotion, 13*, 551–573. doi:10.1080/026999399379186

Gross, J. J., & Levenson, R. W. (1993). Emotional suppression: Physiology, self-report, and expressive behavior. *Journal of Personality and Social Psychology, 64*, 970–986. doi:10.1037/0022-3514.64.6.970

Gross, J. J., & Munoz, R. F. (1995). Emotion regulation and mental-health. *Clinical Psychology: Science and Practice, 2*, 151–164. doi:10.1111/j.1468-2850.1995.tb00036.x

Halfon, N., & Hochstein, M. (2002). Life course health development: An integrated framework for developing health, policy, and research. *The Milbank Quarterly, 80*, 433–479. doi:10.1111/1468-0009.00019

Hazan, C., & Zeifman, D. (1994). Sex and the psychological tether. In D. Perlman & K. Bartholomew (Eds.), *Advances in personal relationships: A research annual* (Vol. 5, pp. 151–177). London, England: Jessica Kingsley.

Hicks, A. M., & Diamond, L. M. (2008). How was your day? Couples' affect when telling and hearing daily events. *Personal Relationships, 15*, 205–228. doi:10.1111/j.1475-6811.2008.00194.x

Horwitz, A. V., McLaughlin, J., & White, H. R. (1998). How the negative and positive aspects of partner relationships affect the mental health of young married people. *Journal of Health and Social Behavior, 39*, 124–136. doi:10.2307/2676395

Kamen-Siegel, L., Rodin, J., Seligman, M. E., & Dwyer, J. (1991). Explanatory style and cell-mediated immunity in elderly men and women. *Health Psychology, 10*, 229–235. doi:10.1037/0278-6133.10.4.229

Kemeny, M. E. (2003). The psychobiology of stress. *Current Directions in Psychological Science, 12*, 124–129. doi:10.1111/1467-8721.01246

Kemeny, M. E. (2009). Psychobiological responses to social threat: Evolution of a psychological model in psychoneuroimmunology. *Brain, Behavior, and Immunity, 23*, 1–9. doi:10.1016/j.bbi.2008.08.008

Kemeny, M. E., & Gruenewald, T. L. (1999). Affect, cognition, the immune system and health. *Progress in Brain Research, 122,* 291–308. doi:10.1016/S0079-6123(08)62146-9

Kemeny, M. E., & Shestyuk, A. (2008). Emotions, the neuroendocrine and immune systems, and health. In M. Lewis, J. M. Haviland-Jones, & L. F. Barrett (Eds.), *Handbook of emotions* (3rd ed., pp. 661–675). New York, NY: Guilford Press.

Kiecolt-Glaser, J. K., Bane, C., Glaser, R., & Malarkey, W. B. (2003). Love, marriage, and divorce: Newlyweds' stress hormones foreshadow relationship changes. *Journal of Consulting and Clinical Psychology, 71,* 176–188. doi:10.1037/0022-006X.71.1.176

Kiecolt-Glaser, J. K., Fisher, L. D., Ogrocki, P., & Stout, J. C. (1987). Marital quality, marital disruption, and immune function. *Psychosomatic Medicine, 49,* 13–34.

Kiecolt-Glaser, J. K., Glaser, R., Cacioppo, J. T., MacCallum, R. C., Snydersmith, M., Kim, C., & Malarkey, W. B. (1997). Marital conflict in older adults: Endocrinological and immunological correlates. *Psychosomatic Medicine, 59,* 339–349.

Kiecolt-Glaser, J. K., Glaser, R., Cacioppo, J. T., & Malarkey, W. B. (1998). Marital stress: Immunologic, neuroendocrine, and autonomic correlates. *Annals of the New York Academy of Sciences, 840,* 656–663. doi:10.1111/j.1749-6632.1998.tb09604.x

Kiecolt-Glaser, J. K., Gouin, J.-P., & Hantsoo, L. (2009). Close relationships, inflammation, and health. *Neuroscience and Biobehavioral Reviews, 35,* 33–38.

Kiecolt-Glaser, J. K., Loving, T. J., Stowell, J. R., Malarkey, W. B., Lemeshow, S., Dickinson, S. L., & Glaser, R. (2005). Hostile marital interactions, proinflammatory cytokine production, and wound healing. *Archives of General Psychiatry, 62,* 1377–1384. doi:10.1001/archpsyc.62.12.1377

Kiecolt-Glaser, J. K., Malarkey, W. B., Chee, M., & Newton, T. (1993). Negative behavior during marital conflict is associated with immunological down-regulation. *Psychosomatic Medicine, 55,* 395–409.

Kiecolt-Glaser, J. K., McGuire, L., Robles, T. F., & Glaser, R. (2002a). Emotions, morbidity, and mortality: New perspectives from psychoneuroimmunology. *Annual Review of Psychology, 53,* 83–107. doi:10.1146/annurev.psych.53.100901.135217

Kiecolt-Glaser, J. K., McGuire, L., Robles, T. F., & Glaser, R. (2002b). Psychoneuroimmunology: Psychological influences on immune function and health. *Journal of Consulting and Clinical Psychology, 70,* 537–547. doi:10.1037/0022-006X.70.3.537

Krieder, R. M. (2005). Number, timing, and duration of marriages and divorces: 2001. *Current Population Reports, P70–97.* Washington, DC: U.S. Census Bureau.

Lacey, K., Zaharia, M. D., Griffiths, J., Ravindran, A. V., Merali, Z., & Anisman, H. (2000). A prospective study of neuroendocrine and immune alterations associated with the stress of an oral academic examination among graduate students. *Psychoneuroendocrinology, 25,* 339–356. doi:10.1016/S0306-4530(99)00059-1

Larsen, R. J. (2000). Toward a science of mood regulation. *Psychological Inquiry, 11,* 129–141. doi:10.1207/S15327965PLI1103_01

Larson, R. W., & Almeida, D. M. (1999). Emotional transmission in the daily lives of families: A new paradigm for studying family process. *Journal of Marriage and Family, 61*, 5–20. doi:10.2307/353879

Loving, T. J., Heffner, K. L., & Kiecolt-Glaser, J. K. (2006). Physiology and interpersonal relationships. In A. L. Vangelisti & D. Perlman (Eds.), *The Cambridge handbook of personal relationships* (pp. 385–405). New York, NY: Cambridge University Press. doi:10.1017/CBO9780511606632.022

Lupien, S. J., Ouellet-Morin, I., Hupbach, A., Tu, M. T., Buss, C., Walker, D., . . . McEwen, B. S. (2006). Beyond the stress concept: Allostatic load—a developmental biological and cognitive perspective. In D. Cicchetti & D. J. Cohen (Eds.), *Developmental psychopathology: Vol 2. Developmental neuroscience* (2nd ed., pp. 578–628). Hoboken, NJ: Wiley.

Magai, C., Cohen, C., Gomberg, D., Malatesta, C., & Culver, C. (1996). Emotion expression in late stage dementia. *International Psychogeriatrics, 8*, 383–395. doi:10.1017/S104161029600275X

Marin, T. J., Martin, T. M., Blackwell, E., Stetler, C., & Miller, G. E. (2007). Differentiating the impact of episodic and chronic stressors on hypothalamic-pituitary-adrenocortical axis regulation in young women. *Health Psychology, 26*, 447–455. doi:10.1037/0278-6133.26.4.447

Marsland, A. L., Cohen, S., Rabin, B. S., & Manuck, S. B. (2006). Trait positive affect and antibody response to hepatitis B vaccination. *Brain, Behavior, and Immunity, 20*, 261–269. doi:10.1016/j.bbi.2005.08.009

Mastekaasa, A. (1994). Marital-status, distress, and well-being: An international comparison. *Journal of Comparative Family Studies, 25*, 183–205.

McEwen, B. S. (2008). Understanding the potency of stressful early life experiences on brain and body function. *Metabolism: Clinical and Experimental, 57*, S11–S15. doi:10.1016/j.metabol.2008.07.006

Miller, G. E., Chen, E., & Zhou, E. S. (2007). If it goes up, must it come down? Chronic stress and the hypothalamic-pituitary-adrenocortical axis in humans. *Psychological Bulletin, 133*, 25–45. doi:10.1037/0033-2909.133.1.25

Mills, P. J., Parker, B., Dimsdale, J. E., Sadler, G. R., & Ancoli-Israel, S. (2005). The relationship between fatigue and quality of life and inflammation during anthracycline-based chemotherapy in breast cancer. *Biological Psychology, 69*, 85–96. doi:10.1016/j.biopsycho.2004.11.007

Miyazaki, T., Ishikawa, T., Iimori, H., Miki, A., Wenner, M., Fukunishi, I., & Kawawura, N. (2003). Relationship between perceived social support and immune function. *Stress and Health, 19*, 3–7.

Murphy, M., Glaser, K., & Grundy, E. (1997). Marital status and long-term illness in Great Britain. *Journal of Marriage and Family, 59*, 156–164. doi:10.2307/353669

Murray, S. L., Holmes, J. G., & Collins, N. L. (2006). Optimizing assurance: The risk regulation system in relationships. *Psychological Bulletin, 132*, 641–666. doi:10.1037/0033-2909.132.5.641

Murray, S. L., Holmes, J. G., & Griffin, D. W. (1996). The self-fulfilling nature of positive illusions in romantic relationships: Love is not blind, but prescient. *Journal of Personality and Social Psychology, 71*, 1155–1180. doi:10.1037/0022-3514.71.6.1155

Murray, S. L., Holmes, J. G., & Griffin, D. W. (2004). The benefits of positive illusions: Idealization and the construction of satisfaction in close relationships. In H. T. Reis & C. E. Rusbult (Eds.), *Close relationships: Key readings* (pp. 317–338). Philadelphia, PA: Taylor & Francis.

O'Cleirigh, C., Ironson, G., Fletcher, M. A., & Schneiderman, N. (2008). Written emotional disclosure and processing of trauma are associated with protected health status and immunity in people living with HIV/AIDS. *British Journal of Health Psychology, 13*, 81–84. doi:10.1348/135910707X250884

O'Leary, A. (1990). Stress, emotion, and human immune function. *Psychological Bulletin, 108*, 363–382. doi:10.1037/0033-2909.108.3.363

Pasupathi, M. (2001). The social construction of the personal past and its implications for adult development. *Psychological Bulletin, 127*, 651–672. doi:10.1037/0033-2909.127.5.651

Pennebaker, J. W. (1993). Inhibition and psychosomatic processes. In H. C. Traue (Ed.), *Emotion inhibition and health* (pp. 146–163). Ashland, OH: Hogrefe & Huber.

Picardi, A., Battisti, F., Tarsitani, L., Baldassari, M., Copertaro, A., Mocchegiani, E., & Biondi, M. (2007). Attachment security and immunity in healthy women. *Psychosomatic Medicine, 69*, 40–46. doi:10.1097/PSY.0b013e31802dd777

Quan, N., Avitsur, R., Stark, J. L., He, L., Shah, M., Caligiuri, M., . . . Sheridan, J. F. (2001). Social stress increases the susceptibility to endotoxic shock. *Journal of Neuroimmunology, 115*, 36–45. doi:10.1016/S0165-5728(01)00273-9

Repetti, R. L., Taylor, S. E., & Seeman, T. E. (2002). Risky families: Family social environments and the mental and physical health of offspring. *Psychological Bulletin, 128*, 330–366. doi:10.1037/0033-2909.128.2.330

Ridker, P. M., Hennekens, C. H., Buring, J. E., & Rifai, N. (2000). C-reactive protein and other markers of inflammation in the prediction of cardiovascular disease in women. *The New England Journal of Medicine, 342*, 836–843. doi:10.1056/NEJM200003233421202

Ross, C. E. (1995). Reconceptualizing marital-status as a continuum of social attachment. *Journal of Marriage and Family, 57*, 129–140. doi:10.2307/353822

Rottenberg, J., Salomon, K., Gross, J. J., & Gotlib, I. H. (2005). Vagal withdrawal to a sad film predicts subsequent recovery from depression. *Psychophysiology, 42*, 277–281. doi:10.1111/j.1469-8986.2005.00289.x

Ryff, C. D., & Singer, B. H. (Eds.). (2001). *Emotions, social relationships, and health.* New York, NY: Oxford University Press.

Ryff, C. D., Singer, B. H., Wing, E., & Love, G. D. (2001). Elective affinities and uninvited agonies: Mapping emotion with significant others onto health. In

C. D. Ryff & B. H. Singer (Eds.), *Emotions, social relationships, and health* (pp. 133–174). New York, NY: Oxford University Press.

Saxbe, D., & Repetti, R. L. (2010). For better or worse? Coregulation of couples' cortisol levels and mood states. *Journal of Personality and Social Psychology, 98,* 92–103. doi:10.1037/a0016959

Sbarra, D. A., & Hazan, C. (2008). Coregulation, dysregulation, self-regulation: An integrative analysis and empirical agenda for understanding adult attachment, separation, loss, and recovery. *Personality and Social Psychology Review, 12,* 141–167. doi:10.1177/1088868308315702

Scheier, M. F., Weintraub, J. K., & Carver, C. S. (1986). Coping with stress: Divergent strategies of optimists and pessimists. *Journal of Personality and Social Psychology, 51,* 1257–1264. doi:10.1037/0022-3514.51.6.1257

Schoebi, D. (2008). The coregulation of daily affect in marital relationships. *Journal of Family Psychology, 22,* 595–604. doi:10.1037/0893-3200.22.3.595

Seeman, T. E. (2003). Integrating psychosocial factors with biology: The role of protective factors in trajectories of health and aging. In F. Kessel, P. L. Rosenfield, & N. B. Anderson (Eds.), *Expanding the boundaries of health and social science: Case studies in interdisciplinary innovation* (pp. 206–227). New York, NY: Oxford University Press.

Seeman, T. E., & Gruenewald, T. L. (2006). Allostasis and allostatic load over the life course. In W. W. Eaton (Ed.), *Medical and psychiatric comorbidity over the course of life* (pp. 179–196). Washington, DC: American Psychiatric Publishing.

Seeman, T. E., Singer, B. H., Ryff, C. D., Dienberg Love, G., & Levy-Storms, L. (2002). Social relationships, gender, and allostatic load across two age cohorts. *Psychosomatic Medicine, 64,* 395–406.

Segerstrom, S. C., Glover, D. A., Craske, M. G., & Fahey, J. L. (1999). Worry affects the immune response to phobic fear. *Brain, Behavior, and Immunity, 13,* 80–92. doi:10.1006/brbi.1998.0544

Segerstrom, S. C., & Miller, G. E. (2004). Psychological stress and the human immune system: A meta-analytic study of 30 years of inquiry. *Psychological Bulletin, 130,* 601–630. doi:10.1037/0033-2909.130.4.601

Segerstrom, S. C., & Roach, A. R. (2008). On the physical health benefits of self-enhancement. In E. C. Chang (Ed.), *Self-criticism and self-enhancement: Theory, research, and clinical implications* (pp. 37–54). Washington, DC: American Psychological Association. doi:10.1037/11624-003

Segerstrom, S. C., Schipper, L. J., & Greenberg, R. N. (2008). Caregiving, repetitive thought, and immune response to vaccination in older adults. *Brain, Behavior, and Immunity, 22,* 744–752. doi:10.1016/j.bbi.2007.11.004

Segerstrom, S. C., Solomon, G. F., Kemeny, M. E., & Fahey, J. L. (1998). Relationship of worry to immune sequelae of the Northridge earthquake. *Journal of Behavioral Medicine, 21,* 433–450. doi:10.1023/A:1018732309353

Segerstrom, S. C., Taylor, S. E., Kemeny, M. E., Reed, G. M., & Visscher, B. R. (1996). Causal attributions predict rate of immune decline in HIV-seropositive gay men. *Health Psychology, 15*, 485–493. doi:10.1037/0278-6133.15.6.485

Seyle, H. (1956). *The stress of life*. New York, NY: McGraw-Hill.

Sgoutas-Emch, S. A., Cacioppo, J. T., Uchino, B. N., Malarkey, W., Pearl, D., Kiecolt-Glaser, J. K., & Glaser, R. (1994). The effects of an acute psychological stressor on cardiovascular, endocrine, and cellular immune response: A prospective study of individuals high and low in heart rate reactivity. *Psychophysiology, 31*, 264–271. doi:10.1111/j.1469-8986.1994.tb02215.x

Stack, S. (1998). Marriage, family and loneliness: A cross-national study. *Sociological Perspectives, 41*, 415–432.

Stack, S., & Eshleman, J. R. (1998). Marital status and happiness: A 17-nation study. *Journal of Marriage and Family, 60*, 527–536. doi:10.2307/353867

Stark, J. L., Avitsur, R., Padgett, D. A., Campbell, K. A., Beck, F. M., & Sheridan, J. F. (2001). Social stress induces glucocorticoid resistance in macrophages. *American Journal of Physiology. Regulatory, Integrative and Comparative Physiology, 280*, R1799–R1805.

Story, L. B., & Repetti, R. (2006). Daily occupational stressors and marital behavior. *Journal of Family Psychology, 20*, 690–700. doi:10.1037/0893-3200.20.4.690

Strauman, T. J., Lemieux, A. M., & Coe, C. L. (1993). Self-discrepancy and natural killer cell activity: Immunological consequences of negative self-evaluation. *Journal of Personality and Social Psychology, 64*, 1042–1052. doi:10.1037/0022-3514.64.6.1042

Taylor, S. E., Dickerson, S. S., & Klein, L. C. (2002). Toward a biology of social support. In C. R. Snyder & S. J. Lopez (Eds.), *Handbook of positive psychology* (pp. 556–569). London, England: Oxford University Press.

Taylor, S. E., Kemeny, M. E., Reed, G. M., Bower, J. E., & Gruenewald, T. L. (2000). Psychological resources, positive illusions, and health. *American Psychologist, 55*, 99–109. doi:10.1037/0003-066X.55.1.99

Taylor, S. E., Lerner, J. S., Sherman, D. K., Sage, R. M., & McDowell, N. K. (2003). Are self-enhancing cognitions associated with healthy or unhealthy biological profiles? *Journal of Personality and Social Psychology, 85*, 605–615. doi:10.1037/0022-3514.85.4.605

Thompson, R. A. (1994). Emotion regulation: A theme in search of definition. *Monographs of the Society for Research in Child Development, 59*(2–3, Serial No. 240), 25–52.

Thomsen, D. K., Mehlsen, M. Y., Hokland, M., Viidik, A., Olesen, F., Avlund, K., . . . Zachariae, R. (2004). Negative thoughts and health: Associations among rumination, immunity, and health care utilization in a young and elderly sample. *Psychosomatic Medicine, 66*, 363–371. doi:10.1097/01.psy.0000127688.44363.fb

Tomkins, S. S. (1984). Affect theory. In P. Ekman (Ed.), *Emotion in the human face* (2nd ed., pp. 353–395). New York, NY: Cambridge University Press.

Trinke, S. J., & Bartholomew, K. (1997). Hierarchies of attachment relationships in young adulthood. *Journal of Social and Personal Relationships*, *14*, 603–625. doi:10.1177/0265407597145002

Uchino, B. N. (2006). Social support and health: A review of physiological processes, potentially underlying links to disease outcomes. *Journal of Behavioral Medicine*, *29*, 377–387. doi:10.1007/s10865-006-9056-5

Weiner, H. (1992). *Perturbing the organism: The biology of stressful experience*. Chicago, IL: University of Chicago Press.

II

RELATIONSHIPS
IN EARLY LIFE

5

PARENT–CHILD AND CHILD–PEER CLOSE RELATIONSHIPS: UNDERSTANDING PARENTAL INFLUENCES ON PEER RELATIONS FROM A CULTURAL CONTEXT

NANCY E. HILL

The realms of parents and peers are fabled as separate and even conflicting, especially in late childhood and early adolescence, as parents and peers are assumed to provide different developmental resources for youth (Ladd & Pettit, 2002; Renshaw & Parke, 1992). Some have suggested that "peers are bad" and lead to maladaptive outcomes, whereas others have suggested that peers provide a unique context for developing an independent sense of self (Cooper & Cooper, 1992). Without question, positive peer relationships have the potential to provide a sense of belonging, self-identification, and affirmation (Hamm & Faircloth, 2005; Hill, Bromell, Tyson, & Flint, 2007; Kuperminc, Blatt, Shahar, Henrich, & Leadbeatter, 2004). These connections between parents and peers can be competitive, compensate for one another, or complement each other (Cooper & Cooper, 1992). For example, domains of authority may be debated between parents and youth, resulting in conflict (Smetana, 2000), whereas parents and youth tend to agree about important aspects of life, including morality, life goals, and aspirations (Kandel & Lesser, 1982). Furthermore, families prepare youth for meaningful relationships by providing children with a context to learn relationship skills that are later used in cultivating and maintaining friendships (Clark & Ladd, 2000). Despite knowledge that peers and parents have significant influence on the social development of children and youth, connections between these socialization forces are complex and not well understood (Knoester, Haynie, & Stephens, 2006).

The realms of parents and peers are both distinct and enmeshed, with similar skills needed and cultivated in both worlds (Laursen, Wilder, Noack, & Williams, 2000). For example, the worlds of peers and parents are, at times, similar with regard to reciprocity but distinct with regard to authority. In the context of friendships, opinions and perspectives are developed through negotiation rather than authority (Cooper & Cooper, 1992). In addition, whereas similarities between teens and their friends may be attributed to homophily—that is, selecting friends who are similar to them and affirm their emerging identities (Ryan, 2000)—parents likely influence the friendship selection process and prepare them to be good friends. Theoretical paradigms, including those on attachment, emotional security, and social cognition, suggest that parents and families provide the first models for relationship characteristics such as trust, warmth, and unconditional love that are key for developing social competence and friendships (Bowlby, 1973; Ladd, 1992; Ladd & Pettit, 2002; see also Chapter 6, this volume).

Research has shifted away from the question of whether families influence peer relationships to understanding the connections between the family and peer contexts and the transfer of skills from one to the other (Collins, Maccoby, Steinberg, Hetherington, & Bornstein, 2000). There has been increased interest in understanding the interplay between families and peers, the linkages between family influence and social competence, and the mechanisms between them (Ladd, 1992).

Although our understanding of family–peer linkages has increased, the research has largely been limited to Euro-American, middle-class samples or samples of convenience, thereby limiting the generalizability to the increasingly diverse U.S. population. Almost 20 years ago, Parke and Ladd (1992), in their seminal book on family–peer linkages, criticized the field for its failure to attend to the ethnic and economic generalizability of the theories and findings linking family and peer worlds, yet few studies have filled this gap since then (see Steinberg & Monahan, 2007, for a notable exception). This chapter begins to fill this void by reviewing theories that link families and peers and their impact on youths' social development. Extant theory and research on ethnic and economic variations in parenting are highlighted as they might impact the generalizability of theory and research on family–peer linkages. Finally, preliminary findings are presented on ethnic and economic variations in the linkages among parenting, friendship dynamics, and social competence for African American and Euro-American youth and their families.

Among the outcomes that are posited to be most affected by peers and the intersection of families and peers are social competence and social development. Social competence and social development include "the competencies children gain that serve them as they engage interpersonally, internalize their society's and their culture's values, and their mental and behavioral health" (Hill & Witherspoon, 2011, p. 327). Also included are the abilities to develop and maintain positive interactions with peers and avoid debilitating social roles and emotional experiences such as victimization, loneliness, and social anxiety (Ladd & Pettit, 2002). Others include prosocial orientations in their definition and include youths' capacity to empathize with friends' needs and/or emotions (Clark & Ladd, 2000). Whereas parenting and peer/friendship dynamics influence a wide range of developmental outcomes including academic achievement and mental health, social development and friendship dynamics are the focus of this chapter. Theories about the connections between parents and peers have a long and storied history. The most substantiated theories are outlined here.

THEORIES AND FRAMEWORKS LINKING FAMILIES AND PEERS

Research and theory on the influences between families and peers suggest that there are both indirect and direct influences (Knoester et al., 2006; Ladd & Pettit, 2002). Direct influences include parents' efforts to directly manage children's social development and friendship experiences. These efforts include arranging playdates and selecting schools and neighborhoods to influence the peer group from whom friends are selected, and ensuring that parents' friends have children with whom their own children can engage (Ladd & Pettit, 2002). Indirect influences are those that are not explicitly connected to the children's peer relationships, friendship quality, and social competence but nevertheless provide children and youth with the experiences and skills that transfer and prepare them for high-quality friendships and peer interactions. General or global parent–child relationships that provide experiences that prepare children and youth for successfully negotiating peer and friendship relationships are among the indirect influences (e.g., attachment relationships and warmth and discipline that provide templates for interpersonal interactions and expectations for relationships; Ladd & Pettit, 2002). These family interactions are designed to prepare youth for friendship interactions. In this section, family-to-peer influences as they pertain to global relationship processes, direct interventions, and parenting practices that shape peer interactions are discussed.

GLOBAL RELATIONSHIP PROCESSES

Among general developmental theories, psychoanalytic, socialization, and cognitive theories represent three classic models or theories that explain the linkages among more global parenting processes, parent–child relationships, and peers (Cooper & Cooper, 1992). In addition, attachment security and parenting practices have an impact (Ladd & Pettit, 2002). Psychoanalytic theories hold that as children mature, they naturally separate themselves from parents and the family and move more directly into the peer context. This transition is seen as a signal of maturity (Blos, 1979). It is believed that peers appropriately compensate for what parents cannot provide (Douvan & Adelson, 1966). As youth reinvent themselves and develop identities separately from their families, psychoanalytic theories suggest that they need peers and friends to affirm their budding identities. Thus, peers and families function in conflict and at odds, according to psychoanalytic theories.

Socialization models and theories also place parents and peers at odds and in conflict. Parents and peers represent two distinct socialization streams, with the peer culture often deemed "antiadult." The assumption is that the goals of youth and parents are different, and therefore the socialization messages heard from peers may undermine or compete with those heard from parents. Immigrant parents who find their children acculturating at a faster pace than themselves especially feel these competing messages between home life and peers (Hill & Torres, 2010). To the extent that parents and peers represent distinct and competing worlds, they then reflect different sources of socialization. Parents may find this disconcerting and want to counteract it because they believe themselves to be models and socializers of societal norms and desirable behaviors and beliefs. However, some have argued that the benefits of peer relationships for an individual's development are dependent on whether the individual has had the family experiences that equip him or her to establish and maintain friendships (Cooper & Cooper, 1992).

According to cognitive models, peers and families provide unique developmental contexts, and both are needed for adequate development (Piaget, 1932; Vygotsky, 1978). The peer context provides opportunities to hone negotiation and conflict-resolution skills and to develop one's own opinions and perspectives. Because of the equal status among friends and peers (compared with parent–child relationships), there are more opportunities for independent and abstract thinking among friends than with parents (Fuligni & Eccles, 1993). Youths' identity development is strengthened in the peer context, especially in cultures that are focused on independence and autonomy. In these cultures, youth often select friends who match their interests and shape their emerging identities. The potential costs of peer influences from a cognitive perspective are that peers and friends become more alike over time in both adaptive and potentially maladaptive ways (Ryan, 2000).

A final, but often deemed as the most important, aspect of the global parent–child relationship that affects peer relationships and friendship quality is the attachment relationship between parents and youth. Emotional and relational attachment between parents and children provides youth with a template of how relationships work and provides a secure base that promotes the development of autonomy and confidence to forge relationships (Bowlby, 1973; Ladd & Pettit, 2002; see also Chapter 7). Through their attachment relationships with parents, youth learn to trust, to experience warmth and responsiveness in relationships, and to have appropriate expectations for relationships (Erikson, 1964), and this impacts their ability to trust and care about others including peers and friends. Secure attachments between parents and children foster interpersonal competence, whereas insecure attachments are associated with problems interacting with peers. Although attachments are deemed as key for understanding relationships across the life span, a meta-analysis of 63 studies (Schneider, Atkinson, & Tardif, 2001) shows only a moderate relation between secure attachment and peer competence, suggesting that other significant factors influence peer relations and friendships.

Friendship quality also may be influenced by the emotional depth and quality of the parent–child relationship. Youth may be inclined to select friends of whom their parents will approve and thereby have higher quality friendships (Knoester et al., 2006). Youth who are emotionally secure and have their basic emotional needs met at home may have less of a sense of urgency about being accepted among their peers, be more selective about their friendships, and therefore have higher quality friendships. In addition to parental influences affecting youths' social competence, and thereby youths' skill at developing and maintaining friends, parents also influence their children's friendships indirectly through their own social networks. The children of parents' friends allow for greater opportunities for youth to spend time with peers, especially peers about whom parents know a great deal.

PARENTAL ORCHESTRATION OF PEER RELATIONS AND FRIENDSHIPS

Three of the five mechanisms through which parents may impact youths' friendships that were identified by Knoester et al. (2006) could be defined as orchestrations or interventions in the peer context and youth–peer relationships. For example, parents may manipulate the environment to change or influence the pool of peers from whom youth select friends. This can occur through the selection or changing of neighborhoods, schools, and extracurricular activities, which dictate the peer group from whom friends are selected (Ladd & Pettit, 2002; Parke & Bhavnagri, 1989). Friends tend to live closer to one another. In addition, neighborhoods that are flat, with houses that are closer together, with playgrounds, and with sidewalks promote friendship development. Parents influence friendships by supervising and monitoring youths' whereabouts, often reducing the amount of time spent with peers and determining with whom time is spent (Knoester et al., 2006).

Parents may serve as mediators of friendships. That is, parents may initiate playdates and social opportunities for their youth (Ladd, 1992). Through their parents' modeling the arrangement of peer interactions, children learn interaction skills and how to regulate peer interactions. Further, parental arrangement of peer interactions increases the number and diversity of peer experiences (Ladd & Pettit, 2002). Indeed, young children whose parents initiate and arrange for interactions with peers have more friends in preschool than those whose parents do not engage at these levels (Ladd & Golter, 1988).

Further, adults, including parents and teachers, may supervise peer interactions and coach children on conflict resolution, empathy, and negotiations. In fact, among older children, coaching and providing advice and support were the most likely forms of intervention (Ladd, 1992). Parents often coach their children on how to make and maintain friendships and how to resolve conflicts with friends (Laird, Pettit, Mize, Brown, & Lindsey, 1994). According to a study examining processes associated with adjustment to a new school, even seventh and eighth graders find it helpful when their parents meet with parents of potential friends, provide a context in which they meet age-mates, encourage activities with age-mates, and talk with them about making friends (Mounts, 2001). However, more direct intervention may be less desired by older adolescents not in transition. In fact, as youth get older, they are more likely to deem the peer domain as one over which they, and not their parents, have control (Smetana, 2000).

Parenting practices themselves affect youths' peer relationships and friendship quality. Moving away from global styles and typologies, research has begun to focus on specific parenting strategies (Ladd & Pettit, 2002). In the next sections, specific parenting practices that both directly and indirectly influence peer relationships are discussed.

INFLUENCING FRIENDSHIPS THROUGH GENERAL PARENTING

Linkages between parents and peers may also be understood as a transfer of relational skills from one context to the other (Brown, Bransford, Ferrara, & Campione, 1983). Relationship interaction styles, empathy, negotiation, and expectations develop in interactions among family members and are then used in developing peer and friendship relationships (Ladd, 1992). In contrast, overly directive or overbearing parents may prevent youth from developing the initiative and emotional control needed to foster meaningful friendships. However, Brown et al. (1983) suggested that it is not as straightforward as it might seem, as youth need to recognize that situations are similar between family and peer contexts before they might apply knowledge and solutions learned in one context to another. Parents and other adults in youths' lives can coach them to see these similarities.

Parental disciplinary strategies have a significant influence on peer relations (Ladd, 1992). Youth may learn negotiation and reasoning skills, which are skills that benefit peer relationships and friendships, through parental discipline. Further, parental disciplinary styles and strategies help youth develop expectations for how relationships function. For example, parents who use more power-assertive disciplinary strategies may not focus enough attention on the relationship or consequences because of the emphasis on compliance and instrumental rather than relational outcomes (Hart, DeWolf, Wozniak, & Burts, 1992). Some have suggested that these types of parenting strategies may undermine children's prosocial skills (Ladd, 1992). Youth learn how to escalate oppositional and conflictual interactions through coercive parenting practices, which in turn generalizes to peer interactions (G. R. Patterson, Reid, & Dishion, 1992). Overly controlling or psychologically controlling parenting undermines children's sense of confidence, is associated with higher levels of anxiety and depression (Barber, 2002), and impacts youth's interpretations of interpersonal events (Dodge, Greenberg, & Malone, 2008).

Whether parenting practices are specific (e.g., discipline or negotiation) or more global (including psychoanalytical, attachment, and social–cognitive paradigms), the evidence is strong that parenting and family dynamics are associated with children's social competence, friendship quality, and in turn other outcomes, including mental health and academic achievement. In the following sections, building on the theories presented, evidence is provided for the theoretical paradigms presented. Included are dynamic effects between parenting and children's social competence, direct effects between parenting and children's social competence, and indirect effects through which parenting shapes social competence.

PARENTING AND CHILDREN'S SOCIAL COMPETENCE: CONTINUITY AND DYNAMIC RELATIONS

There is evidence for a transfer of skills and relationship dynamics between parent–child relationships and child–peer–friend relationships. The parent–child and child–friend relationships impact each other. As an example of the transfer of skills, parent–child closeness is related to reciprocity (i.e., mutual exchange) among children's friendships (Laursen et al., 2000). Similarly, close relationships with friends or with parents are marked by similar or increased reciprocity in the other relationship (Laursen et al., 2000). Moreover, perceptions of support are similar across relationships. Adolescents who rate their parents as supportive also rate their friends as supportive (Bokhorst, Sumter, & Westenberg, 2010). Conversely, higher levels of conflict between parents and youth are associated with higher levels of fighting among friends (Knoester et al., 2006). Also, dynamics within parent–child relationships are associated with or mirror dynamics within children's friendships. That is, correlations between reciprocity and authority among children's friendships are similar to correlations between reciprocity and authority between children and their parents (Laursen et al., 2000).

However, adolescents may seek to compensate for what they hope to get in their parent relationships through their friendships, although these youth may lack the social competence they need to maintain relationships in which these needs can be met. Youth need the skills they learn in one relationship to benefit from or within another relationship (Ladd & Pettit, 2002).

DIRECT EFFECTS BETWEEN PARENTING AND CHILDREN'S SOCIAL COMPETENCE AND FRIENDSHIPS

There is ample evidence linking parenting directly to children's social competence, mental health, and achievement. Parent–child connections or relationship quality is positively related to the number of mutual friends and acceptance among peers (Clark & Ladd, 2000; Knoester et al., 2006). Similarly, secure attachments are positively related to the development of close and larger friendship groups among adolescents, quality of friendships, feelings of integration and acceptance among peers, and the ability to regulate emotions (LaFreniere & Srouft, 1985; Zimmermann, 2004). In contrast, those with insecure representations of their attachment relationships are more anxious and evidence more hostility in their friendships (Kobak & Sceery, 1988). Similarly, children who feel less companionship and affection from their parents are more likely to be rejected by peers (C. J. Patterson, Kupersmidt, & Griesler, 1990). Further, adolescents who have more disagreements with their parents and are more assertive in their negotiations with their parents are more argumentative in their friendships (Cooper & Cooper, 1992).

With regard to parenting practices that reflect an orchestration of friendships and peer relationships, there is evidence that parental selection of neighborhoods because of the quality of the schools and higher levels of supervision and monitoring are associated with youth having fewer friends who are involved in delinquent activities and fewer friends who fight (Knoester et al., 2006). Similarly, poor monitoring and supervision is associated with higher levels of delinquency among adolescent boys (Cooper & Cooper, 1992). In contrast, high levels of monitoring are associated with children having friends with higher GPAs.

Parent–child interaction patterns and disciplinary strategies also have direct effects on children's social competence and friendships. Parents who are consistent in their disciplinary practices and use discipline in ways that are more contingent on children's behavior have children who display greater levels of social competence (LaFreniere & Dumas, 1992). There is ample evidence that power-assertive parenting is associated with lower levels of social competence. Directive and coercive parenting strategies have been shown to undermine peer relationship quality including peer adjustment and acceptance (Ladd, 1992). Lower levels of autonomy granting by parents is associated with higher levels of self-focus and more aggressive and domineering interactions with peers (Putallaz, 1987). In contrast, more inductive discipline is associated with more prosocial behavior. Whereas much of the research has examined direct relations between parenting and peer relationships, there is evidence of mediated effects as well.

MEDIATED PATHWAYS THROUGH WHICH THE PARENTING CONTEXT AFFECTS FRIENDSHIP

In addition to being related to direct friendship outcomes, attachment security is related to relationship mechanisms that undoubtedly increase friendship quality, such as cooperative conflict resolution and lower levels of social anxiety (Zimmermann, 2004). Further, parenting and parent–child relationships may be associated with peer relationships because they communicate to the child his or her sense of worth and self-efficacy. For example, when parents show interest in their child's thoughts and ideas, especially about friendship encounters, they are communicating that the child has a worthwhile perspective and thereby promoting the development of empathy among peers (Clark & Ladd, 2000). Further, connectedness and autonomy support among parenting practices are associated with the development of empathy, which in turn is associated with higher quality friendships (Clark & Ladd, 2000). Conversely, coerciveness between parents and children is associated with higher levels of peer rejection, and this relation is mediated by children's aggressive interaction style with peers (MacKinnon-Lewis et al., 1994). Parents clearly equip youth to effectively participate in peer interactions and develop friendships. They do so directly through orchestration and coaching and indirectly through the development of the child's sense of self, prosocial orientations, empathy, and perspective taking.

Despite this robust and long-standing focus on the intersection between parents and peers and their interrelations, the field lacks a significant perspective and thus only represents a small proportion of the population. The vast majority of research on the linkages between parents and peers and the influences between parenting and children's social competence and friendship quality has been conducted on Euro-American/White and middle-class samples. As the American population is becoming increasingly diverse and the science of psychology and human development is purposefully and necessarily taking a more global perspective (Hill, 2006; Hill & Witherspoon, 2011), such absences of representation and implicit assumptions that findings from one population are generalizable to all limit the impact and usefulness of the field. As Cooper and Cooper (1992) stated almost 20 years ago, "Bringing issues of diversity into mainstream developmental theory will enrich our accounts of intra group variability and provide a more complete normative-developmental picture" (p. 154). Since then, there have been a few studies that examined ethnic, cultural, or economic variations and family–peer dynamics and children's social competence and peer interactions. Such studies have demonstrated that the theories and findings, especially on the effects of parenting practices, that are based on Euro-American, middle-class samples cannot be systematically generalized to other populations.

DEMOGRAPHIC VARIATIONS IN PARENTING AND PEER RELATIONSHIPS

Among the few studies that have examined the generalizability of extant theories across ethnicity and socioeconomic status (SES), there are differences in the processes that link parenting and peer influences and the interrelationships among these constructs. For example, children from lower socioeconomic backgrounds tend to have lower levels of prosocial orientation, such as empathy (Clark & Ladd, 2000). The association between socioeconomic background and prosocial orientation is mediated by parent–child interaction patterns. These researchers concluded that the stressors associated with poverty disrupt the emotional relationships between parents and children and undermine the development of social competence. In addition, SES impacts the context in which friendships are developed. Children from families from lower socioeconomic backgrounds are less likely to have high-quality peer interactions at school and are more socially isolated in activities outside of school (Ladd & Pettit, 2002), especially as lower SES parents attempt to protect their children from unsafe neighborhoods. Consistent with these differences, the rationales offered for the original allocation of neighborhood resources and building of playgrounds in the early 20th century also differ across SES. Urban playgrounds are seen as a solution for youth wandering the streets and deemed as a replacement for the lower socioeconomic "unstable" family, whereas for middle-class youth, playgrounds are developed and managed as an extension of the family and are highly controlled and monitored by families (Renshaw & Parke, 1992).

Culturally embedded beliefs matter as well. The interrelations among relationship characteristics among children, parents, and friends vary by nationality (Laursen, Wilder, Noack, & Williams, 2000). In examining variations between German and American families, Laursen et al. (2000) proposed that cultures that place a greater emphasis on social and geographic mobility (i.e., individualism; e.g., the United States) would be characterized by faster cultivation of relationships and relationships with greater levels of reciprocity and cooperation, compared with cultures with a greater emphasis on relational and geographic stability (e.g., Germany). This is based on the premise that, in societies with high levels of mobility, family members are dispersed and are not in regular contact, which increases the significance of peers and friendships and therefore the reciprocity needed within friend relationships to sustain them. Indeed, there are differences across nationalities. Greater levels of reciprocity are reported in youth friendships in the United States compared with those in Germany. There are more positive associations among reciprocity, closeness, and authority within friendships and parental relationships among German adolescents. Laursen et al. concluded that whereas closeness is more universal across relationships, the significance of authority and reciprocity is culturally embedded.

These studies represent the small body of research on cross-national and cross-socioeconomic variations among parenting, despite a large and growing body of research documenting ethnic, cultural, and socioeconomic variations in parenting beliefs, parenting practices, and their associations with youths' social development and social competence (Hill, 2009; Hill & Torres, 2010; Hill & Witherspoon, 2011). Further, there are ethnic differences in the beliefs about the role friends should have in youths' development. In the remaining sections of this chapter, empirical and theoretical foundations for why relations between parenting and peer influences might be different for African American and Latino youth, compared with their Euro-American counterparts, are presented on the basis of the existing literature on parenting and children's development. The focus is on African American and Latino families because they are from the two largest ethnic minority groups in the United States. Preliminary findings are presented on the basis of quantitative data for elementary school youth and qualitative data for middle school youth.

ETHNIC DIFFERENCES IN PARENTING BELIEFS AND EFFECTIVE PARENTING

African American culture and parenting practices draw on the traditions and practices of a West African cultural worldview (Boykin, 1983, 1986; Mitchell, 1975), including a positive view of life despite difficult circumstances;

belief in the spiritual realm and spirituality; communalism, including a sense of unity among family and others; and harmony, expressiveness and expressive individualism (i.e., verve; Boykin, 1983; Sankofa, Hurley, Allen, & Boykin, 2005; Tyler, Boykin, Miller, & Hurley, 2006). Among these cultural values and beliefs, communalism and its focus on interdependence and the significance of the extended family are most salient for understanding family–peer linkages among African American youth.

Communalism reflects a fundamental interdependence among people, with an emphasis on sharing and working toward the good of the group (Boykin, 1983), giving priority to family over one's personal or individual goals (Cokley, 2005), and the significance of human relationships (Cokley, 2005). Communalism is evident through strong kinship networks, a unity developed as part of a collective struggle, and a sense of an "African American community" that transcends physical boundaries (Hill, Murry, & Anderson, 2005).

African American families also focus on developing their children's sense of self, although in a different way than do Euro-American families. Rather than focusing on an independent self and individual development, African Americans place greater emphasis on their collective self-identity (group identity). In preparing their children for adulthood, African American parents must consider discrimination and social stratification in American society. For good reason, African American parents find that they are preparing their children for a hostile world that will not always give them a fair chance and will often misinterpret their behavior and actions unfavorably (Hill, 2011). African American parents must prepare their children to cope with and understand discriminatory experiences while maintaining their sense of self and self-concept (Hughes et al., 2006; Stevenson, Davis, & Abdul-Kabir, 2001).

African American parenting has been characterized as authoritarian and "no nonsense" (Brody & Flor, 1998; Steinberg, Dornbusch, & Brown, 1992). American society often views African American children's misbehavior as more dangerous than the same behaviors exhibited by Euro-American children, and teachers and the criminal justice system mete out harsher punishments to African American children than they do for Euro-American children for the same misbehaviors (Cross, 2003, 2011; Flynn, 2011). American society is very willing to label African American children as delinquents and is much less likely to give African American children a "second chance" (Cross, 2003). Because of this, African American parents are often more exacting about their children's behavior and place high demands for obedience. Whereas autonomy granting and promoting independence are often valued and are effective parenting strategies for Euro-American middle-class families, these strategies are less effective for African American families and are less consistent with the emphasis that is placed on family relationships (Hill, 2006; Hill et al., 2005).

Characterizations of African American no-nonsense parenting as harsh are inaccurate. African American socialization strategies must be interpreted and understood within the frame of African American cultural values and beliefs. Seemingly harsher, but clearly stricter, parenting practices are positively related to perceived warmth, love, and acceptance among African American children (Mason, Walker-Barnes, Tu, Simons, & Martinez-Arrue, 2004). Moreover, the combination of high levels of strict or authoritarian parenting and warmth are associated with lower levels of mental health problems (Deater-Deckard & Dodge, 1997; Hill & Bush, 2001) and higher levels of achievement (Steinberg et al., 1992). Although most research on African American families confound ethnicity with lower SES and urban contexts, the usefulness of more authoritarian parenting strategies is consistent for middle-class and rural African American families (Brody, Flor, & Gibson, 1999; Hill, 2001; Hill & Bush, 2001; Smetana & Chuang, 2001).

Similarly, effective parenting among Latino families varies from Euro-American, middle-class norms and is grounded in cultural strengths. The importance of social relationships among Latino cultures is well established. Indeed, cultural values, such as *simpatia* (being nice), *respeto* (respect), *personalismo* (being personable), and *dignidad* (dignity) shape social relationships for Latinos, especially with those outside the family (Marin & Marin, 1991; Simoni & Perez, 1995). *Simpatia* is an expected general disposition when relating to others that includes being agreeable, friendly, sympathetic, polite, and humble (Ramirez-Esparza, Gosling, & Pennebaker, 2008). *Personalismo* is the preference for interacting with and trusting individuals rather than institutions and emphasizes having genuine interest in people and their welfare. Similarly, *respeto* reflects expectations for focusing on others and empathy, respect, and intimacy in relationships (Andrés-Hyman, Ortiz, Anez, Paris, & Davidson, 2006; Simoni & Perez, 1995). Finally, *dignidad* reflects a sense of honor and worthiness between people and an expectation that people deserve respect and reverence regardless of their status in life (Andrés-Hyman et al., 2006). This sense of honor and respect for others is often contrasted with the respect for social hierarchies and the promotion of deference and respect toward powerful others (Simoni & Perez, 1995).

In part because of the high regard placed on the family unit (i.e., *familismo*), developing and basing one's identity on the family is highly important (Blair, Blair, Madamba, Rosier, & Kinney, 2003), more so than with peers. Parenting strategies among Latinos, especially those of Mexican descent, have been characterized as "responsibility oriented," especially for first-generation parents in the United States (Buriel, 1993). Parents expect children to make productive use of their time, take advantage of the opportunities they have, and be more autonomous and responsible at earlier ages, which often results in parenting strategies that are both stricter (e.g., about not wasting time) and more permissive (e.g., expectation that children will handle their responsibilities with little direct assistance; Hill & Torres, 2010). In fact, stricter and more authoritarian parenting strategies are positively correlated with warmth and are associated with better mental health, suggesting that stricter parenting is interpreted as caring and concern (Hill, Bush, & Roosa, 2003; Mason et al., 2004). In focus groups with Latino families, mothers reported being consistent, firm, and responsive to children's misbehavior; they valued strictness as a strategy more so than leniency, although strictness must occur in the context of a warm relationship (Guilamo-Ramos et al., 2007).

In each of these cultural traditions, the primacy of family relationships over other relationships is emphasized. This may change the value parents place on developing friendships and the messages youth receive about the importance of friendships for their healthy development. Indeed, many ethnic minority youth are warned of the ways in which peer groups may undermine their development and achievement (e.g., "acting White" and its effect on academic performance; Hughes, McGill, Ford, & Tubbs, 2011). Indeed, some research has shown that African American and Latino youth are more resistant to peer pressure than their Euro-American counterparts (Steinberg & Monahan, 2007). Further, the types of parenting strategies that have been found to be most strongly associated with peer acceptance, friendship quality, and the development of social competence among Euro-American samples are not the parenting practices that have been consistently found to support healthy social development and mental health among Latinos and African Americans. These findings call into question the generalizability of the vast theory and research on the linkages between parent–child relationships and child–peer relationships. The field lacks research on the generalizability of associations among parenting, family dynamics, youth social development, and friendship quality to African American and Latino youth. To this end, preliminary findings are described from two studies of parenting, peer relations, and youth.

PRELIMINARY EVIDENCE ON THE GENERALIZABILITY OF EXITING THEORY TO ETHNIC MINORITIES

The results of these two studies provide preliminary answers to the question of whether parenting practices are similarly related to friendships and social competence across ethnicity and SES. The first is a quantitative study on African American and Euro-American elementary school-age youth and their families. The second is a qualitative study (i.e., focus groups) of African American and Latino middle-school youth and their parents.

African American and Euro-American Elementary-School-Age Youth

For the elementary school-age sample, 105 African American and Euro-American youth were followed from kindergarten to the fourth grade. This sample is ideal for examining ethnic variations because it was purposefully selected so that the African American and Euro-American samples are similar with regard to family SES (i.e., family income, parental education level, and occupational prestige). Although SES and ethnicity are often confounded, this study disentangles ethnicity and SES so that more confident conclusions can be made about the role of ethnicity vis-à-vis SES (Hill, 2006). Outcomes include those reflecting the friendship quality, such as the extent to which friends get the child in trouble (child report), the extent to which friends have a good or bad influence on the child (teacher report), children's perceived loneliness (child report), and the number of friends the child has relative to classmates (teacher report). In addition, there are assessments of social competence, including emotion regulation and prosocial behavior (mother and teacher reports). Among the parenting practices, parental warmth (i.e., parental acceptance and communication) and control, which included assessments of discipline (i.e., no nonsense and rule enforcement) and psychological control (i.e., love withdrawal/shaming) are included. Controlling for prior assessments of the outcomes, ethnicity, and family income (Time 1 assessments), we examine main effects of parenting on outcomes at Time 2 and interactions between parenting and ethnicity using regression analyses.

Family communication and parental acceptance are positively related to the number of friends youth have for both African American and Euro-American youth. However, parenting was more strongly related to outcomes for Euro-American youth. Euro-American youth whose parents are more accepting of them report that they have fewer friends who got them into trouble. The relation is not significant for African Americans ($\beta = -.43$ and .13 for Whites and Blacks, respectively; $\Delta R^2 = .11$, $p < .05$). Similarly, family communication is more strongly related to child reports of friends getting them in trouble for Euro-Americans than for African Americans ($\beta = -.60$ and $-.06$, for Whites and Blacks, respectively; $\Delta R^2 = .08$, $p < .05$). Finally, parental acceptance is associated with feeling less lonely at school for Euro-Americans, but not African Americans ($\beta = -.44$ vs. $-.03$ for Whites and Blacks, respectively; $\Delta R^2 = .07$, $p < .05$). There are ethnic differences in the influence that friends have on individual students, according to teachers' reports. Teachers said that African American students' friends have a more negative influence than do Euro-American students' friends. This is consistent with concerns African American parents have about negative peer influences.

Associations between parenting and friendship outcomes are stronger for Euro-Americans than for African Americans, and acceptance and communication are key. These findings are consistent with theories of attachment, modeling, and emotional security (see Chapters 3 and 7). However, these theories do not generalize well to African Americans. Extant theories have not tapped into the types of parenting practices that promote friendship quality for African American youth.

For social competence, including emotion regulation and prosocial behaviors, there are many similarities across ethnicity. Communication is similarly and positively related to emotion regulation for African Americans and Euro-Americans ($\beta = .26$, $\Delta R^2 = .062$, $p < .05$ for teachers' reports and .28, $\Delta R^2 = .061$, $p < .05$ for mothers' reports) and similarly related to teachers' reports of prosocial behavior ($\beta = -.37$, $\Delta R^2 = 13$, $p < .05$). In contrast, harsh parenting is negatively related to emotion regulation, as expected ($\beta = -.37$, $\Delta R^2 = 13$), and love withdrawal (psychological control) is negative related to mothers' reports of prosocial behaviors for both African Americans and Euro-Americans ($\beta = -.20$, $\Delta R^2 = 04$, $p < .06$).

In contrast to the friendship outcomes, there are many similarities across ethnicity regarding the parenting practices that promote social competence. Parental acceptance and communication are key in supporting the development of social competence, and harsh parenting and psychologically controlling disciplinary strategies undermine the development of social competence. In contrast, for friendship outcomes, additional theory and research is needed for African American youth; the extant theory does not adequately explain these processes of friendship quality and loneliness. However, there is evidence that the role of parenting, especially parenting that conveys warmth and acceptance, in development of social competence functions similarly across ethnicity.

Perspectives on Peer Influences: Voices of Latino and African American Parents and Teens

These findings are based on 12 focus groups with middle school students of African American and Latino descent and their parents. Groups were conducted separately for each ethnic group. Focus groups for Latino parents were conducted in Spanish, and the transcriptions were translated. These focus groups included 44 seventh graders (18 Latino and 26 Black), who were performing at grade level or above, and 42 parents (22 Black and 20 Latino). These focus groups were specifically designed to assess parental involvement in education during middle school and did not directly focus on peers and friendships. However, when discussing strategies for supporting youths' academic success and the role of the school context on academic achievement, all focus groups discussed the influence of peers and friendships. Given the lack of research on parental influence on peer relationships for ethnic minority youth, these data provide solid preliminary information for hypothesis development.

The responses of the African American and Latino youth and their parents are similar in their characterizations of peer relationships and friendships and their discussions of the strategies parents use to shape friendships and peer relations. In characterizing peer relations and peer environment, African American and Latino teens and parents focused on problems and concerns. For example, teens described the peer environment in the following ways:

Latina teen:	"The school is filled with a lot of drama."
African American girl:	"There's too much drama."
African American girl:	"Yeah, people talk too much junk about somebody."
African American boy:	"There is a lot of peer pressure."
Latina teen, regarding older students:	"If they are older than you, then they think they can hurt you."
African American boy, regarding differences between elementary and middle school:	"Students behave worse."

Parents also expressed concerns, as follows:

African American mother of a son:	"I worry about [child's name]. There are some mean kids here."
African American mother:	"When they were in elementary school, they played with their friends, but their friends [didn't] influence them like they do in middle school."
African American mother:	"I mean, peer pressure is a lot different.... You get to middle school, um, the mix of kids is a lot different."

Finally, when asked about barriers to helping their children do well in school, an African American mother immediately mentioned peers: "Peers . . . I think if you do not talk to your child regularly and let [him or her] know that it is important to keep off the negative influences, she will easily be influenced and maybe distracted from the main course and lose direction."

Although one parent discussed the potential value or need for friends, she was still very cautious and protective: "I think . . . having a social life and teaching that it's not all about work and that you can go and socialize with your friends when it's appropriate to socialize with your friends and not when it's not appropriate. Making sure they understand the boundaries between when it's appropriate and not appropriate and just allowing them to be a kid, basically."

Parents and teens consistently characterized the family and peer realms as competing with one another, as shown by the following quotes:

> *Latina teen:* "My mom knows I'm different at school."
>
> *Latina mother:* "It is important to talk to them because they are getting information from older peers that may not be correct or clear."

Although one African American mother indicated that peers and friendships may compensate for family, it was clear that this is not a desirable outcome: "They've got to know someone cares; because if someone [doesn't] care at home, that means someone cares somewhere else. So, if they're not going to get it from their parents, and it's hard to say, but they are going to get it somewhere else. And that's why you have gang activity because they are going to the wrong places to get this love because they are not getting it at home. You stay there and be their friend—but you draw your boundaries."

In addition to warning about the negative peer pressures on their children, parents communicated messages about how their child should behave in order to be a good friend and manage the peer environment, as shown by the following quotes:

> *Latina teen:* "She'll [mom] tell us, like, not to be mean to people and to stay away from trouble."
>
> *Latina mother:* "The best way to deal with a problem [with a friend] is peacefully, respect your classmates and they will be respectful. And, that's all you can do."
>
> *African American parent of a son who is picked on at school:* "[Child's name] doesn't possess the same internal strength that I have. If my feelings are hurt, I can move on."

Teens and parents discussed a number of ways in which parents assisted teens in navigating the peer context. To a large extent, these strategies centered on how to avoid peers who might be a bad influence or lead the child to trouble and directly orchestrating his or her environment to avoid negative peer influences. Rather than just parents feeling concern, teens also focused on the need to avoid negative peer influences. The following are a sample of quotes from teens and parents:

> *Latina teen:* "She [her mom] just says as long as I stay in school and away from gangs . . . drugs and people who look like they're in a gang."

Latina teen:	"I don't listen to my friends that much. I don't really hang out with my friends that much."
Moderator:	"So, your parents teach you things?
Latino teen:	"It was like, people to hang out with like who behaves and who 'don't' behave."
Moderator:	"So he helps you select your friends too?"
Latino teen:	"Yeah."
Latino teen:	"My parents tell me stuff like what to do, what not to do, like don't join gangs because you might get killed in middle school."
African American girl:	"My mom always tells me that I'm judged by the company I keep. So she tells me to choose who I hang out with, don't mix with the wrong crowd."
African American mother:	"I teach my daughter, you walk with the stupid you going to be stupid. If you walk with the wise, you are going to be wise."

One African American parent's goal for the child was "to develop positive friendships, surround themselves with kids that want to succeed and do well."

This focus on avoiding negative peer influence is consistent with the quantitative data presented previously in which teachers reported that African American students' friends are more likely to get them in trouble than are Euro-American students' friends. Further, it supports prior research that has shown that African American and Latino youth are more resistant to peer pressure than are Euro-American youth (Steinberg & Monahan, 2007). Latino and African American parents prepare their children to avoid the increased negative peer influence during early adolescence.

In addition to direct advice and coaching about how to select friends and the potential pitfalls of "hanging out with the wrong crowd," parents use parenting practices that they themselves described as strict to help assure that their child does not fall into the wrong crowd or "get off track," as evident in the following quotes:

Latino teen:	"So, like, they've [his parents] have seen a lot of gang fights and stuff. And, I think it is helpful for them to be strict . . . because, like, they'll tell me what's bad and good for me."
Latina mother:	"I want to know everything, where he is going, phone numbers, when he will be back—everything."

| Latino father: | "For me, having good communication and trust with my children and being a bit strict with my children as well. If not . . . [sigh]. We're in a country that grants a lot of liberties, so if you are not strict with your children . . . [sigh]." |

When these strategies fail, parents resort to more direct orchestration and intervention, including moving and changing schools, as follows:

| African American teen: | "Well, my mother moved me away from a bad community, well not really a bad community, but a community where I knew too many people. And so . . . now I'm in a quiet place." |
| An African American parent of a different child than the previous one: | "I had to get them out, I am glad I got them away from that environment. It took me a long time, but we did get away from them [gangs]." |

Although these focus groups were not designed to directly target information about peer relations and friendships, these were concerns that both parents and teens had at the forefront of their minds. Focus groups were also conducted with Euro-American parents and teens. However, in contrast to African Americans and Latinos, Euro-American parents and teens did not mention friendships, peer interactions, or peer pressure in their focus groups, suggesting that these problems are particularly significant and poignant for ethnic minority youth. Further, these differences suggest that the linkages between the family and peer/friendship realms are much more distinct and in conflict for African American and Latino families than for Euro-American families. These teens and parents do not see the same type of continuity between family and peer/friendship influences that are described in the extant theory and research.

From a socialization perspective, African American and Latino parents believe that there are greater differences in the messages between parents and peers than do their Euro-American counterparts, on the basis of the qualitative and quantitative analyses presented. From a psychoanalytic perspective, ethnic minority cultures tend to be more collective and interdependent and thereby expect and promote less individuation among youth and see autonomy development as less central to adolescent development. This may render peers, especially the broader peer culture, as less necessary for affirming identity and sense of self.

These two studies did not focus directly on the context of close friendships, which according to cognitive theories, are the central context for the developmental benefits of friendships and peer relations. However, these findings point to the need to broaden our theories to account for differences in effective parenting practices, messages about the role of peers, and significant and poignant concerns about the negative influences of peers on the likelihood that children and adolescents will reach their potential. For African American and Latino youth, the realms of parents and peers are separate and conflicting, indeed.

REFERENCES

Andrés-Hyman, R. C., Ortiz, J., Anez, L. M., Paris, M., & Davidson, L. (2006). Culture and clinical practice: Recommendations for working with Puerto Ricans and other Latinas(os) in the United States. *Professional Psychology: Research and Practice, 37*, 694–701. doi:10.1037/0735-7028.37.6.694

Barber, B. K. (2002). Reintroducing parental psychological control. In B. K. Barber (Ed.), *Intrusive parenting: How psychological control affects children and adolescents* (pp. 3–13). Washington, DC: American Psychological Association. doi:10.1037/10422-000

Blair, S. L., Blair, M. C. L., Madamba, A. B., Rosier, K. B., & Kinney, D. A. (2003). *Race/ethnicity, gender, and adolescents' occupational aspirations: An examination of family context.* New York, NY: Elsevier Science.

Blos, P. (1979). *The adolescent passage: Developmental issues.* New York, NY: International University Press.

Bokhorst, C. L., Sumter, S. R., & Westenberg, P. M. (2010). Social support from parents, friends, classmates, and teachers in children and adolescents aged 9 to 18 years: Who is perceived as most supportive? *Social Development, 19*, 417–426. doi:10.1111/j.1467-9507.2009.00540.x

Bowlby, J. (1973). *Attachment and loss: Vol. 2. Separation.* New York, NY: Basic Books.

Boykin, A. W. (1983). The academic performance of Afro-American children. In J. Spence (Ed.), *Achievement and achievement motives* (pp. 321–371). San Francisco, CA: Freeman.

Boykin, A. W. (1986). The triple quandary and the schooling of Afro-American children. In U. Neisser (Ed.), *The school achievement of minority children* (pp. 57–92). Hillsdale, NJ: Erlbaum.

Brody, G. H., & Flor, D. L. (1998). Maternal resources, parenting practices, and child competence in rural, single parent African American families. *Child Development, 69*, 803–816.

Brody, G. H., Flor, D. L., & Gibson, N. M. (1999). Linking maternal efficacy beliefs, developmental goals, parenting practices, and child competence in rural single-parent African American families. *Child Development, 70*, 1197–1208. doi:10.1111/1467-8624.00087

Brown, A. L., Bransford, J. D., Ferrara, R. A., & Campione, J. C. (1983). Learning, remembering and understanding. In J. H. Flavell & E. M. Markman (Eds.), *Handbook of child psychology: Vol. 3. Cognitive development* (pp. 77–166). New York, NY: Wiley.

Buriel, R. (1993). Childrearing orientations in Mexican American families: The influence of generation and sociocultural factors. *Journal of Marriage and Family, 55,* 987–1000. doi:10.2307/352778

Clark, K. E., & Ladd, G. W. (2000). Connectedness and autonomy support in parent-child relationships: Links to children's socioemotional orientation and peer relationships. *Developmental Psychology, 36,* 485–498. doi:10.1037/0012-1649.36.4.485

Cokley, K. O. (2005). Racial(ized) identity, ethnic identity, and afrocentric values: Conceptual and methodological challenges in understanding African American identity. *Journal of Counseling Psychology, 52,* 517–526. doi:10.1037/0022-0167.52.4.517

Collins, W. A., Maccoby, E. E., Steinberg, L., Hetherington, E. M., & Bornstein, M. H. (2000). Contemporary research on parenting: The case for nature and nurture. *American Psychologist, 55,* 218–232. doi:10.1037/0003-066X.55.2.218

Cooper, C. R., & Cooper, J. R. G. (1992). Links between adolescents' relationships with their parents and peers: Models, evidence, and mechanisms. In R. D. Parke & G. W. Ladd (Eds.), *Family-peer relationships: Modes of linkages* (pp. 135–158). Hillsdale, NJ: Erlbaum.

Cross, W. E. (2003). Tracing the historical origins of youth delinquency & violence: Myths & realities about Black culture. *Journal of Social Issues, 59,* 67–82. doi:10.1111/1540-4560.t01-1-00005

Cross, W. E. (2011). The historical relationship between Black identity and Black achievement motivation. In N. E. Hill, T. L. Mann, & H. E. Fitzgerald (Eds.), *African American children's mental health: Development and context* (1–27). Santa Barbara, CA: Praeger.

Deater-Deckard, K., & Dodge, K. A. (1997). Externalizing behavior problems and discipline revisited: Nonlinear effects and variations by culture, context, and gender. *Psychological Inquiry, 8,* 161–175. doi:10.1207/s15327965pli0803_1

Dodge, K. A., Greenberg, M. T., & Malone, P. S. (2008). Testing an idealized dynamic cascade model of the development of serious violence in adolescence. *Child Development, 79,* 1907–1927. doi:10.1111/j.1467-8624.2008.01233.x

Douvan, E., & Adelson, J. (1966). *The adolescent experience.* New York, NY: Wiley.

Erikson, E. H. (1964). *Childhood and society.* New York, NY: Norton.

Flynn, J. R. (2011). Black youth: The lost boys. In N. E. Hill, T. L. Mann, & H. E. Fitzgerald (Eds.), *African American children's mental health: Development and context* (pp. 29–62). Santa Barbara, CA: Praeger.

Fuligni, A. J., & Eccles, J. S. (1993). Perceived parent-child relationships and early adolescents' orientation toward peers. *Developmental Psychology, 29,* 622–632. doi:10.1037/0012-1649.29.4.622

Guilamo-Ramos, V., Dittus, P., Jaccard, J., Johansson, M., Bouris, A., & Acosta, N. (2007). Parenting practices among Dominican and Puerto Rican mothers. *Social Work, 52,* 17–30.

Hamm, J., & Faircloth, B. S. (2005). Peer context of mathematics classroom belonging in early adolescence. *The Journal of Early Adolescence, 25*, 345–366. doi:10.1177/0272431605276932

Hart, C. H., DeWolf, M., Wozniak, P., & Burts, D. (1992). Maternal and paternal disciplinary styles: Relations with preschoolers' playground behavioral orientations and peer status. *Child Development, 63*, 879–892. doi:10.2307/1131240

Hill, N. E. (2001). Parenting and academic socialization as they relate to school readiness: The roles of ethnicity and family income. *Journal of Educational Psychology, 93*, 686–697. doi:10.1037/0022-0663.93.4.686

Hill, N. E. (2006). Disentangling ethnicity, socioeconomic status, and parenting: Interactions, influences, and meaning. *Vulnerable Children and Youth Studies, 1*, 114–124. doi:10.1080/17450120600659069

Hill, N. E. (2009). Culturally-based world views, family processes, and family school interactions. In S. L. Christenson & A. Reschly (Eds.), *The handbook on school-family partnerships for promoting student competence*. New York, NY: Routledge.

Hill, N. E. (2011). Undermining partnerships between African American families and schools: Legacies of discrimination and inequalities. In N. E. Hill, T. L. Mann, & H. E. Fitzgerald (Eds.), *African American children and mental health: Development and context* (Vol. 1, pp. 199–230). Santa Barbara, CA: Praeger.

Hill, N. E., Bromell, L., Tyson, D. F., & Flint, R. C. (2007). Developmental commentary: Ecological perspectives on parental influences during adolescence. *Journal of Clinical Child and Adolescent Psychology, 36*, 367–377.

Hill, N. E., & Bush, K. R. (2001). Relationships between parenting environment and children's mental health among African American mothers and children. *Journal of Marriage and Family, 63*, 954–966. doi:10.1111/j.1741-3737.2001.00954.x

Hill, N. E., Bush, K. R., & Roosa, M. W. (2003). Parenting and family socialization strategies and children's mental health: Low-income Mexican American and Euro-American mothers and children. *Child Development, 74*, 189–204. doi:10.1111/1467-8624.t01-1-00530

Hill, N. E., Murry, V. M., & Anderson, V. D. (2005). Sociocultural contexts of African American families. In V. C. McLoyd, N. E. Hill, & K. A. Dodge (Eds.), *African American family life: Ecological and cultural diversity* (pp. 21–44). New York, NY: Guilford Press.

Hill, N. E., & Torres, K. (2010). Negotiating the American dream: The paradox of Latino students' goals and achievement and engagement between families and schools. *Journal of Social Issues, 66*, 95–112. doi:10.1111/j.1540-4560.2009.01635.x

Hill, N. E., & Witherspoon, D. (2011). Race, ethnicity, and social class. In M. Underwood & L. H. Rosen (Eds.), *Handbook of social development* (pp. 316–346). New York, NY: Guilford Press.

Hughes, D. L., McGill, R. K., Ford, K. R., & Tubbs, C. (2011). Racial socialization messages from parents, peers, and school contexts: Implications for Black youths' academic success. In N. E. Hill, T. L. Mann, & H. E. Fitzgerald (Eds.), *African American children's mental health: Development and context* (pp. 95–124). Santa Barbara, CA: Praeger.

Hughes, D., Rodriguez, J., Smith, E. P., Johnson, D. J., Stevenson, H. C., & Spicer, P. (2006). Parents' ethnic-racial socialization practices: A review of the research and directions for future study. *Developmental Psychology, 42,* 747–770. doi:10.1037/0012-1649.42.5.747

Kandel, D., & Lesser, G. S. (1982). *Youth in two worlds.* San Francisco, CA: Jossey-Bass.

Knoester, C., Haynie, D. L., & Stephens, C. M. (2006). Parenting practices and adolescents' friendship networks. *Journal of Marriage and Family, 68,* 1247–1260. doi:10.1111/j.1741-3737.2006.00326.x

Kobak, R. R., & Sceery, A. (1988). Attachment in late adolescence: Working models, affect regulation, and presentations of self and others. *Child Development, 59,* 135–146. doi:10.2307/1130395

Kuperminc, G. P., Blatt, S. J., Shahar, G., Henrich, C., & Leadbeater, B. J. (2004). Cultural equivalence and cultural variance in longitudinal associations of young adolescent self-identification and interpersonal relatedness to psychological and school adjustment. *Journal of Youth and Adolescence, 33,* 13–30. doi:10.1023/A:1027378129042

Ladd, G. W. (1992). Themes and theories: Perspectives on processes in family-peer relationships. In R. D. Parke & G. W. Ladd (Eds.), *Family-peer relationships: Modes of linkages* (pp. 3–34). Hillsdale, NJ: Erlbaum.

Ladd, G. W., & Golter, B. (1988). Parents' management of preschoolers' peer relations: Is it related to children's social competence? *Developmental Psychology, 24,* 109–117. doi:10.1037/0012-1649.24.1.109

Ladd, G. W., & Pettit, G. S. (2002). Parenting and the development of children's peer relationships. In M. H. Bornstein (Ed.), *Handbook of parenting: Vol. 5. Practical issues in parenting* (pp. 269–309). Mahwah, NJ: Erlbaum.

LaFreniere, P. J., & Dumas, J. E. (1992). A transactional analysis of early childhood anxiety and social withdrawal. *Development and Psychopathology, 4,* 385–402. doi:10.1017/S0954579400000857

LaFreniere, P., & Srouft, L. A. (1985). Profiles of peer competence in the preschool: Interrelations between measures, influence of social ecology, and relation to attachment history. *Developmental Psychology, 21,* 56–69. doi:10.1037/0012-1649.21.1.56

Laird, R. D., Pettit, G. S., Mize, J., Brown, E. G., & Lindsey, E. (1994). Mother-child conversations about peers: Contributions to competence. *Family Relations, 43,* 425–432. doi:10.2307/585374

Laursen, B., Wilder, D., Noack, P., & Williams, V. (2000). Adolescent perceptions of reciprocity, authority, and closeness in relationships with mothers, fathers, and friends. *International Journal of Behavioral Development, 24,* 464–471. doi:10.1080/016502500750038017

MacKinnon-Lewis, C., Colling, B. L., Lamb, M., Dechman, K., Rabiner, D., & Curtner, M. E. (1994). A cross-contextual analysis of boys' social competence: From family to school. *Developmental Psychology, 30,* 325–333. doi:10.1037/0012-1649.30.3.325

Marin, G., & Marin, B. V. (1991). *Research with Hispanic populations* (Vol. 23). Newbury Park, CA: Sage.

Mason, C. A., Walker-Barnes, C. J., Tu, S., Simons, J., & Martinez-Arrue, R. (2004). Ethnic differences in the affective meaning of parental control behaviors. *The Journal of Primary Prevention, 25,* 59–79. doi:10.1023/B:JOPP.0000039939.83804.37

Mitchell, H. H. (1975). *Black belief: Folk beliefs in America and West Africa.* New York, NY: Harper & Row.

Mounts, N. S. (2001). Young adolescents' perceptions of parental management of peer relationships. *The Journal of Early Adolescence, 21,* 92–122. doi:10.1177/0272431601021001005

Parke, R. D., & Bhavnagri, N. (1989). Parents as managers of children's peer relationships. In D. Belle (Ed.), *Children's social networks and social supports* (pp. 241–259). New York, NY: Wiley.

Parke, R. D., & Ladd, G. W. (1992). *Family-peer relationships: Modes of linkage.* Hillsdale, NJ: Erlbaum.

Patterson, C. J., Kupersmidt, J. B., & Griesler, P. C. (1990). Children's perceptions of self and of relationships with others as a function of sociometric status. *Child Development, 61,* 1335–1349. doi:10.2307/1130746

Patterson, G. R., Reid, J. B., & Dishion, T. J. (1992). *Antisocial boys.* Eugene, OR: Castalia.

Piaget, J. (1932). *The moral judgment of the child.* London, England: Routledge & K. Paul.

Putallaz, M. (1987). Maternal behavior and children's sociometric status. *Child Development, 58,* 324–340. doi:10.2307/1130510

Ramirez-Esparza, N., Gosling, S. D., & Pennebaker, J. W. (2008). Paradox lost: Unraveling the puzzle of simpatia. *Journal of Cross-Cultural Psychology, 39,* 703–715. doi:10.1177/0022022108323786

Renshaw, P. D., & Parke, R. D. (1992). Family and peer relationships in historical perspective. In R. D. Parke & G. W. Ladd (Eds.), *Family-peer relationships: Modes of linkages* (pp. 35–74). Hillsdale, NJ: Erlbaum.

Ryan, A. M. (2000). Peer groups as a context for the socialization of adolescents' motivation, engagement, and achievement in school. *Educational Psychologist, 35,* 101–111. doi:10.1207/S15326985EP3502_4

Sankofa, B. M., Hurley, E. A., Allen, B. A., & Boykin, A. W. (2005). Cultural expression and Black students' attitudes toward high achievers. *The Journal of Psychology: Interdisciplinary and Applied, 139,* 247–260. doi:10.3200/JRLP.139.3.247-260

Schneider, B. H., Atkinson, L., & Tardif, C. (2001). Child-parent attachment and children's peer relations: A quantitative review. *Developmental Psychology, 37,* 86–100. doi:10.1037/0012-1649.37.1.86

Simoni, J. M., & Perez, L. (1995). Latinos and mutual support groups: A case for considering culture. *American Journal of Orthopsychiatry, 65*, 440–445. doi:10.1037/h0079697

Smetana, J. G. (2000). Middle-class African American adolescents' and parents' conceptions of parental authority and parenting practices: A longitudinal investigation. *Child Development, 71*, 1672–1686. doi:10.1111/1467-8624.00257

Smetana, J. G., & Chuang, S. (2001). Middle-class African American parents' conceptions of parenting in early adolescence. *Journal of Research on Adolescence, 11*, 177–198. doi:10.1111/1532-7795.00009

Steinberg, L., Dornbusch, S., & Brown, B. (1992). Ethnic differences in adolescent achievement: An ecological perspective. *American Psychologist, 47*, 723–729. doi:10.1037/0003-066X.47.6.723

Steinberg, L., & Monahan, K. C. (2007). Age differences in resistance to peer influence. *Developmental Psychology, 43*, 1531–1543. doi:10.1037/0012-1649.43.6.1531

Stevenson, H. C., Davis, G., & Abdul-Kabir, S. (2001). *Stickin' to, watchin' over, and gettin' with: An African American parent's guide to discipline*. San Francisco, CA: Jossey-Bass.

Tyler, K. M., Boykin, A. W., Miller, O., & Hurley, E. A. (2006). Cultural values in the home and school experiences of low-income African American students. *Social Psychology of Education, 9*, 363–380. doi:10.1007/s11218-006-9003-x

Vygotsky, L. S. (1978). *Mind in society: The development of higher psychological processes* (M. Cole, V. John-Steiner, S. Scribner, & E. Souberman, Eds. and Trans.). Cambridge, MA: Harvard University Press.

Zimmermann, P. (2004). Attachment representations and characteristics of friendship relations during adolescence. *Journal of Experimental Child Psychology, 88*, 83–101. doi:10.1016/j.jecp.2004.02.002

6

SOCIAL NETWORKS AND ATTACHMENT BONDS DURING ADOLESCENCE: IMPLICATIONS FOR EARLY PAIR BONDING AND RISKY BEHAVIORS

ROGER KOBAK AND JOANNA HERRES

Over the course of adolescence, relationships with peers become an increasingly salient aspect of the adolescent's social environment. Yet as adolescents form new relationships with friends and romantic partners, they maintain long-enduring relationships with adult caregivers in their families. Extensive research literatures have focused exclusively on either family or peer influences on adolescents' social development. Further, both family and peer relationships have demonstrated important effects on a wide range of developmental tasks that mark the transition into adulthood. These tasks include mate selection, reproduction, and the formation of pair bonds with sexual partners. Surprisingly, although adolescents' relationships with peers and adult caregivers have been extensively studied as factors that influence young adult outcomes, there are few conceptual or theoretical models for how adolescents maintain and organize their relationships with adult caregivers as they form new ones with peers (see Chapter 5, this volume).

Methods for assessing social networks provide a potential tool for describing adolescents' relationships with family and peers. However, efforts to assess relationships within a social network often rely on quantitative measures, such as frequency of contact, proximity, or social support, that place different relationships on common dimensions. Although this approach is useful, it fails to capture qualitative differences in the nature and function of relationships with caregivers, kin, and peers. Efforts to reach a more qualitative understanding of adolescents' relationships require a series of steps. First, it is important to distinguish close from more distal relationships. Second, close relationships must then be differentiated in terms of the functions they serve for the adolescent. Third, how adolescents organize their close relationships with adults and peers must be specified. Preferences for individuals within a social network may be relatively equivalent or interchangeable (i.e., there is not a clear preference for one individual or another) or hierarchically ordered. Finally, a description of adolescents' social networks should account for both normative changes in the organization of close relationships and individual differences in how adolescents manage this process.

Attachment theory offers a conceptual framework for identifying a component of social networks that changes over the course of adolescence. In the first part of this chapter, we use an attachment framework to describe the close relationships in adolescents' social networks and an interview technique that distinguishes attachment from other types of affectional bonds. In the second part of the chapter, we discuss how social class, culture, and gender influence the composition and organization of adolescents' bonds with attachment figures. In the final section, we consider how individual differences in adolescents' hierarchies of attachment figures can increase adolescents' vulnerability to engage in risky behaviors with a particular focus on sexual risk and pregnancy outcomes.

RELATIONSHIPS THAT MEET CRITERIA
FOR AN AFFECTIONAL BOND

The notion of an affectional bond provides a useful first step in differentiating close from more distal relationships (Ainsworth, 1989). Ainsworth defined an *affectional bond* as a "relatively long enduring tie" characterized by a "need to maintain proximity," distress on "inexplicable" separation, pleasure or joy on reunion, and grief at loss (p. 711). These criteria are useful in distinguishing close from more distal relationships. Although children form relationships with other children, teachers, day care providers, and grandparents, the majority of these relationships will not readily meet criteria for affectional bonds. In considering relationships that would constitute an affectional bond, we begin with early relationships with caregivers that are motivated by the child's attachment system, and we then move on to relationships formed later in life that are motivated by affiliative, sexual, or caregiving behavioral systems. The behavioral system notion has been a key component of attachment theory since its inception (Bowlby, 1982) and provided Ainsworth (1989) with a basis for differentiating attachment from other affectional bonds formed at later developmental periods.

The bond formed with a primary caregiver early in life clearly meets criteria for an affectional bond, though the age at which a young child can experience grief has been subject to some dispute (Bowlby, 1980). The formation of the child–caregiver bond is primarily motivated by the child's attachment system or need to rely on the caregiver as a source of nurturance, protection, and survival. This system works in a synchronous fashion with fear, so that when infants and young children perceive danger or become distressed, they actively seek contact with a preferred caregiver or attachment figure. The relationship that results from these interactions is marked by distress at separation and joy at reunion. Yet the child's attachment bond with the caregiver differs from later developing affectional bonds insofar as its function of ensuring protection and survival increases the emotional significance of the relationship. As a result, attachments can be distinguished from other affectional bonds by the role that the partner plays as a protective or supportive figure in situations involving threat, danger, or challenge.

Other Affectional Bonds

Whereas the child's bond to his or her caregiver is primarily motivated by the attachment behavioral system and is formed during infancy and early childhood, later developing affectional bonds formed during adolescence and adulthood are motivated by other behavioral systems that result in social contact seeking (see also Chapter 4). The major social motivational systems identified by Ainsworth were affiliative, sexual, and caregiving. Each of these systems serves a biological function. Affiliation facilitates group formation, and in most social species, the group can serve a protective function and provide sense of belonging (Baumeister & Leary, 1995). An individual who strays from or is excluded from the group is more vulnerable to predators and may suffer emotional distress. The sexual system motivates mating behaviors that serve the function of reproduction and maintenance of the species. Caregiving bonds serve the function of promoting survival of offspring.

During adolescence, close friendships that endure for several years may qualify as affectional bonds. These relationships emerge within the broader set of peer relationships that are motivated by a sociability or affiliative system. In peer relationships that become close friendships, the adolescent may actively miss the friend when separated and experience and communicate joy and positive feeling on being reunited. A bond with a close friend can provide opportunities for self-disclosure and exploring aspects of adolescents' emerging identities that test their ability to rely on friends as confidants (Collins & Sroufe, 1999). In a similar manner, close friendships may also provide adolescents with the opportunity to develop listening and support skills that provide them with experience in a caregiving capacity.

The involvement of the sexual system in the formation of bonds with romantic partners gives these relationships the appearance of an affectional bond. The desire to be in the physical presence of the partner and the strong propensity to think about and miss the partner when separated are typically considered hallmarks of "falling in love." However, these intense feelings often occur during the early stages of a romantic relationship long before the adolescent has had a chance to form a "long-enduring" bond with the sexual partner. Adolescents are also aware that many romantic relationships are short-lived and a potential source of vulnerability. As a result, only the romantic relationships that have stood the test of time and elicited some degree of mutual commitment are likely to meet criteria for an attachment bond (Duemmler & Kobak, 2001).

The caregiving system functions to monitor and protect the child as well as to provide guidance and support over the course of the child's development. This is a more complex behavioral system that requires empathetic and cognitive capacities to coordinate caring for offspring with other adult relationship and work demands. The system complements the child's attachment bond to ensure the child's survival and welfare. The formation of the caregiving bond precedes the child's development of an attachment bond, and in the case of biological mothers, the bond may begin to form during pregnancy. The bond that the caregiver forms with the child is characterized by the same emotional reactions to inexplicable separation from the child, joy at reunion and grief at loss that mark other affectional bonds. The caregiving bond has clear evolutionary value in terms of assuring the child's survival and works in a complementary fashion with the child's attachment. Yet it differs from an attachment bond insofar as its primary goal is to ensure the safety and well-being of the child and not the caregiver. In extreme situations, caregivers will often make substantial personal sacrifices and risk their own well-being to protect offspring.

Can Affiliative and Sexual Bonds Become Attachments?

Compared with child–caregiver bonds, affectional bonds that are formed with a close friend or romantic partner are relatively short-lived. Yet during adolescence and adulthood, these relationships penetrate further into the youth's daily life and create a substantial degree of interdependence between relationship partners. As these relationships with close friends or romantic partners persist and become an affectional bond, partners are likely to be gradually tested for their ability to serve as attachment or caregiving figures.

The process through which a relationship partner becomes an attachment figure is likely to occur gradually and over a number of years. The slow developing nature of adolescent and adult attachment bonds is attributable to the relatively infrequent activation of the attachment system. Ainsworth (1989) noted that compared with infancy in which the child's survival depends on access to an attachment figure, situations involving threat and danger are far less frequent during adolescence and adulthood. Nonetheless, occasional events, such as accidents, injuries, and major life transitions, all provide opportunities to test the ability of a relationship partner to serve as a source of protection, comfort, and encouragement. In this respect, the emotional significance of affectional bonds is enhanced to the extent that partners have experienced difficulties that activate the attachment system and successfully test a relationship partner as an attachment or caregiving figure.

Once they have formed, peer attachment bonds differ from child–caregiver bonds insofar as attachments and caregiving roles are reciprocal or interchangeable. In adult attachments, partners must at times be able to rely on their partner and at other times care for their partner's attachment needs (see Chapter 2). Individual differences in how couples negotiate reciprocal caregiving and attachment roles are relatively unexplored areas of adult attachment research. Given gender differences in socialization and reproduction, it is likely that men and women will show some differences in both the types of events that activate the attachment and reliance on a partner and in the type of caregiving support available in the relationship. Ainsworth (1989) noted that pregnancy and childbirth are periods of vulnerability for women that are more likely to test male partners' abilities to serve in a caregiving role. Relationships may also differ in the extent to which caregiving and attachment roles are reciprocal and interchangeable.

When an adult affectional bond also serves a reproductive function and results in offspring, the nature of the bond between mothers and fathers is further motivated by the caregiving system being directed toward the offspring. During pregnancy, infancy, and early childhood periods, the caregiving system is likely to be activated on a frequent basis and couples face the task of protecting and nurturing offspring. The caregiving component of the couples' relationship must be coordinated with other aspects of the couple's relationship. As a result, the task of coordinating reciprocal adult attachment and caregiving systems must accommodate the new challenge posed by the need to ensure the children's survival. This requires a major change in the couple's relationship, often requiring a redirection of how the individuals rely on each other for support. Coordination of different systems and cooperative negotiation of goal conflicts are likely to become important in maintaining the adult affectional bond during this period.

Is There a Hierarchy of Attachment Figures?

The notion of affectional bonds accommodates several types of close relationships and provides a useful way of distinguishing close relationships from the other relationships that constitute an individual's social network. Yet attachment theory makes a further distinction between affectional bonds, suggesting that not all affectional bonds have equal significance for an individual. As previously suggested, a bond formed through activation of the affiliative or sexual systems may meet criteria as a "relatively long enduring tie" characterized by a "need to maintain proximity," distress on inexplicable separation, pleasure or joy on reunion, and grief at loss. Yet the loss of one of these bonds would not result in a threat to an individual's or partner's survival. By contrast, the emotional stakes in maintaining a bond are much higher when an individual has come to rely on a partner as an attachment figure. When an affectional bond has become an attachment bond, loss or threats of loss of the partner are likely to activate fear and be perceived as deeply threatening to the individual's well-being. Infants' and young children's attachment bonds and the complementary caregiving bond to the child are likely to be highly emotionally salient. The emotional significance of these bonds is likely to persist into later developmental periods long after the child's reliance on the caregiver for survival has passed.

Attachment bonds are not only a highly select and more emotionally salient type of affectional bond, but Bowlby also suggested that children organize their preferences for multiple attachment figures in a hierarchical fashion. The hierarchical model posits that although adolescents maintain bonds with multiple attachment figures, they will have a consistent order of preference for whom they would seek out in emergency and challenging situations. A primary attachment figure can be identified from a child's preferences for that person in situations that test the presence of an attachment bond. However, if the primary figure is inaccessible, children will often show selective preferences for a secondary figure. In her observational study of infants in Uganda, Ainsworth (1967) found that most children organized their attachment behavior around a primary caregiver. Subsequent studies have demonstrated that infants show clear discrimination and consistent preferences for a primary caregiver over subsidiary or secondary attachment figures. The notion that young children maintain a hierarchical ordering of preferences for their attachment figures has provided a basis for considering how children, adolescents, and adults maintain attachment bonds and organize attachment behavior in adolescence and adulthood (Kobak, Rosenthal, Zajac, & Madsen, 2007).

The attachment hierarchy provides a framework for conceptualizing how adolescents organize their preferences for parents, romantic partners, and friends as attachment figures. As adolescents' bonds with friends or romantic partners are tested as possible sources of protection and support, it may be useful to consider the possibility of tertiary and quaternary attachment figures. Bowlby (1982) hypothesized that during adolescence, "other adults may come to assume an importance equal to or greater than that of parents, and sexual attraction to age-mates begins to extend the picture" (p. 207). In early adolescence, adult caregivers are likely to constitute the major attachment figures in adolescents' hierarchies. By mid-adolescence, there is likely to be a gradual movement of friends or romantic partners into the hierarchy, and by the later teenage years, many adolescents will likely show evidence of a preference for a peer over a mother or father as an attachment figure. The formation of long-term reciprocal attachment bonds typically results in the peer partner taking on the role of primary attachment figure, with parents moved into secondary or tertiary positions.

Rosenthal and Kobak (2010) tested a new measure, the Important People Interview (IPI), that was designed to (a) determine who adolescents identified as attachment figures, (b) distinguish attachment relationships from others that were primarily motivated by affiliative or support-seeking concerns, and (c) determine whether preferences for attachment figures were hierarchically ordered. To accomplish this, they used the IPI that asks adolescents to nominate the four most important people in their lives as well as four additional peers. Participants were then asked to rank their preferences for which individuals they would contact in situations designed to test attachment bond, affiliation, and support-seeking situations. Attachment situations include threats to the accessibility of an attachment figure (whom an adolescent would miss the most), emergency situations involving danger (whom the adolescent would contact following a life-threatening event), and situations that elicit feelings of closeness (whom the adolescent feels closest to). Conversely, contexts that elicit nonemergency support-seeking behaviors derive from more commonly occurring sources of distress or challenge (whom the adolescent would go to when having a bad day or experiencing a social rejection or anxiety-provoking challenge). These daily events are likely to motivate support-seeking behaviors. In addition to situations that elicit attachment and support-seeking preferences, it is also important to consider social contact seeking that is independent of these concerns.

Individuals showed remarkably consistent preferences for those whom they prefer in the three attachment situations, and their preferences were hierarchically ordered. It is not surprising that in a sample of high school students, biological parents, particularly mothers, predominated as primary attachment figures. However, there was considerable diversity in who served as secondary, tertiary, and quaternary attachment figures for this relatively homogenous sample of European American middle-class students. Biological fathers and kin (i.e., siblings or relatives) occupied many of the positions in adolescents' hierarchies, but many adolescents also indicated that peers, close friends, or romantic partners were beginning to be identified as attachment figures. As expected, there was a developmental trend toward older adolescents showing an increased likelihood of identifying romantic partners or friends as attachment figures.

THE SOCIAL ECOLOGY OF ADOLESCENTS' ATTACHMENT HIERARCHIES

There is a strong evolutionary argument for the universality of the child's need to form an attachment bond with a primary caregiver (Bowlby, 1982). Without such a bond that provides protection and nurturance, human infants would not survive or eventually reproduce. Efforts to study the cultural effects on the formation of the attachment bond have generally relied on using Ainsworth and colleagues' (1978) Strange Situation procedure across different cultures. Most of these comparisons were based on assessments in which the child's security with the biological mother was tested. Although infants' relationships with biological fathers and to some extent infant day-care providers have been assessed in the Strange Situation procedure, there have been few attempts to determine whom infants prefer as a primary attachment figure or whether these preferences are hierarchically organized and vary with caregiving arrangements (Colin, 1996; Main, 1999). In one of the few naturalistic studies of attachment relationships, Ainsworth noted that older female siblings often assumed caretaking roles for young infants that were secondary to those of the biological mothers (Ainsworth, 1967).

The need for descriptive studies of attachment hierarchies becomes more pressing when considering adolescents' preferences for attachment figures. Although reproduction is also critical to the maintenance of all species, there is considerable flexibility in humans in the timing and relationship context for reproduction (Settersten, 2004; see also Chapter 9, this volume). For instance, there is substantial variation within the U.S. population in the age at which adolescents and adults transition to marriage and parenthood. There is also substantial variation in the extent to which individuals assume that marriage will occur before childbirth, with nearly 40% of children in the United States presently being delivered by unmarried mothers (Hamilton, Martin, & Ventura, 2009). Family structure, social class, gender, and culture all contribute to adolescents' attitudes toward the formation of affectional bonds with romantic partners and their attitudes and expectancies for the timing of reproduction and the formation of a caregiving bond with offspring. These factors in turn should influence the composition and structure of their hierarchies of attachment figures.

Following the study of middle-class adolescents and young adults (Rosenthal & Kobak, 2010), we administered the IPI to a sample of 225 economically disadvantaged adolescents. We had several reasons to expect that the social ecology of poverty would influence the composition of adolescents' attachment hierarchies. First, poverty and family structure are closely related in many U.S. families. Many more economically disadvantaged children grow up in single-parent households or households with cohabiting males compared with their middle-class counterparts. Second, many adolescents from low-income families are on an accelerated timetable for transitioning to parenthood (Burton, 1990; Elder, 1998) and possibly forming adult attachments. However, before addressing comparisons between economically disadvantaged and middle-class adolescents, we needed to test the validity of the IPI procedure with our low-income sample.

The IPI was administered to the low-income sample during a second wave of data collection when the adolescents were close to their 15th birthdays. A first question was whether adolescents differentiated between individuals they preferred in the three attachment situations compared with those they preferred in the three affiliative and three support-seeking situations. Principal component analysis confirmed that the nine situations produced the three components, and adolescents' preferences for the eight persons nominated in the IPI are graphed in Figure 6.1. The average placement (4 = primary, 3 = secondary, 2 = tertiary, 1 = quaternary, 0 = not placed) for each of the eight nominees is plotted on the y-axis. Compared with the average placement of individuals in

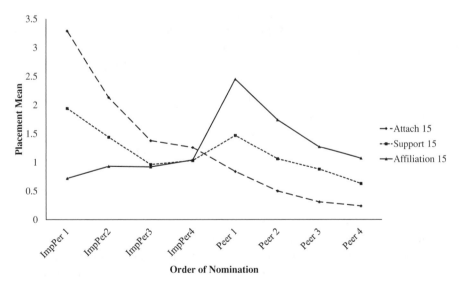

Figure 6.1. Average rankings of eight nominees in attachment, support-seeking, and affiliative situations. ImpPer = important person.

affiliative and social-support situations, placement of individuals in attachment situations tends to follow the order in which individuals nominated the important people in their life. Further, attachment preferences show a linear decline, indicating hierarchical ordering of attachment preferences. By comparison, affiliative and support-seeking preferences are more evenly distributed across nominees, though the first peer nominated was more likely to receive a higher ranking in these situations than were other individuals. This pattern is very similar to that found in our middle-class sample and supports the IPI's validity among economically disadvantaged adolescents.

On the basis of attachment preferences, we identified those who served as adolescents' primary through quaternary attachment figures. This allowed us to compare the composition of the attachment hierarchies of low-income adolescents with those in a middle-income sample. As expected, there was a major difference in the family structure of the two samples. In our largely middle-class sample used to validate the IPI, 81% of the adolescents lived in families with intact marriages between biological mothers and fathers (Rosenthal & Kobak, 2010). Conversely, in our longitudinal study of adolescents from low-income families who met federal criteria for free and reduced lunch, only 21% of the families had intact marriages between biological mothers and fathers (Kobak, Zajac, & Smith, 2009).

Seventy percent of biological mothers were primary attachment figures, and 15% were secondary in the low-SES sample. In the middle-income sample, 59% of biological mothers were primary and 19% occupied secondary positions in adolescents' hierarchies. The lower levels of mothers' placement in the middle-income sample were largely compensated for by biological father involvement. Compared with the low SES sample in which 4% of biological fathers were identified as primary attachment figures, 10% of biological fathers in middle-SES families were identified as primary attachments. The differences in biological fathers' placement between the two groups were most marked in terms of the number of them who were not identified as an attachment figure anywhere in adolescents' hierarchies. As indicated in Figure 6.2, 34% of high-school-age adolescents in the middle-income sample did not identify fathers as attachment figures, compared with 64% of adolescents in the low-income sample. These differences in fathers' placement in adolescents' attachment hierarchies are shaped by the high rates of single parenthood in low-income families and the resulting limited contact with biological fathers.

The largest and most significant difference in the attachment hierarchies of low- and middle-SES adolescents was in terms of the role played by kin (i.e., siblings or other relatives) in the attachment hierarchy. As indicated in Figure 6.3, low-SES adolescents were nearly 3 times more likely to identify kin as an attachment figure in all four positions (primary through quaternary) in their attachment hierarchies. We cannot entirely attribute this sizeable

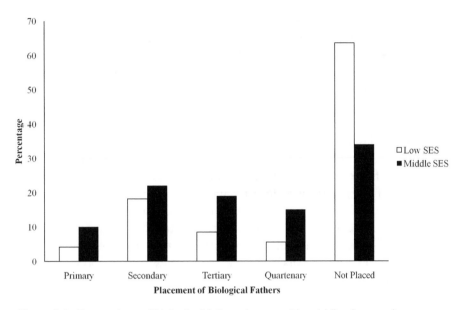

Figure 6.2. Comparison of biological father placement in middle-class and low–socioeconomic status (SES) samples.

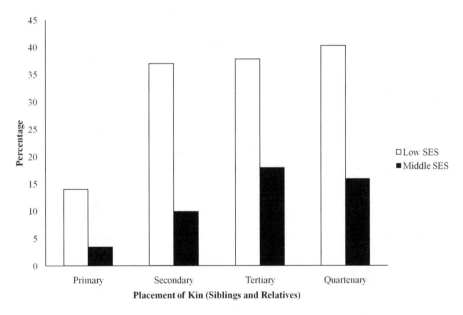

Figure 6.3. Comparison of kin placement (siblings or other relatives) in middle-class and low–socioeconomic status (SES) samples.

effect entirely to social class, as our low-income sample consisted of 74% African American adolescents compared with less than 5% African Americans in our middle-income group (see also Chapter 5, this volume). The maintenance of kin networks among families living in poverty has been identified as a way of coping with the adversities associated with poverty and is especially evident in low-income African American families (Stack, 1974).

In spite of striking social-class differences in the extent to which fathers and kin were identified as attachment figures, there was a notable similarity across social class in the role played by biological mothers. Not only did the vast majority of adolescents in both samples identify biological mothers as primary attachment figures, but the majority of adolescents also identified biological mothers as their primary attachment figure. In addition, there was substantial similarity between samples in the extent to which adolescents had begun to identify close friends and romantic partners as attachment figures. Given the tendency of biological mothers to serve as primary caregivers, they also are likely to serve as "gatekeepers" for adolescents' access to men and kin (Roy & Burton, 2007).

INDIVIDUAL DIFFERENCES IN ADOLESCENTS' ATTACHMENT HIERARCHIES AND RISKY BEHAVIORS

At one extreme are adolescents who cut themselves off from parents, and at the other are those who remain intensely attached and unwilling to direct attachment behavior to others; between these extremes lie the great majority of adolescents whose attachments to parents remain strong but whose ties to others are of much importance also (Bowlby 1982, p. 207).

As adolescents form attachment bonds with peers, the ordering of their preferences for attachment figures may be gradually transformed. In comparing adolescents in early high school (9th and 10th grades) with those in later high school (11th and 12th grades) and early college (freshman and sophomore years), romantic partners moved up in the attachment hierarchies as fathers moved to lower positions (Rosenthal & Kobak, 2010). Although attachment hierarchies go through a normative transformation as adolescents and young adults form attachment bonds with romantic partners, there are also substantial individual differences in the timing of this transformation. Adolescents who identify peers as attachment figures at younger ages are potentially more likely to be at risk for problem behaviors than adolescents who take longer to rely on peers as attachment figures. Adult attachment figures not only serve a protective function, but they are also "older and wiser" and can monitor and supervise adolescents as they face new opportunities to engage in risky behaviors, such as driving cars, experimenting with drugs and alcohol, or engaging in sexual behavior (Steinberg, 2007). By contrast, relying on a friend or romantic partner as an attachment figure may increase rather than decrease the likelihood of engaging in risk-taking behavior.

Support for the hypothesis that prematurely relying on a peer as an attachment figure may represent a maladaptive process comes from several sources. Numerous studies have identified adolescents who generally disengage from parents during early adolescence and, as a result, are increasingly susceptible to peer influence (Bronfenbrenner, 1967; Fuligni & Eccles, 1993; Silverberg & Steinberg, 1987). Premature autonomy has been described as adolescents' detachment from parents and early engagement with peers and has been shown to be a risk factor in the development of problem behavior (Dishion, Spracklen, & Medici Skaggs, 2000). These adolescents are at increased risk for associating with deviant peers and engaging in aggressive and delinquent behaviors (Dishion, Nelson, & Bullock, 2004). Further, when adolescents make decisions without any parental input, they are at greater risk for poorer academic achievement, deviance, and problem behavior (Dornbusch, Ritter, Mont-Reynaud, & Chen, 1990; Lamborn, Dornbusch, & Steinberg, 1996). Adolescents' maladaptive reliance on peers may be more systematically examined by considering the extent to which they have relinquished parents and prematurely promoted peers in their attachment hierarchies.

The Rosenthal and Kobak (2010) study provided initial support for the hypothesis that early reliance on peers as attachment figures is associated with risky or problem behaviors. In that sample of middle-class high school and college students, participants who identified a close friend as a primary, secondary, or tertiary attachment figure reported high levels of both internalizing and externalizing symptoms. In our sample of economically disadvantaged adolescents, we tested the hypothesis by identifying the highest placement of either a friend or romantic partner in adolescents' hierarchies at age 15. We then graphed adolescents' reports of their externalizing (aggressive and delinquent) behaviors at ages 13, 15, and 17 (see Figure 6.4). There was a linear increase across all three reporting periods between reliance on a peer as an attachment figure and adolescents' problem behaviors. Whereas not identifying a peer was associated with the least risk for problem behaviors, risk increased with the peers' placement in the adolescent's attachment hierarchy.

Early reliance on a romantic partner as an attachment figure may have very different implications for economically disadvantaged adolescents than for their middle-income counterparts. The latter are much less likely than low-income youth to expect that a romantic attachment will result in reproduction and transition to parenthood. Although they may have long-term plans for marriage and parenthood, these transitions are typically delayed because they are associated with higher "opportunity costs" in terms of education and future employment (Plotnick, 2007). Conversely, low-income adolescents who have

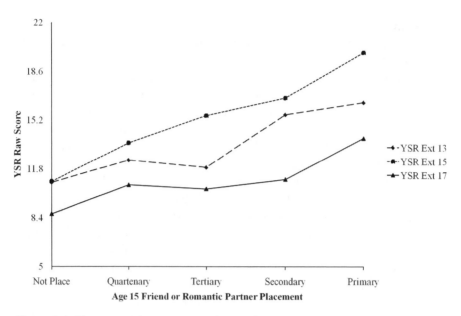

Figure 6.4. Placement of peers as attachment figures at age 15 years and externalizing behaviors at ages 13, 15, and 17 years.

disengaged from school and face limited opportunities for employment are more likely to have an accelerated transition to parenthood, an alternative life course strategy (Burton, 1990). The differences in the timing of parenthood between low- and middle-income adolescents and young adults are evident in substantially higher rates of teenage childbearing and unwed motherhood in low-income communities (Sassler, 2010; Smock & Greenland, 2010).

The implications of transition to parenthood are substantially different for low-income females than for their male partners. Many economically disadvantaged females anticipate raising children as unwed parents and face difficulties finding male partners who have the educational or employment opportunities to sustain marriage (Huston & Melz, 2004). Although low-income females still value marriage and would prefer to be married before having children, they do not perceive any stigma in childbearing outside of marriage (Cherlin, Cross-Barnet, Burton, & Garrett-Peters, 2008). Adolescents growing up in single-parent families may lack models of pair bonds between mothers and fathers that persist through the transition to parenthood and involve shared responsibility for caring for offspring. This increases the importance of maintaining attachment bonds with the adolescent's mother and other members of the kin network. Grandmothers and other kin networks are likely to be important sources of support for teenage mothers (Oberlander, Black, & Starr, 2007).

SUMMARY AND IMPLICATIONS

Attachment bonds are highly selective and form an emotionally salient component of adolescents' social networks. Bonds formed early in life to biological mothers are the most typical and long-enduring attachments, and even in late adolescence and early adulthood biological mothers are most likely to be identified as attachment figures. By contrast, relationships with biological fathers vary considerably and are more subject to ecological and developmental factors. Not surprisingly, family structure has a major effect on adolescents' likelihood of identifying biological fathers as attachment figures, but fathers are also more likely than mothers to be relinquished as attachment figures as adolescents form new affectional bonds with friends or romantic partners.

Major questions remain to be addressed about the stability and enduring nature of friends and romantic partners whom adolescents identify in the IPI as attachment figures. Many of the bonds that adolescents form with a friend or sexual partner are fragile and vulnerable to disruptions and terminations. Thus, the movement of a peer into a position as a primary or secondary attachment figure may only be temporary, and the maintenance of parents as attachment figures in reserve can buffer the adolescent from some of the stresses associated with disruptions in their relationships with peers.

More generally, the relationships that the adolescents form with friends and romantic partners must stand the test of time to become attachment bonds. Adolescents motivated by the immediacy of sexual attraction or intimacy with a friend may identify their partner as someone whom they would count on when confronted with danger or an emergency. However, such preferences need to be tested, and opportunities for testing are relatively infrequent compared with the daily attachment needs of young children. As a result, only longitudinal studies of adult attachment can determine the extent to which these relationships constitute actual attachment bonds.

Yet in spite of substantial variability in the formation of peer attachment bonds, adolescents' preferences for friends and romantic partners have important implications for their adaptation. There is evidence that increased risky and problem behaviors occur among younger adolescents who identify a friend or romantic partner as an attachment figure. At a conceptual level, this is not surprising insofar as adolescents can benefit from continued adult monitoring of their safety and welfare. For instance, identifying a romantic partner as a primary or secondary attachment figure not only signals a substantial emotional investment in the relationship but also may result in increased sexual risk-taking behaviors and unintended pregnancy. Some risky behaviors have long-term effects on adolescents' developmental pathways that include not only the possibility of serious injury or death from reckless driving but also effects on the transition to adult work and family roles. Such effects can result from teenage pregnancy or arrest for delinquent behaviors. Individual differences in the timing of how adolescents continue to rely on parents while forming new bonds with peers remain an area that is ripe for further investigation.

REFERENCES

Ainsworth, M. D. S. (1967). *Infancy in Uganda*. Baltimore, MD: Johns Hopkins University Press.

Ainsworth, M. D. S. (1989). Attachments beyond infancy. *American Psychologist, 44,* 709–716. doi:10.1037/0003-066X.44.4.709

Ainsworth, M. D. S., Blehar, M., Waters, E., & Wall, S. (1978). *Patterns of attachment: A psychological study of the Strange Situation*. Hillsdale, NJ: Erlbaum.

Baumeister, R. F., & Leary, M. R. (1995). The need to belong: Desire for interpersonal attachments as a fundamental human motivation. *Psychological Bulletin, 117,* 497–529. doi:10.1037/0033-2909.117.3.497

Bowlby, J. (1980). *Attachment and loss: Vol. 3. Loss*. New York, NY: Basic Books.

Bowlby, J. (1982). *Attachment and loss: Vol. 1. Attachment* (2nd ed.). New York, NY: Basic Books.

Bronfenbrenner, U. (1967). Response to pressure from peers versus adults among Soviet and American school children. *International Journal of Psychology, 2,* 199–207. doi:10.1080/00207596708247216

Burton, L. (1990). Teenage childbearing as an alternative life-course strategy in multigeneration black families. *Human Nature, 1,* 123–143. doi:10.1007/BF02692149

Cherlin, A., Cross-Barnet, C., Burton, L. M., & Garrett-Peters, R. (2008). Promises they can keep: Low-income women's attitudes toward motherhood, marriage and divorce. *Journal of Marriage and Family, 70,* 919–933. doi:10.1111/j.1741-3737.2008.00536.x

Colin, V. (1996). *Human attachment*. New York, NY: McGraw-Hill.

Collins, W. A., & Sroufe, L. A. (1999). Capacity for intimate relationships: A developmental construction. In W. Furman, B. B. Brown, & C. Feiring (Eds.), *The development of romantic relationships in adolescence* (pp. 125–147). Cambridge, England: Cambridge University Press.

Dishion, T. J., Nelson, S. E., & Bullock, B. M. (2004). Premature adolescent autonomy: Parent disengagement and deviant peer process in the amplification of problem behavior. *Journal of Adolescence, 27,* 515–530. doi:10.1016/j.adolescence.2004.06.005

Dishion, T. J., Spracklen, K. M., & Medici Skaggs, N. (2000). The ecology of premature autonomy in adolescence: Biological and social influences. In K. A. Kerns, J. M. Conteras, & A. M. Neal-Barnett (Eds.), *Family and peers: Linking two social worlds* (pp. 27–45). Westport, CT: Praeger.

Dornbusch, S. M., Ritter, P. L., Mont-Reynaud, R., & Chen, Z. (1990). Family decision making and academic performance in a diverse high school population. *Journal of Adolescent Research, 5*, 143–160. doi:10.1177/074355489052003

Duemmler, S. L., & Kobak, R. (2001). The development of attachment and commitment in dating relationships: Attachment security as a relationship construct. *Journal of Adolescence, 24*, 401–415. doi:10.1006/jado.2001.0406

Elder, G., Jr. (1998). The life course as developmental theory. *Child Development, 69*(1), 1–12.

Fuligni, A. J., & Eccles, J. S. (1993). Perceived parent-child relationships and early adolescents' orientation toward peers. *Developmental Psychology, 29*, 622–632. doi:10.1037/0012-1649.29.4.622

Hamilton, B., Martin, J., & Ventura, S. (2009). Births: Preliminary Data for 2007. *National Vital Statistics Reports, 57*(12). Hyattsville, MD: National Center for Health Statistics.

Huston, T., & Melz, H. (2004). The case for (promoting) marriage: The devil is in the details. *Journal of Marriage and Family, 66*, 943–958. doi:10.1111/j.0022-2445.2004.00064.x

Kobak, R., Rosenthal, N., Zajac, K. & Madsen, S. (2007). Adolescent attachment hierarchies and the search for an adult pair bond. *New Directions for Child and Adolescent Development: Attachment in Adolescence, 117*, 57–72.

Kobak, R., Zajac, K., & Smith, C. H. (2009). Preoccupied states of mind and trajectories of hostile-impulsive behavior: Implications for the development of personality disorders. *Development and Psychopathology, 21*, 839–851. doi:10.1017/S0954579409000455

Lamborn, S. D., Dornbusch, S. M., & Steinberg, L. (1996). Ethnicity and community context as moderators of the relations between family decision making and adolescent adjustment. *Child Development, 67*, 283–301. doi:10.2307/1131814

Main, M. (1999). Epilogue. Attachment theory: Eighteen points with suggestions for future studies. In J. Cassidy & P. Shaver (Eds.), *Handbook of attachment: Theory, research and clinical applications* (pp. 845–887). New York, NY: Guilford Press.

Oberlander, S. E., Black, M., & Starr, R. (2007). African American adolescent mothers and grandmothers: A multigenerational approach to parenting. *American Journal of Community Psychology, 39*(1–2), 37–46. doi:10.1007/s10464-007-9087-2

Plotnick, R. D. (2007). Adolescent expectations and desires about marriage and parenthood. *Journal of Adolescence, 30*, 943–963. doi:10.1016/j.adolescence.2007.01.003

Rosenthal, N. L., & Kobak, R. (2010). Assessing adolescents' attachment hierarchies: Differences across developmental periods and associations with individual adaptation. *Journal of Research on Adolescence, 20*, 678–706. doi:10.1111/j.1532-7795.2010.00655.x

Roy, K., & Burton, L. (2007). Mothering through recruitment: Kinscription of nonresidential fathers and father figures in low-income families. *Family Relations, 56*, 24–39. doi:10.1111/j.1741-3729.2007.00437.x

Sassler, S. (2010). Partnering across the life course: Sex, relationships, and mate selection. *Journal of Marriage and Family, 72,* 557–575. doi:10.1111/j.1741-3737.2010.00718.x

Settersten, R. (2004). The age structuring and rhythm of the life course. In J. T. Mortimer & M. J. Shanahan (Eds.), *Handbook of the life course* (pp. 81–98). New York, NY: Springer Science.

Silverberg, S. B., & Steinberg, L. (1987). Adolescent autonomy, parent-adolescent conflict, and parental well-being. *Journal of Youth and Adolescence, 16,* 293–312. doi:10.1007/BF02139096

Smock, P. J., & Greenland, F. R. (2010). Diversity in pathways to parenthood: Patterns, implications, and emerging research directions. *Journal of Marriage and Family, 72,* 576–593. doi:10.1111/j.1741-3737.2010.00719.x

Stack, C. (1974). *All our kin: Strategies for survival in a Black community.* New York, NY: Random House.

Steinberg, L. (2007). Risk taking in adolescence: New perspectives from brain and behavioral science. *Current Directions in Psychological Science, 16,* 55–59. doi:10.1111/j.1467-8721.2007.00475.x

III

ADULT RELATIONSHIPS

7

AN ORGANIZATIONAL–DEVELOPMENTAL PERSPECTIVE ON FUNCTIONING IN ADULT ROMANTIC RELATIONSHIPS

JESSICA E. SALVATORE, W. ANDREW COLLINS, AND JEFFRY A. SIMPSON

The building blocks of successful adult romantic relationships, such as trust, intimacy, and effective conflict resolution, do not appear ex nihilo. Rather, competence in adult romantic relationships relies on capacities developed in earlier relationships with parents and peers (see Chapters 3, 5, and 6, this volume). Identifying the legacy of early experience on adult romantic relationship functioning is significant for both theoretical and practical reasons. Moreover, examining a person's developmental history in combination with his or her concurrent relationship functioning allows one to generate novel hypotheses about the future outcomes for both the person and his or her relationship.

In this chapter, we adopt an organizational–developmental perspective on couple functioning in early adulthood. We begin by outlining the principles of an organizational perspective on development, paying particular attention to the implications for individual differences in adult romantic relationship functioning. We then discuss findings from a prospective longitudinal study that links individuals' adult romantic relationship outcomes with their early caregiving experiences. These findings illustrate how a developmental perspective can illuminate the origins of individual differences in romantic competence. Finally, we discuss a promising future direction for developmental research on adult romantic relationships.

AN ORGANIZATIONAL PERSPECTIVE ON DEVELOPMENT AND ITS IMPLICATIONS FOR STUDYING RELATIONSHIPS ACROSS THE LIFE SPAN

The organizational perspective rests on the assumption that the intensity or frequency of any thought, feeling, or behavior is less important than its orchestration with other thoughts, feelings, and behaviors. Though widely accepted today, this premise was controversial during the third quarter of the 20th century when Mischel (1968, 1973) and others (e.g., Masters & Wellman, 1974) demonstrated that the frequency and intensity of discrete behaviors such as smiling or crying fluctuate across time and situations. One conclusion from this body of work was that individual differences in behavior at a single point in time were poor predictors of future behavior. The organizational perspective on development (Sroufe, Egeland, Carlson, & Collins, 2005) emerged from foundational concepts that existed at the dawn of developmental psychology (Collins & Hartup, in press). This perspective emphasizes the processes through which behavioral expectancies developed in early relationships are carried forward into novel social contexts. Expectations must be adjusted by building on the past, but also by gaining sensitivity to how present circumstances vary from past ones (Piaget, 1952; Sander, 1962, 1975; Spitz, Emde, & Metcalf, 1970; Vygotsky, 1962, 1978; Waddington, 1957; Werner, 1948). Bowlby (1982) and Ainsworth (1989) advanced views that were complementary to earlier formulations by emphasizing the significance of the quality of care experienced by children across different developmental periods.

When focusing on how behavior in relationships is organized rather than frequency of events, the problem of prediction becomes tractable. A primary advantage of an organizational perspective is that one can improve the prediction of interpersonal behavior across both time and different contexts. Imagine, for example, a romantic couple in which both partners rely on each other for emotional support when one or both partners are upset. The discrete behaviors that partners enact toward one another on a daily basis, especially in situations that do not call for caregiving, are unlikely to be a good predictor of the quality and amount of support one partner gives the other when he or she is distressed (see Chapter 8). From an organizational perspective such as attachment theory, however, one would interpret the quality and amount of support seeking and support giving displayed when partners are upset as an expression of the quality of the secure base that characterizes their relationship. Moreover, the extent to which partners serve as a secure base for each other ought to be manifested differently in other situations, such as encouraging partners to engage in greater exploration in nonstressful situations.

Given that any discrete behavior can take on different meaning depending on the behaviors with which it co-occurs, a second advantage of adopting an organizational perspective is that it allows one to make different predictions about concurrent versus future couple functioning. Consider the following examples of negative affect in two romantic dyads. In both dyads, one partner implores the other to make it home for dinner on time. The partner in the first dyad responds by raising his or her voice and blaming rush-hour traffic for his or her tardiness. In contrast, the partner in the second dyad averts his or her gaze, walks away, and mumbles sarcastically about needing to "try harder" to get home on time in the future. Although the partners in both dyads respond to the punctuality request with negative affect and displeasure, the specific coordination of their affect with other behaviors reflects their actual interest in solving the problem. One person responds angrily but advocates his or her position with the goal of receiving leniency in the future. The second person walls-off, shielding himself or herself from further criticism and limiting the opportunity for a collaborative resolution to the problem. Thus, the pattern of behavior within which negative affect is embedded may be more important than the presence versus absence of negative affect. This, in fact, is the basis for distinguishing between anger (in the first couple) and hostility (in the second couple), or what Bowlby (1973) called the "anger of hope" versus the "anger of despair."

A third guiding principle of the organizational perspective is that the patterning of thoughts, feelings, and behaviors in close relationships is rooted in early experiences with caregivers, particularly parents (Sroufe et al., 2005; see also Chapter 3, this volume). Early experiences with caregivers carry unique importance because they are the "initiating conditions" that foreshadow how individuals are likely to behave in future social environments. Early experiences with caregivers, including those that occur before children can talk, establish initial expectations about the benevolence and availability of significant others and, correspondingly, beliefs about the worth of the self. Furthermore, overlearned interaction patterns that become established in early relationships often lay the groundwork for interpersonal organized action sequences (i.e., automatized behavioral routines) that are drawn on when similar situations occur in the future (Berscheid, 1983). Similar to Bowlby's (1982, 1973) concept of internal working models, organized action sequences exist outside of conscious awareness and control. As a consequence, once a sequence is activated, it usually runs off until completed.

This early foreshadowing, of course, is probabilistic, not deterministic. Negative early experiences do not condemn individuals to a lifetime of dissatisfying close relationships, nor do positive early experiences inoculate against unhappiness. True to its roots in attachment theory (Bowlby, 1973), the organizational perspective holds that individual functioning reflects both an individual's history and his or her current circumstances. We consider this assertion later in the chapter.

TRANSACTIONS BETWEEN RELATIONSHIP REPRESENTATIONS AND SOCIAL BEHAVIOR ACROSS DEVELOPMENT

An emphasis on the significance of early caregiving experiences across the life span raises the question, What is the mechanism that brings these early experiences forward? Relationship representations (i.e., internal working models) are one probable mechanism (Bowlby, 1973; Bretherton & Munholland, 1999, 2008). Relationship representations involve expectations, attitudes, and beliefs about the accessibility and responsiveness of significant others in relationships and, therefore, one's worth and value as a relationship partner. These representations begin to develop on the basis of repeated patterns of interaction with initial caregivers (Isabella & Belsky, 1991; Isabella, Belsky, & von Eye, 1989), and they continue to develop (and sometimes change) in response to interaction patterns with subsequent caregivers later in life (Carlson, Sroufe, & Egeland, 2004; Vaughn, Egeland, Sroufe, & Waters, 1979; see also Chapter 2, this volume). Relationship representations operate in a top-down manner, guiding expectations, perceptions, and behavior in future interpersonal situations.

Consistent with Bowlby's (1973) theorizing, the organizational perspective views infant attachment security as marking the beginning of a transactional process between representations and social behavior that plays out across the life span (Carlson et al., 2004). This process is transactional in that representations and social behavior are mutually influential across time. In other words, instead of exerting unilateral influence, relationship representations affect social behavior and are also affected by it. A natural extension of this logic is that relationship representations are changeable in the face of new experiences that contradict previously held representations (Vaughn et al., 1979).

The complicated process of predicting a person's future social functioning based on his or her past requires identifying the salient developmental experiences and issues that individuals confront at each period of the life span. Each period presents a novel set of culturally defined socioemotional developmental issues that must be mastered (Erikson, 1963; Masten & Coatsworth, 1995; Sroufe, Egeland, & Carlson, 1999; Sroufe et al., 2005). In infancy, the most salient task is forming an attachment to a stronger/wiser caregiver who can help to modulate arousal and promote infant survival. The prominence of infant–caregiver attachment begins to wane in the preschool years as the child enters the world of same-age peers. Although caregivers remain important features of the child's social environment, attention is increasingly shifted toward peers as the child's social world expands. Peers continue to play a prominent role during middle childhood and adolescence as the individual balances group functioning with the establishment of close, same-sex and opposite-sex relationships (Sroufe et al., 2005).

These developmental issues are cumulative. Failure to successfully negotiate issues that are salient in the interpersonal experiences of earlier periods interferes with the ability to engage in later ones effectively because the individual is ill-equipped to handle increasingly sophisticated and challenging interpersonal demands. Consider the most salient socioemotional task of early childhood, which is to engage with peers successfully. Maintaining constructive, satisfying interactions with peers builds the intrapersonal behavioral and emotional regulatory capacities that were scaffolded by parents during infancy and toddlerhood (Sameroff & Emde, 1989; Sander, 1975; see also Chapter 6, this volume). For example, a preschooler who lacks these abilities and immediately becomes physically aggressive when frustrated is less likely to be integrated in group interactions over time. In addition, such children may also be excluded from positive peer interactions, thus losing opportunities to develop new skills that are needed to negotiate the socioemotional issues of middle childhood successfully.

Carlson et al. (2004) translated the transaction between relationship representations and social behavior across development into a measurement model using data from the Minnesota Longitudinal Study of Risk and Adaptation. According to this model, the connection between early caregiving experiences and late adolescent social behavior is a result of transactions between relationship representations and social behavior across time. Relationship representations in early childhood, middle childhood, and early adolescence were assessed using interviews and projective drawings. Social behavior was measured using teachers' rankings of participants' peer competence and emotional health obtained during each of these developmental periods. For the teacher rankings, participants' classroom teachers were given an age-appropriate description of peer competence and emotional health, which included criteria such as sociability, peer acceptance, and leadership (peer competence) and confidence, curiosity, self-assuredness, and engagement in new experiences and challenges (emotional health). Teachers then rank-ordered all students in their classrooms in terms of how well each child fit the description. Structural equation modeling was used to test the parsimony and fit of the transactional (i.e., cross-lagged) model compared with six others. Some of these alternative models examined the cumulative and noninteractive contributions of relationship representations and social behavior. Other models omitted data from specific developmental periods. The transactional model shown in Figure 7.1 provided the best fit to the data. These findings are

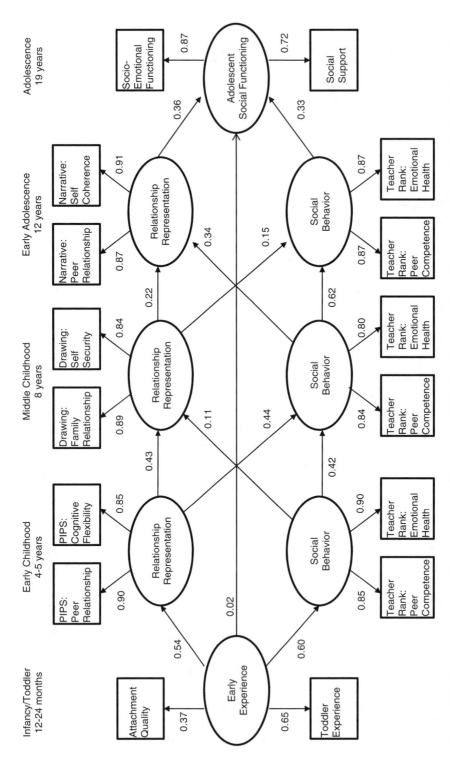

Figure 7.1. Cross-lagged model linking representations and social behavior across time. Numbers represent standardized path coefficients. PIPS = Preschool Interpersonal Problem-Solving Assessment. From "The Construction of Experience: A Longitudinal Study of Representation and Behavior," by E. A. Carlson, L. A. Sroufe, and B. Egeland, 2004, *Child Development, 75,* p. 78. Copyright 2007 by Blackwell Publishing. Reprinted with permission.

consistent with Bowlby's (1982, 1973) claim that early caregiving experiences initiate pathways of social functioning that are propagated through relationship representations and social experiences from each successive developmental period.

AN ORGANIZATIONAL–DEVELOPMENTAL PERSPECTIVE ON ATTACHMENT AND BEHAVIOR IN ROMANTIC RELATIONSHIPS

Most successful relationships, defined as those that promote a positive sense of self and of one's partner and that have high levels of trust, intimacy, and sensitivity (Collins & van Dulmen, 2006; Sroufe et al., 2005), contain features of the good relationships that precede them. Individuals draw on the emotion regulation, peer engagement, and close relationship skills (e.g., intimacy, conflict resolution) from earlier developmental periods to meet the interpersonal challenges that arise in later relationships, such as balancing needs for autonomy and intimacy.

As mentioned previously, attachment theory (Ainsworth, 1989; Ainsworth, Blehar, Waters, & Wall, 1978; Bowlby, 1973, 1980, 1982) provides a comprehensive account of behavioral organization in relationships across successive periods of the life span. This conceptual premise, coupled with measurement advances in attachment research during the past 3 decades (e.g., the development of the Adult Attachment Interview [AAI]; George, Kaplan, & Main, 1985; Main, Kaplan, & Cassidy, 1985), has enriched our understanding of the important role of developmental history in adult social functioning, including the most salient socioemotional task of adulthood, establishing and maintaining romantic relationships (Ainsworth, 1989). The AAI is a semi-structured interview that assesses recollections of childhood experiences with parents and other attachment figures. The AAI is scored for discourse properties and violations of norms regarding clear and coherent communication. The degree to which respondents describe their childhoods with their parents in a clear, credible, and coherent manner is the primary criterion for determining attachment classifications on the AAI. As a result, some people who claim in the interview to be "secure" or to have had secure relationships with their parents during childhood are classified as insecure on the basis of the manner and coherence (rather than the content) of how they describe their childhoods. The AAI was designed to measure individuals' current state of mind with respect to past attachment issues rather than their childhood attachment to parents per se (Main et al., 1985). Unless individuals have unusual, unresolved attachment issues or cannot be classified in a single attachment category, most people are assigned to one of three general categories: secure, dismissing (avoidant), and preoccupied.

Persons classified as secure on the AAI present a clear, well-supported description of their past relationship with both parents. Their episodic memories of childhood are vivid and coherent, and they have little difficulty recalling important childhood experiences, even if their upbringing was difficult. Persons classified as dismissing on the AAI typically view their parents and upbringing as normal or even ideal, but cannot support these claims with specific, episodic memories of significant childhood events. Others classified as dismissing actively disregard or dismiss the importance of attachment figures or attachment-related emotions and behavior. Individuals who are classified as preoccupied on the AAI usually discuss their childhood experiences with attachment figures extensively during the interview. Their interviews often reveal deep-seated, unresolved anger toward one or both parents, which taints their descriptions and interpretations of past experiences.

In one of the first studies to investigate how representations of early attachment experiences are related to perceptions and behavior in adulthood, Kobak and Sceery (1988) tested whether secure, dismissing, and preoccupied working models are associated with unique patterns of self–other representations and social behavior. They found that individuals who have secure representations of their parents on the AAI are rated by their peers as more ego resilient and less anxious than either of the insecure groups. In addition, the peers of secure adolescents rated them as less hostile than dismissing adolescents and less anxious than preoccupied adolescents. Kobak and Sceery (1988) also found that secure individuals report greater social competence and less psychological distress compared with preoccupied adolescents. Secure individuals also report less loneliness and greater social support from family than do dismissing adolescents. Similar attachment-related differences have been found in observational studies of peer problem solving (e.g., Zimmermann, Maier, Winter, & Grossmann, 2001), which reveal that secure individuals respond more constructively than do insecure people when their partners act negatively.

Kobak and Sceery's (1988) investigation foreshadowed numerous studies on how representations of early caregiving contribute to functioning in adult romantic relationships. Most of these studies have involved observational assessments of couples in contexts (e.g., support provision, conflict resolution) in which attachment-related behaviors should be witnessed. Stressful situations such as these ought to activate the attachment system (Bowlby, 1982; Simpson & Rholes, 2004). Moreover, they are ideal for understanding continuity in relationship functioning across time because stressful situations are "high-potential" contexts in which overlearned interaction patterns developed in prior attachment relationships, such as parent–child relationships, should be displayed. Consistent with this hypothesis, Creasey (2002) found that differences between secure and insecure individuals' negative behavior (e.g., contempt, belligerence, domineering, stonewalling, defensiveness, sadness, anger) were more pronounced in a mildly stressful conflict management condition than in a low stress waiting-room condition. As predicted, insecure individuals exhibited more of these negative behaviors than did secure individuals (cf. Simpson, Rholes, & Nelligan, 1992).

Roisman, Madsen, Hennighausen, Sroufe, and Collins (2001) found conceptually similar effects in their observational study of developmentally at-risk young adult romantic couples during a series of conflict and collaborative tasks. Specifically, they found that dyads that had secure individuals had higher quality interactions, resolved conflicts better, displayed more positive affect and secure base behaviors, and demonstrated better balance between good individual functioning and good couple functioning. Similar results, whereby more secure individuals displayed a higher ratio of positive-to-negative behaviors during a problem-solving discussion, were also documented in a young adult middle-class sample (Holland & Roisman, 2010). Above and beyond this contemporaneous correlation, Holland and Roisman (2010) also found that AAI security predicted increases in effective couple functioning over a 1-year period. Studying emotion regulation in marital dyads during a problem-solving task, Bouthillier Julien, Dubé, Bélanger, and Hamelin (2002) found that secure husbands engaged in more positive communication behaviors and were more responsive to, and less withdrawn from, their wives. Secure wives also displayed more supportive and responsive behaviors.

Individual differences in adult attachment representations of parents are also related to unique patterns of secure base behavior in romantic relationships. Crowell et al. (2002), for example, coded videotaped observations of engaged couples during a problem task on scales conceptualized as the adult analogs to Ainsworth and colleagues' description of secure base use and secure base support in parent–child relationships (Ainsworth et al., 1978; Waters, Kondo-Ikemura, Posada, & Richters, 1991). Secure base use scores reflected the degree to which an individual clearly signaled his or her distress, maintained distress signals (if necessary), made direct bids for partner support, and was soothed by the partner's response (or by the self if the partner was unresponsive). Secure base support scores reflected the degree to which an individual expressed interest in the partner, recognized his or her distress, showed empathic understanding, and responded sensitively. As hypothesized, secure men and women scored higher in both secure base use and secure base support relative to their insecure counterparts. The same positive relation between secure base behavior and attachment security was also evident when the AAI coherence score was used instead of the secure versus insecure categories (Treboux, Crowell, & Waters, 2004).

Only one AAI study has examined how individuals who have different attachment representations of their parents respond to different forms of care. In a videotaped problem-solving discussion that investigated the degree to which instrumental and emotional forms of care provided by romantic partners calmed individuals who had different AAI classifications, secure individuals were rated as being more calmed when their partners gave them more emotional care, particularly when they were distressed. Conversely, dismissing individuals reacted more favorably to instrumental care from their partners, especially when they were distressed (Simpson, Winterheld, Rholes, & Oriña, 2007).

Other studies of adult attachment representations and behavior in romantic relationships have documented that secure individuals exhibit better functioning than insecure ones, though some studies have found gender differences. For example, Cohn, Silver, Cowan, Cowan, and Pearson (1992) examined young married couples who engaged in structured and unstructured interaction tasks with their preschool-age child. Secure men displayed more positive (i.e., pleasurable, warm, responsive, and interactive) and less negative (i.e., angry, displeasurable, disagreeing, and competitive) behavior than did insecure men. Women's behavior, however, did not differ as a function of their attachment representations. Gender differences explaining the connection between attachment security and the emotional tone of the marriage remained even when the AAI coherence score was used instead of the secure and insecure categories (Cowan, Cohn, Cowan, & Pearson, 1996). Paley, Cox, Burchinal, and Payne (1999), in contrast, found that preoccupied wives were less positive than secure wives, and dismissing wives displayed more withdrawal than did secure wives in a similar study. With respect to the provision of support, Simpson, Rholes, Oriña, and Grich (2002) also found that secure women gave more and better "contingent" support to their romantic partners, but only when their partners were distressed and requested help.

In sum, although occasional gender differences are found, individuals classified as secure on the AAI tend to display more constructive behaviors, whereas those classified as insecure (preoccupied or dismissing) exhibit more destructive behaviors in attachment-relevant situations. There is some evidence that this same pattern also holds in distressed marital couples (e.g., Babcock, Jacobson, Gottman, & Yerington, 2000; Wampler, Shi, Nelson, & Kimball, 2003). Viewed together, these findings suggest that insecure individuals may have a dual disadvantage when it comes to romantic relationship functioning. Not only do they carry "emotional baggage" from earlier attachment relationships, they also lack many of the skills necessary to offset or repair potentially detrimental interactions with their current attachment figures (Gottman, 1994).

DEVELOPMENTAL PERSPECTIVE ON ROMANTIC RELATIONSHIPS: THE CASE OF THE EXPERIENCE AND EXPRESSION OF EMOTIONS IN ROMANTIC RELATIONSHIPS

Until recently, relatively little was known about how the nature and quality of early attachment experiences, measured prospectively, systematically forecast romantic relationship functioning and outcomes in adulthood. In an attempt to fill that gap, we and our colleagues have conducted longitudinal analyses with measures collected from birth forward. The research addresses whether, how, and why relationship experiences with parents and peers earlier in life are linked to the experience and expression of emotions in adult romantic relationships. The hypotheses were grounded in the organizational–developmental perspective. Previous research has explored how early attachment experiences are associated with behavioral outcomes in preschool (Kochanska, Aksan, Knaack, & Rhines, 2004; Sroufe, 1983; Troy & Sroufe, 1987; Waters, Wippman, & Sroufe, 1979), middle childhood (Elicker, Englund, & Sroufe, 1992; Sroufe, Bennett, Englund, Urban, & Shulman, 1993), adolescence (Carlson et al., 2004; Sroufe et al., 1999), and early adult romantic relationships (Collins, Hennighausen, Schmit, & Sroufe, 1997; Collins & van Dulmen, 2006). However, no research had tested structural relations between the unique relational challenges of different developmental periods (e.g., early childhood, middle childhood, adolescence) and the subsequent experience and expression of emotion in adult romantic relationships. This study, therefore, provides an important test of the core hypothesis that experiences within close relationships across development systematically predict emotional functioning in adult romantic relationships.

A Longitudinal Study of Emotion in Relationships

To test whether infant attachment experiences initiate pathways of social functioning that are eventually tied to adult romantic relationship outcomes, Simpson, Collins, Tran, and Haydon (2007) focused on participants who had been studied continuously from infancy into their mid-20s as part of the Minnesota Study of Risk and Adaptation from Birth to Adulthood (Sroufe et al., 2005). Between the ages of 20 and 23, each target participant and his or her current romantic partner completed a battery of self-report relationship measures. Each couple was also videotaped while engaging in both conflict resolution and collaborative tasks.

The primary structural equation model tested was a double-mediation developmental model (see Simpson, Collins, et al., 2007). According to this model, the emotional qualities of romantic relationships in early adulthood should be predicted by a set of sequential links from attachment security status in infancy, to competent functioning in childhood peer groups, to the establishment of high quality friendships in adolescence. The relation between early attachment security and the emotional tenor of adult romantic relationships was predicted to be indirect, with middle-childhood peer and adolescent friendship variables functioning as mediators. Individuals classified as secure in infancy should be rated as more socially competent by their grade-school teachers. Middle-childhood social competence, in turn, should predict more strongly rated secure-base behavior in the context of a close adolescent friendship. Finally, friendship security during adolescence should predict a more favorable ratio of positive to negative emotions in adult romantic relationships.

The Sample and Early Developmental Measures

Our longitudinal study (Simpson, Collins, et al., 2007) examined a subset of the full sample, namely, study participants who took part in the romantic relationship assessments in early adulthood ($n = 78$). Target participants who had been involved in a romantic relationship for at least 4 months participated with their partners when targets were between the ages of 20 and 23. The mean age of participants was 21.60 years, and the mean length of their relationships was 25.06 months. All couples were heterosexual.

Target participants and their partners were first interviewed separately, after which they completed self-report measures that assessed the functioning and perceptions of their relationship. Each couple then discussed and tried to resolve a major point of disagreement or contention in their relationship, which was followed by a collaborative problem-solving task. All interactions were videotaped and then coded by trained observers on theoretically relevant constructs.

During earlier phases of the Minnesota Study of Risk and Adaptation from Birth to Adulthood, measures were collected at three critical stages of social development: (a) during early childhood (at 12 months); (b) during early elementary school (Grades 1–3); and (c) during adolescence (at age 16). Assessments were conducted at these periods of social development because each one is a unique stage at which new and different kinds of relationships are being formed and developed. The measurement approach we used is consistent with this conceptualization and with the principle of heterotypic continuity (Caspi & Roberts, 2001; Rutter & Sroufe, 2000), which posits that latent traits are manifested differently at different ages and stages of social development. Accordingly, measures of competence in relationships were selected to reflect the salient relationship issues that individuals face at each stage of development. The infancy measures obtained from target participants at 12 months assessed their attachment behaviors with their caregivers in the

Strange Situation procedure (Ainsworth et al., 1978). The middle-childhood measures at ages 6 to 8 assessed target participants' competence at engaging peers in social interactions and their attunement to interpersonal dynamics in organized peer groups in Grades 1 through 3. The adolescence measure at age 16 assessed the nature and quality of target participants' behaviors indicative of having a secure attachment representation of a close same-sex best friend (e.g., greater disclosure, more trust, greater authenticity). The early adulthood measures at ages 20 to 23 indexed the experience and expression of emotions evident in target participants' current romantic relationships. Even though target participants' behaviors, relationships, and relationship representations were assessed by different measures in different relationships at different points of social development, the meaning and function of those behaviors and representations should be consistent across time because they tap the general coherence of social competence within each developmental stage. The measures we collected at each developmental stage were as described in the following subsections.

Infant Attachment Security

The quality of parent–infant attachment relationships was assessed at 12 months in the Strange Situation procedure (Ainsworth et al., 1978). Raters classified each infant's attachment pattern as Secure, Avoidant, or Anxious/ Resistant. We used the conventional Secure versus Insecure scoring distinction, in which Avoidant and Anxious/Resistant classifications were collapsed into a single insecure group; 61% of target participants were classified as secure at 12 months, and 39% were classified as insecure.

Peer Competence

Peer competence was assessed in Grades 1, 2, and 3. Each target participant's classroom teacher was given a one-paragraph description of a hypothetical child who was well liked and respected by peers, had mutual friendships, demonstrated understanding of other children's perspectives and ideas, and constructively engaged peers in activities. Each teacher then rank-ordered all of the children in her classroom on the basis of how closely each student matched these criteria. Teachers did not know which child in their classroom was the target (study participant). Thus, peer competence scores reflected teachers' perceptions of each target participant's percentile rank in their classes during Grades 1, 2, and 3, divided by the total number of students in each class. Each target participant received a mean peer competence percentile ranking relative to his or her classmates averaged across the three grades.

Friendship Security

Each target participant's level of friendship security was evaluated by raters at age 16 from an hour-long audiotaped interview. This measure was developed from the premise that attachment security in later relationships should be facilitated by security in earlier relationships (Ainsworth, 1989; Bowlby, 1982; Thompson, 1999). Specifically, target participants were asked to describe their closest friendship, including whether and how they disclosed behaviors and feelings indicative of trust and authenticity to that person. Ratings assessed the degree to which each adolescent felt comfortable telling private details to the friend, how the friend responded to such disclosures, and the psychological closeness of the relationship. This scale, therefore, indexed the extent to which target participants felt that they could be themselves with their best friend, expected the friend to be available and supportive, and could mutually share positive and negative emotional and interpersonal experiences with him or her.

Contemporary Self-Report Measures

At ages 20 to 23, target participants and their current romantic partners both completed the following relationship-based measures.

Emotional Tone of the Relationship

The Emotional Tone Index (ETI; Berscheid, Snyder, & Omoto, 1989) is a self-report instrument that measures the extent to which individuals experience different emotions in their current relationship. The ETI assesses 12 positive emotions and 15 negative ones that vary in intensity from high (e.g., elated, angry) to low (e.g., content, disappointed). It has three subscales: (a) the extent to which individuals experience positive emotions (the sum of the 12 positive emotion items); (b) the extent to which they experience negative emotions (the sum of the 15 negative emotion items); and (c) the relative balance of positive versus negative emotions (i.e., the mean of the positive emotion index minus the mean of the negative emotion index). A modified version of the scale including 10 positive emotions and 14 negative emotions was used in the present study, and we focused primarily on the relative balance score.

Contemporary Relationship Observation Measures

Couples also completed a videotaped observational procedure in the lab that involved two interaction tasks: the Markman-Cox procedure (Cox, 1991) and the Ideal Couple Q-sort (Collins et al., 1999). The Markman-Cox procedure is designed to elicit conflict between relationship partners. In the first phase of the procedure, each partner identified and rated the most salient problems in the relationship. Each couple then chose the one problem that generated the most conflict. In the second phase, each couple discussed the problem and tried to reach a solution within 10 min.

After a 5-min cool-down period, each couple completed an Ideal Couple Q-sort, which is designed to elicit collaborative behaviors. Each couple was given 45 cards, each of which listed a potential quality of a hypothetical romantic couple (e.g., make sacrifices for each other, have the same interests). Each couple read each card aloud and decided which of three baskets it should be placed in: "Most like an ideal couple"; "Least like an ideal couple"; or "Middle/Unsure." Couples were told to base their decisions on their ideas of an "ideal couple" rather than on their own relationship.

Trained observers then rated each of the interactions on scales assessing the amount of Shared Positive Affect, Shared Negative Affect, Anger, Hostility, Conflict Resolution, Secure Base Behavior, and Overall Quality (see Roisman et al., 2001; Sroufe et al., 2005). Ratings were also made on three "balance scales" that indexed the extent to which the partners facilitated (a) acceptance of openness and vulnerability, (b) individual growth in the relationship, and (c) effective completion of the problem-solving task. All scales were coded at the dyadic level, meaning that each dyad received a score on each rated measure. The affect scales assessed the extent to which each couple engaged in reciprocal exchanges of positive affect, negative affect, anger, and hostility. Two composite relationship observation measures were calculated (see Roisman et al., 2001). The first measure, Romantic Relationship Process, was a composite (z-score) of Positive Affect, Secure Base, two of the Balance Scales, Conflict Resolution, and Overall Quality. The second measure, Romantic Relationship Negative Affect, was a composite of the Anger, Hostility, and Dyadic Negative Affect scales.

Primary Findings

We tested the hypothesized structural relations between the antecedent measures and the nature and quality of emotions experienced in adult romantic relationships in early adulthood (both self-reported and observer rated) using structural equation modeling. More specifically, we tested a structural model for each of the three dependent variables: (a) observer-rated adult romantic relationship process scores (from the videotaped discussions), (b) observer-rated negative affect scores (from the videotaped discussions), and (c) targets' self-reported emotion balance scores on the ETI. We also tested a model in which the three dependent variables were summed into a single composite dependent variable.

Our first model tested whether the link between infant attachment security and the adult romantic relationship process measure was mediated through

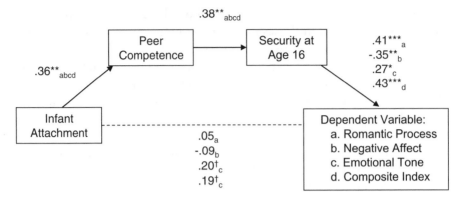

Figure 7.2. Double mediation model linking infant attachment security and early adulthood romantic relationship outcomes. Numbers represent standardized path coefficients. Four tests of the structural model were conducted, each with one of the four dependent variables: a—adult romantic relationship process, b—adult romantic negative affect, c—adult romantic emotional tone, and d—the composite score for dependent variables a, b, and c. $^{\dagger}p < .10$, $^{*}p < .05$, $^{**}p < .01$, $^{***}p < .001$. From "Attachment and the Experience and Expression of Emotions in Romantic Relationships: A Developmental Perspective," by J. A. Simpson, W. A. Collins, S. Tran, and K. C. Haydon, 2007, *Journal of Personality and Social Psychology, 92,* p. 362. Copyright 2007 by the American Psychological Association.

the middle-childhood peer competence composite and friendship security in adolescence. As shown in Figure 7.2 (see subscript a), this model provided a good fit. The second model tested whether the association between infant attachment security and the adult negative affect measure was mediated through peer competence and security at age 16 (Figure 7.2, subscript b). Once again, this model fit the data well. The third model tested whether the link between infant attachment security and ETI balance scores were mediated by middle-childhood peer competence and adolescent friendship security at age 16 (Figure 7.2, subscript c). Unlike the dyadic dependent variables in the first two models, the ETI balance scales were collected from both the target participant and his or her current romantic partner. If our basic hypothesis is correct, antecedent relationship experiences in an individual's life should predict the emotional tone (i.e., positive relative to negative emotions) of his or her current romantic relationship, even when reports of emotional tone provided by the partner are statistically controlled. To control for the partner's influence on each target participant's emotional tone scores, we created a residualized variable in which the ETI balance scores reported by each partner were partialed from each target participant's ETI balance scores. This residualized measure was then treated as the dependent measure in the third model. As expected, Model 3 also fit the data well.

If the hypothesized double-mediation model is robust, it should emerge when the three dependent measures are aggregated. Accordingly, Model 4 tested whether the association between infant attachment security and the composite measure of all three dependent variables—adult romantic relationship process, adult negative affect, and adult emotional tone—was mediated through peer competence and security at age 16 (Figure 7.2, subscript d). As expected, this model fit the data well.

From an organizational–developmental perspective, these findings reconfirm that adult relationship experiences are embedded in processes that begin with early caregiving, and that the qualities of early caregiving are then carried forward through important relationships across successive developmental periods (Collins & Sroufe, 1999; Sroufe, 1989). This carry-forward process is complex, involving the continuous interplay of internal working models and social relationships associated with different developmental periods between infancy and adolescence (see Carlson et al., 2004). The current findings suggest that this process continues into early adulthood and partially explains the pattern of emotions that people experience and express in their adult romantic relationships.

LOOKING AHEAD: DIFFERENTIAL PREDICTIONS BASED ON DEVELOPMENTAL HISTORY AND CURRENT FUNCTIONING

One of the advantages of the organizational–developmental perspective is its ability to make differential predictions about an individual's future functioning, given his or her current and past functioning with regard to developmental issues (e.g., the maintenance of a high-quality romantic relationship; Sroufe et al., 2005). Consistent with systems theory principles of equifinality and multifinality (von Bertalanffy, 1968), this perspective holds that individuals can arrive at the same outcome from different starting points. They can also arrive at different outcomes from the same starting point. In other words, individuals who have distinct developmental histories can show the same adaptation at one moment in time, but then exhibit different adaptations at later points of development (Sroufe, Egeland, & Kreutzer, 1990). These differences should be predictable if an individual's functioning reflects his or her cumulative developmental history, rather than being fully specified by either past or current life circumstances.

Consider, for example, two individuals who are involved in different romantic relationships. Each individual reports a low positive-to-negative emotion ratio in his or her current relationship, which videotaped observations of each couple corroborate. Despite their similarities on concurrent relationship measures, these two individuals may have arrived at this common outcome via different pathways. One individual could have a secure attachment history and a good network of close, caring friends from late childhood onward. This person has been with his or her current romantic partner for several years but was shattered by the recent discovery of infidelity by his or her partner. The couple decided to repair the relationship and is currently in therapy, but the emotional difficulties of the past few months are reflected in the couple's rather negative emotions and social interactions. In contrast, the other low-scoring individual could have an insecure attachment history and poor support networks from late childhood onward. No specific event precipitated the second individual's more negative relationship emotions and social interaction tendencies. Instead, these outcomes are driven primarily by emotional baggage from prior relationships.

When the emotional profiles of these two individuals are examined cross-sectionally, they appear almost identical to one another. Given this limited amount of information, one would expect each individual to have similar relationship trajectories and outcomes (in terms of satisfaction, conflict, stability, etc.) in the near future. However, differential predictions about future functioning emerge when current adaptation is considered in conjunction with each person's unique developmental history. For instance, assuming that the first couple's therapy is successful and lingering issues of trust are resolved, one might anticipate that the individual who has a secure attachment history will show a rebound in relationship functioning a year from now, given his or her working models and the couple's concerted efforts to repair the relationship. In contrast, the individual who has an insecure attachment history may not rebound nearly as well. An empirical test of these differential predictions would provide another key test of the hypothesis that romantic relationship outcomes are the product of both an individual's relationship history and his or her current relationship circumstances.

CONCLUSION

The organizational–developmental perspective highlights the coherence of behavior in salient relationships across time. The patterning of relationship-relevant thoughts, feelings, and actions is the common thread that connects early experiences with caregivers to later experiences with peers and eventually to romantic partners in adulthood. Although social competence is manifested differently at each relational stage, the underlying meaning of competent and incompetent behavior remains the same. As the findings of our research on the experience and expression of emotions in adult romantic relationships indicate, adult romantic outcomes are meaningfully related to relationship experiences encountered earlier in life. Indeed, in many relationships, the past may be an integral part of the present.

REFERENCES

Ainsworth, M. (1989). Attachments beyond infancy. *American Psychologist, 44,* 709–716. doi:10.1037/0003-066X.44.4.709

Ainsworth, M., Blehar, M., Waters, E., & Wall, S. (1978). *Patterns of attachment.* Hillsdale, NJ: Erlbaum.

Babcock, J. C., Jacobson, N. S., Gottman, J. M., & Yerington, T. P. (2000). Attachment, emotional regulation, and the function of marital violence: Differences between secure, preoccupied, and dismissing violent and nonviolent husbands. *Journal of Family Violence, 15,* 391–409. doi:10.1023/A:100 7558330501

Berscheid, E. (1983). Emotion. In H. H. Kelley, E. Berscheid, A. Christensen, J. H. Harvey, T. L. Huston, G. Levinger, . . . D. R. Peterson (Eds.), *Close relationships* (pp. 110–168). New York, NY: Freeman.

Berscheid, E., Snyder, M., & Omoto, A. M. (1989). The relationship closeness inventory: Assessing the closeness of interpersonal relationships. *Journal of Personality and Social Psychology, 57,* 792–807. doi:10.1037/0022-3514.57.5.792

Bouthillier, D., Julien, D., Dubé, M., Bélanger, I., & Hamelin, M. (2002). Predictive validity of adult attachment measures in relation to emotion regulation behaviors in marital interactions. *Journal of Adult Development, 9,* 291–305. doi:10.1023/A:1020291011587

Bowlby, J. (1973). *Attachment and loss: Vol. 2. Separation: Anxiety and anger.* New York, NY: Basic Books.

Bowlby, J. (1980). *Attachment and loss: Vol. 3. Loss: Sadness and depression.* New York, NY: Basic Books.

Bowlby, J. (1982). *Attachment and loss: Vol. 1. Attachment* (2nd ed.). New York, NY: Basic Books.

Bretherton, I., & Munholland, K. A. (1999). Internal working models in attachment relationships: A construct revisited. In J. Cassidy & P. R. Shaver (Eds.), *Handbook of attachment: Theory, research, and clinical applications* (pp. 89–111). New York, NY: Guilford Press.

Bretherton, I., & Munholland, K. A. (2008). Internal working models in attachment relationships: Elaborating a central construct in attachment theory. In J. Cassidy & P. R. Shaver (Eds.), *Handbook of attachment: Theory, research, and clinical applications* (2nd ed., pp. 102–127). New York, NY: Guilford Press.

Carlson, E. A., Sroufe, L. A., & Egeland, B. (2004). The construction of experience: A longitudinal study of representation and behavior. *Child Development, 75,* 66–83. doi:10.1111/j.1467-8624.2004.00654.x

Caspi, A., & Roberts, B. W. (2001). Personality development across the life course: The argument for change and continuity. *Psychological Inquiry, 12,* 49–66. doi:10.1207/S15327965PLI1202_01

Cohn, D. A., Silver, D. H., Cowan, C. P., Cowan, P. A., & Pearson, J. (1992). Working models of childhood attachment and couple relationships. *Journal of Family Issues, 13*, 432–449. doi:10.1177/019251392013004003

Collins, W. A., Aguilar, B., Hennighausen, K., Hyson, D., Jimerson, S., Levy, A., . . . Sesma, A. (1999). *Scales and coding manual for observed interactions in romantic relationships.* Unpublished manuscript, University of Minnesota, Minneapolis.

Collins, W. A., & Hartup, W. W. (in press). History of research in developmental psychology. In P. D. Zelazo (Ed.), *Oxford handbook of developmental psychology.* New York, NY: Oxford University Press.

Collins, W. A., Hennighausen, K. H., Schmit, D. T., & Sroufe, L. A. (1997). Developmental precursors of romantic relationships: A longitudinal analysis. In S. Shulman & W. A. Collins (Eds.), *Romantic relationships in adolescence: Developmental perspectives* (pp. 69–84). San Francisco, CA: Jossey-Bass.

Collins, W. A., & Sroufe, L. A. (1999). Capacity for intimate relationships: A developmental construction. In W. Furman, B. B. Brown, & C. Feiring (Eds.), *The development of romantic relationships in adolescence* (pp. 125–147). New York, NY: Cambridge University Press.

Collins, W. A., & van Dulmen, M. (2006). "The course of true love(s) . . . ": Origins and pathways in the development of romantic relationships. In A. Crouter & A. Booth (Eds.), *Romance and sex in adolescence and emerging adulthood: Risks and opportunities* (pp. 63–86). Mahwah, NJ: Erlbaum.

Cowan, P. A., Cohn, D. A., Cowan, C. P., & Pearson, J. L. (1996). Parents' attachment histories and children's externalizing and internalizing behaviors: Exploring family systems models of linkage. *Journal of Consulting and Clinical Psychology, 64*, 53–63. doi:10.1037/0022-006X.64.1.53

Cox, M. J. (1991). *Marital and parent-child relationships study.* Unpublished manuscript, University of North Carolina, Chapel Hill.

Creasey, G. (2002). Associations between working models of attachment and conflict management behavior in romantic couples. *Journal of Counseling Psychology, 49*, 365–375. doi:10.1037/0022-0167.49.3.365

Crowell, J. A., Treboux, D., Gao, Y., Fyffe, C., Pan, H., & Waters, E. (2002). Assessing secure base behavior in adulthood: Development of a measure, links to adult attachment representations, and relations to couples' communication and reports of relationships. *Developmental Psychology, 38*, 679–693. doi:10.1037/0012-1649.38.5.679

Elicker, J., Englund, M., & Sroufe, L. A. (1992). Predicting peer competence and peer relationships in childhood from early parent-child relationships. In R. Parke & G. Ladd (Eds.), *Family-peer relationships: Modes of linkage* (pp. 77–106). Hillsdale, NJ: Erlbaum.

Erikson, E. (1963). *Childhood and society.* New York, NY: Norton.

George, C., Kaplan, N., & Main, M. (1985). *The Adult Attachment Interview.* Unpublished manuscript, University of California, Berkeley.

Gottman, J. M. (1994). *What predicts divorce? The relationship between marital processes and marital outcomes.* Hillsdale, NJ: Erlbaum.

Holland, A. S., & Roisman, G. I. (2010). Adult attachment security and young adults' dating relationships over time: Self-reported, observational, and physiological evidence. *Developmental Psychology, 46,* 552–557. doi:10.1037/a0018542

Isabella, R. A., & Belsky, J. (1991). Interactional synchrony and the origins of infant-mother attachment: A replication study. *Child Development, 62,* 373–384. doi: 10.2307/1131010

Isabella, R. A., Belsky, J., & von Eye, A. (1989). Origins of infant-mother attachment: An examination of interactional synchrony during the infant's first year. *Developmental Psychology, 25,* 12–21. doi:10.1037/0012-1649.25.1.12

Kobak, R. R., & Sceery, A. (1988). Attachment in late adolescence: Working models, affect regulation, and representations of self and others. *Child Development, 59,* 135–146. doi:10.2307/1130395

Kochanska, G., Aksan, N., Knaack, A., & Rhines, H. M. (2004). Maternal parenting and children's conscience: Early security as a moderator. *Child Development, 75,* 1229–1242. doi:10.1111/j.1467-8624.2004.00735.x

Main, M., Kaplan, N., & Cassidy, J. (1985). Security in infancy, childhood, and adulthood: A move to the level of representation. *Monographs of the Society for Research in Child Development, 50*(1–2), 66–104. doi:10.2307/3333827

Masten, A. S., & Coatsworth, J. D. (1995). Competence, resilience, & psychopathology. In D. Cicchetti & D. Cohen (Eds.), *Developmental psychopathology: Vol 2. Risk, disorder, and adaptation* (pp. 715–752). New York, NY: Wiley.

Masters, J. C., & Wellman, H. (1974). The study of human infant attachment: A procedural critique. *Psychological Bulletin, 81,* 218–237. doi:10.1037/h0036184

Mischel, W. (1968). *Personality and assessment.* New York, NY: Wiley.

Mischel, W. (1973). Toward a cognitive social learning reconceptualization of personality. *Psychological Review, 80,* 252–283. doi:10.1037/h0035002

Paley, B., Cox, M. J., Burchinal, M. R., & Payne, C. C. (1999). Attachment and marital functioning: Comparison of spouses with continuous-secure, earned-secure, dismissing, and preoccupied attachment stances. *Journal of Family Psychology, 13,* 580–597. doi:10.1037/0893-3200.13.4.580

Piaget, J. (1952). *The origins of intelligence in children.* New York, NY: Norton. doi:10.1037/11494-000

Roisman, G. I., Madsen, S. D., Hennighausen, K. H., Sroufe, L. A., & Collins, W. A. (2001). The coherence of dyadic behavior across parent-child and romantic relationships as mediated by the internalized representation of experience. *Attachment & Human Development, 3,* 156–172. doi:10.1080/14616730126483

Rutter, M., & Sroufe, L. A. (2000). Developmental psychopathology: Concepts and challenges. *Development and Psychopathology, 12,* 265–296. doi:10.1017/S0954579400003023

Sameroff, A. J., & Emde, R. (1989). *Relationship disturbances in early childhood.* New York, NY: Basic Books.

Sander, L. (1962). Issues in early mother-child interaction. *Journal of the American Academy of Child Psychiatry, 1,* 141–166. doi:10.1016/S0002-7138(09)60013-3

Sander, L. (1975). Infant and caretaking environment. In E. J. Anthony (Ed.), *Explorations in child psychiatry* (pp. 129–165). New York, NY: Plenum Press.

Simpson, J. A., Collins, W. A., Tran, S., & Haydon, K. C. (2007). Attachment and the experience and expression of emotions in romantic relationships: A developmental perspective. *Journal of Personality and Social Psychology, 92,* 355–367. doi:10.1037/0022-3514.92.2.355

Simpson, J. A., & Rholes, W. S. (2004). Stress and secure base relationships in adulthood. In K. Bartholomew & D. Perlman (Eds.), *Advances in personal relationships: Vol. 5. Attachment processes in adulthood* (pp. 181–204). London, England: Kingsley.

Simpson, J. A., Rholes, W. S., & Nelligan, J. S. (1992). Support-seeking and support-giving within couples in an anxiety-provoking situation: The role of attachment styles. *Journal of Personality and Social Psychology, 62,* 434–446. doi:10.1037/0022-3514.62.3.434

Simpson, J. A., Rholes, W. S., Oriña, M. M., & Grich, J. (2002). Working models of attachment, support giving, and support seeking in a stressful situation. *Personality and Social Psychology Bulletin, 28,* 598–608. doi:10.1177/0146167202288004

Simpson, J. A., Winterheld, H. A., Rholes, W. S., & Oriña, M. M. (2007). Working models of attachment and reactions to different forms of caregiving from romantic partners. *Journal of Personality and Social Psychology, 93,* 466–477. doi:10.1037/0022-3514.93.3.466

Spitz, R. A., Emde, R., & Metcalf, D. (1970). Further prototypes of ego formation. *The Psychoanalytic Study of the Child, 25,* 417–441.

Sroufe, L. A. (1983). Infant-caregiver attachment and patterns of adaptation in preschool: The roots of maladaptation and competence. In M. Perlmutter (Ed.), *The Minnesota Symposia on Child Psychology: Vol. 16. Development and policy concerning children with special needs* (pp. 41–83). Hillsdale, NJ: Erlbaum.

Sroufe, L. A. (1989). Relationships, self, and individual adaptation. In A. J. Sameroff & R. N. Emde (Eds.), *Relationship disturbances in early childhood: A developmental approach* (pp. 70–94). New York, NY: Basic Books.

Sroufe, L. A., Bennett, C., Englund, M., Urban, J., & Shulman, S. (1993). The significance of gender boundaries in preadolescence: Contemporary correlates and antecedents of boundary violation and maintenance. *Child Development, 64,* 455–466. doi:10.2307/1131262

Sroufe, L. A., Egeland, B., & Carlson, E. A. (1999). One social world: The integrated development of parent-child and peer relationships. In W. A. Collins, B. P. Laursen, & W. W. Hartup (Eds.), *The 30th Minnesota Symposium on Child Psychology: Relationships as developmental contexts* (pp. 241–261). Mahwah, NJ: Erlbaum.

Sroufe, L. A., Egeland, B., Carlson, E. A., & Collins, W. A. (2005). *The development of the person: The Minnesota Study of Risk and Adaptation from Birth to Adulthood.* New York, NY: Guilford Press.

Sroufe, L. A., Egeland, B., & Kreutzer, T. (1990). The fate of early experience following developmental change: Longitudinal approaches to individual adaptation in childhood. *Child Development, 61,* 1363–1373. doi:10.2307/1130748

Thompson, R. A. (1999). Early attachment and later development. In J. Cassidy & P. R. Shaver (Eds.), *Handbook of attachment: Theory, research, and clinical applications* (pp. 265–286). New York, NY: Guilford Press.

Treboux, D., Crowell, J. A., & Waters, E. (2004). When "new" meets "old": Configurations of adult attachment representations and their implications for marital functioning. *Developmental Psychology, 40,* 295–314. doi:10.1037/0012-1649.40.2.295

Troy, M., & Sroufe, L. A. (1987). Victimization among preschoolers: The role of attachment relationship history. *Journal of the American Academy of Child and Adolescent Psychiatry, 26,* 166–172. doi:10.1097/00004583-198703000-00007

Vaughn, B., Egeland, B., Sroufe, L. A., & Waters, E. (1979). Individual differences infant-mother attachment at twelve and eighteen months: Stability and change in families under stress. *Child Development, 50,* 971–975. doi:10.2307/1129321

von Bertalanffy, L. (1968). *General systems theory: Foundations, development, applications.* New York, NY: George Braziller.

Vygotsky, L. (1962). *Thought and language.* Cambridge, MA: MIT Press. doi:10.1037/11193-000

Vygotsky, L. (1978). *Mind and society.* Cambridge, MA: Harvard University Press.

Waddington, C. (1957). *The strategy of the genes.* London, England: Allen & Unwin.

Wampler, K. S., Shi, L., Nelson, B. S., & Kimball, T. G. (2003). The Adult Attachment Interview and observed couple interaction: Implications for an intergenerational perspective on couple therapy. *Family Process, 42,* 497–515. doi:10.1111/j.1545-5300.2003.00497.x

Waters, E., Kondo-Ikemura, K., Posada, G., & Richters, J. (1991). Learning to love: Mechanisms and milestones. In M. R. Gunnar & L. A. Sroufe (Eds.), *The 23rd Minnesota Symposium on Child Psychology: Self processes and development* (pp. 217–255). Hillsdale, NJ: Erlbaum.

Waters, E., Wippman, J., & Sroufe, L. A. (1979). Attachment, positive affect, and competence in the peer group: Two studies in construct validation. *Child Development, 50,* 821–829. doi:10.2307/1128949

Werner, H. (1948). *The comparitive psychology of mental development.* New York, NY: International Universities Press.

Zimmermann, P., Maier, M. A., Winter, M., & Grossmann, K. E. (2001). Attachment and adolescents' emotion regulation during a joint problem-solving task with a friend. *International Journal of Behavioral Development, 25,* 331–343. doi:10.1080/01650250143000157

8

PUTTING MARRIAGE IN ITS CONTEXT: THE INFLUENCE OF EXTERNAL STRESS ON EARLY MARITAL DEVELOPMENT

LISA A. NEFF

On entering marriage, newlywed spouses profess a deep love for their partner, as well as an unwavering commitment to preserving the marriage over time (Neff & Karney, 2002, 2005b). In fact, most people agree that maintaining a satisfying marriage is one of the most important things in life (Conger & Conger, 2002; Karney & Bradbury, 2005). Unfortunately, an ironic and poignant fact is that this seemingly ubiquitous desire for marital happiness often fails to translate into relationship success, as divorce rates more than doubled over the last half of the 20th century (Singh, Matthews, Clarke, Yannicos, & Smith, 1995; see also Chapter 10, this volume). Recent estimates have suggested that between 40% and 50% of first marriages end in divorce or permanent separation, with the rate of dissolution being even higher in remarriages (Cherlin, 2005, 2010). Thus, although marriages begin optimistically, it has become normative for initially satisfying marriages to deteriorate and dissolve. A key question, then, is why people have so much difficulty sustaining their initial feelings of happiness and love. In other words, how can we account for the frequency of this drastic and unwanted transformation within the marriage?

To answer this question, many theories of intimate relationships have argued that the experience of change or stability in marital satisfaction is, at its heart, the result of the interpersonal transactions taking place within the marriage. Namely, maintaining those initially positive marital feelings requires that spouses successfully cope with the inevitable ups and downs of their daily experiences with their partners (see Chapter 4). On many days, partners may experience primarily positive, supportive interactions with each other, but on other days their interactions may be characterized by conflict and negativity. Recognizing this, several theoretical perspectives agree that relationship success hinges on intimates' adaptive relationship processes, or the manner in which intimates process, interpret, and respond to varying relationship experiences (e.g., Karney & Bradbury, 1995; Kelley & Thibaut, 1978; Murray, Holmes, & Collins, 2006). In other words, preserving satisfying relationships requires that spouses invest energy into minimizing negative relationship events by thinking and behaving in relationship-promoting ways (Rusbult, Verette, Whitney, Slovik, & Lipkus, 1991).

Accordingly, much research has taken a microanalytic approach to understanding marital well-being, demonstrating reliable links between particular relationship processes and future marital outcomes. For instance, partners who exchange positive behaviors during their interactions with each other tend to maintain their initial satisfaction more effectively than do partners who are prone to exchanging punishing behaviors (Gottman, Coan, Carrere, & Swanson, 1998). These effects are especially clear when researchers have observed the way couples engage in problem-solving and conflict interactions (Weiss & Heyman, 1990). Other work has pointed to the importance of relying on temporary, situational attributions to describe a partner's transgressions (Holtzworth-Munroe & Jacobson, 1985), as spouses who rely on nonblaming attributions report greater and more stable levels of marital satisfaction over time (Bradbury & Fincham, 1990; Karney & Bradbury, 2000). In sum, although the particular adaptive process being studied has varied, a notable bulk of the literature converges on the message that marital well-being is a consequence of factors situated squarely within the dyad.

The limitation of this microanalytic approach, however, is that these internal relationship processes often are studied without regard to the context in which they are occurring. Marriages are embedded within broader environmental contexts that may play important roles in accounting for relationship development (Bronfenbrenner, 1989). Thus, other perspectives on marital outcomes have taken a macroanalytic approach, arguing that change in marital quality may not be fully understood without examining variables external to partners and their interactions. For instance, surveys examining divorce rates in the United States have revealed that although marital disruption touches all segments of society, its effects are disproportionately experienced by the economically disadvantaged (see Chapter 1). Whereas divorce is declining among middle-class, better-educated individuals, divorce is on the rise among lower income, less-educated individuals (Cherlin, 2005). Even among marriages that remain intact, low-income spouses report significantly higher levels of marital distress than middle- or high-income spouses (Amato, Johnson, Booth, & Rogers, 2003; Karney, Garvan, & Thomas, 2003). Understanding this disparity in rates of marital distress and disruption across levels of income draws attention to the unique factors that shape and constrain the development of low-income marriages compared with more affluent marriages. The most notable differences lie in the context within which couples form and maintain their marriages: Low-income marriages take place in an environment characterized by a host of negative stressors, such as unemployment, accumulating debts, inadequate child care, health problems, poor housing, lack of transportation, etc., all of which may place an enormous strain on couples (Ooms & Wilson, 2004). In other words, some contexts may render it more difficult for spouses to maintain a marriage than others.

Indeed, growing evidence confirms that when the marital context contains numerous stressful life events, such as work stress, financial strain, or illness, marriages tend to suffer (Bodenmann, 1997; Conger, Rueter, & Elder, 1999; Lavee, McCubbin, & Olson, 1987). Yet, research in this area, although showing important links between stress and marital outcomes, generally has failed to clarify the potential mechanisms through which stress may influence relationship development. In other words, how do stressors originating in domains external to the relationship destabilize marriages over time? A premise of the current chapter is that developing a complete model of marital change and stability requires bridging the gap between theories of internal relationship processes and research on the marital context (see Chapter 2). To this end, the chapter presents a model highlighting how spouses' varying stressful life circumstances may interfere with their capacity to effectively engage in relationship-promoting behaviors and thereby contribute to marital declines over time.

INTEGRATING LEVELS OF ANALYSIS: THE TWO-ROUTE MODEL OF STRESS EFFECTS ON MARRIAGE

Stressors originating in domains external to the marriage consistently have been associated, both cross-sectionally and longitudinally, with lowered marital quality and greater marital instability, a phenomenon referred to as *stress spillover* (for reviews, see Randall & Bodenmann, 2009; Story & Bradbury, 2004). For example, between-subjects comparisons of couples experiencing high versus low levels of external stress have indicated that it is harder for even initially satisfied spouses to maintain their relationships when facing important stressors (Bodenmann, 1997; Karney, Story, & Bradbury, 2005; Tesser & Beach, 1998). In one study, couples who were in the first 6 months of their marriage were asked to report on the chronic stressors they were currently facing (e.g., ongoing health problems, lack of financial security, job instability), as well as their marital satisfaction (Karney et al., 2005). These couples were then followed over 4 years to assess their marital outcomes. In general, couples facing higher levels of chronic stress reported lower levels of marital satisfaction, even as newlyweds. Moreover, when controlling for differences in their general levels of satisfaction, couples facing more severe chronic stress as newlyweds also experienced greater declines in their marital satisfaction over the early years of marriage (Karney et al., 2005).

Further work has provided a more refined analysis of the within-subject changes in spouses' stress and their appraisals of their partners and the marriages over time. Such within-subject analyses allows researchers to partial out spouses' stable tendencies to view their stress and their relationships in a particular manner, thereby limiting the possibility that third variables may be influencing the results. For instance, daily diary studies have shown that increases in individuals' daily work stress are linked to less accepting views of family members (Crouter & Bumpus, 2001). Similarly, longitudinal research examining changes in acute stress (e.g., increase in workload, temporary injury) and changes in marital satisfaction at multiple time points over the early years of marriage has revealed that spouses' marital satisfaction tends to be lower after periods during which they faced many acute stressors and higher after periods that were relatively low in acute stressors (Karney et al., 2005; Neff & Karney, 2004, 2007). Moreover, spouses whose marital evaluations are most vulnerable to fluctuations in their acute stress tend to experience the greatest declines in marital satisfaction during the early years of marriage (Neff & Karney, 2004).

Though the propensity for marital satisfaction to deteriorate after couples are exposed to external stressors has long been established, only recently has research elaborated on the precise mechanisms underlying these stress spillover effects. In particular, my colleagues and I have proposed a model highlighting how intrapersonal and dyadic relationship processes may mediate the effects of stress on marital quality (Neff & Karney, 2004, 2009). Namely, stress may influence marital quality through two independent routes (see Figure 8.1): Stressors external to the marriage may increase the frequency of negative events experienced within the marriage while simultaneously hindering spouses' capacity to respond to negative relationship events in a constructive and adaptive manner.

Route 1: Stress Gives Rise to Relationship Problems

The first and most direct route through which external stress may affect marital well-being involves the content of the relationship. Stressors external to a marriage tend to alter family dynamics by diverting time and atten-

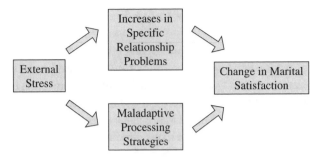

Figure 8.1. Two-route model of stress effects on marriage.

tion away from activities that serve to promote the relationship. For instance, spouses facing increased demands at work often modify their behavior at home by reducing their social interactions and expressions of emotion with their partners (Repetti, Wang, & Saxbe, 2009). A study of male air traffic controllers' daily work stress revealed that both the air traffic controllers and their wives described husbands' behavior as more withdrawn after work shifts that were busier and more difficult (i.e., were characterized by higher air traffic volume) than after work shifts that were relatively stress free (Repetti, 1989). Daily diary studies of dual-earner couples have found that after more stressful days at work, both husbands and wives report being more distracted and less responsive toward their partner (Story & Repetti, 2006) and generally less involved in the daily activities of home life, as they tend to engage in fewer household tasks and fewer family leisure events (Bolger, DeLongis, Kessler, & Wethington, 1989; Crouter, Perry-Jenkins, Huston, & Crawford, 1989). Furthermore, higher levels of daily stress tend to predict less engagement in sexual activity with the partner for women (Bodenmann, Ledermann, & Bradbury, 2007).

Given that spouses appear to disengage from marital interactions under stressful conditions, it is perhaps not surprising that couples report experiencing more severe relationship problems during periods of relatively high stress than they do during periods of low stress (Neff & Karney, 2004). Couples facing serious stressors report having less time to interact with each other, and therefore they experience fewer opportunities for expressing affection. When spouses do have opportunities to interact, external stressors often require active coping efforts on the part of the couple (Randall & Bodenmann, 2009), again displacing activities that foster intimacy and closeness within the relationship. In this way, stress outside of the marital relationship shapes and constrains spouses' experiences within the relationship, resulting in lowered overall relationship satisfaction.

Route 2: Stress Hinders Adaptive Responding to Relationship Problems

The second route through which stress may affect marital well-being is more indirect. In addition to affecting the nature of spouses' experiences within the marriage, stress also may render spouses less likely to interpret and respond to any negative events that do arise in an adaptive, relationship-enhancing manner. When navigating the ups and downs of a relationship, spouses are presumed to have some flexibility in how they choose to adapt and respond to each other. For instance, when faced with potentially discordant relationship experiences, spouses can decide to retaliate by engaging in destructive acts, such as blaming the partner for negative relationship events or exacerbating conflict discussions by reciprocating a partner's negative comments with further negativity. Alternatively, spouses can diffuse any negativity by choosing to respond in more constructive, relationship-promoting behaviors, such as making situational, rather than dispositional, attributions for a partner's negative behaviors. It is important that a sizable literature has argued that although engaging in constructive behaviors may be beneficial for relationship well-being, these behaviors are not automatic in nature and require greater cognitive resources to enact compared with destructive behaviors (Rusbult, Yovetich, & Verette, 1996; Yovetich & Rusbult, 1994). For this reason, the expression of prorelationship behaviors is often described as a two-step process in which spouses must first inhibit any self-centered, immediate impulses to respond destructively and then choose to engage in more positive, relationship-focused behaviors (Rusbult et al., 1996).

If resisting the impulse to enact retaliatory behaviors is an effortful process, it stands to reason that spouses may find it more difficult to engage in prorelationship behaviors at times when their resources and energy are divided among multiple tasks. Theories of self-regulation argue that self-control is a limited resource that can become depleted through use, making further acts of self-control more difficult (Baumeister, 2002). Thus, to the extent that coping with stressful events outside the marriage taxes spouses' self-regulatory resources, this coping should leave spouses with less energy to manage relationship issues, thereby reducing their capacity to respond to those issues effectively (McCubbin & Patterson, 1983). Moreover, the detrimental effects of stress on relationship behaviors may occur regardless of spouses' motivation to maintain the relationship, as level of self-control has been shown to predict the performance of prorelationship behaviors independent of commitment level (Finkel & Campbell, 2001). Put another way, even the most motivated spouses may find it difficult to engage in prorelationship behaviors if they do not also possess the resources necessary for enacting those behaviors.

Several recent findings are consistent with this idea. For instance, increases in stress seem to impede effective communication between spouses.

Husbands in blue-collar occupations display more negative affect in their marital interactions than do husbands in white-collar occupations (Krokoff, Gottman, & Roy, 1988). This association was nonsignificant when controlling for job distress, suggesting that stressful working conditions rather than status influenced these behaviors. Similarly, a study of African American couples revealed that couples residing in neighborhoods characterized by greater economic disadvantage exhibited lower levels of warmth during observed marital interactions than did couples from higher income neighborhoods (Cutrona et al., 2003). Daily diary studies have indicated that on days when spouses report experiencing more stress at work, their partners describe them as more irritable and angry (Schulz, Cowan, Cowan, & Brennan, 2004; Story & Repetti, 2006). In fact, arguments in the home are more likely to be reported on days in which individuals report more distressing encounters with coworkers and supervisors at work (Bolger, DeLongis, Kessler, & Wethington 1989; Repetti & Wood, 1997). Perhaps the strongest evidence, however, comes from an experimental study in which couples' interactions were observed before and after couples engaged in a stress-induction task. Following the stressor, the quality of couples' marital communication decreased by 40% (Bodenmann & Shantinath, 2004).

Spouses' capacity to engage in more forgiving responses to a partner's transgressions also appears diminished under conditions of stress. One longitudinal study of newlywed couples examined the within-person association between spouses' stress and their attributions for their partner's negative behaviors over eight assessments during a 4-year period (Neff & Karney, 2004). At times when spouses were experiencing higher levels of stress than normal, they were more likely to rely on a maladaptive attributional style, viewing the partner as blameworthy for negative marital events. In contrast, during times of low stress, these same spouses tended to excuse any transgressions and give the partner the benefit of the doubt. It is important that these findings held when controlling for any increases in the number of negative relationship events experienced during stressful periods.

Finally, a series of studies by Neff and Karney (2009) revealed links between spouses' external stress and their general reactivity to daily relationship events. Prior daily diary studies have shown that some spouses are highly reactive to daily relationship events, such that on days when daily events are positive, they report high levels of marital satisfaction, whereas on days when daily events are negative, they report decreased satisfaction. Other spouses seem to maintain a separation between their overall marital evaluations and their specific relationship experiences such that their daily global satisfaction remains high and stable regardless of their fluctuating specific experiences (Jacobson, Follette, & McDonald, 1982; McNulty & Karney, 2001). Controlling for differences in the frequency of positive and negative daily events, spouses who are more reactive to those events (i.e., exhibit a stronger covariance between daily events and daily global satisfaction) are more likely to experience marital distress (Jacobson et al., 1982). Thus, maintaining a low reactivity to daily events seems to represent a more adaptive relationship behavior.

Traditionally, research aimed at identifying sources of reactivity in relationships has focused on the idea that certain individuals are predisposed, on the basis of their personality and background, to exhibit maladaptive response patterns in their relationships. For example, individuals with low self-esteem and anxious attachment styles seem to magnify the importance of daily experiences by exhibiting strong links between these specific experiences and global relationship judgments (Campbell, Simpson, Boldry, & Kashy, 2005; Murray, Rose, Bellavia, Holmes, & Kusche, 2002; see also Chapter 7, this volume). However, drawing from the two-route model described here, we demonstrated the power of external stress to constrain spouses' responses to daily relationship experiences, above and beyond the influence of various personality factors (Neff & Karney, 2009). Study 1 examined whether spouses experiencing greater stress in nonrelationship domains, as assessed in a face-to-face interview, were more reactive to specific relationship experiences, as assessed through a 7-day daily diary, controlling for spouses' level of self-esteem and attachment style. Partially replicating prior work, results revealed that wives, but not husbands, who were lower in self-esteem, higher in anxious attachment, and lower in their comfort with dependence in relationships were more reactive to specific relationship events. Turning to the associations between observed stress and spouses' reactivity, results first revealed that spouses under greater stress reported experiencing more negative daily relationship experiences, supporting the notion that stress may give rise to additional problems within the marriage. Controlling for the nature of their daily experiences, however, husbands and wives coping with higher levels of external stress also were more reactive to those daily relationship experiences. In other words, spouses facing greater stress were prone to experiencing more negative relationship events and independently were less likely to process those events in an adaptive, less reactive manner. Furthermore, stress remained a significant predictor of reactivity when controlling for self-esteem and attachment style.

Study 2 examined whether changes in spouses' stress were associated with corresponding changes in their reactivity to daily events over a 4-year period. Newlywed couples completed a 7-day daily diary assessing their daily global satisfaction and their daily specific relationship experiences at three different time points during the first 4 years of marriage. Thus, three repeated measures of reactivity could be derived for each spouse. At each of these three assessments, spouses also reported on the level of external stress they were currently experiencing. Consistent with the idea that coping with greater levels of external stress may deplete spouses of the resources necessary for positive relationship functioning, at times when spouses were experiencing higher levels of stress than normal, they also were more reactive than usual to daily relationship events. Conversely, at times when stress was lower, these same individuals seemingly found it easier to dismiss the importance of these daily events, as they maintained a greater separation between their global satisfaction and specific experiences. Again, this association held when controlling for self-esteem and attachment style (Neff & Karney, 2009).

Contrasting the Two-Route Model to Traditional Stress Buffering Models

Overall, a growing number of studies have indicated that stress appears to act as a double-edged sword: Under stress, spouses not only are more likely to experience negative relationship events but also are less likely to interpret and respond to marital events in an adaptive manner (see Chapter 4). These findings are particularly intriguing as they challenge prior research suggesting that possessing good relationship skills should protect marital satisfaction from the detrimental effects of stress. Most research examining links between stress and relationship quality has argued for a stress-buffering model of prorelationship behaviors, such that spouses with better adaptive processes should be less prone to experiencing stress spillover effects (Gottman, 1994; Showers, & Kling, 1996). However, support for the stress-buffering approach has been based on studies examining whether a single, between-subjects assessment of spouses' relationship behaviors may moderate the link between stress and relationship outcomes. This reliance on a single measurement seemingly assumes that the relationship processes being assessed represent a chronic ability and thus will remain stable throughout the relationship, regardless of the stress spouses are facing.

Research considering changes in spouses' adaptive processes over time offers new perspective by suggesting that positive relationship behaviors may deteriorate in a stressful context (Neff & Karney, 2004, 2009). Rather than acting as a protective buffer, adaptive processes may actually represent the mechanism through which stress impacts marital quality. Ironically, the very times when spouses need their relationship skills the most may be precisely the times when it is most difficult to draw on those skills. Thus, simply having the proper skill set in one's "relationship toolbox" does not ensure that spouses will have the capacity to use those skills at any given moment. Instead, spouses' tendency to engage in adaptive relationship behaviors should also depend on the broader context in which those behaviors are occurring; that is, having a supportive environment within which to exercise one's skills. In this way, even spouses who generally exhibit positive behaviors within the marriage may find themselves unable to engage in adaptive relationship functioning under conditions of stress, resulting in satisfaction declines among initially happy and healthy couples.

STRESS CROSSOVER EFFECTS: HOW DOES STRESS AFFECT EACH PARTNER IN THE MARRIAGE?

Thus far, the research reviewed has examined stress as an intraindividual phenomenon, addressing how spouses' external stress may influence their own relationship behaviors. Yet, the consequences of spouses' stressors likely extend beyond their own relationship happiness, as the stressful life events of one individual can lead to changes in the emotions and behaviors of significant others as well, a phenomenon referred to as *stress crossover* (Larson & Almeida, 1999; Westman, 2001). For instance, research on emotional transmission between family members has indicated that what happens to one family member outside the home often affects other family members' health and well-being. Mothers' daily anxiety has been shown to predict the subsequent anxiety of their adolescent children even when controlling for adolescents' initial levels of anxiety (see Chapters 5 and 6). This transmission of anxiety from mother to child was particularly likely at times when mothers were under higher levels of stress (Larson & Gillman, 1999). Similarly, independent observers have rated children's affect as increasingly dysphoric on days in which their mothers reported higher levels of work stress (Repetti & Wood, 1997).

Within the marital literature, cross-sectional studies have revealed that husbands' job stress is associated with elevated levels of psychological distress (Rook, Dooley, & Catalano, 1991) and depression (Katz, Monnier, Libet, Shaw, & Beach, 2000), as well as increased psychosomatic symptoms (see Westman, 2001, for a review) in wives. Interestingly, these crossover effects are often stronger among happy couples than among distressed couples (Rook et al., 1991), suggesting that a healthy marriage ironically may act as a conduit for the transmission of stress across partners. More direct evidence that spouses' stress contributes to partners' relationship satisfaction was found in a daily diary study of couples in which one partner was preparing for the bar exam. Thompson and Bolger (1999) measured the examinees' mood as well as their partners' relationship feelings each day for the 35 days preceding the exam. Results indicated that if the examinee reported an increase in depression on a given day, the partner reported less positive feelings about the relationship on the following day.

Unfortunately, most studies taking a dyadic perspective on stress have been limited in two very important ways. First, though husbands' and wives' experiences of stress are often highly correlated, prior research generally has failed to control for partner's own levels of stress when examining crossover effects (see Westman, 2001, for a review). In other words, the assessment of stress crossover is complicated by the fact that the stressors found in a marital context can be divided into three subsets: stressors originating in the context of Partner A but not Partner B (e.g., Partner A's heavy workload); stressors originating in the context of Partner B but not Partner A (e.g., Partner B's argument with a sibling); and stressors shared by both members of the couple (e.g., financial strains). Ignoring Partner B's own stress level when examining crossover effects leaves open the question of whether Partner A's stress has a unique influence on Partner B's marital satisfaction, independent of the influence of Partner B's stress. If spouses share many of the same stressors, then what appears to be a crossover effect from Partner A's stress to Partner B's satisfaction may actually be the spurious result of those common stressors, producing a spillover effect for Partner B (see Chapter 2).

Second, most research on crossover effects has focused narrowly on how one spouse's work stress may affect the other partner's general well-being. Thus, few studies have used partner's marital happiness as an outcome. Even more problematic, many of these studies either have examined specifically how husbands' stress affects wives' well-being or have examined job stress in careers that tend to be predominately held by men. Consequently, less is known about the links between wives' stress and husbands' well-being.

To tease apart the unique influences of each spouse's stress on marital well-being and provide a more stringent examination of stress crossover processes, Neff and Karney (2007) asked newlywed couples to report on their general external stress (e.g., stress with work, friends, health) and their marital satisfaction at seven assessments over the first 3.5 years of marriage. Replicating prior spillover effects, at times when spouses were experiencing higher levels of stress than usual, they reported declines in their own marital satisfaction. It was then examined whether, at the within-couple level, increases in spouses' stress were associated with decreases in their partners' marital satisfaction, controlling for changes in partners' own stress (e.g., partners' spillover effects). Controlling for partners' spillover effects served to control not only for partners' unique stressors but also for those stressors shared by both members of the couple when examining crossover effects. Thus, this analysis isolated the association between spouses' unique stress and partners' satisfaction. Results revealed a crossover effect for husbands but not for wives. Namely, at times when wives were experiencing increases in external stress, their husbands reported being less satisfied in the marriage. Changes in husbands' stress, however, did not predict corresponding fluctuations in their wives' marital happiness.

In addition to isolating pure crossover effects, this study further examined whether partners' own stress may moderate their vulnerability to stress crossover experiences (see Figure 8.2). As previously reviewed, spouses under higher levels of stress exhibit more negative behaviors in the relationship. Whether this increased negativity from the spouse results in lowered marital happiness in the partner should depend on the partner's response to that negativity. In general, positive responses (e.g., providing support, attributing a spouse's negative behavior to the stressor) should help contain the negative influence of stress on a marriage, whereas negative responses (e.g., engaging in negative reciprocity) are likely to exacerbate the transmission of stress between partners. As indicated by the two-route model of stress effects on marriage, if partners have little stress of their own to manage, they may be more likely to engage in supportive and forgiving responses, thereby limiting crossover effects. Alternatively, if partners are distracted by their own stressful life circumstances, their coping resources will be depleted, rendering them less able to respond to their spouses' stress in an adaptive manner. As a result, stress crossover should be especially high at times when partners are experiencing greater levels of their own stress.

To address this possibility, the interactive effects of each spouse's stress on marital satisfaction were examined at the within-couple level. Results revealed that husbands' susceptibility to stress crossover was not moderated by their current stress levels. However, a moderating effect was found for wives, such that increases in husbands' stress were more strongly associated with decreases in wives' satisfaction at those times when wives also reported higher levels of their own stress. Together, the findings from this study suggest that when wives were faced with greater external stress, both husbands and wives were less happy in the marriage. When husbands were experiencing greater external stress, husbands were less happy, but

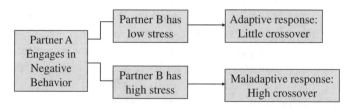

Figure 8.2. Partner's own stress as a moderator of stress crossover processes within couples.

their wives were only less happy if they too were under greater stress (Neff & Karney, 2007).

One possible explanation for this gender difference may involve the level of support spouses receive from their partners during times of stress. Wives often are more likely to support their husbands during stressful periods than vice versa (Bolger, DeLongis, Kessler, & Wethington, 1989; Neff & Karney, 2005a). If wives tend to provide support for their husbands' stressors, this positive coping response should help suppress crossover effects. Likewise, if husbands are not providing support to their wives, wives' stress may be more likely to infiltrate the marriage and affect both members of the dyad. Though further work is needed in this area, results such as these point to the importance of assessing the stressors and coping resources found in the context of both marital partners when addressing the role of stress in marriage.

THE NEXT STEP: IS STRESS ALWAYS DETRIMENTAL?

Generally, theories incorporating external stress as a prominent factor influencing marital development have focused on the detrimental impact of stress on relationship quality. As the previous review indicates, a key idea emerging from this literature is that stress seems to adversely affect the relationship functioning of both partners in the marriage. Yet, this perspective fails to account for accumulating evidence indicating that although many relationships do crumble in the face of hardships, others may emerge from stressful experiences relatively unscathed. Negative life events such as cancer (Gritz, Wellisch, Siau, & Wang, 1990), the death of a child (Lehman, Lang, Wortman, & Sorenson, 1989), and experiencing a natural disaster (Cohan & Cole, 2002) have actually predicted marital improvements among some couples. Thus, to obtain a fuller appreciation of the links between stress and marital quality, an important future direction is to address the conditions under which couples may be more or less susceptible to stress spillover and stress crossover effects. Initial evidence for two potentially important conditions is reviewed in the next section.

The Role of Stressor Salience: Can Awareness of Stress Reduce Its Impact?

When asked to explain the success or failure of their relationships, individuals rarely acknowledge the role the relationship context may have played in shaping those outcomes (e.g., Berscheid, Lopes, Ammazzalorso, & Langenfeld, 2001), suggesting that external stress often affects relationship processes without couples' awareness. Thus, one condition that may help reduce spillover and crossover effects is an increased recognition of how stressful events may constrain marital functioning. To explore the potential influence of stressor salience on marital well-being, Tesser and Beach (1998) examined changes in marital satisfaction as spouses' stress increased from low to moderate to high. Results indicated a complex and nonlinear relationship between the severity of external stressors experienced and judgments of marital satisfaction. As level of stress increased from low to moderate, spouses exhibited typical spillover effects, reporting more negative evaluations of their marriage. Interestingly, these spillover effects disappeared under conditions of moderate stress, as the link between stress and satisfaction was substantially weaker. As stressors continued to accumulate beyond this point, though, increases in stress again were associated with lowered marital satisfaction. To explain these findings, Tesser and Beach (1998) postulated that low levels of stress may negatively impact spouses' mood (e.g., create general feelings of irritability), which then unknowingly colors their appraisals of the relationship. Under moderate stress, however, spouses may become cognizant that stress could be contaminating their relationship judgments and thus work to correct for the effects of their mood on their appraisals (cf. Clore, 1992). Unfortunately, this correction process requires effort (Martin, Seta, & Crelia, 1990), and consistent with the themes of the two-route model described earlier, coping with high levels of stress may overwhelm spouses' capacity to engage in such compensatory efforts. In other words, spouses may be able to limit spillover effects when their stress reaches a level that is salient yet not overly exacting.

Stressor salience also may encourage correction efforts in the partner of the stressed spouse, thereby weakening crossover effects. In the previously reviewed Thompson and Bolger (1999) study of couples in which one partner was preparing for the bar exam, it was noted that in the weeks leading up to the exam, examinees' stress predicted a reduction in positive relationship feelings in the partner. However, results also revealed that, immediately before the exam, when the source of the examinee's stress was clear and obvious, examinees' stress was no longer associated with partners' satisfaction. These findings suggest that when individuals clearly may attribute the source of a partner's distress to the stressful situation, they may not react as negatively to the partner's distress. In fact, further analyses indicated that individuals increased their support provision to the partner as the exam drew near (Bolger, Zuckerman, & Kessler, 2000). In this way, awareness of the stress may increase the likelihood of support exchanges within the relationship, which, to the extent that the support is effective, can help nullify the impact of stress on the relationship.

Finally, stressor salience has been invoked as an explanation for the differential influence of major (e.g., severe illness) versus minor (e.g., daily hassles) stressors on couples' functioning. Some recent findings have suggested that although links between major stressors and marital quality can be unclear and inconsistent, minor stressors strongly predict lowered marital quality (see Randall & Bodenmann, 2009, for a review). Why might this be? Major stressors are clearly perceptible and thus are likely to foster greater coping and support efforts on the part of the couple, particularly as such responses are considered normative in the face of important stressful events (Bodenmann, 2005). Again, if coping efforts are successful, the association between stress and marital quality should be weakened. Conversely, minor stressors may be particularly insidious for relationships as they tend to occur on the fringe of conscious awareness, and thus may fail to incite these adaptive responses.

Overall, then, several lines of research point to the potential of stressor salience to modify the links between stress and marital well-being. Nevertheless, a critical limitation of this existing work is that awareness of the stressor has been assumed rather than directly measured or manipulated. Thus, further research testing this assumption is needed.

Stress Resilience in Early Marriage: Can Practice Make Perfect?

Some theories have shifted away from an emphasis on the negative effects of stress to consider whether, under certain conditions, stress can serve to enhance well-being (see Updegraff & Taylor, 2000, for a review). For instance, Meichenbaum's (1985) stress inoculation theory suggests that the experience of coping with mild, manageable stressors may help protect individuals from the potentially harmful effects of subsequent, more severe stressors. Just as a vaccine exposes individuals to a weakened form of a harmful disease to promote the creation of antibodies for fighting stronger forms of the disease, exposure to mildly stressful experiences may help individuals develop an increased ability to handle larger stressors in the future (Meichenbaum, 1985). From this perspective, stressful life events provide opportunities for positive growth by promoting new coping skills, mobilizing previously untapped personal and social resources for effective coping, and increasing confidence in one's ability to surmount stress (Holahan & Moos, 1990; McCubbin & Patterson, 1983; Updegraff & Taylor, 2000).

Empirical evidence for the positive effects of stressful experiences is growing. A study of female rape victims revealed that those who had experienced the death of a family member more than 2 years before recovered more quickly from the rape than women who did not have this prior stress experience (Burgess & Holmstrom, 1978). Further work highlights how stress may interact with individuals' coping resources to predict future well-being. In other words, to benefit from the "inoculation" experience, individuals not only must be exposed to mild stress but also must possess a level of resources necessary to successfully surmount that initial stress. For instance, studies of daily stress have revealed that individuals report a more positive mood on the day following a stressful event than on other stress-free days (Bolger, DeLongis, Kessler, & Schilling, 1989; DeLongis, Folkman & Lazarus, 1988). This effect is particularly strong when individuals receive high levels of social support for the event (Caspi, Bolger, & Eckenrode, 1987). Moreover, individuals who experience stress, and manage to cope well with that stress, have shown an increase in resources, such as improved family support and reduced family conflict 1 year later (Holahan & Moos, 1990).

To date, however, there has been very little research examining these kinds of stress inoculation effects within marriage. One longitudinal study of newlywed couples found that for couples with poor problem-solving skills, experiencing stress early in the marriage predicted declines in satisfaction over time, but for couples with more effective problem-solving skills, experiencing early stress predicted more satisfying relationships 18 months later (Cohan & Bradbury, 1997). Though these results are encouraging, this study nonetheless did not examine how experiences with early stress may affect responses to later stressors. More recently, Neff and Broady (in press) directly examined whether spouses who encounter moderate stress early in the relationship, and possess the relationship skills needed to effectively manage that stress, may have relationship appraisals that are more resilient to future stress spillover effects. In Study 1, newlywed couples provided data regarding their stressful life events, relationship skills (i.e., observed conflict resolution behaviors), and marital satisfaction at five assessments over 2.5 years. To measure stress spillover effects, the within-person association between changes in stress and changes in satisfaction over the 2-year period that followed the initial assessment (i.e., Time 2 through Time 5) was estimated for each spouse. Thus, a stronger, negative association would indicate greater spillover, or a stronger tendency for increases in a spouse's external stressors to be associated with decreases in marital satisfaction. We then examined whether early stress and early relationship skills, both assessed when the couples were first married (Time 1), would interact to predict the strength of those future spillover effects. Results revealed that spouses who experienced moderate stress during the early months of marriage and possessed good relationship skills exhibited fewer future stress spillover effects than did spouses who possessed good relationship skills but had experienced little to no early stress.

Study 2 examined stress resilience in the context of the transition to parenthood. The transition to parenthood has been recognized as a stressful period for couples, which often can be associated with declines in marital satisfaction (Lawrence, Rothman, Cobb, Rothman, & Bradbury, 2008). Thus, this study examined whether spouses who possessed good relationship skills, and who had some prior experience coping with stress in the marriage, were most successful in navigating this transition. To examine this idea, data were drawn from a larger study of marital development that followed newlywed couples over the first 4 years of marriage. For the purposes of this study, only data from couples who underwent the transition to parenthood at some point during those 4 years were used. Similar to Study 1, when couples were first married, they were asked to provide data on their marital satisfaction, stressful life events, and relationship skills (e.g., the observed ability to effectively ask for spousal support). Then, 6 months after the birth of the child, spouses were asked to rate how parenthood had affected their marriage, from 1 (*made the marriage much worse*) to 9 (*made the marriage much better*). Again, spouses who possessed good relationships skills and had experienced moderate stress during the early months of marriage reported better marital adjustment following the transition to parenthood, compared with spouses who possessed good relationship skills but had little prior experience coping with stress.

Together, these results indicate yet again that simply possessing good relationship skills may not be sufficient to protect spouses from the detrimental effects of stress. Yet, extending the previously reviewed spillover work, they suggest that perhaps spouses may overcome stress if they have both good relationship skills and some practice effectively using those skills in the face of mild and manageable stressors. These results are preliminary, however, and much further research exploring this possibility is warranted.

CONCLUSIONS AND IMPLICATIONS FOR PUBLIC POLICY

How are couples able to maintain their marital happiness over the course of a long-term relationship? Surveying prior attempts to address this question reveals an important tension within the close relationships literature. Traditionally, many theoretical perspectives have argued that the course of a marriage is influenced by the intrapersonal and dyadic processes taking place inside the relationship. Thus, couples exhibiting positive relationship behaviors should fare better in their marriage over time than those lacking in relationship skills. Other perspectives maintain that the antecedents of marital deterioration may stem from contextual rather than interpersonal influences, as even the happiest couples experience stressful events external to the relationship that may strain the marriage, despite the initial absence of difficulties within the relationship (Robinson & Jacobson, 1987). To integrate these micro- and macroanalytic perspectives on marital development, this chapter reviewed evidence highlighting how spouses' immediate capacity to draw on and use their relationship skills may be constrained by unstable elements of their environmental context. Conditions of high external stress may interfere with efforts to engage in positive relationship functioning by draining resources and energy that spouses might otherwise spend on each other (Baumeister, 2002; Neff & Karney, 2004, 2009). Thus, a crucial point emerging from the literature is that under conditions of stress, even couples that normally possess adequate relationship skills may find it difficult or impossible to express those skills effectively.

This point becomes especially important when one considers that the federal government recently has devoted unprecedented levels of resources toward marital intervention programs designed to improve marriages by teaching couples more adaptive ways of relationship functioning. The major assumption guiding these skills training programs is that distressed couples simply never learned how to engage in those behaviors necessary for successful relationship maintenance (Markman, Stanley, & Blumberg, 1994). Often, this training takes place in controlled settings in which couples can practice their skills away from the distractions of their everyday lives. It is presumed that once couples have acquired better relationship skills, those skills will remain intact when the couple leaves the therapy setting, resulting in stronger, more resilient marriages. Yet, research on the role stress plays in shaping relational processes raises the possibility that such efforts to improve marriages may be ineffective or misguided. Teaching couples more adaptive behaviors may do little to improve marriage if the marriage is taking place in a context filled with many stressors. In fact, the few studies examining the effectiveness of these programs have shown mixed results (Halford, Sanders, & Behrens, 2001), with at least some evidence suggesting that couples who return to lives filled with stressful events benefit less from therapy interventions (Jacobson, Schmaling, & Holtzworth-Munroe, 1987).

The research reviewed here helps explain why couples may encounter difficulty using the relationship skills learned in therapy and points to new avenues for marital interventions. If stress impedes couples' capacity to engage in the behaviors they know to be beneficial for the marriage, then a focus on enhancing couples' basic relationship skills is necessary but not sufficient to ensure positive marital outcomes. Rather, interventions may want to incorporate an additional focus on aiding couples in their stress management techniques. For instance, as a first step toward successful stress management, couples may benefit from insight into how stressors encountered outside of the marriage may influence their thoughts and behaviors within the marriage. As suggested by the previous literature review, recognizing the influence of stress may encourage spouses not only to work on correcting their own relationship behavior but also to be less judgmental of the partner's behaviors during times of stress (Bodenmann & Shantinath, 2004). Once couples identify the stressors surrounding their marriages and recognize the ways that stress may influence their marital processes, another important step may be to equip couples with better coping skills for managing or even reducing their stress and ensure that couples gain practice applying these skills to small stressors. In this way, when faced with larger stressors in the future, that stress may be less likely to spill over and affect processes within the marriage (Bodenmann, 2005). In sum, understanding both the internal dynamics and the external contexts that account for successful marital outcomes is imperative not only to advance the science of relationships but also to inform government policy and direct resources toward interventions most likely to be effective in strengthening families.

REFERENCES

Amato, P. R., Johnson, D. R., Booth, A., & Rogers, S. J. (2003). Continuity and change in marital quality between 1980 and 2000. *Journal of Marriage and Family, 65*, 1–22. doi:10.1111/j.1741-3737.2003.00001.x

Baumeister, R. F. (2002). Ego depletion and self-control failure: An energy model of the self's executive function. *Self and Identity, 1*, 129–136. doi:10.1080/152988 602317319302

Berscheid, E., Lopes, J., Ammazzalorso, H., & Langenfeld, N. (2001). Causal attributions of relationship quality. In V. Manusov & J. H. Harvey (Eds.), *Attribution, communication behavior, and close relationships* (pp. 115–133). New York, NY: Cambridge University Press.

Bodenmann, G. (1997). The influence of stress and coping on close relationships: A two-year longitudinal study. *Swiss Journal of Psychology, 56*, 156–164.

Bodenmann, G. (2005). Dyadic coping and its significance for marital functioning. In T. R. Revenson, K. Kayser, & G. Bodenmann (Eds.), *Couples coping with stress: Emerging perspectives on dyadic coping* (pp. 33–49). Washington, DC: American Psychological Association. doi:10.1037/11031-002

Bodenmann, G., Ledermann, T., & Bradbury, T. (2007). Stress, sex, and satisfaction in marriage. *Personal Relationships, 14*, 551–569. doi:10.1111/j.1475-6811.2007. 00171.x

Bodenmann, G., & Shantinath, S. D. (2004). The couples coping enhancement training (CCET): A new approach to prevention of marital distress based upon stress and coping. *Family Relations, 53*, 477–484. doi:10.1111/j.0197-6664.2004.00056.x

Bolger, N., DeLongis, A., Kessler, R. C., & Schilling, E. A. (1989). Effects of daily stress on negative mood. *Journal of Personality and Social Psychology, 57*, 808–818. doi:10.1037/0022-3514.57.5.808

Bolger, N., DeLongis, A., Kessler, R. C., & Wethington, E. (1989). The contagion of stress across multiple roles. *Journal of Marriage and Family, 51*, 175–183. doi:10. 2307/352378

Bolger, N., Zuckerman, A., & Kessler, R. C. (2000). Invisible support and adjustment to stress. *Journal of Personality and Social Psychology, 79*, 953–961.

Bradbury, T. N., & Fincham, F. D. (1990). Attributions in marriage: Review and critique. *Psychological Bulletin, 107*, 3–33. doi:10.1037/0033-2909.107.1.3

Bronfenbrenner, U. (1989). Ecological systems theory. *Annals of Child Development, 6*, 187–249.

Burgess, A. W., & Holmstrom, L. L. (1978). Recovery from rape and prior life stress. *Research in Nursing & Health, 1*, 165–174. doi:10.1002/nur.4770010404

Campbell, L., Simpson, J. A., Boldry, J., & Kashy, D. A. (2005). Perceptions of conflict and support in romantic relationships: The role of attachment anxiety. *Journal of Personality and Social Psychology, 88*, 510–531. doi:10.1037/0022-3514.88.3.510

Caspi, A., Bolger, N., & Eckenrode, J. (1987). Linking person and context in the daily stress process. *Journal of Personality and Social Psychology, 52*, 184–195. doi:10.1037/0022-3514.52.1.184

Cherlin, A. J. (2005). American marriage in the early twenty-first century. *The Future of Children, 15*, 33–55. doi:10.1353/foc.2005.0015

Cherlin, A. J. (2010). Demographic trends in the United States: A review of research in the 2000s. *Journal of Marriage and Family, 72*, 403–419. doi:10.1111/j.1741-3737.2010.00710.x

Clore, G. L. (1992). Cognitive phenomenology: Feelings and the construction of judgment. In L. L. Martin & A. Tesser (Eds.), *The construction of social judgments* (pp. 133–163). Hillsdale, NJ: Erlbaum.

Cohan, C. L., & Bradbury, T. N. (1997). Negative life events, marital interaction and the longitudinal course of newlywed marriage. *Journal of Personality and Social Psychology, 73*, 114–128. doi:10.1037/0022-3514.73.1.114

Cohan, C. L., & Cole, S. W. (2002). Life course transitions and natural disaster: Marriage, birth, and divorce following Hurricane Hugo. *Journal of Family Psychology, 16*, 14–25. doi:10.1037/0893-3200.16.1.14

Conger, R. D., & Conger, K. J. (2002). Resilience in Midwestern families: Selected findings from the first decade of a prospective longitudinal study. *Journal of Marriage and Family, 64*, 361–373. doi:10.1111/j.1741-3737.2002.00361.x

Conger, R. D., Rueter, M. A., & Elder, G. H. (1999). Couple resilience to economic pressure. *Journal of Personality and Social Psychology, 76*, 54–71. doi:10.1037/0022-3514.76.1.54

Crouter, A. C., & Bumpus, M. F. (2001). Linking parents' work stress to children's and adolescents' psychological adjustment. *Current Directions in Psychological Science, 10*, 156–159. doi:10.1111/1467-8721.00138

Crouter, A. C., Perry-Jenkins, M., Huston, T. L., & Crawford, D. E. (1989). The influence of work-induced psychological states on behavior at home. *Basic and Applied Social Psychology, 10*, 273–292. doi:10.1207/s15324834basp1003_5

Cutrona, C. E., Russell, D., Abraham, W., Gardner, K., Melby, J., Bryant, C., & Conger, R. D. (2003). Neighborhood context and financial strain as predictors of marital interaction and marital quality in African American couples. *Personal Relationships, 10,* 389–409. doi:10.1111/1475-6811.00056

DeLongis, A., Folkman, S., & Lazarus, R. S. (1988). The impact of daily stress on health and mood: Psychological and social resources as mediators. *Journal of Personality and Social Psychology, 54,* 486–495. doi:10.1037/0022-3514.54.3.486

Finkel, E. J., & Campbell, W. K. (2001). Self-control and accommodation in close relationships: An interdependence analysis. *Journal of Personality and Social Psychology, 81,* 263–277. doi:10.1037/0022-3514.81.2.263

Gottman, J. M. (1994). *What predicts divorce? The relationship between marital processes and marital outcomes.* Hillsdale, NJ: Erlbaum.

Gottman, J. M., Coan, J., Carrere, S., & Swanson, C. (1998). Predicting marital happiness and stability from newlywed interactions. *Journal of Marriage and Family, 60,* 5–22. doi:10.2307/353438

Gritz, E. R., Wellisch, D. K., Siau, J., & Wang, H. (1990). Long-term effects of testicular cancer on marital relationships. *Psychosomatics, 31,* 301–312.

Halford, W. K., Sanders, M. R., & Behrens, B. C. (2001). Can skills training prevent relationship problems in at-risk couples? Four-year effects of a behavioral relationship education program. *Journal of Family Psychology, 15,* 750–768. doi:10.1037/0893-3200.15.4.750

Holahan, C. J., & Moos, R. H. (1990). Life stressors, resistance factors, and improved psychological functioning: An extension of the stress resistance paradigm. *Journal of Personality and Social Psychology, 58,* 909–917. doi:10.1037/0022-3514.58.5.909

Holtzworth-Munroe, A., & Jacobson, N. S. (1985). Causal attributions of married couples: When do they search for causes? What do they conclude when they do? *Journal of Personality and Social Psychology, 48,* 1398–1412. doi:10.1037/0022-3514.48.6.1398

Jacobson, N. S., Follette, W. C., & McDonald, D. W. (1982). Reactivity to positive and negative behavior in distressed and nondistressed married couples. *Journal of Consulting and Clinical Psychology, 50,* 706–714. doi:10.1037/0022-006X.50.5.706

Jacobson, N. S., Schmaling, K. B., & Holtzworth-Munroe, A. (1987). Component analysis of behavioral marital therapy: 2-year follow-up and prediction of relapse. *Journal of Marital and Family Therapy, 13,* 187–195. doi:10.1111/j.1752-0606.1987.tb00696.x

Karney, B. R., & Bradbury, T. N. (1995). The longitudinal course of marital quality and stability: A review of theory, methods, and research. *Psychological Bulletin, 118,* 3–34. doi:10.1037/0033-2909.118.1.3

Karney, B. R., & Bradbury, T. N. (2000). Attributions in marriage: State or trait? A growth curve analysis. *Journal of Personality and Social Psychology, 78,* 295–309. doi:10.1037/0022-3514.78.2.295

Karney, B. R., & Bradbury, T. N. (2005). Contextual influences on marriage: Implications for policy and intervention. *Current Directions in Psychological Science, 14,* 171–174. doi:10.1111/j.0963-7214.2005.00358.x

Karney, B. R., Garvan, C. W., & Thomas, M. S. (2003). *Family formation in Florida: 2003 baseline survey of attitudes, beliefs, and demographics relating to marriage and family formation*. Gainesville: University of Florida.

Karney, B. R., Story, L. B., & Bradbury, T. N. (2005). Marriages in context: Interactions between chronic and acute stress among newlyweds. In T. A. Revenson, K. Kayser, & G. Bodenmann (Eds.), *Couples coping with stress: Emerging perspectives on dyadic coping* (pp. 13–32). Washington, DC: American Psychological Association.

Katz, J., Monnier, J., Libet, J., Shaw, D., & Beach, S. R. H. (2000). Individual and crossover effects of stress on adjustment in medical student marriages. *Journal of Marital and Family Therapy, 26*, 341–351. doi:10.1111/j.1752-0606.2000.tb00303.x

Kelley, H. H., & Thibaut, J. W. (1978). *Interpersonal relations: A theory of interdependence*. New York, NY: Wiley.

Krokoff, L. J., Gottman, J. M., & Roy, A. K. (1988). Blue-collar and white-collar marital interaction and communication orientation. *Journal of Social and Personal Relationships, 5*, 201–221. doi:10.1177/026540758800500205

Larson, R. W., & Almeida, D. M. (1999). Emotional transmission in the daily lives of families: A new paradigm for studying family process. *Journal of Marriage and Family, 61*, 5–20. doi:10.2307/353879

Larson, R. W., & Gillman, S. (1999). Transmission of emotions in the daily interactions of single-mother families. *Journal of Marriage and Family, 61*, 21–37. doi:10.2307/353880

Lavee, Y., McCubbin, H. I., & Olson, D. H. (1987). The effect of stressful life events and transitions on family functioning and well-being. *Journal of Marriage and Family, 49*, 857–873. doi:10.2307/351979

Lawrence, E., Rothman, A. D., Cobb, R. J., Rothman, M. T., & Bradbury, T. N. (2008). Marital satisfaction across the transition to parenthood. *Journal of Family Psychology, 22*, 41–50. doi:10.1037/0893-3200.22.1.41

Lehman, D. R., Lang, E. L., Wortman, C. B., & Sorenson, S. B. (1989). Long-term effects of sudden bereavement: Marital and parent-child relationships and children's reactions. *Journal of Family Psychology, 2*, 344–367. doi:10.1037/h0080505

Markman, H. J., Stanley, S. M., & Blumberg, S. L. (1994). *Fighting for your marriage: Positive steps for a loving and lasting relationship*. San Francisco, CA: Jossey Bass.

Martin, L. L., Seta, J. J., & Crelia, R. A. (1990). Assimilation and contrast as a function of people's willingness and ability to expend effort in forming an impression. *Journal of Personality and Social Psychology, 59*, 27–37. doi:10.1037/0022-3514.59.1.27

McCubbin, H. I., & Patterson, J. M. (1983). Family transitions: Adaptation to stress. In H. I. McCubbin & C. R. Figley (Eds.), *Stress and the family: Coping with normative transitions* (Vol. 1, pp. 5–25). New York, NY: Brunner/Mazel.

McNulty, J. K., & Karney, B. R. (2001). Attributions in marriage: Integrating specific and global evaluations of close relationships. *Personality and Social Psychology Bulletin, 27*, 943–955. doi:10.1177/0146167201278003

Meichenbaum, D. (1985). *Stress inoculation training*. New York, NY: Pergaman.

Murray, S. L., Holmes, J. G., & Collins, N. L. (2006). Optimizing assurance: The risk regulation system in relationships. *Psychological Bulletin, 132*, 641–666. doi: 10.1037/0033-2909.132.5.641

Murray, S. L., Rose, P., Bellavia, G. M., Holmes, J. G., & Kusche, A. G. (2002). When rejection stings: How self-esteem constrains relationship-enhancement processes. *Journal of Personality and Social Psychology, 83*, 556–573. doi:10.1037/0022-3514.83.3.556

Neff, L. A., & Broady, E. F. (in press). Stress resilience in early marriage: Does practice make perfect? *Journal of Personality and Social Psychology*.

Neff, L. A., & Karney, B. R. (2002). Judgments of a relationship partner: Specific accuracy but global enhancement. *Journal of Personality, 70*, 1079–1112. doi: 10.1111/1467-6494.05032

Neff, L. A., & Karney, B. R. (2004). How does context affect intimate relationships? Linking external stress and cognitive processes within marriage. *Personality and Social Psychology Bulletin, 30*, 134–148. doi:10.1177/0146167203255984

Neff, L. A., & Karney, B. R. (2005a). Gender differences in social support: A question of skill or responsiveness? *Journal of Personality and Social Psychology, 88*, 79–90. doi:10.1037/0022-3514.88.1.79

Neff, L. A., & Karney, B. R. (2005b). To know you is to love you: The implications of global adoration and specific accuracy for marital relationships. *Journal of Personality and Social Psychology, 88*, 480–497. doi:10.1037/0022-3514.88.3.480

Neff, L. A., & Karney, B. R. (2007). Stress crossover in early marriage: A longitudinal and dyadic perspective. *Journal of Marriage and Family, 69*, 594–607. doi:10.1111/j.1741-3737.2007.00394.x

Neff, L. A., & Karney, B. R. (2009). Stress and reactivity to daily relationship experiences: How stress hinders adaptive processes in marriage. *Journal of Personality and Social Psychology, 97*, 435–450. doi:10.1037/a0015663

Ooms, T., & Wilson, P. (2004). The challenges of offering relationship and marriage education to low-income populations. *Family Relations, 53*, 440–447. doi:10.1111/j.0197-6664.2004.00052.x

Randall, A. K., & Bodenmann, G. (2009). The role of stress on close relationships and marital satisfaction. *Clinical Psychology Review, 29*, 105–115. doi:10.1016/j.cpr.2008.10.004

Repetti, R. L. (1989). Effects of daily workload on subsequent behavior during marital interaction: The roles of social withdrawal and spouse support. *Journal of Personality and Social Psychology, 57*, 651–659. doi:10.1037/0022-3514.57.4.651

Repetti, R. L., Wang, S., & Saxbe, D. (2009). Bringing it all back home: How outside stressors shape families' everyday lives. *Current Directions in Psychological Science*, 18, 106–111. doi:10.1111/j.1467-8721.2009.01618.x

Repetti, R. L., & Wood, J. (1997). Families accommodating to chronic stress: Unintended and unnoticed processes. In B. H. Gottlieb (Ed.), *Coping with chronic stress* (pp. 191–220). New York, NY: Plenum Press.

Robinson, E. A., & Jacobson, N. S. (1987). Social learning theory and family psychopathology: A Kantian model in behaviorism? In T. Jacob (Ed.), *Family interaction and psychopathology* (pp. 117–162). New York, NY: Plenum Press.

Rook, K., Dooley, D., & Catalano, R. (1991). Stress transmission: The effects of husbands' job stressors on the emotional health of their wives. *Journal of Marriage and Family*, 53, 165–177. doi:10.2307/353141

Rusbult, C. E., Verette, J., Whitney, G. A., Slovik, L. F., & Lipkus, I. (1991). Accommodation processes in close relationships: Theory and preliminary empirical evidence. *Journal of Personality and Social Psychology*, 60, 53–78. doi:10.1037/0022-3514.60.1.53

Rusbult, C. E., Yovetich, N. A., & Verette, J. (1996). An interdependence analysis of accommodation processes. In G. J. O. Fletcher & J. Fitness (Eds.), *Knowledge structures in close relationships: A social psychological approach* (pp. 63–90). Mahwah, NJ: Erlbaum.

Schulz, M. S., Cowan, P. A., Cowan, C. P., & Brennan, R. T. (2004). Coming home upset: Gender, marital satisfaction, and the daily spillover of workday experience into couple interactions. *Journal of Family Psychology*, 18, 250–263. doi:10.1037/0893-3200.18.1.250

Showers, C., & Kling, K. C. (1996). Organization of self-knowledge: Implications for recovery from sad mood. *Journal of Personality and Social Psychology*, 70, 578–590.

Singh, G. K., Matthews, T. J., Clarke, S. C., Yannicos, T., & Smith, B. L. (1995). Annual summary of births, marriages, divorces, and deaths: United States, 1994. *Monthly Vital Statistics Report*, 43(No. 13). Atlanta, GA: National Center for Health Statistics.

Story, L. B., & Bradbury, T. N. (2004). Understanding marriage and stress: Essential questions and challenges. *Clinical Psychology Review*, 23, 1139–1162. doi:10.1016/j.cpr.2003.10.002

Story, L. B., & Repetti, R. L. (2006). Daily occupational stressors and marital behavior. *Journal of Family Psychology*, 20, 690–700. doi:10.1037/0893-3200.20.4.690

Tesser, A., & Beach, S. R. H. (1998). Life events, relationship quality, and depression: An investigation of judgment discontinuity in vivo. *Journal of Personality and Social Psychology*, 74, 36–52. doi:10.1037/0022-3514.74.1.36

Thompson, A., & Bolger, N. (1999). Emotional transmission in couples under stress. *Journal of Marriage and Family*, 61, 38–48. doi:10.2307/353881

Updegraff, J. A., & Taylor, S. E. (2000). From vulnerability to growth: Positive and negative effects of stressful life events. In J. Harvey & E. Miller (Eds.), *Loss and trauma: General and close relationship perspectives* (pp. 3–28). Philadelphia, PA: Brunner-Routledge.

Yovetich, N. A., & Rusbult, C. E. (1994). Accommodative behavior in close relationships: Exploring transformation of motivation. *Journal of Experimental Social Psychology, 30*, 138–164. doi:10.1006/jesp.1994.1007

Weiss, R. L., & Heyman, R. E. (1990). Observation of marital interaction. In F. D. Fincham & T. N. Bradbury (Eds.), *The psychology of marriage* (pp. 87–117). New York, NY: Guilford Press.

Westman, M. (2001). Stress and strain crossover. *Human Relations, 54*, 717–751. doi:10.1177/0018726701546002

9

THE UTILITY OF EVOLUTIONARY PERSPECTIVES ON ROMANTIC RELATIONSHIPS: WOMEN'S ESTRUS AS ILLUSTRATION

STEVEN W. GANGESTAD

The past 3 decades have witnessed the emergence of a robust science of relationships (e.g., Berscheid, 1999). Relationship science, in Berscheid's (1999) view, develops a traditional focus of social psychology on interactions between individuals, in contrast to a more individualistic perspective on internal processes that roots much psychological inquiry. Relationship scientists seek to understand the causal processes that produce regularities that govern interactions between people—how each person of a pair (or more generally, multiperson group) affects the behavior of the other—giving rise to the "rhythm" of influence observed in interpersonal interactions, as it unfolds over time (see also Chapters 1 and 12, this volume). As such, relationship science is not limited to an individualistic, psychological level of analysis. It is inherently multidisciplinary in nature, encompassing, for instance, sociology, anthropology, communication studies, epidemiology, and economics as well as psychology. The further "greening" of relationship science (Berscheid, 1999) will require articulation of metatheories, and at this time it may not be clear precisely what metatheories will productively guide its major trajectories of growth (e.g., some scholars may view dynamic systems approaches as being critical; others might argue for behavioral perspectives that focus on context; see Chapter 8). What seems clear is that individualistic perspectives with an exclusive focus on processes "inside the head" will not, by themselves, be fully adequate for this emerging science.

In parallel, the past 3 decades have also witnessed the emergence of a robust evolutionary behavioral science. Evolutionary psychology draws its inspiration from evolutionary biology. It asks, in part, how past selection has given rise to adaptations in individuals that significantly affect how they engage with their worlds, importantly including their social worlds. Evolutionary behavioral science perspectives too are multidisciplinary, encompassing, for instance, biology, anthropology, and economics as well as psychology (see Buss, 2007; Crawford & Krebs, 2008; Dunbar & Barrett, 2009; Gangestad & Simpson, 2007).

In the current chapter, I address some issues pertaining to how the perspectives within evolutionary behavioral science may inform relationship science. In brief, I address what it means to adopt an evolutionary perspective. What are the fundamental assumptions of this approach? Does evolutionary biology/psychology constitute a metatheory for psychology and, more specifically, relationship science? Does it offer a methodology? If it is at all useful, what is its utility? I ultimately argue that evolutionary science serves as a good example of how an interdisciplinary approach can lead to novel discoveries. Like evolutionary science, relationship science should take an interdisciplinary approach (see Chapters 1, 11, and 12).

EVOLUTIONARY PERSPECTIVES ON RELATIONSHIPS: WHAT DO THEY OFFER?

Evolutionary psychology has offered understandings of all sorts of relationship phenomena. Its contributions to understanding romantic relationships are probably best known (e.g., criteria of mate selection, romantic attraction, assortative mating, romantic and sexual jealousy, mate poaching; see, e.g., Buss, 2007). But it offers unique perspectives on other close relationships as well, including mother–child, father–child, sibling, and friend relationships (e.g., Buss, 2007; Crawford & Krebs, 2008; DeScioli & Kurzban, 2009; Dunbar & Barrett, 2009; Ellis & Bjorklund, 2005; Salmon & Shackelford, 2007; Tooby & Cosmides, 1996).

Metatheory in Psychology

A number of scholars have proposed that, as one article's title proclaimed, "evolutionary psychology is a metatheory for psychology" (Duntley & Buss, 2008). What does it mean for evolutionary theory to offer a metatheory for psychology? A standard definition is that a *metatheory* is a theory about other theories. The seminal metatheory was that of David Hilbert, who proposed at the beginning of the 20th century that all mathematical theories were consistent and set out to prove that claim. The claim itself was a metatheoretical one. Within psychology and other sciences, metatheory functions to specify what theories of phenomena in the domain should "look like." That is, metatheory defines the nature of the entities, objects, and phenomena of study to be explained within a discipline or domain of inquiry and the processes through which they are explained. Overton (1998) more specifically defined metatheory as "a set of interlocking rules, principles, or a story (narrative) that both describes and prescribes what is acceptable and unacceptable as theory—the means of conceptual exploration—in a scientific discipline" (p. 1). Mechanistic approaches to information processing assume that particular kinds of explanation are perfectly acceptable, which radical behaviorism would reject as unacceptable. At the same time, explanations offered within a radical behaviorist framework would typically be viewed as insufficient from a mechanistic cognitive psychology perspective. These two perspectives illustrate contrasting metatheories for psychology. Similarly, within developmental psychology, some approaches permit transformational change, whereas other, more mechanistic, frameworks reject it. These perspectives constitute differing metatheories. Evolutionary psychology might therefore be viewed as a metatheory.

Not everyone accepts evolutionary psychology as metatheory for psychology, of course. I recently cotaught a graduate seminar with a developmental psychologist who had his own well-defined metatheory, developmental systems theory. This view sees development as emergent phenomena that occur within contexts or systems of entities. Explanation within this approach constitutes description of these systems and their transformations that constitute development. This developmental psychologist had no qualms with evolutionary biology. He simply did not see how it added anything to his explanations. For instance, one could argue that a particular developmental phenomenon (system) had been selected historically, and selection may explain its current existence. Another particular phenomenon may be novel and perhaps even maladaptive. The different histories of these systems, in his mind, had nothing to do with how they are to be explained qua development. That is, saying one is adaptive and ancestrally selected and one is maladaptive or evolutionary novel says nothing about the developmental processes involved. Development is not predetermined. It must unfold anew in real time on each occasion (see Chapter 7). Whether it has occurred many times in the past and been selected or occurred just once—this one time we're observing it now—does not change the fact that developmental processes are involved and must be described.

This developmental psychologist went so far as to argue that evolutionary perspectives may be counterproductive or obfuscating. A perspective that argues that some developmental systems have long histories whereas others do not may suggest that the former are more real, more fundamental, more basic, and more "ingrained." Such a perspective could also imply, even if unintentionally, that long-standing developmental phenomena are, in some sense, predetermined in a way in which they are "there" before they even occur. If so, that is inappropriate, as every instance of development is equally "real" and demands explanation in terms of developmental processes. Evolutionary explanations do not stand in for developmental explanations. Applied to relationships, the argument is that relationship phenomena occurring in the here and now are all equally real. Whether they have a long history of being selected has no bearing on how they are to be explained qua relationship phenomena in the here and now.

Does Evolutionary Biology Offer a Metatheory for Psychology?

I agree with my colleague in developmental psychology. Evolutionary theory, in my view, does not offer a metatheory for psychology. That is not to say that evolutionary biology is not useful for psychology or relationship science; indeed, in my view it has already proven to be very useful. Hence, my statement that evolutionary theory does not offer a metatheory for psychology can be taken to mean that the reason evolutionary theory has been very useful for psychology and relationship science is not because it offers metatheory. Rather, evolutionary theory is useful because it offers methodologies for exploring psychological and relationship phenomena. A distinction between metatheory and methodology is hence critical. Why does evolutionary theory not offer metatheory for psychology? And how can it fruitfully offer methodology?

The Relevance of Tinbergen's Four Questions

Niko Tinbergen (1963) famously argued that one can ask four distinct questions about any behavior of an organism (or, in fact, any feature of an organism): What are the behavior's function, phylogeny, proximate cause, and development? One must ask and answer all four questions to achieve a complete explanation of the feature.

Depending on one's interests, however, one need not necessarily ask all four questions. The questions concern distinct causal or explanatory phenomena. An explanation in response to one question does not constrain one's explanation in response to any other question.

Explanatory frameworks relevant to specific questions fall into different disciplines. The first two issues are domains of evolutionary biology. Function has a very specific meaning within evolutionary biology. Adaptations are features that were maintained and spread within populations because they enhanced the reproductive success (or more generally the inclusive fitness) of their bearers. That is, they provided fitness benefits. The function of an adaptation is the means through which it increased fitness. Crudely put, the function of eyes is sight. The function of wings is flight. Not all features of organisms are adaptations. Indeed, most are not. Many are nonbeneficial by-products of features that were selected because of fitness benefits. The whiteness of bones and the bellybutton are purportedly such by-products. Whereas adaptations were directly selected, by-products evolved through indirect selection (i.e., were "carried along" with adaptations).

Evolutionary biologists are interested in distinguishing adaptations from by-products. The way they do so typically involves exploration of special design. Features that were selected because they offered fitness benefits very often exhibit telltale signs of that selection process. Specifically, they often possess details indicative of having been "designed" to offer those fitness benefits (e.g., Thornhill, 1997; G. C. Williams, 1966, 1992). The classic example is the vertebrate eye. It possesses numerous details that indicate that they were selected for their optical properties, such that it is extraordinarily improbable that they evolved through any scenario that excludes selection for sight (G. C. Williams, 1992). By-products lack special design. Moreover, once one possesses an understanding of selection and design, one can often appreciate what arose as by-product. How belly buttons evolved is not a mystery once we understand that umbilical cords were directly selected and entail, as by-products, belly buttons.

Questions of phylogeny concern additional evolutionary phenomena. Even if one knows the selective pressures that favored a human trait, a number of other questions remain. When did it arise within our lineage? Did it first appear in hominids? Apes? Primates? An ancestral species common to mammals? All vertebrates? And how was it modified over time? These questions concern the evolution of the feature but go beyond the question of selection per se (for further discussion, see Eastwick, 2009; Fraley et al., 2005; Gosling & Graybeal, 2007; Thornhill, 2007).

Some evolutionary biologists reframe Tinbergen's two questions in terms of origin and maintenance. The question of origin concerns how a trait first appeared within a lineage. When did it first appear, and how did it appear? Through what process did it appear? Traits typically originate through a perturbation of a developmental process, giving rise to a novelty. Once a novel trait appears, it may be maintained. If it is maintained, one can ask what process maintained it. Was it an adaptation (i.e., a trait directly selected because of fitness benefits), and if so, what is its function—the benefits resulting in its selection? Was it maintained as a by-product of other favored features? Or was it maintained by some other evolutionary process, such as random drift? In general, questions of phylogeny map onto questions of origins, and questions of function map onto questions of maintenance. But maintenance processes are broader than those that concern function per se, and some questions of phylogeny accordingly are questions of maintenance.

The distinction between origins and maintenance can be illustrated with a topic I speak to later, the evolution of estrogen receptors. All modern chordates—all vertebrates plus lampreys—have functional estrogen receptors (Thornton, 2001; Thornton, Need, & Crews, 2003). On the basis of our current understanding of common ancestors of these species, we can infer that estrogen receptors originated in the tree of life about 450 million years ago in the ancestor common to all modern chordates. In all of these species aside from chordates (i.e., all modern vertebrates), estrogen receptors are distributed in a sexually dimorphic way, with estrogen being more important in females than males. This feature, therefore, arose about 400 million years ago in the species ancestral to all modern vertebrates. Once estrogen receptors originated, they were maintained in all lineages of vertebrates with modern descendants. The causal process through which they were maintained is a matter quite different from the causal process through which they were originated. Because estrogen hormones have effects and are not readily interpreted as mere by-products (in contrast to, say, belly buttons), direct selection for estrogen hormones appears to have operated to maintain them. But what were the precise benefits of estrogens? This question concerns function, which itself is embedded within the larger issue of evolutionary maintenance.

The remaining two questions in Tinbergen's scheme do not fall within evolutionary biology. They are addressed by different disciplines. Take the first, proximate causation underlying a particular behavior. The proximate causes of behavior lie within the purview of psychology. Causal processes that, in the here and now, give rise to behavior are, in fact, primarily the domain of psychology. If one is interested in digging deeper into underlying causal processes or understanding proximate causal processes giving rise to nonpsychological traits, fields of neurobiology or physiology or endocrinology or another field dedicated to understanding some specific organismic systems might be pertinent.

The point can be illustrated with estrogen receptors again. A question quite separate from issues of evolutionary origin and maintenance concerns how estrogens affect behavior in a variety of ways in any particular species, such as humans. Fields dealing with the question include endocrinology, neurobiology, and psychology.

The remaining question concerns development, and here the developmental sciences apply: developmental psychology, developmental neurobiology, possibly developmental genetics. Once again, questions of how development occurs qua development are not questions within evolutionary biology per se.

Tinbergen (1963), once again, separated the four questions because different causes are pertinent to answering the different questions. The causes giving rise to evolutionary origins are distinct from the causes of evolutionary maintenance, which are distinct from causes operating proximately, which are different from developmental causes of features. Philosophers of science speak of the "object language" of a discipline or approach—the descriptive and explanatory terms put to use within a scientific discipline. Put otherwise, then, Tinbergen's distinctions imply that the object language put forward to offer explanatory frameworks of, say, proximate causes of behavior are different from the explanatory frameworks put forward to explain evolutionary origins and maintenance. This is not to say that all psychologists are in agreement about the object language pertinent to psychology; again, to take an example, information processing theorists may talk about psychological processes in terms quite different from more those of committed behavioral persuasions, a reflection of their contrasting metatheories. Nonetheless, whatever language one applies to proximate causes is not the one appropriate to explain evolutionary maintenance, and vice versa.

Metatheory, as I have used the term, offers claims about what explanation should look like, which entails specification of the object language of a discipline. For this reason, evolutionary biology is not a metatheory for psychology and cannot supply a metatheory for psychology (at least in the sense in which I have used the term). Psychology and evolutionary biology fundamentally concern different causal phenomena. The object language pertinent to explanation of origins and maintenance of traits in evolutionary biology cannot be imported into psychology to explain distinct causal phenomena of proximate causation.

It should be noted that Duntley and Buss (2008), whose article's title claimed that evolutionary biology offers a metatheory for psychology, may define the term *metatheory* in a way different from how I define it. Perhaps their meaning is akin to a *scientific paradigm*, the term used by Buss (1995) to describe evolutionary psychology in an earlier article. Relatedly, evolutionary perspectives may suggest that certain kinds of psychological outcomes are much more likely than others—for example, extensive modularity is likely to be involved in psychological processing (e.g., Tooby & Cosmides, 1996)—but that point is distinct from the claim that evolutionary biology specifies what a proximate causal account should look like at a psychological level of explanation.

The Methodological Utility of Evolutionary Biology for Psychology and Relationship Science

Another distinction that philosophers of science have written of is that between the context of justification and the context of discovery (Reichenbach, 1938). The former pertains to how one justifies scientific claims or interpretations of data within a discipline. What are established rules of evidence, on the basis of general thinking about scientific inference as well as rules specifically pertaining to the object language adopted? The latter concerns how one arrives at hypotheses and decides what empirical data to collect in the first place. From where does one derive ideas?

The source of one's ideas (i.e., the sources of inspiration within the context of discovery) need not be restricted to theories in the object language of one's own discipline. Although explanation of function and explanation of phylogeny are distinct from proximate explanation of behavior and must be stated in wholly different terms, that is not to say that they are not terribly useful to think about when exploring phenomena responsible for proximate causation. More specifically, based on evolutionary biology, evolutionary psychologists have proposed methodologies designed to advance reasonable hypotheses about how psychological or relationship phenomena work and to systematically explore domains of those phenomena. These methodologies do not require that the explanatory processes pertinent to evolutionary biology are those that apply to proximate psychological or interpersonal processes. Evolution-mindedness offers not a metatheory for psychology and relationship science; rather, it offers a set of useful methodological approaches to explore psychological phenomena.

Are evolutionary biology and evolution-mindedness necessary for researchers to identify and explain interesting relationship phenomena in proximate terms? Of course not. Introductory texts in psychology or relationship science offer hundreds of examples of how scientists have come to understand proximate processes in absence of any guidance from evolutionary biology whatsoever. Can evolutionary biology help researchers do so? Yes. Can it uniquely do so? That is, are there some phenomena that would be unlikely to be discovered in absence of guidance from evolutionary biology? Might evolution-mindedness lead researchers to ask questions about relationship phenomena that they would otherwise simply not ask, as there would be no basis other than an evolution-minded one to ask such questions? Once again, the answer would appear to be yes.

This final claim demands evidence. In the remainder of this chapter, I attempt to illustrate it using an example that borrows heavily from my own work. But the same point could be illustrated with a variety of research programs in evolutionary psychology (for one notable example, see Lieberman et al., 2007).

ESTRUS: WHAT FUNCTION AND PHYLOGENY CAN TELL US ABOUT FORM

Estrus has been defined as "the periodic state of sexual excitement in the female of most mammals . . . that immediately precedes ovulation and during which the female is most receptive to mating" (American Heritage Stedman's

Medical Dictionary, 2002). Put otherwise, it is a distinct fertile-phase period of sexual excitement of female mammals, also commonly known as *heat*. The term itself derives from the Greek word for a botfly. When a botfly lays its eggs on the hide of a cow, the cow often experiences a frenzy. Even in ancient times, the Greeks used the term *oestrus* to refer to frenzy. Around 1890, reproductive biologists co-opted the term to refer to the sexual excitement or frenzy of a fertile female mammal (see Thornhill & Gangestad, 2008).

At this time, important reproductive hormones had not yet been discovered. In 1923, Allen and Doisy identified the first such hormone, estrogen. Estrogen was named for estrus. It was the proposed *gen* or generator of estrus—that is, a chemical at least partly responsible for female fertile-phase sexual excitement. Though the endocrinology underlying estrous sexuality is more complicated than this claim implies (as later-discovered hormones such as progesterone and testosterone also play roles, at least in some species), estrogen is a fertile-phase hormone in most if not all mammalian species and influences female sexual behavior (as well as fertility) in many species.

As I noted earlier, estrogen is important in not just mammals but in chordates in general, and particularly so in females in all vertebrates. One might reasonably infer, then, that estrus first evolved in the ancestor common to all vertebrates, about 400 million years ago (Thornhill & Gangestad, 2008).

The Search for Women's Estrus

Of course, humans are descendants of that common ancestor. And estrogen levels characteristically peak during the fertile phase in women, as in other vertebrate females.

Hence, it was reasonable for researchers to think they might find evidence of estrus, a distinct fertile-phase sexuality, in women. Beginning around 1930, researchers looked for it. Findings were mixed, but overall far less than compelling. Much more recently, for instance, Brewis and Meyer (2005) looked for evidence of increased human female sexual desire in about 20,000 women's reports of recent sexual intercourse with their primary partners in 13 developing countries. They found no evidence of changes in frequency across the cycle aside from a drop during menses. Although women do not initiate all sex with partners, one would suspect that in a sample size of over 20,000, one would have the power to detect even a small increase in female sexual interest midcycle.

Even by about 1960, then, reproductive biologists and anthropologists drew the conclusion that evolutionarily, women "lost" estrus. That is, although our common ancestors with at least nearly all vertebrates possessed estrus, something remarkable happened in the distinctly human lineage that evolved in the past 5 million years: Women evolved to lack it, presumably because it was no longer advantageous and hence selected against. As Donald Symons (1979) claimed in his classic monograph *The Evolution of Human Sexuality*, "Estrus is the relatively brief period of proceptivity, receptivity, and attractivity in female mammals that usually, but not invariably, coincides with their brief period of fertility. *Human females do not experience estrus. . . . [E]strus must have been lost at some point in human ancestry* [italics added]" (p. 97).

This conclusion naturally led theorists to ask why women lost estrus, why this rather extraordinary event occurred. It was thought that this unique human trait held the key to understanding something very important about uniquely hominin evolution. A number of theories emerged, the most prominent of which argued that it facilitated pair-bonding (see Alexander & Noonan, 1979; Symons, 1979). The basic idea is that when males in a group-living species know which females are fertile, it may pay for them to attend to those that are fertile. By contrast, when males do not know which females are fertile, they are more likely to benefit most from attending to one primary female partner and invest in her well-being and that of her offspring (largely fathered by the attending male). Continuous sexual proceptivity and lack of any other cue of fertility (aside from menses, which does not pinpoint the fertile phase) achieve the concealment of ovulation and the fertile state. This argument did not claim that loss of estrus by itself led to the evolution of pair-bonding and paternal care. Rather, in the presence of other factors favoring pair-bonding, loss of estrus facilitated it and paternal care (see Thornhill & Gangestad, 2008, for a fuller discussion of this and other theories of women's loss of estrus).

Evidence That Women Do Possess Estrus

In fact, research accumulated over the past dozen years has indicated that the long-standing conclusion that women lost estrus must be rethought. Recently, Randy Thornhill and I have argued that it is likely to be wrong (Gangestad & Thornhill, 2008; Thornhill & Gangestad, 2008). Women probably do possess estrus. Estrus itself, however, has been misconstrued by reproductive biologists. When properly construed, evidence for women's estrus is abundant. That women probably do experience estrus has a number of deep and broad downstream implications for thinking about human mating in an evolutionary context.

About a dozen years ago, researchers began to examine whether women particularly prefer male features that, ancestrally, may have been associated with genetic benefits for offspring when they are fertile in their cycles. This research was explicitly guided by evolution-minded thinking—specifically, the idea that selection may have shaped women to weight features associated with genetic benefits for offspring, as opposed to features with nongenetic benefits (e.g., willingness to care for offspring, kindness and cooperativeness), during the sole phase of the cycle when women could garner genetic benefits, the fertile phase (e.g., Gangestad & Thornhill, 1998). As amended by Penton-Voak et al. (1999), this idea implies that changes in women's preferences should be most profound when they evaluate men's sexual attractiveness rather than their attractiveness as a long-term, invested, pair-bonded partner.

In fact, normally ovulating women's preferences do change across the cycle in predicted and varied ways. Just prior to ovulation, compared with the nonfertile luteal phase, women exhibit stronger preferences for masculine faces (Johnston et al., 2001; Little, Jones, & DeBruine, 2008; Penton-Voak et al., 1999; Penton-Voak & Perrett, 2000; cf. Peters et al., 2009; Scarbrough & Johnston, 2005; see also Roney & Simmons, 2008; Welling et al., 2007), masculine voices (Feinberg et al., 2006; Puts, 2005; see also Puts, 2006), masculine or muscular bodies (Gangestad, Garver-Apgar, Simpson, & Cousins, 2007; Little, Jones, & Burriss, 2007; cf. Peters et al., 2009), arrogant and intrasexually confrontative behavior (Gangestad et al., 2007; Gangestad, Simpson, Cousins, Garver-Apgar, & Christensen, 2004), male scents associated with social dominance (Havlicek, Roberts, & Flegr, 2005) or body symmetry (Gangestad & Thornhill, 1998; Rikowski & Grammer, 1999; Thornhill & Gangestad, 1999; Thornhill et al., 2003; see also Garver-Apgar et al., 2008), and male tallness (Pawlowski & Jasienska, 2005). But changes in preferences are specific to women's evaluations of men's sexiness; their preferences for long-term stable partners do not appear to change across the cycle (see Gangestad & Thornhill, 1998, for a review). Furthermore, women do not increasingly esteem all valued male features when fertile. Women value men's kindness, faithfulness, and ability to be a good father, especially in long-term, investing partners, but these features are not any more attractive to fertile women than women nonfertile in their cycles (Gangestad et al., 2007; for mixed evidence with regard to preference for male intelligence, see Gangestad, Thornhill, & Garver-Apgar, 2010a, 2010b; Haselton & Miller, 2006; Prokosch et al., 2008).

The dimensions along which women discriminate men's attractiveness, then, systematically change across the ovarian cycle in multiple and systematic ways. In a nutshell, when fertile in their cycles, normally ovulating women find masculine features assessed through multiple modalities, as well as social and physical traits potentially effective in male intrasexual competition, sexier. But estrus, as traditionally defined, refers to a peak in female sexual receptivity and proceptivity during the fertile phase. What do changes in the features women find sexually appealing in men have to do with estrus?

If estrus is conceptualized in its traditional form, these findings perhaps have nothing to do with it. But perhaps this traditional conceptualization does not adequately reflect changes in female sexuality during the fertile phase more generally across species. That is, perhaps the traditional construal of estrus is misconceived. A common notion implied by this construal, even in the reproductive biology literature, is that estrous females seek sex, unqualified by what kind of male with whom they might have sex (for a discussion, see Nelson, 2000). That is, heightened female estrous sexual desire has typically been assumed to be indiscriminant. This idea in turn derives from the common assumption that the function of estrous sexual desire is to obtain sperm. Fertile females need sperm to conceive. They seek it through sex. And one male's sperm has thought to be as good at achieving conception as any other's sperm.

This thinking is likely to be incorrect for both theoretical and empirical reasons. From a theoretical standpoint, females do not typically have to worry about finding males who are willing and able to inseminate them. Males are selected to be motivated to have sex with females. The problem that females typically face is not that they must actively seek sex from males to find it, lest no male be willing to inseminate them; rather, it is that far too many males, from their standpoint, are willing and ready to inseminate them.

Most males may well be able to deliver sperm that leads to conception. But from the female's standpoint, conception with one male is not just as reproductively successful as conception with any other male. When it comes to what promotes offspring fitness, and hence what promotes the fitness of the choosing female, the DNA in sperm are not all equal. Because of the accumulation of random mutations (and possibly other deleterious genes) in the genome and their uneven distribution across males, some males offer genetic benefits to offspring relative to what other males offer. Estrous female sexuality, then, should not have been shaped by selection to be indiscriminant. Estrous females should be very discriminating, particularly so in species in which males deliver nothing but genes to offspring (that is, they do not care for offspring).

Empirically, this pattern is precisely what is typically found. Research has found that estrous females are particularly attracted to specific males in a variety of species. For instance, in pronghorn antelope (Byers et al., 1994), Asian elephants (Schulte & Rasmussen, 1999), American bison (Wolff, 1998), pygmy loris (Fisher et al., 2003), and common chimpanzees (Stumpf & Boesch, 2005), estrous females are particularly attracted to dominant or competitive males. In red deer (Charlton et al., 2007) and guinea pigs (Hohoff et al., 2003), they prefer large, robust males. In Asian elephants (Schulte & Rasmussen, 1999) and rhesus macaques (Waitt, Gerald, Little, & Kraiselburd, 2006), estrous preferences favor testosterone-facilitated traits. In snow voles (Luque-Larena, López, & Gosálbez, 2003), estrous females find symmetrical males attractive. And in house mice (Potts et al., 1991; J. R. Williams & Lenington, 1993), during the fertile phase females favor males possessing particular genes (major histocompatibility complex genes [MHC]) that are compatible with their own (see Thornhill & Gangestad, 2008, for a fuller discussion).

Humans' closest relatives, chimpanzees, illustrate the discriminating nature of female estrous sexual interests. Female chimpanzees are highly promiscuous. They mate effectively with all adult male residents of a group each cycle, purportedly to confuse paternity or, perhaps better stated, to not allow any male to rule out that he might be the father. Females are sexually receptive and proceptive about 10 days out of each 30-day cycle. They are fertile, however, only 2 to 3 days of this 10-day period. The traditional construal of estrus expects that females will be especially sexually active and promiscuous during this brief fertile phase. In fact, precisely the opposite pattern is found. Females are least promiscuous during the estrous phase (Stumpf & Boesch, 2005). They reject the advances of an increased proportion of males in the group. They do seek out sex with males, but their sexual advances are more selective and converge on males that all estrous females prefer. In this study, estrous females especially preferred up-and-coming dominant males (for an alternative interpretation of this mating pattern, see Muller & Wrangham, 2009). For evidence of estrus changes in female orangutans, see Knott et al. (2010).

Women's preference shifts at estrous fit the general comparative pattern. Once again, estrous women particularly prefer men with masculine features and behavioral and physical features that promote intrasexual competition. On the basis of this comparative pattern, Thornhill and I provisionally concluded that, in fact, women did not evolve to lose estrus. They possess estrus, as demonstrated by these preference shifts. Researchers failed to find evidence for women's estrus not because it does not exist; rather, guided by a misconceived notion of estrus, they looked for evidence of estrus in the wrong places. Estrus is marked by discriminating sexual desires favoring particular males. It may or may not (as illustrated by chimpanzees) also be associated with increased sexual desire (indeed, we suggest that only in species completely lacking any sexual phase other than estrus will estrus be associated with enhanced sexual receptivity; see Thornhill & Gangestad, 2008).

Of course, to say that women and chimpanzees both possess estrus is not to claim that women's estrus and sexuality more generally are just like the estrus or sexuality of female chimpanzees and other close relatives. Women are not typically promiscuous in the way that female chimpanzees are. Humans, unlike chimps, did evolve biparental care and pair-bonding, which has many implications for human sexuality. Women's "extended sexuality"—their nonconceptive sexual receptivity and proceptivity outside of estrus—probably functions in the context of pair-bonding, along lines related to the ideas of Symons (1979) and Alexander and Noonan (1979; though, unlike those ideas, pertaining to sexuality outside of estrus rather than loss of estrus). Nonetheless, the fact that women are continuously receptive should not blind us from seeing that embedded within their cycles is a distinct fertile phase, appropriately referred to as estrus.

Implications of Women's Estrus for an Understanding of the Dynamics of Romantic Relationships

Again, the reason that researchers have not found evidence for women's estrus is that they looked for it in the wrong place. Most research designed to assess whether women experience increased sexual desire when fertile has examined whether women have greater sexual desire (e.g., greater frequency of sex or female-initiated sex) with their primary male partners. On average, however, male primary partners are, of course, just average on the traits that women prefer midcycle. Women should hence not be expected to experience greater sexual desire toward their primary partners when fertile compared with during the luteal phase. And indeed, in multiple studies we have found no changes in normally ovulating women's sexual interest in or attraction to male primary partners across the cycle (Gangestad, Thornhill, & Garver, 2002; Gangestad, Thornhill, & Garver-Apgar, 2005).

By contrast, women nearly always encounter in their social spheres men other than primary partners who do possess those features sexy to women midcycle. And hence, in these same studies we have found that, on average, women report that they have experienced sexual attraction to or interest in a male other than their primary partners during estrus (Gangestad et al., 2002; Gangestad et al., 2005).

These studies and others have further found, however, variation across women in changes in patterns of attraction to men in their lives. In particular, women most dramatically experience increased attraction to "extra-pair" men, relative to partners, when their own partners lack the features that women find particularly sexy midcycle—in particular, when partners are asymmetrical (Gangestad et al., 2005), unattractive (whether judged by the women themselves or independent raters; Haselton & Gangestad, 2006; Pillsworth & Haselton, 2006), or facially feminine (Gangestad et al., 2010b) or possess incompatible MHC genes with their partners (Garver-Apgar et al., 2006; not all research has found changes across the cycle in preference for MHC-compatible genes; see, e.g., Thornhill et al., 2003).

The fact that women have retained estrus, then, has real implications for an understanding of human mating and romantic relationships. Although adaptations for pair-bonding and biparental care have very likely evolved in humans (e.g., Kaplan et al., 2000; Marlowe, 2003), conflicts of interest between partners persist. For instance, women may find men other than partners attractive, particularly when they can conceive. Perhaps relatedly, near ovulation women in committed relationships are more likely to endorse statements such as, "The thought of an illicit sex affair excites me" and "If an attractive person (of my preferred sex) approached me sexually, it would be hard to resist, no matter how well I knew him/her" (Gangestad, Thornhill, & Garver-Apgar,

2010a). That women retain estrus has implications for an understanding of the evolution of human mating, as well as the dynamics of romantic relationships in contemporary times.

If, in fact, certain conflicts of interest between partners become particularly acute when women are fertile, we might expect men to have evolved to pick up on subtle cues of women's fertility status. In many species, males detect female fertility status on the basis of its by-products—probably, often, by-products of estrogen production, such as particular scents associated with estrogen. And, in fact, men apparently can detect subtle cues of fertility status too, as they prefer the scent of fertile females (e.g., Havlicek, Dvorakova, Bartos, & Flegr, 2006; Singh & Bronstad, 2001; Thornhill et al., 2003); indeed, men's testosterone levels appear to rise in response to the scent of fertile, relative to infertile, women (S. L. Miller & Maner, 2010). In all likelihood, they do so not because women advertise their fertility status, but rather because men have evolved to detect and prefer scents associated with physiological changes in women's bodies that occur when they are fertile (see Thornhill & Gangestad, 2008).

Men may pick up on other changes across women's cycles. One study examined the tip earnings of female lap dancers over a 2-month period. Normally ovulating women earned significantly more in tips from their customers when they were fertile (G. F. Miller, Tybur, & Jordan, 2007). The cause of this effect remains unknown (changes in women's scent, appearance, behavior, perhaps). As lap dancers in general should be interested in earning tips, however, it is likely that the effects are driven by changes in women's desire to make money.

On the basis of cues available to them, women's primary partners act differently toward them when they are fertile relative to when they are in the luteal phase. Multiple studies have found that men engage in greater levels of behavior interpreted as "mate-guarding" behavior when their partners are ovulating (vigilance of their whereabouts, attempts to spend time with them, jealousy, show of affection or need for them; Gangestad et al., 2002; Haselton & Gangestad, 2006; Pillsworth & Haselton, 2006). In turn, women behave toward their partners differently too; they become more self-assertive and report engaging in more behaviors that "resist" mate-guarding (Gangestad et al., 2010; see also Haselton & Gangestad, 2006). More generally, the dynamic in men's and women's relationships tends to change across the cycle, on average, becoming more conflictual when women are fertile.

Couples vary in the extent to which male partners become proprietary and women become more self-asserting during the fertile phase. Consistently, research has found that increases in women's attraction to other men when they are fertile predict these changes in behavior (as opposed to, for instance, increases in women's or men's attraction to their partners). This pattern suggests that there has been a conflict of interest over male detection of female fertility status, with men benefiting from detection and women not. Hence, perhaps, selection has favored suppression of fertility status by-products (but not complete elimination, which may not be possible without disrupting fertility itself) in women. This is what constitutes selection for concealed estrus. The best evidence for it is the rather informal observation that men appear to be rather poor at detecting female fertility status compared with most male primates (see Thornhill & Gangestad, 2008).

Hormonal contraceptives change the pattern of changes in hormones across the cycle. Estrogen levels peak less markedly midcycle, whereas most contraceptive pills tend to increase levels of progesterone, a hormone that reaches peak levels during the luteal phase. As should be expected, women who use hormonal contraceptives do not experience the preferences characteristic of estrus midcycle. As a result, hormonal contraceptive may change the dynamics of relationships in a host of ways. This possibility is ripe for detailed empirical investigation (e.g., Alvergne & Lummaa, 2010).

THE UTILITY OF AN EVOLUTIONARY PERSPECTIVE IN UNDERSTANDING THESE PHENOMENA

I now return to the general points laid out in the first half of this chapter. I argued for two primary claims: first, that evolutionary biology does not constitute or offer a metatheory for relationship science or psychology, and second, that evolutionary biology nonetheless offers useful methodology that can help relationship scientists discover phenomena within relationship science and psychology. The latter half of this chapter was intended to illustrate these points.

The language of evolutionary biology is not necessary to explain men's and women's behavior across the cycle in terms of proximate causation. We can and should discuss those causes in psychological terms, with no reference to evolutionary biology and its concepts—selection, adaptation, phylogeny—whatsoever. That is to say, the metatheory of relationship science or psychology is not dictated by evolutionary considerations. This illustrates my first claim.

Evolutionary science nonetheless offers potentially powerful methodology for identifying relationship phenomena by leading researchers to ask interesting, probing questions that explore the landscape of relationship phenomena. Indeed, evolution-mindedness may lead researchers to explore regions of that landscape that they would simply never otherwise think to explore. Though relationship scientists may stumble on certain kinds of findings I presented concerning changes in women's preferences across the cycle or their implications for relationship dynamics in absence of an evolutionary perspective, certain findings here are extremely unlikely to have been discovered in the absence of specific evolutionary reasoning.

REFERENCES

Alexander, R. D., & Noonan, K. M. (1979). Concealment of ovulation, parental care, and human social evolution. In N. A. Chagnon & W. G. Irons (Eds.), *Evolutionary biology and human social behavior: An anthropological perspective* (pp. 436–453). Scituate, MA: North Duxbury Press.

Alvergne, A., & Lummaa, V. (2010). Does the contraceptive pill alter mate choice in humans? *Trends in Ecology & Evolution, 25,* 171–179. doi:10.1016/j.tree.2009.08.003

American Heritage Stedman's Medical Dictionary. (2002). Boston, MA: Houghton Mifflin.

Berscheid, E. (1999). The greening of relationship science. *American Psychologist, 54,* 260–266. doi:10.1037/0003-066X.54.4.260

Brewis, A., & Meyer, M. (2005). Demographic evidence that human ovulation is undetectable (at least in pair bonds). *Current Anthropology, 46,* 465–471. doi:10.1086/430016

Buss, D. M. (1995). Evolutionary psychology: A new paradigm for psychological science. *Psychological Inquiry, 6,* 1–30. doi:10.1207/s15327965pli0601_1

Buss, D. M. (2005). *The handbook of evolutionary psychology.* New York, NY: Wiley.

Buss, D. M. (Ed.). (2007). *Evolutionary psychology: The new science of the mind.* New York, NY: Allyn & Bacon.

Byers, J. A., Moodie, J. D., & Hall, N. (1994). Pronghorn females choose vigorous mates. *Animal Behaviour, 47,* 33–43. doi:10.1006/anbe.1994.1005

Charlton, B. D., Reby, D., & McComb, K. (2007). Female red deer prefer the roars of larger males. *Biology Letters, 3,* 382–385. doi:10.1098/rsbl.2007.0244

Crawford, C., & Krebs, D. (Eds.). (2008). *Foundations of evolutionary psychology.* London, England: Psychology Press.

DeScioli, P., & Kurzban, R. (2009). The alliance hypothesis for human friendship. *PLoS ONE, 4,* e5802. doi:10.1371/journal.pone.0005802

Dunbar, R., & Barrett, L. (Eds.). (2009). *The Oxford handbook of evolutionary psychology.* Oxford, England: University of Oxford Press.

Duntley, J. D., & Buss, D. M. (2008). Evolutionary psychology is a metatheory for psychology. *Psychological Inquiry, 19,* 30–34.

Eastwick, P. W. (2009). Beyond the Pleistocene: Using phylogeny and constraint to inform the evolutionary psychology of human mating. *Psychological Bulletin, 135,* 794–821. doi:10.1037/a0016845

Ellis, B. J., & Bjorklund, D. F. (Eds.). (2005). *Origins of the social mind: Evolutionary psychology and child development.* New York, NY: Guilford Press.

Feinberg, D. R., Jones, B. C., Law Smith, M. J., Moore, F. R., DeBruine, L. M., Cornwell, R. E., . . . Perrett, D. I. (2006). Effects of menstrual cycle and trait estrogen level on masculinity preferences in the human voice. *Hormones and Behavior, 49,* 215–222. doi:10.1016/j.yhbeh.2005.07.004

Fisher, H. S., Swaisgood, R. R., & Fitch-Snyder, H. (2003). Countermarking by male pygmy lorises (*Nycticebus pygmaeus*): Do females use odor cues to select mates with high competitive ability? *Behavioral Ecology and Sociobiology, 53,* 123–130.

Fraley, R. C., Brumbaugh, C. C., & Marks, M. J. (2005). The evolution and function of adult attachment: A comparative and phylogenetic analysis. *Journal of Personality and Social Psychology, 89,* 731–746. doi:10.1037/0022-3514.89.5.751

Gangestad, S. W., Garver-Apgar, C. E., Simpson, J. A., & Cousins, A. J. (2007). Changes in women's mate preferences across the ovulatory cycle. *Journal of Personality and Social Psychology, 92,* 151–163. doi:10.1037/0022-3514.92.1.151

Gangestad, S. W., & Simpson, J. A. (Eds.). (2007). *The evolution of mind: Fundamental issues and controversies.* New York, NY: Guilford Press.

Gangestad, S. W., Simpson, J. A., Cousins, A. J., Garver-Apgar, C. E., & Christensen, P. N. (2004). Women's preferences for male behavioral displays shift across the menstrual cycle. *Psychological Science, 15,* 203–207. doi:10.1111/j.0956-7976.2004.01503010.x

Gangestad, S. W., & Thornhill, R. (1998). Menstrual cycle variation in women's preference for the scent of symmetrical men. *Proceedings of the Royal Society B: Biological Sciences, 265,* 927–933. doi:10.1098/rspb.1998.0380

Gangestad, S. W., & Thornhill, R. (2008). Human oestrus. *Proceedings of the Royal Society B: Biological Sciences, 275,* 991–1000. doi:10.1098/rspb.2007.1425

Gangestad, S. W., Thornhill, R., & Garver, C. E. (2002). Changes in women's sexual interests and their partners' mate retention tactics across the menstrual cycle: Evidence for shifting conflicts of interest. *Proceedings of the Royal Society B: Biological Sciences, 269,* 975–982. doi:10.1098/rspb.2001.1952

Gangestad, S. W., Thornhill, R., & Garver-Apgar, C. E. (2005). Women's sexual interests across the ovulatory cycle depend on primary partner fluctuating asymmetry. *Proceedings of the Royal Society B: Biological Sciences, 272,* 2023–2027. doi:10.1098/rspb.2005.3112

Gangestad, S. W., Thornhill, R., & Garver-Apgar, C. E. (2010a). Fertility in the cycle predicts women's interest in sexual opportunism. *Evolution and Human Behavior, 31,* 400–411.

Gangestad, S. W., Thornhill, R., & Garver-Apgar, C. E. (2010b). Men's facial masculinity predicts changes in their female partners' sexual interests across the ovulatory cycle, whereas men's intelligence does not. *Evolution and Human Behavior, 31,* 412–424.

Garver-Apgar, C. E., Gangestad, S. W., & Thornhill, R. (2008). Hormonal correlates of women's mid-cycle preference for the scent of symmetry. *Evolution and
Human Behavior, 29,* 223–232.

Garver-Apgar, C. E., Gangestad, S. W., Thornhill, R., Miller, R. D., & Olp, J. (2006).
MHC alleles, sexually responsivity, and unfaithfulness in romantic couples. *Psychological Science, 17,* 830–835. doi:10.1111/j.1467-9280.2006.01789.x

Gosling, S. D., & Graybeal, A. (2007). Tree thinking: A new paradigm for integrating
comparative data in psychology. *The Journal of General Psychology, 134,* 259–277.
doi:10.3200/GENP.134.2.259-278

Haselton, M. G., & Gangestad, S. W. (2006). Conditional expression of women's
desires and male mate retention efforts across the ovulatory cycle. *Hormones and
Behavior, 49,* 509–518. doi:10.1016/j.yhbeh.2005.10.006

Haselton, M., & Miller, G. F. (2006). Women's fertility across the cycle increases the
short-term attractiveness of creative intelligence compared to wealth. *Human
Nature, 17,* 50–73. doi:10.1007/s12110-006-1020-0

Havlicek, J., Dvorakova, R., Bartos, L., & Flegr, J. (2006). Non-advertized does not
mean concealed: Body odour change across the human menstrual cycle. *Ethology,
112,* 81–90. doi:10.1111/j.1439-0310.2006.01125.x

Havlicek, J., Roberts, S. C., & Flegr, J. (2005). Women's preference for dominant
male odour: Effects of menstrual cycle and relationship status. *Biology Letters, 1,*
256–259. doi:10.1098/rsbl.2005.0332

Hohoff, C., Franzin, K., & Sachser, N. (2003). Female choice in a promiscuous wild
guinea pig, the yellow-toothed cavy (*Galea musteloides*). *Behavioral Ecology and
Sociobiology, 53,* 341–349.

Johnston, V. S., Hagel, R., Franklin, M., Fink, B., & Grammer, K. (2001). Male facial
attractiveness: Evidence for hormone-mediated adaptive design. *Evolution and
Human Behavior, 22,* 251–267. doi:10.1016/S1090-5138(01)00066-6

Kaplan, H., Hill, K., Lancaster, J. B., & Hurtado, A. M. (2000). A theory of human life
history evolution: Diet, intelligence, and longevity. *Evolutionary Anthropology, 9,*
156–185. doi:10.1002/1520-6505(2000)9:4<156::AID-EVAN5>3.0.CO;2-7

Knott, C. E., Emery Thompson, M., Stumpf, R. M., & McIntyre, M. H. (2010).
Female reproductive strategies in female orangutans: Evidence for female choice
and counter strategies to infanticide in a species with frequent sexual coercion.
Proceedings of the Royal Society, 277, 105–113.

Lieberman, D., Tooby, J., & Cosmides, L. (2007, February 15). The architecture of
human kin detection. *Nature, 445,* 727–731. doi:10.1038/nature05510

Little, A. C., Jones, B. C., & Burriss, R. P. (2007). Preferences for masculinity in male
bodies change across the menstrual cycle. *Hormones and Behavior, 51,* 633–639.
doi:10.1016/j.yhbeh.2007.03.006

Little, A. C., Jones, B. C., & DeBruine, L. M. (2008). Preferences for variation in masculinity in real male faces change across the menstrual cycle: Women prefer more
masculine faces when they are fertile. *Personality and Individual Differences, 45,*
478–482. doi:10.1016/j.paid.2008.05.024

Luque-Larena, J. J., López, P., & Gosálbez, J. (2003). Male dominance and female chemosensory preferences in the rock-dwelling snow vole. *Behaviour, 140,* 665–681. doi:10.1163/156853903322149496

Marlowe, F. W. (2003). A critical period for provisioning by Hadza men: Implications for pair bonding. *Evolution and Human Behavior, 24,* 217–229. doi:10.1016/S1090-5138(03)00014-X

Miller, G. F., Tybur, J., & Jordan, B. (2007). Ovulatory cycle effects on tip earnings by lap dancers: Economic evidence for human estrus? *Evolution and Human Behavior, 28,* 375–381. doi:10.1016/j.evolhumbehav.2007.06.002

Miller, S. L., & Maner, J. K. (2010). The scent of a woman: Men's testosterone responses to olfactory ovulation cues. *Psychological Science, 21,* 276–283. doi:10.1177/0956797609357733

Muller, M. N., & Wrangham, R. W. (Eds.). (2009). *Sexual coercion in primates and humans: An evolutionary perspective on male aggression against females.* Cambridge, MA: Harvard University Press.

Nelson, R. J. (2000). *An introduction to behavioral endocrinology* (2nd ed.). Sunderland, MA: Sinauer Associates.

Overton, W. F. (1998). *Metatheory and methodology in developmental psychology.* Retrieved from http://astro.ocis.temple.edu/~overton/metatheory.html

Pawlowski, B., & Jasienska, G. (2005). Women's preferences for sexual dimorphism in height depend on menstrual cycle phase and expected duration of relationship. *Biological Psychology, 70,* 38–43. doi:10.1016/j.biopsycho.2005.02.002

Penton-Voak, I. S., & Perrett, D. I. (2000). Female preference for male faces changes cyclically: Further evidence. *Evolution and Human Behavior, 21,* 39–48. doi:10.1016/S1090-5138(99)00033-1

Penton-Voak, I. S., Perrett, D. I., Castles, D. L., Kobayashi, T., Burt, D. M., Murray, L. K., & Minamisawa, R. (1999, June 24). Female preference for male faces changes cyclically. *Nature, 399,* 741–742. doi:10.1038/21557

Peters, M., Simmons, L. W., & Rhodes, G. (2009). Preferences across the menstrual cycle for masculinity and symmetry in photographs of male faces and bodies. *PLoS ONE, 4,* e4138. doi:10.1371/journal.pone.0004138

Pillsworth, E. G., & Haselton, M. G. (2006). Male sexual attractiveness predicts differential ovulatory shifts in female extra-pair attraction and male mate retention. *Evolution and Human Behavior, 27,* 247–258. doi:10.1016/j.evolhumbehav.2005.10.002

Potts, W. K., Manning, C. J., & Wakeland, E. K. (1991). Mating patterns in semi-natural populations of mice influenced by MHC genotype. *Nature, 352,* 619–621. doi:10.1038/352619a0

Prokosch, M. D., Coss, R. G., Scheib, J. E., & Blosiz, S. A. (2008). Intelligence and mate choice: Intelligent men are always appealing. *Evolution and Human Behavior, 30,* 11–20. doi:10.1016/j.evolhumbehav.2008.07.004

Puts, D. A. (2005). Mating context and menstrual phase affect women's preferences for male voice pitch. *Evolution and Human Behavior, 26*, 388–397. doi:10.1016/j.evolhumbehav.2005.03.001

Puts, D. A. (2006). Cyclic variation in women's preferences for masculine traits: Potential hormonal causes. *Human Nature, 17*, 114–127. doi:10.1007/s12110-006-1023-x

Reichenbach, H. (1938). *Experience and prediction*. Chicago, IL: University of Chicago Press. doi:10.1037/11656-000

Rikowski, A., & Grammer, K. (1999). Human body odour, symmetry and attractiveness. *Proceedings of the Royal Society of London B, 266*, 869–874.

Roney, J. R., & Simmons, Z. L. (2008). Women's estradiol predicts preference for facial cues of men's testosterone. *Hormones and Behavior, 53*, 14–19.

Salmon, C., & Shackelford, T. K. (Eds.) (2007). *Family relationships: An evolutionary perspective*. New York, NY: Oxford University Press.

Scarbrough, P. S., & Johnston, V. S. (2005). Individual differences in women's facial preferences as a function of digit ratio and mental rotation ability. *Evolution and Human Behavior, 26*, 509–526. doi:10.1016/j.evolhumbehav.2005.03.002

Schulte, B. A., & Rasmussen, L. E. L. (1999). Signal receiver interplay in the communication of male condition by Asian elephants. *Animal Behaviour, 57*, 1265–1274. doi:10.1006/anbe.1999.1092

Singh, D., & Bronstad, P. M. (2001). Female body odour is a potential cue to ovulation. *Proceedings of the Royal Society of London B: Biological Sciences, 268*, 797–801.

Stumpf, R. M., & Boesch, C. (2005). Does promiscuous mating preclude female choice? Female sexual strategies in chimpanzees (*Pan troglodytes verus*) of the Tai National Park, Cote d'Ivoire. *Behavioral Ecology and Sociobiology, 57*, 511–524).

Symons, D. (1979). *The evolution of human sexuality*. New York, NY: Oxford University Press.

Thornhill, R. (1997). The concept of an evolved adaptation. In M. Daly (Ed.), *Characterizing human psychological adaptations* (pp. 4–13). New York, NY: Wiley.

Thornhill, R. (2007). The importance of developmental biology to evolutionary biology and vice versa. In S. W. Gangestad & J. A. Simpson (Eds.), *The evolution of mind: Fundamental questions and controversies* (pp. 203–209). New York, NY: Guilford Press.

Thornhill, R., & Gangestad, S. W. (1999). The scent of symmetry: A human sex pheromone that signals fitness? *Evolution and Human Behavior, 20*, 175–201. doi:10.1016/S1090-5138(99)00005-7

Thornhill, R., & Gangestad, S. W. (2008). *The evolutionary biology of human female sexuality*. New York, NY: Oxford University Press.

Thornhill, R., Gangestad, S. W., Miller, R., Scheyd, G., Knight, J., & Franklin, M. (2003). MHC, symmetry, and body scent attractiveness in men and women. *Behavioral Ecology, 14*, 668–678. doi:10.1093/beheco/arg043

Thornton, J. W. (2001). Evolution of vertebrate steroid receptors from an ancestral estrogen receptor by ligand exploitation and serial genome expansions. *Proceedings of the National Academy of Sciences, USA, 98,* 5671–5676. doi:10.1073/pnas.091553298

Thornton, J. W., Need, E., & Crews, D. (2003, September 19). Resurrecting the ancestral steroid receptor: Ancient origin of estrogen signaling. *Science, 301,* 1714–1717. doi:10.1126/science.1086185

Tinbergen, N. (1963). On aims and methods in ethology. *Zeitschrift für Tierpsychologie, 20,* 410–433. doi:10.1111/j.1439-0310.1963.tb01161.x

Tooby, J., & Cosmides, L. (1996). Friendship and the banker's paradox: Other pathways to the evolution of adaptations for altruism. *Proceedings of the British Academy, 88,* 119–143.

Waitt, C., Gerald, M. S., Little, A. C., & Kraiselburd, E. (2006). Selective attention toward female secondary sexual color in male rhesus monkeys. *American Journal of Primatology, 68,* 738–744. doi:10.1002/ajp.20264

Welling, L. L. M., Jones, B. C., DeBruine, L. M., Conway, C. A., Law Smith, M. J., Little, A. C., . . . Al-Dujaili, E. A. S. (2007). Raised salivary testosterone in women is associated with increased attraction to masculine faces. *Hormones and Behavior, 52,* 156–161. doi:10.1016/j.yhbeh.2007.01.010

Williams, G. C. (1966). *Adaptation and natural selection.* Princeton, NJ: Princeton University Press.

Williams, G. C. (1992). *Natural selection: Domains, levels and challenges.* New York, NY: Oxford University Press.

Williams, J. R., & Lenington, S. (1993). Factors modulating preferences of female house mice for males differing in T-complex genotype: Role of T-complex genotype, genetic background, and estrous condition of females. *Behavior Genetics, 23,* 51–58. doi:10.1007/BF01067553

Wolff, J. O. (1998). Breeding strategies, mate choice, and reproductive success in American bison. *Oikos, 83,* 529–544. doi:10.2307/3546680

10

EXAMINING DIVORCE CONSEQUENCES AND POLICIES AND THE QUESTION: IS MARRIAGE MORE THAN A PIECE OF PAPER?

ROBERT E. EMERY, HYUN JOO SHIM, AND ERIN HORN

Intimate relationships are always tricky, and they have become a lot more complicated in the past 50 years. In 1959, the median age at first marriage in the United States was 20.2 for women and 22.5 for men (U.S. Census Bureau, 2009). College students ideally got "pinned" and then engaged while in school, with a wedding shortly after graduation. Young people had sex, but an "out of wedlock" pregnancy was routinely followed by a "shotgun wedding." Non-marital childbearing, cohabitation, and divorce all existed but were rare exceptions to the rule of an expectation of life-long marriage.

By 2009, the median age at first marriage had risen to 25.9 for women and 28.1 for men (U.S. Census Bureau, 2009). Young people continued to have sex, sometimes "hooking up" casually without romantic involvement. Rates of teen childbearing were lower than in 1959, largely because of better birth control and legal abortion. But with later age at first marriage and shotgun weddings an anachronism, almost 40% of children in the United States were born outside of marriage in 2007 (data for 2009 are not yet available) versus about 5% in 1959 (Ventura, 2009). Over half of young people cohabited prior to or as an alternative to marriage in 2009 (Cherlin, 2009), whereas cohabitation was so rare in 1959 that no one thought to track it. Finally, in 2008 (data for 2009 are not yet available) there were 3.5 divorces per 1,000 population, compared with 2.2 in 1959 (Emery, 1999; Tejada-Vera & Sutton, 2009; see also Chapter 8, this volume).

Dramatic changes in family life are not limited to the United States but have occurred throughout the industrialized world. Global changes are important to recognize for many reasons. One is that they cause us to question some explanations of family change—for example, a decline in family values. Family values have changed in the United States (Cherlin, 2009), and new attitudes surely must contribute to divorce and family upheavals. Yet, a loss of family values cannot explain the skyrocketing rates of divorce in South Korea in the last decade, because by Western standards family values remain incredibly strong and traditional in South Korea. A global perspective also calls attention to innovative and sometimes controversial family policies. For example, in New Zealand, where cohabitation has become the norm, a new version of common law marriage binds cohabiting couples together in essentially the same contract as traditional marriage (Lind, 2008).

Our primary focuses in this chapter are the broad consequences of divorce for adults and children and the policies designed to ameliorate adverse psychological, social, and economic outcomes. Our more unique, secondary focus is examining divorce to get insight into marriage. Research on divorce has suggested that young people are wrong when they say, "Marriage is just a piece of paper." Through the lens of divorce, we can see that marriage is much more.

INTERNATIONAL TRENDS IN MARRIAGE AND DIVORCE

To get a picture of changes in families around the world, we compared crude marriage and divorce rates over the past 4 decades across six countries.[1] Figure 10.1 shows changes in marriage rates from 1963 to 2007. Marriages rates gradually declined in all six countries over this time period, despite a variety of short-term fluctuations. The most noticeable declines are observed in Japan (10.0 in 1964 and 5.7 in 2007) and in Italy (8.2 in 1963 and 4.2 in 2007). The patterns for the United Kingdom and Australia are strikingly similar, showing a rise in the 1960s followed by a progressive decline. In Sweden, a sharp downturn in marriage was observed from the middle 1960s to the middle 1970s, with a record low of 3.6 in 1998. In general, marriage rates are lower in Sweden than the other five countries because of high rates of Swedish cohabitation. Finally, in South Korea, marriage rates have been consistently high in comparison with those in the other five countries. However, there was a recent sharp decline from a record high of 9.5 in 1996 to a record low of 6.3 in 2003.

---

[1]Crude marriage and divorce rates each track the annual number of marriages/divorces per 1,000 population (United Nations, 2007).

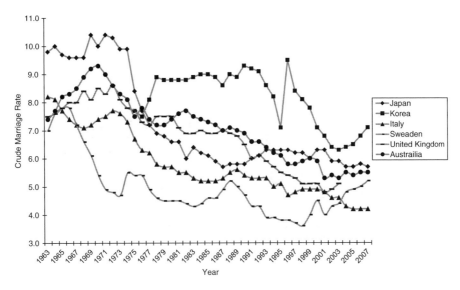

Figure 10.1. Crude marriage rates in six countries over 4 decades. Data from United Nations (2007).

Figure 10.2 shows crude divorce rates from 1963 to 2007 for the same six countries. Divorce rates rose substantially for all countries, with the relatively gradual increase in Italy standing out as an exception.[2] Different countries show sharp temporary increases in divorce attributable to important social events, such as the passage of no-fault divorce law in Australia in 1975 and the economic crisis in South Korea in 1998. Still, the international trend reveals an overall increase in divorce across our diverse sample of countries.

Taken as a whole, a clear pattern is discernable across these (and other) industrialized countries. Divorce is on the rise internationally, whereas marriage is on the decline. At the individual level, there are a great many reasons to delay marriage or get divorced, but we also need to consider the big picture. The overall decline in marriage and increase in divorce are at least partially due to industrialization and its weakening of family ties (e.g., increased mobility), altering of gender roles (e.g., increased employment among women), and consequent changes in social attitudes (e.g., greater acceptance of alternatives to life-long marriage) and legal norms (e.g., policies supporting single parents, no-fault divorce). Industrialization produces many benefits including economic growth and greater individual and family

---

[2]We suspect that rates of marital separation, without legal divorce, are considerably higher in Italy. Divorce was illegal in Italy until the 1970s, and today a 3-year separation is required for divorce on the grounds of living apart.

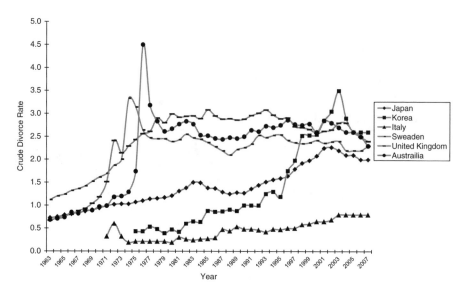

Figure 10.2 Crude divorce rates of six countries over 4 decades. Data from United Nations (2007).

autonomy. At the margin, divorce is one cost. Still, as readers will see, there is considerable individual variation between, and within, families in the costs or potential benefits of divorce.

CHILDREN: PSYCHOLOGICAL CONSEQUENCES AND SOCIAL POLICIES

The extent to which children are affected by their parents' divorce has been a topic of considerable debate, with some concluding that the effects are devastating and long enduring (Wallerstein, Lewis, & Blakeslee, 2000) and others pointing to minimal increases in psychological problems (Allison & Furstenberg, 1989). For reasons we have addressed in detail elsewhere, we conclude that both sides of this debate are right—and wrong (Emery, 1999, 2004; Laumann-Billings & Emery, 2000). The magnitude of the effects depends on what consequences are emphasized.

Psychological Consequences of Divorce for Children

Overall, research has indicated that (a) divorce is almost always stressful for children, particularly in the short term; (b) divorce increases the risk for psychological problems for a minority of children; (c) the majority of children from divorced families are resilient, not "at risk"; (d) even resilient young people commonly report painful memories and ongoing worries about their parents' divorce; and (e) how parents (and the legal system) manage divorce largely determines children's risk or resilience.

Stress

Extensive research documents multiple stressors of divorce for children. First, the transition itself is difficult, as the year or two immediately before and after divorce is a time of emotional and practical upheaval (Hetherington & Kelly, 2002). A second major stressor is exposure to and involvement in parental conflict, as many distraught, divorcing parents fight about, around, and through their children (Emery, 1982, 1994). The stress of conflict also is supported by evidence that divorce is a relief for children when conflict was high during the marriage but a shock for children when conflict was low (Amato & Booth, 1997). Third, divorce leads to diminished parenting quality, at least for a period of time, especially for fathers (Buchanan, Maccoby, & Dornbusch, 1996; Hetherington & Kelly, 2002). A fourth stressor is lost contact with one parent, usually the father (Amato, Meyers, & Emery, 2009; Seltzer, 1991). Fifth, the economic challenges of divorce can create many additional stressors for children, including decreased availability of parents because of increased employment, changes in residence and schools, and increased child care or time alone for older children.

Risk, Resilience, and Pain

On average, parental divorce is associated with an increased risk for a variety of psychological problems among children and adolescents. The risk is greatest for externalizing problems but also elevated for internalizing, academic, and interpersonal concerns (Amato, 2001; Amato & Keith, 1991; Emery, 1999; Hetherington & Kelly, 2002; McLanahan & Sandefur, 1994). Still, the majority of children from divorced families have no more psychological problems than do children from married families, implying that most children are resilient in the face of parental divorce (Emery, 1999; Emery & Forehand, 1994). At the same time, the absence of psychological problems is not the same as the absence of psychological pain. Even resilient, well-functioning young people from divorced families are likely to report painful childhood memories, ongoing concerns about family relationships, and worries about future events like graduations and weddings, where both parents will be present (Laumann-Billings & Emery, 2000).

The divorce process determines risk and resilience. How parents and the legal system manage a divorce process determines, in large part, whether the children are at risk or resilient as a result of a parental divorce. Not coincidentally, the keys to a more or less "family friendly" divorce are successfully managing the major stressors reviewed previously. However, not all stressors are equally good predictors of children's outcomes. Listed in order of importance, the strongest correlates of a child's successful adjustment are having (a) a good relationship with at least one parent, (b) minimal or contained parental conflict, (c) economic stability, and (d) a good relationship with the second parent. Although social policies rightly encourage all four factors, this cannot be achieved in all cases, thus the hierarchical ranking (Emery, 1999). For example, policies designed to minimize children's emotional turmoil wisely discourage, in the face of enduring and intense parental conflict, children's frequent contact with both parents, because entrapment in conflict is more detrimental to children psychologically than lost contact with one parent. Of course, there may be other reasons for wanting to promote substantial contact with both parents in high-conflict divorces (e.g., fairness to the parents).

Policies Designed to Protect Children in Divorce

Should parents stay together for their children's sake? On average, children fare better psychologically in happy, married families, and for this reason (and others), we advocate for enduring, happy marriage. We emphasize "happy" because children fare better in a well-functioning, divorced family than in a high-conflict, married one. At the same time, children are better adjusted if parents stay together in unfulfilling, low-conflict marriages than when such marriages end in divorce (Amato & Booth, 1997). Because of the harmful effects of conflict on children, we suggest promoting marriage by improving marriage, not by making divorce more difficult (Emery, 2001).

In fact, most social and legal policies designed to facilitate children's adjustment have the goal of making divorce less disruptive; we focus on the following three: (a) less adversarial dispute resolution, (b) laws and policies designed to maintain children's relationships with both parents, and (c) educational and therapeutic interventions to assist divorced families and their children.

Making Dispute Resolution Less Adversarial

Divorce and custody disputes form the largest single category of legal action in the United States today (Schepard, 2004), and the process of settling these disputes in the adversary system creates problems for courts, parents, and children.[3] Courts are overburdened with contentious cases. Parents may become embroiled in expensive, threatening, and often personally devastating contro-

---

[3]The adversary legal system in the United States embraces a fundamental theory of procedure: Litigants are adversaries and their attorneys must "zealously represent" the interests of their own client and only their client.

versies in negotiations and perhaps in the open courtroom. And children find themselves in the middle of escalating parental conflict, which is clearly counter to their interests, even though promoting children's best interests is the overriding goal of the law (Emery & Wyer, 1987).

A great many judges, lawyers, mental health professionals, and divorced adults are well aware of the harms caused by overly adversarial divorce, particularly to children. As such, a major goal of policy in recent decades has been to make the legal system less adversarial, particularly by promoting alternative forms of dispute resolution (ADR; Emery, 1994; Schepard, 2004).

The investment in ADR is evident in the range of dispute resolution alternatives that have been invented in recent decades. Innovations include collaborative law, in which specially trained lawyers agree to negotiate in good faith and with full disclosure of information by both sides. Most critically, collaborative lawyers and their clients sign a contract indicating that the lawyers will no longer represent the parties if they fail to reach a settlement outside of court (Tesler & Thompson, 2007). Parenting coordinators are usually mental health experts who engage in a mediation–arbitration procedure, typically in an effort to keep high-conflict couples from constantly relitigating cases. A parenting coordinator helps parents negotiate disputes about custody-related matters, such as an impending holiday schedule, but if the parents fail to agree, the parenting coordinator has quasi-judicial authority and can impose a decision—the process shifts from mediation to arbitration (Coates et al., 2004). Yet another new form of divorce ADR is early neutral evaluation, an innovative twist on more traditional custody evaluations (an assessment of children and parents that often includes a recommendation about a preferred custody arrangement). In early neutral evaluation, an experienced evaluator completes a relatively brief and confidential evaluation that leads to a nonbinding recommendation that is shared with the parents, all done with the intent of encouraging a settlement, which it often does (Santeramo, 2004).

Mediation is the oldest, best-established, and most carefully studied form of ADR in divorce and custody disputes. A mediator is a neutral third party, often a mental health professional or a lawyer, who meets with parents to help them negotiate their own settlement to their parenting and perhaps financial disputes. Evidence has indicated that mediators typically settle half to three quarters of cases otherwise destined for court, and parties report higher satisfaction with the process in comparison with traditional adversary settlement (Emery, Sbarra, & Grover, 2005). Most important, a 12-year longitudinal randomized trial of mediation and litigation found that mediation caused dramatic increases in children's contact with both parents, led to improved parenting quality, and decreased parent conflict (Emery et al., 2001; Sbarra & Emery, 2008).

Increasing Children's Contact With Both Parents

Mediation increases children's contact with both parents by short-circuiting adversary procedures and the parting parents' own anger, grief, hurt, and pain (Emery, in press). A vexing problem for the legal system, parents, and professionals is what to do when parents fail to reach an agreement on their own, in ADR, or through traditional attorney negotiations. Some advocate joint physical custody in such cases (Kruk, 2005); others believe that joint physical custody is a good arrangement for children in many circumstances but not when parents are high conflict (Buchanan et al., 1996; Emery, Otto, & O'Donohue, 2005). One operational definition of high conflict is litigating custody, which only a minority (10% or less) of divorcing parents do (Maccoby & Mnookin, 1992).

Joint custody is associated with improved adjustment among children, according to one meta-analysis (Bauserman, 2002), but (a) cooperative parents self-select into joint custody, (b) joint legal custody (legal authority but not increased contact) was as strongly linked to children's adjustment as joint physical custody (shared parenting) in this meta-analysis, (c) the observed effect sizes were small in any case, (d) most studies (22 of 33) in the meta-analysis were unpublished dissertations, and (e) no interaction was found with level of conflict, contrary to some of the best research of joint physical custody (Buchanan et al., 1996; Johnston, Kline, & Tschann, 1989). Moreover, research evidence on the harm caused by parental conflict is clear (Cummings & Davies, 2010; Emery, 1982), but research has indicated that increased contact with both parents is only weakly associated with improved adjustment among children (Amato & Gilbreth, 1999). At this time, no U.S. state has a statute clearly indicating a preference for joint physical custody in contested cases, although several states have considered such a law. National experiments with such laws currently are under way in Australia and Belgium, although the new laws were passed in response to "fathers' rights" concerns, not evidence on what benefits children.

Educational and Therapeutic Interventions

In addition to changing the substance and procedure of the law, various efforts have been made to promote the well-being of children in divorce through education, prevention, and therapy. Mandatory divorce education classes for parents are probably the most widespread of these efforts; however, the programs typically are quite brief, and evidence supporting their effectiveness is limited (Emery, Kitzmann, & Waldron, 1999). School-based groups run for children from divorced families include a variety of innovative psycho-educational activities and are supported by sound empirical research (Pedro-Carroll & Alpert-Gillis, 1997). Similarly, parent support and education groups also fall into the category of evidence-based practice (DeGarmo & Forgatch, 2005; Wolchik et al., 1993). Unfortunately, these latter two interventions can be expensive and more difficult to disseminate because they involve new procedures rather than replacing existing ones, as is the case of ADR.

Easing Divorce for Children: Shared Goals With Parenting in Marriage

We conclude our overview of the consequences of divorce for children, and efforts to ameliorate them, with an observation: Policy in divorce focuses on encouraging parents to take the long view, to control their own understandable anger and pain to recognize that they are tied together throughout their life by their children, and to work together as coparents. In so doing, divorced parents can not only help their children but also help and support each other. This is a laudable set of goals in divorce. Yet, we cannot help but note that there already is a family policy designed to promote the same goals: marriage. Children can and do thrive in divorced families. Doing so is easier for children, and for parents, in happily married families. We believe it is possible, and beneficial, for policies both to encourage happy marriage and to ease the pain of divorce.

ADULTS: PSYCHOLOGICAL CONSEQUENCES AND SOCIAL POLICIES RELATED TO DIVORCE

Children have been the primary focus of research and policies directed toward the psychological consequences of divorce. Still, there has been a long-standing and recently renewed interest in the effects of divorce on adults, particularly in reaction to recent, vigorous debates in the United States about whether the government should actively promote marriage or accept and support a variety of alternative family forms.

Psychological Consequences of Divorce for Adults

Research consistently shows that adults who are married score higher than those who are not on a long list of indicators of individual well-being, including measures of (a) psychological functioning, such as less depression (Wade & Pevalin, 2004) and substance abuse (Power et al., 1999), and greater happiness/subjective well-being (Gove, Hughes, Style, 1983; Johnson & Wu, 2002); (b) intimate relationship quality, including sexuality (Laumann, Gagnon, Michael, & Michaels, 1994; Pedersen & Blekesaune, 2003) and decreased violence (Waite & Gallagher, 2000); and (c) physical health functioning, including general health (Hughes & Waite, 2009), chronic diseases (Dupre & Meadows, 2007), and longevity (Sbarra & Nietert, 2009; see also Chapter 1, this volume).

The benefits associated with marriage are impressive, but they lead to a number of important questions. What are the benefits of a first marriage versus those of never having been married, of cohabiting, separation or divorce, widowhood, or remarriage? Does marital quality matter? Does individual well-being improve near the time of marriage (or remarriage) and decline near the time of separation, divorce, or widowhood (see Chapter 8)? Are the benefits of marriage or costs of dissolution temporary or enduring? Is it healthier to be married for a longer time (or divorced/single for a shorter time)? Precisely why would we expect marriage to promote individual well-being, particularly improved physical health (see Chapter 4)? Are the benefits of marriage universal, or do they differ according to cultural traditions and societal supports? Is marriage equally beneficial for men and for women? Does marriage cause good outcomes, or are some, most, or all of the purported "outcomes" due to selection into or out of marriage?

We can at least partially answer some of these questions. The largest effect sizes typically are found when comparing married to separated/divorced adults on indices of psychological distress (Blekesaune, 2008; Wade & Pevalin, 2004). Still, getting married, as opposed to remaining single, is associated with some benefits like less depression (Gove et al., 1983) and better sex (Pedersen & Blekesaune, 2003). In addition, when compared with marriage, cohabitation is linked with less commitment and relationship satisfaction (Nock, 1995) and less dissolution distress (Blekesaune, 2008). Moreover, the psychological (Barrett, 2000; Blekesaune, 2008) and health benefits tied to remarriage are short-lived and less positive compared with those associated with first marriage (Hughes & Waite, 2009). Longitudinal evidence has indicated that alcohol use increases (Power et al., 1999) and psychological distress rises (Booth & Amato, 1991; Hope, Rodgers, & Power, 1999) near the time of marital dissolution, but many important psychological changes precede relationship breakups and are relatively short-lived (Blekesaune, 2008). Longitudinal evidence has also indicated, however, that the lower subjective well-being reported by divorced versus married adults remains even years after the crisis is resolved (Johnson & Wu, 2002; Lucas, 2005). The duration of single status also is linked to an increased risk for more perceived health problems (Hughes & Waite, 2009), chronic illnesses (among men; Dupre & Meadows, 2007), and earlier mortality (Dupre, Beck, & Meadows, 2009). Finally, although some researchers have found that marital status is more strongly linked to men's well-being and marital quality is more strongly linked to women's well-being, both factors are linked to improved well-being among both men and women (Waite & Gallagher, 2000). One analysis suggested that the magnitude of the benefits actually are functionally equivalent for men and women but are observed according to gender-typed expressions of emotional distress, less depression for women and less alcohol use for men (Simon, 2002).

Whether marital status or marital quality causes these various outcomes remains an unanswered question, one that we plan to address using twin studies, which offer the best available method of controlling for nonrandom selection into different experiences, including marriage. We have been involved in several twin studies of consequences of divorce for children, and this research suggested that although selection is important in some ways, many of the outcomes of divorce appear to be true consequences (D'Onofrio et al., 2005, 2006, 2007).

Policies Designed to Protect Adults in Divorce

Few legal or social policy initiatives have been directed at protecting adults from the psychological consequences of divorce. True, efforts to protect children also may benefit adults (e.g., less adversarial legal procedures and parenting support programs), but doing so has not been a primary objective of these efforts. Instead, policy directed toward adults has focused on marriage promotion.

The extent to which marriage promotion policies are effective is an open question. Policies currently in place have been fairly ineffective in increasing marriage rates, particularly among lower income couples (Graefe & Lichter, 2008; McLanahan, 2003; see also Chapter 1, this volume). On the other hand, premarital education may benefit marrying couples. Participation in programs such as the Prevention and Relationship Enhancement Program (Markman, Floyd, Stanley, & Lewis, 1986) is associated with reduced odds of divorcing (Stanley, Amato, Johnson, & Markman, 2006). It is important that the prevention effect is robust across race and socioeconomic status (Stanley, Amato, et al., 2006), both of which predict relationship dissolution. Furthermore, meta-analyses of marriage education programs have indicated that, on average, participants are better off than 79% of those who have never participated on a variety of measures of relationship skills and quality (Carroll & Doherty, 2003). Overall, the evidence has suggested that policies can enhance marriage, perhaps in part by discouraging mismatched couples from marrying, but policy to date is failing to get more couples to marry.

ECONOMIC CONSEQUENCES OF DIVORCE

Divorce also has important economic consequences for children and adults that sometimes are overlooked by psychologists but are of great concern to policy makers and divorced families. In fact, the large number of single mothers who receive welfare has motivated a variety of legal and policy efforts, including welfare reform, stringent child support enforcement, and marriage promotion.

There is a basic reason why divorce leads to economic difficulties: It is cheaper to live in one household than two. Lost economies of scale and their consequences for living standards differ by income level (with only the very wealthy being unaffected), but the effects can be substantial, particularly for lower income families. To illustrate this, consider that, in 2008, the official U.S. poverty threshold was $21,834 for a family of four. For a family of three, the equivalent threshold was $17,346; for a single-person household, it was $11,201. Thus, if a family of four living at the poverty level divorced, they needed over 30% more money ([$17,346 + $11,201] / $21,834) to maintain the same standard of living.

Empirical evidence has shown that the inevitable decline in living standards is not shared equally by men and women. In the United States, women's living standards fall by an average of 27% following divorce, whereas men's living standards actually increase by 10% (Peterson, 1996). Very similar patterns are found across European countries, although different welfare policies partially cushion the impact (Jansen, Mortelmans, & Snoeckx, 2009; Uunk, 2004).

Welfare clearly ameliorates some of the economic consequences of divorce, but welfare policies have been called into question because of their expense and rising numbers of recipients, among other political reasons. There are limits to welfare as a policy solution for these reasons and because of the fundamental problem of economies of scale. It is no coincidence that the first finding of the Personal Responsibility and Work Opportunity Reconciliation Act of 1996, the major welfare reform act in the United States, was "(1) Marriage is the foundation of a successful society." This philosophical assertion precedes a litany of statistics on increases in single parenting and surging welfare rolls.

The limited ability of state support to cushion the economic consequences of divorce leaves adults with two choices: (re)employment or repartnering. Both strategies can help substantially, but for women, repartnering (remarriage or cohabitation) clearly is more efficient. Women who repartner reach predivorce living standards within 2 years following a separation; those who do not repartner require 10.6 to 13.4 years. Men also benefit from repartnering, but the benefits are significantly lower than for women, and men who do not repartner require less than half the time to attain preseparation living standards (4.4 to 6.3 years; Jansen et al., 2009).

COHABITATION: WHY AREN'T MORE PEOPLE GETTING MARRIED?

Enduring, happy marriage is one solution to the adverse psychological and economic consequences of divorce for children and adults. Yet, even as we have outlined many benefits accruing from happy marriage, we are aware of a paradox. If marriage is such a good deal, why aren't more people buying it? From a perspective of self-interest, young people should be flocking to marriage where they would find themselves happier, healthier, and sexier and would have better adjusted children and higher living standards. As we showed at the beginning of the chapter, however, young people are doing the opposite. Why? There must be hidden costs associated with marriage, including opportunity costs (e.g., the possibility of finding a better mate, sexual variety) and, we think, the costs associated with divorce risk. Instead of marrying, in fact, young people are cohabitating.

Today, nearly half of all individuals in the United States under the age of 44 have cohabited outside of marriage, and over half of all first marriages are preceded by cohabitation (Bumpass & Lu, 2001). It varies by both culture and individual whether young people view cohabitation as a prelude or an alternative to marriage (Guzzo, 2009; Kiernan, 2002; Manning, Longmore, & Giordano, 2007; Seltzer, 2004), but the message everywhere is the same: Cohabitation is here to stay.

Who Cohabits and Why?

Not surprisingly, younger adults are more likely to cohabit than are older adults (Seltzer, 2004). So too are individuals of lower socioeconomic status, those with lower educational attainment (Bumpass & Lu, 2001), nonmarital childbearers (Manning & Landale, 1996), and individuals who attend religious services less frequently (Thornton, Axinn, & Hill, 1992). In addition, and perhaps critically, those who experienced parental divorce or separation (Thornton, 1991) or their own divorce (Bumpass & Sweet, 1989) are also more likely to be more accepting of cohabitation, as well as to engage in the practice itself.

An analysis of who cohabits, however, does not reveal why people cohabit. Researchers have identified many reasons for cohabitation, ranging from economic convenience and spending more time together to sexual benefits without the commitment of marriage and "trying out" marriage (Rhoades, Stanley, & Markman, 2009a).

Avoiding Divorce?

We believe that a desire to avoid divorce is one overarching reason why people cohabit in the United States today. Cohabitors can avoid divorce by avoiding marriage, by delaying it, or by trying to find the right partner by sniffing out the wrong one(s) (notwithstanding evidence that cohabitation predicts increased divorce risk, discussed next). In support of this reasoning, we note that individuals whose parents divorced before the age of 15 are more likely to cohabit than their counterparts from intact families, especially if their parents cohabited following divorce (Sassler, Cunningham, & Lichter, 2009). Furthermore, many young adults from divorced families report apprehension about the potential for their own divorce despite their hope for a long-lasting marriage (Wallerstein, 1985); they are more ambivalent about intimate relationships than are young people from intact families (Jacquet & Surra, 2001), and they indicate less desire for long-term relationships (Gabardi & Rosen, 1993).

Parental divorce is one predictor of cohabitation; so is experiencing your own divorce. Among cohabiting households, a majority have at least one member who was married previously (U.S. Census Bureau, 1998). Previously married cohabiters, especially the middle-aged, often view living together as an alternative to marriage, rather than as its precursor (Manning, Longmore, & Giordano, 2007).

Finally, we note that, whether they have experienced divorce personally or not, young people in the United States now know that marriage is no longer for "ever after," happily or not. In fact, we believe that the biggest effects of the divorce revolution have been on the culture as a whole, not solely on children or adults who experienced divorce personally. The logic may sound (and be) twisted, but many people today appear to be avoiding marriage in order to decrease their risk for divorce.

A Transition Into Marriage?

Still, the vast majority of teens expect to marry someday, and most young people in the United States view cohabitation as part of their life trajectory, not as a substitute for marriage (Manning, Longmore, & Giordano, 2007). Although modern cohabiting unions tend to be relatively short-lived (roughly half last less than a year, one sixth last 3 years, and just one in 10 lasts 5 years or longer; Bumpass & Lu, 2001), roughly half of these couples do eventually marry (Bumpass & Sweet, 1989).

Some cohabitors marry to have children within wedlock, others to follow the tradition of marriage (Carmichael & Whittaker, 2007), and still others because it's the next step in their relationship (Stanley, Rhoades, & Markman, 2006). Cohabiting couples who have a child together are likely to marry, whereas those who have a child from a prior relationship are not. People, particularly men, are more likely to marry their current partners if they entered the cohabiting union with the intention to marry, but this is observed only among Whites (Guzzo, 2009). Cohabiting African Americans and Hispanics report more intentions to marry than do Whites, yet they are less likely to realize their marriage plans (Guzzo, 2009; Manning & Smock, 1995).

Finally, we note that aspects of a cohabiting relationship also predict whether the couple will eventually marry. Of particular interest, relationship quality assessed by females affects whether a cohabiting union dissolves, whereas poor relationship quality assessed by males decreases the likelihood of marrying (Brown, 2000). This suggests that female cohabitors may be looking for the "right" marriage partner, whereas male cohabitors marry when they are afraid of losing a desirable mate.

The Cohabitation Paradox

That nearly one in two marriages ends in divorce no doubt weighs heavily in the minds of all young people today, not simply those who have experienced it firsthand. Divorces are messy financially, socially, and emotionally—certainly no one enters a marriage wishing for one. It is understandable for young people to make attempts to avoid such a possibility ahead of time, and these attempts often come in the form of cohabiting—"test driving" the relationship. But using cohabitation to avoid divorce is a paradox. Research has consistently demonstrated a detrimental impact of cohabitation on marriage permanency (e.g., Bumpass & Sweet, 1989; Dush, Cohan, & Amato, 2003; Jose, O'Leary, & Moyer, 2010), and these findings have held when controlling for relationship duration (Teachman & Polonko, 1990) and other selection effects (Woods & Emery, 2002).

Perhaps the trend is shifting. A recent investigation of Australian cohorts found that, for marriages occurring after 1988, cohabitation may serve as a protective factor against marital instability (Hewitt & de Vaus, 2009). A recent meta-analysis reached a similar conclusion: Cohabitation with a future spouse is not associated with a greater risk of marital instability (Jose et al., 2010). Similarly, recent investigations have found a pronounced effect for divorce risk only among those married couples who initiated cohabitation before engagement (Kline et al., 2004; Rhoades, Stanley, & Markman, 2009b).

This implies yet another paradox: The way to avoid the divorce risk associated with cohabitation is to make cohabitation a commitment. Commitment may also explain why cohabitation is more enduring in countries where it is an alternative to marriage than in the United States (Cherlin, 2009). But committed cohabitation, like marriage, is more than a piece of paper, as evidenced by legal movements to register cohabitations or treat cohabitations of some minimal duration as common law marriages (Lind, 2008).

"MOM-AND-POP" FAMILIES OR "WALMART" FAMILIES?

We conclude our broad, if brief, overview of divorce, family change, and social policy with a few, even broader, historical observations. In particular, we call attention to the fact that, over the course of relatively recent history, family functions have become state functions. Prior to the Industrial Revolution, families served multiple functions, including protecting their members; providing them with economic support; educating them; defining a role in the larger community; providing religious training; and offering each other socialization, affection, and recreation (Ogburn, 1953). Since industrialization, the state has assumed more and more of these family functions, leaving socialization, affection, recreation, and religious training as the primary family responsibilities. Indeed, the state even peers over parents' shoulders as they fulfill, or fail to fulfill, today's tasks of loving, socializing, and entertaining children.

To offer a more concrete example, we find ourselves reflecting on the changing views of intergenerational obligations. A common piece of economic advice to today's American parents is: "Save for your retirement first and your children's college education second." The rationale is that your independence in later life really is the best gift you can give your children. Yet, why not advise parents to educate their children so they will prosper and take care of you when you need it? Certainly, in countries like Italy (Cigoli & Scabini, 2006) and South Korea (Miller, 1994), children traditionally have incurred such intergenerational obligations, as indicated, for example, by the extensive coresidence found between adult children and their elderly parents in South Korea (Rindfuss, Choe, Bumpass, & Byun, 2004). Yet, such practices seem like an anachronism as families assume fewer functions and as people become less tied to their families, or their marriages, and more individualistically connected to their workplaces and governments. In South Korea, in fact, not only has divorce skyrocketed, but there has also been a tenfold increase in "early study abroad" students (Kim, 2006)—young people who leave their families prior to college to pursue individual economic and educational opportunities elsewhere.

Or consider a much different perspective and country, Sweden, the paradigm of family policy, a country that provides far more extensive and family friendly policies than the United States (Gauthier, 1996). One historian referred to Swedish family policy as "the triumph of the state over the family" (Carlson, 1990, p. 197) in promoting gender equality, child care, employment opportunities, and economic support.

We do not doubt that compared with policies promoting traditional families, Swedish family policy offers many benefits, or indeed, that there are numerous improvements in quality of life that contribute to and grow out of rapidly evolving family structures and supports throughout the industrialized world today. We also do not doubt that WalMart—an economic product of the Industrial Revolution—offers lower prices than traditional mom-and-pop stores. Yet, we worry that the triumph of the state over the family in Sweden and, to a lesser extent, in other industrialized countries, also comes at a price. WalMart's lower prices carry hidden costs; WalMart puts mom-and-pop stores out of business. Our societal transitions from mom-and-pop families to Wal-

Mart families, which do offer many benefits, also carry such hidden costs. We will not try to detail them here. Rather, we encourage the reader—and young people—to think more deeply and systemically about whether WalMart really is just about lower prices and whether marriage really is just a piece of paper.

REFERENCES

Allison, P. D., & Furstenberg, F. F. (1989). How marital dissolution affects children: Variations by age and sex. *Developmental Psychology, 25*, 540–549. doi:10.1037/0012-1649.25.4.540

Amato, P. R. (2001). Children of divorce in the 1990s: An update of the Amato and Keith (1991) meta-analysis. *Journal of Family Psychology, 15*, 355–370. doi:10.1037/0893-3200.15.3.355

Amato, P. R., & Booth, A. (1997). *A generation at risk: Growing up in an era of family upheaval.* Cambridge, MA: Harvard University Press.

Amato, P. R., & Gilbreth, J. G. (1999). Nonresident fathers and children's well-being: A meta-analysis. *Journal of Marriage and Family, 61*, 557–573. doi:10.2307/353560

Amato, P. R., & Keith, B. (1991). Consequences of parental divorce for children's well-being: A meta-analysis. *Psychological Bulletin, 110*, 26–46. doi:10.1037/0033-2909.110.1.26

Amato, P. R., Meyers, C. E., & Emery, R. E. (2009). Changes in nonresident father-child contact from 1976 to 2002. *Family Relations, 58*, 41–53. doi:10.1111/j.1741-3729.2008.00533.x

Barrett, A. E. (2000). Marital trajectories and mental health. *Journal of Health and Social Behavior, 41*, 451–464. doi:10.2307/2676297

Bauserman, R. (2002). Child adjustment in joint-custody arrangements: A meta-analytic review. *Journal of Family Psychology, 16*, 91–102. doi:10.1037/0893-3200.16.1.91

Blekesaune, M. (2008). Partnership transitions and mental distress: Investigating temporal order. *Journal of Marriage and Family, 70*, 879–890. doi:10.1111/j.1741-3737.2008.00533.x

Booth, A., & Amato, P. R. (1991). Divorce and psychological stress. *Journal of Health and Social Behavior, 32*, 396–407.

Brown, S. L. (2000). Union transitions among cohabitors: The significance of relationship assessments and expectations. *Journal of Marriage and Family, 62*, 833–846. doi:10.1111/j.1741-3737.2000.00833.x

Buchanan, C. M., Maccoby, E. E., & Dornbusch, S. M. (1996). *Adolescents after divorce.* Cambridge, MA: Harvard University Press.

Bumpass, L., & Lu, H. (2001). Trends in cohabitation and implications for children's family contexts in the United States. *Population Studies, 54*, 29–41. doi:10.1080/713779060

Bumpass, L. L., & Sweet, J. A. (1989). National estimates of cohabitation. *Demography, 26*, 615–625. doi:10.2307/2061261

Carlson, A. (1990). *The Swedish experiment in family politics*. New Brunswick, NJ: Transaction.

Carmichael, G. A., & Whittaker, A. (2007). Living together in Australia: Qualitative insights into a complex phenomenon. *Journal of Family Studies, 13*, 202–223. doi:10.5172/jfs.327.13.2.202

Carroll, J. S., & Doherty, W. J. (2003). Evaluating the effectiveness of premarital prevention programs: A meta-analytic review of outcome research. *Family Relations, 52*, 105–118. doi:10.1111/j.1741-3729.2003.00105.x

Cherlin, A. J. (2009). *The marriage go-round: The state of marriage and the family in America today*. New York, NY: Knopf.

Cigoli, V., & Scabini, E. (2006). *The family identity: Ties, symbols and transitions*. Mahwah, NJ: Erlbaum.

Coates, C. A., Deutsch, R., Starnes, H., Sullivan, M. J., & Syldlik, B. (2004). Parenting coordination for high conflict families. *Family Court Review, 42*, 246–262. doi:10.1177/1531244504422006

Cummings, E. M., & Davies, P. T. (2010). *Marital conflict and children: An emotional security perspective*. New York, NY: Guilford Press.

DeGarmo, D. S., & Forgatch, M. S. (2005). Early development of delinquency within divorced families: Evaluating a randomized preventive intervention trial. *Developmental Science, 8*, 229–239. doi:10.1111/j.1467-7687.2005.00412.x

D'Onofrio, B. M., Turkheimer, E., Emery, R. E., Harden, K. P., Slutske, W. S., Heath, A. C., . . . Martin, N. G. (2007). A genetically informed study of the intergenerational transmission of relationship instability. *Journal of Marriage and Family, 69*, 793–809. doi:10.1111/j.1741-3737.2007.00406.x

D'Onofrio, B. M., Turkheimer, E., Emery, R., Slutske, W., Heath, A., Madden, P., & Martin, N. (2005). A genetically informed study of marital instability and its association with offspring psychopathology. *Journal of Abnormal Psychology, 114*, 570–586.

D'Onofrio, B. M., Turkheimer, E., Emery, R., Slutske, W., Heath, A., Madden, P., & Martin, N. (2006). A genetically informed study of the processes underlying the association between parental marital instability and offspring life course patterns. *Developmental Psychology, 42*, 486–499. doi:10.1037/0012-1649.42.3.486

Dupre, M. E., Beck, A. N., & Meadows, S. O. (2009). Marital trajectories and mortality among U.S. adults. *American Journal of Epidemiology, 170*, 546–555. doi:10.1093/aje/kwp194

Dupre, M. E., & Meadows, S. O. (2007). Disaggregating the effects of marital trajectories on health. *Journal of Family Issues, 28*, 623–652. doi:10.1177/0192513X06296296

Dush, C. M. K., Cohan, C. L., & Amato, P. R. (2003). The relationship between cohabitation and marital quality and stability: Change across cohorts? *Journal of Marriage and Family, 65*, 539–549. doi:10.1111/j.1741-3737.2003.00539.x

Emery, R. E. (1982). Interparental conflict and the children of discord and divorce. *Psychological Bulletin, 92*, 310–330. doi:10.1037/0033-2909.92.2.310

Emery, R. E. (1994). *Renegotiating family relationships: Divorce, child custody, and mediation.* New York, NY: Guilford Press.

Emery, R. E. (1999). *Marriage, divorce, and children's adjustment* (2nd ed.). Thousand Oaks, CA: Sage.

Emery, R. E. (2001). Promoting a positive, pluralistic, and inclusive model of marriage. *Virginia Journal of Social Policy and the Law, 9*, 153–162.

Emery, R. E. (2004). *The truth about children and divorce: Dealing with the emotions so you and your children can thrive.* New York, NY: Viking/Penguin.

Emery, R. E. (in press). *Renegotiating family relationships: Divorce, child custody, and mediation* (2nd ed.). New York, NY: Guilford Press.

Emery, R. E., & Forehand, R. (1994). Parental divorce and children's well-being: A focus on resilience. In R. J. Haggerty, L. Sherrod, N. Garmezy, & M. Rutter (Eds.), *Risk and resilience in children* (pp. 64–99). London, England: Cambridge University Press.

Emery, R. E., Kitzmann, K. M., & Waldron, M. (1999). Psychological interventions for separated and divorced families. In E. M. Hetherington (Ed.), *Coping with divorce, single parenting, and remarriage: A risk and resiliency perspective* (pp. 323–344). Mahwah, NJ: Erlbaum.

Emery, R. E., Laumann-Billings, L., Waldron, M., Sbarra, D. A., & Dillon, P. (2001). Child custody mediation and litigation: Custody, contact, and co-parenting 12 years after initial dispute resolution. *Journal of Consulting and Clinical Psychology, 69*, 323–332. doi:10.1037/0022-006X.69.2.323

Emery, R. E., Otto, R. K., & O'Donohue, W. (2005). Custody disputed. *Scientific American Mind, 16*, 64–67. doi:10.1038/scientificamericanmind1005-64

Emery, R. E., Sbarra, D. S., & Grover, T. (2005). Divorce mediation: Research and reflections. *Family Court Review, 43*, 22–37. doi:10.1111/j.1744-1617.2005. 00005.x

Emery, R. E., & Wyer, M. M. (1987). Child custody mediation and litigation: An experimental evaluation of the experience of parents. *Journal of Consulting and Clinical Psychology, 55*, 179–186. doi:10.1037/0022-006X.55.2.179

Gabardi, L., & Rosen, L. A. (1993). Intimate relationships: College students from divorced and intact families. *Journal of Divorce & Remarriage, 18*, 25–56.

Gauthier, A. H. (1996). *The state and the family: A comparative analysis of family policies in industrialized countries.* Oxford, England: Clarendon Press.

Gove, W. R., Hughes, M., & Style, C. B. (1983). Does marriage have positive effects on psychological well-being of the individual? *Journal of Health and Social Behavior, 24*, 122–131. doi:10.2307/2136639

Graefe, D. R., & Lichter, D. T. (2008). Marriage patterns among unwed mothers: Before and after PRWORA. *Journal of Policy Analysis and Management, 27,* 479–497. doi:10.1002/pam.20352

Guzzo, K. B. (2009). Marital intentions and the stability of first cohabitations. *Journal of Family Issues, 30,* 179–205. doi:10.1177/0192513X08323694

Hetherington, E. M., & Kelly, J. (2002). *For better or for worse: Divorce reconsidered.* New York, NY: Norton.

Hewitt, B., & de Vaus, D. (2009). Change in the association between premarital cohabitation and separation, Australia 1945-2000. *Journal of Marriage and Family, 71,* 353–361. doi:10.1111/j.1741-3737.2009.00604.x

Hope, S., Rodgers, B., & Power, C. (1999). Marital status transitions and psychological distress: Longitudinal evidence from a national population sample. *Psychological Medicine, 29,* 381–389.

Hughes, M. E., & Waite, L. J. (2009). Marital biography and health at midlife. *Journal of Health and Social Behavior, 50,* 344–358. doi:10.1177/002214650905000307

Jacquet, S. E., & Surra, C. A. (2001). Parental divorce and premarital couples: Commitment and other relationship characteristics. *Journal of Marriage and Family, 63,* 627–638. doi:10.1111/j.1741-3737.2001.00627.x

Jansen, M., Mortelmans, D., & Snoeckx, L. (2009). Repartnering and (re)employment: Strategies to cope with the economic consequences of partnership dissolution. *Journal of Marriage and Family, 71,* 1271–1293. doi:10.1111/j.1741-3737.2009.00668.x

Johnson, D. R., & Wu, J. (2002). An empirical test of crisis, social selection, and role explanations of the relationship between marital disruption and psychological distress: A pooled time-series analysis of four-wave panel data. *Journal of Marriage and Family, 64,* 211–224. doi:10.1111/j.1741-3737.2002.00211.x

Johnston, J. R., Kline, M., & Tschann, J. M. (1989). Ongoing post-divorce conflict in families contesting custody: Effects on children of joint custody and frequent access. *American Journal of Orthopsychiatry, 59,* 576–592. doi:10.1111/j.1939-0025.1989.tb02748.x

Jose, A., O'Leary, D., & Moyer, A. (2010). Does premarital cohabitation predict subsequent marital instability and marital quality? A meta-analysis. *Journal of Marriage and Family, 72,* 105–116. doi:10.1111/j.1741-3737.2009.00686.x

Kiernan, K. (2002). Cohabitation in Western Europe: Trends, issues, and implications. In A. Booth & A. C. Crouter (Eds.), *Just living together: Implications of cohabitation on families, children, and social policy* (pp. 3–31). Mahwah, NJ: Erlbaum.

Kim, K. H. (2006). *Statistics for early study abroad students* (Korean Education Department, in Korean). Retrieved from http://www.mest.go.kr/me_kor/inform/1/2/1207871_10862.html

Kline, G. H., Stanley, S. M., Markman, H. J., Olmos-Gallo, P. A., St. Peters, M., Whitton, S. W., & Prado, L. M. (2004). Timing is everything: Pre-engagement cohabitation and increased risk for poor marital outcomes. *Journal of Family Psychology, 18,* 311–318. doi:10.1037/0893-3200.18.2.311

Kruk, E. (2005). Shared parental responsibility: A harm reduction-based approach to divorce law reform. *Journal of Divorce & Remarriage, 43,* 119–140. doi:10.1300/J087v43n03_07

Laumann, E., Gagnon, J. H., Michael, R. T., & Michaels, S. (1994). *The social organization of sexuality: Sexual practices in the United States.* Chicago, IL: University of Chicago Press.

Laumann-Billings, L., & Emery, R. E. (2000). Distress among young adults from divorced families. *Journal of Family Psychology, 14,* 671–687. doi:10.1037/0893-3200.14.4.671

Lind, G. (2008). *Common law marriage: A legal institution for cohabitation.* New York, NY: Oxford University Press.

Lucas, R. E. (2005). Time does not heal all wounds: A longitudinal study of reaction and adaptation to divorce. *Psychological Science, 16,* 945–950. doi:10.1111/j.1467-9280.2005.01642.x

Maccoby, E. E., & Mnookin, R. H. (1992). *Dividing the child: Social and legal dilemmas of custody.* Cambridge, MA: Harvard University Press.

Manning, W. D., & Landale, N. S. (1996). Racial and ethnic differences in the role of cohabitation and premarital childbearing. *Journal of Marriage and Family, 58,* 63–77. doi:10.2307/353377

Manning, W. D., Longmore, M. A., & Giordano, P. C. (2007). The changing institution of marriage: Adolescent expectations to cohabit and to marry. *Journal of Marriage and Family, 69,* 559–575. doi:10.1111/j.1741-3737.2007.00392.x

Manning, W. D., & Smock, P. J. (1995). Why marry? Race and the transition to marriage among cohabitors. *Demography, 32,* 509–520. doi:10.2307/2061671

Markman, H. J., Floyd, F., Stanley, S. M., & Lewis, H. C. (1986). Prevention. In N. Jacobson & A. Gurman (Eds.), *Clinical handbook of marital therapy* (pp. 173–195). New York, NY: Guilford Press.

McLanahan, S. S. (2003). Fragile families and the marriage agenda. In L. Kowaleski-Jones & N. H. Wilfinger (Eds.), *Fragile families and the marriage agenda* (pp. 1–21). New York, NY: Springer.

McLanahan, S., & Sandefur, G. D. (1994). *Growing up with a single parent: What hurts? What helps?* Cambridge, MA: Harvard University Press.

Miller, J. G. (1994). Cultural diversity in the morality of caring: Individually oriented versus duty-based interpersonal moral codes. *Cross-Cultural Research, 28,* 3–39. doi:10.1177/106939719402800101

Nock, S. L. (1995). A comparison of marriages and cohabiting relationships. *Journal of Family Issues, 16,* 53–76. doi:10.1177/019251395016001004

Ogburn, W. F. (1953). *The changing functions of the family: Selected studies in marriage and the family.* New York, NY: Holt.

Pedersen, W., & Blekesaune, M. (2003). Sexual satisfaction in young adulthood: Cohabitation, committed dating or unattached life? *Acta Sociologica, 46*, 179–193. doi:10.1177/00016993030463001

Pedro-Carroll, J. L., & Alpert-Gillis, L. J. (1997). Preventive interventions for children of divorce: A developmental model for 5 and 6 year old children. *The Journal of Primary Prevention, 18*, 5–23. doi:10.1023/A:1024601421020

Peterson, R. R. (1996). A re-evaluation of the economic consequences of divorce. *American Sociological Review, 61*, 528–536. doi:10.2307/2096363

Power, C., Rodgers, B., & Hope, S. (1999). Heavy alcohol consumption and marital status: Disentangling the relationship in a national study of young adults. *Addiction, 94*, 1477–1487. doi:10.1046/j.1360-0443.1999.941014774.x

Rhoades, G. K., Stanley, S. M., & Markman, H. J. (2009a). Couples' reasons for cohabitation: Associations with individual well-being and relationship quality. *Journal of Family Issues, 30*, 233–258. doi:10.1177/0192513X08324388

Rhoades, G. K., Stanley, S. M., & Markman, H. J. (2009b). The pre-engagement cohabitation effect: A replication and extension of previous findings. *Journal of Family Psychology, 23*, 107–111. doi:10.1037/a0014358

Rindfuss, R. R., Choe, M. K., Bumpass, L. L., & Byun, Y. C. (2004). Intergenerational relations. In N. O. Tsuya & L. L. Bumpass (Eds.), *Marriage, work, and family life in a comparative perspective* (pp. 54–75). Honolulu, HI: University of Hawaii Press.

Santeramo, J. L. (2004). Early neutral evaluation in divorce cases. *Family Court Review, 42*, 321–341. doi:10.1177/1531244504422011

Sassler, S., Cunningham, A., & Lichter, D. T. (2009). Intergenerational patterns of union formation and relationship quality. *Journal of Family Issues, 30*, 757–786. doi:10.1177/0192513X09331580

Sbarra, D. A., & Emery, R. E. (2008). Deeper into divorce: Using actor-partner analyses to explore systemic differences in coparenting following mediation and litigation of custody disputes. *Journal of Family Psychology, 22*, 144–152. doi: 10.1037/0893-3200.22.1.144

Sbarra, D. A., & Nietert, P. J. (2009). Divorce and death: Forty years of the Charleston Heart Study. *Psychological Science, 1*, 107–133.

Schepard, A. I. (2004). *Children, courts, and custody: Interdisciplinary models for divorcing families*. New York, NY: Cambridge University Press.

Seltzer, J. A. (1991). Relationships between fathers and children who live apart: The father's role after separation. *Journal of Marriage and Family, 53*, 79–101.

Seltzer, J. A. (2004). Cohabitation in the United States and Britain: Demography, kinship, and the future. *Journal of Marriage and Family, 66*, 921–928. doi:10.1111/j.0022-2445.2004.00062.x

Simon, R. W. (2002). Revisiting the relationships among gender, marital status, and mental health. *American Journal of Sociology, 107*, 1065–1096. doi:10.1086/339225

Stanley, S. M., Amato, P. R., Johnson, C. A., & Markman, H. J. (2006). Premarital education, martial quality, and marital instability: Findings from a large, random household survey. *Journal of Family Psychology, 20*, 117–126. doi:10.1037/0893-3200.20.1.117

Stanley, S. M., Rhoades, G. K., & Markman, H. J. (2006). Sliding versus deciding: Inertia and the premarital cohabitation effect. *Family Relations, 55*, 499–509. doi:10.1111/j.1741-3729.2006.00418.x

Teachman, J. D., & Polonko, K. A. (1990). Cohabitation and marital stability in the United States. *Social Forces, 69*, 207–220. doi:10.2307/2579614

Tejada-Vera, B., & Sutton, P. D. (2009). *Births, marriages, divorces, and deaths: Provisional data for 2008. National Vital Statistics Reports, 57*(19). Hyattsville, MD: National Center for Health Statistics.

Tesler, P. H., & Thompson, P. (2007). *Collaborative divorce: The revolutionary new way to restructure your family, resolve legal issues, and move on with your life*. New York, NY: ReganBooks.

Thornton, A. (1991). Influence of marital history of parents on the marital and cohabitational experiences of children. *American Journal of Sociology, 96*, 868–894. doi:10.1086/229611

Thornton, A., Axinn, W. G., & Hill, D. H. (1992). Reciprocal effects of religiosity, cohabitation, and marriage. *American Journal of Sociology, 98*, 628–651. doi:10.1086/230051

Uunk, W. (2004). The economic consequences of divorce for women in the European Union: The impact of welfare state arrangements. *European Journal of Population, 20*, 251–285. doi:10.1007/s10680-004-1694-0

United Nations. (2007). *Demographic yearbook*. New York, NY: Author. Retrieved from http://unstats.un.org/unsd/demographic/products/dyb/dyb2.htm

U.S. Census Bureau. (1998). Household and family characteristics: March 1998 (update). *Current Population Reports, Series P20–515, Special Censuses*. Washington, DC: U.S. Government Printing Office.

U.S. Census Bureau. (2009). *Family and living arrangements characteristics: Estimated median age at first marriage, by sex: 1890 to the present* (Historical Time Series, Table MS-2). Washington, DC: U.S. Government Printing Office. Retrieved from http://www.census.gov/population/www/socdemo/hh-fam.html#ht

Ventura, S. J. (2009). *Changing patterns of nonmarital childbearing in the United States* (NCHS Data Brief No. 18). Hyattsville, MD: National Center for Health Statistics.

Wade, T. J., & Pevalin, D. J. (2004). Marital transitions and mental health. *Journal of Health and Social Behavior, 45*, 155–170. doi:10.1177/002214650404500203

Waite, L. J., & Gallagher, M. (2000). *The case for marriage: Why married people are happier, healthier, and better off financially*. New York, NY: Doubleday.

Wallerstein, J. S. (1985). Children of divorce: Preliminary report of a ten-year follow-up of older children and adolescents. *Journal of the American Academy of Child Psychiatry, 24*, 545–553. doi:10.1016/S0002-7138(09)60055-8

Wallerstein, J. S., Lewis, J. M., & Blakeslee, S. (2000). *The unexpected legacy of divorce: The 25 year landmark study.* New York, NY: Hyperion.

Wolchik, S. A., West, S. G., Westover, S., Sandler, I. N., Martin, A., Lustig, J., . . . Fisher, J. (1993). The Children of Divorce Intervention Project: Outcome evaluation of an empirically based parenting program. *American Journal of Community Psychology, 21*, 293–331. doi:10.1007/BF00941505

Woods, L. N., & Emery, R. E. (2002). The cohabitation effect on divorce: Causation or selection? *Journal of Divorce & Remarriage, 37*, 101–122. doi:10.1300/J087 v37n03_06

IV

CONCLUSIONS

11

A PATH TO INTERDISCIPLINARY SCHOLARSHIP

ALETHA C. HUSTON

Social scientists and funding agencies have repeatedly touted the value of interdisciplinary approaches for extending knowledge beyond the silos of particular disciplines. Much of the research on close relationships has interdisciplinary roots or important intellectual, theoretical, and empirical connections with a range of disciplines, but true interdisciplinary scholarship is often elusive, in part because individual scholars learn modes of thought, theoretical models, and methodological preferences that are strongly maintained and reinforced by the universities, journals, and granting agencies attached to their disciplines (see Chapters 1 and 12, this volume).

I would not classify myself as a relationships scholar, but my experience in practicing interdisciplinary scholarship can apply across many topics in the social sciences. Over the 40-some years of my career, I have come to appreciate and take for granted the value of cross-disciplinary collaborations, particularly for investigating such applied topics as understanding the effects of public policies on family functioning and children's development. My training and early work as a developmental psychologist formed the core of my thinking, but the theories and tools of developmental psychology no longer seem sufficient to understand important social phenomena. The process by which this change came about and the value it has added to my work are the topics of this chapter. In the final section, using illustrations from my work on children's development, I attempt to draw some generalizations about the processes and structures that create environments for truly interdisciplinary scholarship.

DEFINITIONS OF INTERDISCIPLINARY

The terms *interdisciplinary*, *multidisciplinary*, and *cross-disciplinary* are sometimes used interchangeably, but interdisciplinary conveys most clearly the idea of true integration of disciplines at the levels of concepts, assumptions, theories, methods, and interpretation. The stages of young children's peer interactions provide a metaphor for different levels of such integration. The first is parallel play—side-by-side but essentially independent (e.g., drawing pictures on adjacent easels). In research, collections of papers or conferences bringing together people from different disciplines might be examples. Associative play occurs when children interact somewhat independently around a set of materials (e.g., building separate structures with one set of blocks). Research projects with both quantitative and qualitative components may fall in this category if the two approaches are pursued relatively independently. Cooperative play involves interdependent interactions (e.g., building one structure with each child placing blocks on those placed by the other); reaching truly integrated scholarship at this level involves interactions among disciplines in which each builds on and is responsive to the others. Over the course of my career, I have been involved in some multidisciplinary activities that probably qualify for the parallel play level, but in the last 20 years, I have had the good fortune to take part in research that is more truly interdisciplinary.

THEMES IN MY RESEARCH

Like many college students, I majored in psychology because I wanted to help people. Interventions in childhood seemed most promising for changing the course of dysfunctional or deviant behavior; hence, the natural pathway was graduate training in child clinical psychology. Although I chose to pursue research rather than clinical practice after my degree, a strong commitment to generating knowledge about important social problems led to research on several topic areas, united under the broad rubric of socialization influences outside the family. No one disputes the importance of families for child development (see Chapters 5, 6, and 10), but families live in broader contexts, a point that has been imprinted on the thinking of many in our field by Bronfenbrenner's ecological model placing the child at the center of (and in interaction with) a set of systems representing proximal and distal contexts

(Bronfenbrenner & Morris, 1998). Encompassing those multiple contexts requires the knowledge and tools of several disciplines.

Gender

Gender development, particularly for females, was the first topic to occupy several years of my life. This work began with efforts to understand how sex stereotypes affected achievement effort, using conventional laboratory research approaches. The women's movement exploded into full bloom a few years after this line of investigation began, leading the field to scholarship that incorporated psychology, sociology, and anthropology and, more important, making obvious the interplay between social values and assumptions of social scientists. Psychological theorists made a 180-degree turn away from assuming that "good" socialization outcomes were masculinity for boys and femininity for girls to assuming that sex stereotyping was "bad" and androgyny was "good." Suddenly, we were asking what processes reduced adherence to stereotypes rather than investigating the child-rearing practices that led to "appropriate" sex roles. Despite these changes, for the most part the scholarship around gender, including my own, was not interdisciplinary. That is, individual scholars addressed the issues within their own disciplinary theories and approaches. At best, it might be classified as cross-disciplinary (see Huston, 1983).

Television and Children

My second foray into a pressing social problem—the effects of television on children—came about as a result of an invitation from the National Institute of Mental Health (NIMH) to apply for a grant in its program of research on television and social behavior. The NIMH program was conducted at the direction of Congress to inform the Surgeon General's Scientific Advisory Committee on Television and Social Behavior. During a period of urban riots, student protests, and the war in Indochina, policy makers wanted to know whether television violence contributed to aggression.

Rather than organizing one large, comprehensive study, NIMH funded approximately 20 projects ranging from content analyses of media to surveys of viewing to experiments guided largely by psychological theories (e.g., Bandura, 1977; Berkowitz, 1990). Although a range of disciplines was represented, each study remained a separate entity brought together in a series of volumes, along with one or two meetings of the investigators after the research was conducted. I would argue that this approach is at the very lowest level of interdisciplinarity. Research from different disciplines was assembled in a multivolume series and one summary volume (Surgeon General's Scientific Advisory Committee on Social Behavior, 1971), but there is little evidence that the approaches represented in the various studies influenced the assumptions, theories, methods, or interpretations in individual papers. The metaphor of parallel play characterizes this approach.

Although I continued doing media research for many years, creating with my husband, John Wright, the Center for Research on the Influences of Television on Children, our work was guided primarily by psychological theories of children's cognitive and social development. We had occasional collaboration with mass communication researchers (http://www.he.utexas.edu/web/CRITC). I do not mean to dismiss the value of the work, but it was not interdisciplinary.

Poverty and Public Policy

My research in more recent years on a set of related issues—poverty, public policy, child care, and child development—provides a good case study of interdisciplinary research. Poverty among children became a salient issue in the United States in the 1980s, partly because, after record low levels of child poverty in the late 1960s and 1970s, the percentage of children living in poverty rose sharply in the 1980s. At the same time, public policy became an explicit topic for child development research through the visible contributions of such scholars as Ed Zigler and Urie Bronfenbrenner. The question for some of us revolved around how to do scientifically respectable and valid research that went beyond political rhetoric. I turned to the people who have been studying political life for a long time—the political scientists.

Learning About Policy Analysis

The University of Kansas, where I was a faculty member at the time, had a program called an "intrauniversity professorship"—an internal sabbatical for faculty members to study a discipline outside their major fields—that allowed me to spend a year studying public policy analysis in the Department of Political Science, sitting in on courses, talking with faculty, and reading extensively about policy research on welfare, employment, and poverty programs. That intensive period of immersion in political science, or more accurately, the field of policy analysis within political science, opened my eyes to basic disciplinary differences in underlying assumptions.

First and most important, individual and social-structural levels of analysis offer different perspectives. An experience in a women's consciousness-raising group in the early 1970s provides an illustrative example. One of the women said, "All women are prostitutes. Some marry as part of selling their bodies, and others don't." My gut reaction was to dismiss her comment as radical feminist rhetoric. At an individual level, I and other married people I knew did not feel that we were selling our bodies, but I came to appreciate that her comments had some truth as a statement about the structure of a society in which alliances with men were the primary and expected pathways for women to achieve financial support and security. Structural analyses help to define the social and economic parameters within which individual variations in ability and personality operate.

Second, although children's welfare is central to such disciplines as developmental psychology and education, children are relatively unimportant in the world of policy analysis. The tables of contents in most policy textbooks rarely included family policy, and never child policy. Children were discussed in connection with welfare policy primarily as economic burdens of their parents that posed impediments to employment. During the long debates about welfare "reform" in the 1990s, policy makers often had to be reminded that children were involved in the families they were discussing. In one hearing in which there was a debate about requiring women to work if their children were at least 3 years old, a staff member continually whispered reminders to the representative conducting the hearing that child care would be necessary.

Third, in policy analysis, the grounds for policy decisions are often economic rather than the social good. Child developmentalists tend to assume that demonstrating the efficacy of a policy to enhance child development is sufficient to lead to its adoption. In political science, a great deal of theory and empirical study is devoted to understanding the processes by which policies move from proposals to being adopted and implemented. Economic criteria—costs and benefits—play a major role not only in policy adoption, but also in evaluation. Since that time, economists and child developmentalists have developed effective collaborations around early childhood education and intervention—an illustration of interdisciplinary interactions that not only benefit the science but also increase its impact on policy (e.g., Karoly, Kilburn, & Cannon, 2005).

Finally, there is a difference between policy research and research "with implications for policy." Although psychological research is often valuable for informing choices among policies or practices, much of it does so indirectly. For example, research showing the influences of maternal employment on development does not provide information about the best policies to address those influences.

> According to one definition, *policy research* is: "research on, or analysis of, a fundamental social problem in order to provide policymakers with pragmatic, action oriented recommendations for alleviating the problem" (Majchrzak, 1984, p. 12). That is, policy research is designed to answer a question about what *actions* will or will not be effective in dealing with the problem studied, not just to understand its antecedents or consequences. . . . In the case of maternal employment, for example, one might study the effect of paid parental leave and/or quality infant child care on

parents' returns to work, family income, or child development. (Huston, 2005, p. 3)

Learning About Poverty Intervention Research

Because the year allowed me time to read a great deal, I discovered random-assignment experiments designed to test issues of public policy directly. In my academic world, research questions were generated by theory or sometimes by salient social issues (e.g., television), but this work was different; it was designed specifically to test policy solutions. The most interesting studies were several large-scale experiments testing the effects of a "negative income tax" on low-income families. In the late 1960s, proposals were floated to adjust the tax system to ensure that all families would have a minimum income—the mechanism would be a refundable tax credit that enhanced total income for individuals below some minimum level. The designs and interpretations of these studies were generated primarily by economists; for example, they tested different rates by which the credit was reduced as income increased. Most salient, from my point of view, was the fact that the dependent variables were almost all related to adult labor force participation. The major question addressed was whether the negative income tax would reduce work effort. Subsidiary questions dealt with the effects on marriage, divorce, and fertility. As I read these works, I kept asking myself, "Where are the children?" Even if labor force participation declined, which it did for some subgroups, might that be a positive influence on children? For example, in one study that included many large families, wives reduced work hours. Perhaps the families benefitted from mothers having more time at home. In another, teenagers reduced work hours, probably allowing them to devote more time to school (Rossi, & Lyall, 1978). A few scattered measures of children's school performance and health were collected (Salkind & Haskins, 1982), but few of the reports from these studies considered impacts on parenting, child development, or family relationships (with the exception of marriage and divorce).

Poverty Study Group

Invigorated by my newfound knowledge, I organized a small study group on children and poverty. The group consisted of eight people, including myself, an economist (Greg Duncan), a sociologist (Sara McLanahan), an education scholar (Henry Levin), a public health scholar (Lorraine Klerman), two psychologists (Vonnie McLoyd and Deborah Phillips), and a policy expert (Lizbeth Schorr). Prior to our meeting, many of these people did not know one another, but 3 days of discussion revolving around papers prepared ahead of time produced an exciting mix that led to the edited book *Children and Poverty* (Huston, 1991) as well as some later collaborations. Instead of having people present their papers, the group read them ahead of time, and a discussant appointed for each paper started the conversation, summarizing the major points and leaving plenty of time for productive discussion.

MacArthur Network

Policy research is difficult to conduct on the small scale that is available to most individual investigators. It requires "big science." The tricks are organizing the right mix of people and obtaining enough funding. My opportunity came through membership in the MacArthur Network on Successful Pathways Through Middle Childhood, which began in 1994 (http://childhood.isr.umich. edu/). The Human Development program at the MacArthur Foundation made a decision sometime in the early 1980s to be proactive in organizing programs of research on topics of importance rather than responding to field-initiated proposals. They formed a number of networks, each dealing with a particular age period (e.g., infancy, adolescence, middle age). The early networks were modeled on program project grants, with several groups of investigators doing coordinated studies, but by the time our network was formed, the model had changed. The group comprised 13 to 15 scholars from different institutions and different disciplines, carefully selected to represent a range of perspectives and methodological preferences. We were told that we had 7 years and a healthy budget to design and carry out some research on middle childhood (approximately ages 6–12) within some broad parameters. It should investigate successful development rather than concentrating on deviant or dysfunctional patterns; it should be applicable to important social problems; and it should be a bit risky, testing ideas and using methods that might be too unconventional for National Institutes of Health (NIH) funding.

We organized into groups around three topics: poverty, ethnic issues, and schools. One of the network members was Robert Granger, at that time a vice president at MDRC, a major nonprofit policy research organization known for random-assignment studies. At one of our early meetings, Granger offered the poverty group the opportunity to add some assessments of children and families to ongoing studies testing variations on welfare and employment policies for low-income adults. Here was the opportunity to address the frustration I had felt about the absence of such information in the early negative income tax experiments. After reviewing several ongoing studies, we identified the New Hope Project in Milwaukee as particularly interesting because it had features that seemed most likely to improve the well-being of families and children.

New Hope

Most of the 1990s experiments conducted at MDRC were designed to test potential changes in the welfare system (e.g., earnings disregards, time limits, mandatory job search), but New Hope was a community-initiated intervention intended to reduce poverty by making work pay. Its creators believed that work is the best route out of poverty and that public policies should ensure that people who work full time will not be poor. For participants who worked full time (30 hr a week), it offered wage supplements to bring total income above the poverty threshold, health care subsidies, and child care subsidies. All participants had access to supportive and respectful "project representatives" and to opportunities for community service jobs if they could not find full-time work. Because New Hope was likely to increase family incomes and to provide access to health care and to formal child care, we thought it had good potential to promote the development of children.

The true random-assignment experimental design of the evaluation offered a unique opportunity to test the effects of this package of benefits without concerns about confounding omitted variables. There was and is no doubt that children in poor families are disadvantaged in almost every area of development; they have lower levels of cognitive performance, more behavior problems, and worse health than children in more affluent families. The questions revolve around why. Is it material deprivation, low parent education, single-mother families, ethnic backgrounds, schools, or any of many factors known to correlate with poverty? Economists and policy makers are particularly interested in the importance of income per se, as opposed to other components of poverty, in part because income can be readily changed through policy (see, e.g., Duncan & Brooks-Gunn, 1997; Mayer 1997). The experimental design of New Hope was especially appealing because it allowed us to make causal statements about the effects of the package of benefits that it offered.

The collaboration to study New Hope evolved over time. When the MacArthur Network entered the scene, MDRC already had a contract to do a 2-year follow-up of the adult applicants to the program, who had been randomly assigned to be eligible for benefits or to be in a control group. Adult income, earnings, workforce participation, and welfare use were the primary dependent variables to be collected. Adding a multidisciplinary team interested in children and families not only expanded the scope of the study but also led to a conceptual framework laying out the theoretical basis for expecting program impacts on children. Evaluation research sometimes suffers from a "black box" approach—does it work or doesn't it? Having individuals with theoretical interest in the processes that connect a policy with an outcome can make such studies more useful and informative for both science and policy.

Our first step was to meet with staff, both local and national advisory boards, and representatives of the community to get their approval to add a child and family component to the planned 2-year survey. Some staff members were initially apprehensive about intruding on families' privacy with questions about children and parenting. (Ironically, it turned out that people were often happier to talk about their children than about their incomes.) We dealt with these fears by working closely with staff and with groups of adults in the community to review the measures we planned to use and, in one or two instances, changing measures they deemed inappropriate for the families, who were predominantly African American and Latino.

The 2-year follow-up demonstrated clear advantages of the program for children. In brief, teachers rated children in New Hope families higher on achievement, classroom behavior, and positive social skills, as well as lower on behavior problems (Huston et al, 2001). As a result, members of the MacArthur Network and MDRC collaborated in further follow-ups conducted 5 and 8 years after random assignment. These results are described elsewhere but are not detailed here because my major goal is to extract some possible generalizations from the process (Duncan, Huston, & Weisner, 2007).

Because the MacArthur Network included both quantitative and qualitative researchers, the New Hope study took on an important added dimension—an intensive ethnographic study of 40 families supervised by anthropologist Tom Weisner. Interviewers met frequently with the families over 3 years and then interviewed them again near the end of our 8-year follow-up. Qualitative and quantitative studies sometimes take place in tandem with little communication, but we were able to incorporate cross-talk in both design and interpretation. One example arose from the unexpected finding that New Hope had larger impacts on boys than on girls. Analyses of the ethnographic data led to a plausible interpretation—parents of children in middle childhood worried about their boys getting into gangs or being co-opted by older drug dealers. When parents had a little extra money, they were inclined to spend it on their boys. One mother talked about buying a $100 pair of shoes so her son would not steal to get them (Gibson-Davis & Duncan, 2005). Information from the ethnographic interviews informed the questions for the subsequent surveys, and survey results informed the topics explored in the ethnographic interviews, though we never fully understood the gender differences.

Next Generation

Still another sequel to the New Hope collaboration was the Next Generation Project, organized by Granger at MDRC, incorporating some of the MacArthur Network members with MDRC staff and some new investigators. While we had been collecting data on children and families in New Hope, others were obtaining quantitative and qualitative data on children and families in several of the welfare and employment experiments in which MDRC participated. The goal of the Next Generation Project was to synthesize the results of these studies through secondary analysis, using the variations in policies tested to draw conclusions about what policies or policy components were more positive (or perhaps more negative) for children.

Next Generation was organized differently from the MacArthur Network, in part because it had a specific set of policy research questions and in part because it was "housed" in a policy research firm. The investigators included senior and junior researchers and quantitative and qualitative experts from economics, psychology, sociology, public health, evaluation research, and anthropology. MDRC had had mixed experiences collaborating with academics, sometimes feeling as though they were being treated as research assistants to the academics who did the science. Granger's careful planning avoided that pitfall by creating three teams devoted to investigating three of the major paths by which welfare and employment policies were expected to affect children and families: parent employment, income, and child care. Each team was headed by a relatively junior, very talented staff member.

Next Generation produced substantive findings as well as methodological advances. Using a range of econometric techniques that were unfamiliar to psychologists, we were able to isolate the effects of employment, income, and child care, reaching the conclusion that policies produced positive effects on children's achievement and social behavior when they increased income and/or use of center-based child care (Morris, Gennetian, Duncan, & Huston, 2009). The employment team carried out a series of studies using qualitative and quantitative data to understand the nuances of employment effects on low-income women's families and children (Yoshikawa, Weisner, & Lowe, 2006). On the methodological side, we extended instrumental variables analyses in new ways that included multiple instruments based on multiple random assignment studies (Gennetian, Magnuson, & Morris, 2008).

Center for the Analysis of Pathways From Childhood to Adulthood

The MacArthur Network had initially elected to carry out a set of relatively discreet studies rather than one omnibus investigation of middle childhood. The school team conducted a mixed-methods longitudinal study to understand the relations of schools to development, following low-income children from kindergarten through fifth grade in three communities. The products included reports of quantitative data (e.g., Hauser-Cram, Warfield, Stadler, & Sirin, 2007) as well as narratives used in a set of "teaching cases" for students of education. Several mixed-method investigations of ethnic identity and diversity were gathered in an edited volume (Cooper, Garcia Coll, Bartko, Davis, & Chatman, 2007).

Nevertheless, as we approached the last few years of the network's existence, some members felt that we had not quite addressed the big question—

What environmental contexts are important influences on development in middle childhood? Put another way, does middle-childhood experience make a unique contribution to development (see Chapters 6 and 7)? Freud defined middle childhood as the "latency period," an uninteresting interlude between the early years and adolescence. In many respects, the developmental literature reflected that assumption. It was no coincidence that the network on middle childhood was almost the last to be created, well after networks on the infant/toddler period, adolescence, middle age, and old age.

To address the question of middle-childhood influences directly, we organized a group of scholars with longitudinal data to do analyses and write papers about family, school, out-of-school activities, peers, and poverty policy as contexts for development. To the extent possible, they examined how middle-childhood experiences made unique contributions, above and beyond those of experiences in early childhood, and whether middle-childhood influences endured through adolescence. The MacArthur Network sponsored meetings of the investigators to plan coordinated data analyses (a critical component for eventually integrating the results), a 2-day conference presenting the findings, and preparation of an edited book integrating the data (Huston & Ripke, 2006).

From this experience, a group of investigators at the University of Michigan was inspired by the promise of integrating results from different longitudinal studies. They created a center (Center for Analysis of Pathways From Childhood to Adulthood [CAPCA]) funded by the National Science Foundation (NSF), expanding the scope to understanding development across the life span with members drawn largely from the MacArthur-sponsored project. The center was sufficiently successful that NSF awarded another 5 years of support for its successor (http://www.rcgd.isr.umich.edu/capca/). Although the CAPCA projects dealt primarily with psychological questions of individual development, they retained some interdisciplinary flavor through the participation of key economists and through incorporating members from several European countries.

One sign of success is transmission to the next generation. Edward Lowe and Rashmita Mistry were both junior researchers in New Hope—Lowe on the ethnographic side and Mistry on the quantitative side. They and their students carried out a fine mixed-methods analysis of New Hope, deriving hypotheses about the role of material resources in family life from the ethnographic data that were then tested on the large sample with structural models (Mistry, Lowe, Benner, & Chien, 2008). Several of the graduate students studying with Greg Duncan at Northwestern University served as ethnographic interviewers, giving them new perspectives on data obtained by quantitative methods that influenced their subsequent work. The experience even increased their economist advisor's enthusiasm for qualitative information.

Child Care

The National Institute of Child Health and Human Development (NICHD) Study of Early Child Care and Youth Development (SECCYD) represents a different kind of collaborative big science and helps to illustrate both the advantages and disadvantages of the cross-disciplinary research I have described thus far (NICHD Early Child Care Research Network, 2005). In the late 1980s, NICHD issued a request for applications to participate in a study investigating the effects of infant child care on young children's development. The study would be naturalistic, not an experimental intervention, and longitudinal, following children from birth to age 3 years. Individual investigators applied to be part of a multisite study using a common protocol of measures. The exact design and measures were to be decided by a steering committee composed of a chairperson who did not represent any research site, the principal investigators, the NICHD project officer, and a representative of the data center that coordinated all data collection and analysis.

Of the 10 sites selected, most had coinvestigators, so the original contingent of people planning the study numbered over 20. In monthly meetings of the steering committee, we hammered out a design, a sampling plan, and initial measures, finally launching data collection about 18 months later. We identified mothers giving birth in selected hospitals during selected 24-hr time blocks as the initial sampling frame, beginning data collection when their infants were 1 month old. Ultimately, the study was continued beyond age 3 to the most recent wave measuring children at age 15 (Vandell, Belsky, Burchinal, Steinberg, & Vandergrift, 2010). It is one of the best if not the best longitudinal study of child development in the literature. The measures are comprehensive and theoretically based, and the quality of data collection is excellent (e.g., reliability of observers and testers, precision with which protocols were followed). It has yielded publications on a wide range of topics, including child care but going well beyond it into family processes, health, policy, schools, and neighborhoods (NICHD Early Child Care Research Network, 2005).

Although the SECCYD is an extremely valuable study conducted by excellent scholars, it is not interdisciplinary. Virtually all of the initial investigators and most of those who were added in the middle childhood and adolescent phases are developmental psychologists. They brought the best that their discipline had to offer to the study, but the absence of other disciplines led to some weaknesses as well. First, although the sample was drawn from 10 geographic areas in the United States, it was not designed to be nationally representative—a problem that might have been avoided if the team had included more sociologists. Second, many economists rejected causal claims about the effects of child care because the analytic methods relied on regressions with controls for a range of covariates—the standard procedure for many psychologists and other social scientists. Again, the issues of causal inference might have been dealt with earlier if the team had been more interdisciplinary. In a study designed to inform a public policy issue, it is important that the results are accepted as valid by people outside psychology.

Process: What Facilitates and What Inhibits Interdisciplinary Collaborations?

Universities and funding agencies frequently tout the value of interdisciplinary scholarship, but the efforts to create it often meet with limited success. The barriers can be formidable, particularly for junior scholars. Professional recognition and career advancement occur primarily within disciplines, represented by academic departments, professional organizations, and publication outlets (see Chapter 1). In my field, a publication in the most prestigious developmental journals is given more credit than one in another journal. Even when the work is interdisciplinary, publishing in a journal outside one's discipline can be difficult because its reviewers have different assumptions and standards than those internal to the discipline. It is often problematic to identify a journal that is appropriate and that reaches the intended audience.

A similar problem exists with grant reviews. The NIH Social Science and Population Studies Study Section, on which I served for 4 years, reviewed applications in economics, sociology, anthropology, historical demography, some aspects of child development, and gerontology. Pleasing reviewers from all of those disciplines was difficult, and qualitative studies fared very poorly, but at least there was a venue for research crossing some of the disciplines represented. When review committees are organized around disciplines, it is difficult to fit interdisciplinary research into any niche.

Interdisciplinary studies almost inevitably involve collaborations, often on the scope of big science. The reward structures in universities, on the other hand, are based on evaluating independent scholarship, making it especially difficult for early career scholars to participate in large-scale studies. Tenure committees look for first-authored and lone-authored papers. If a senior investigator is involved, others assume that person is the intellectual leader of the effort.

Academic departments face the same issues of reduced credit for the collaborative research done by their faculty. At the University of Texas, for example, credit for a grant goes to one department, giving no recognition to a department whose faculty members have shared grants on which a member of another department is principal investigator or a grant administered by a research center that promotes interdisciplinary collaboration.

Finally, for those of us doing policy research, the different cultures of academe and policy research organizations can pose problems. Policy research organizations work largely on contracts, taking on the questions that funders want answered. By definition, they usually study the policies that exist, not ones they create from theory. Compared with academic institutions, their time frames are typically shorter, the reward structures for employees are different, and their publication outlets are reports rather than journal articles or scholarly books.

Despite these barriers, I have been fortunate to participate in a number of successful and productive interdisciplinary collaborations. In what follows, I offer some observations from my own experiences about what made these efforts work as well as some observations about why they did not always do so. There are undoubtedly many other models and many routes by which some of the same goals can be achieved, but I believe these principles have some generality.

First, truly interdisciplinary scholarship requires participants to learn how to think in the lexicon of other disciplines, at least to some degree (see Chapter 12). Studying public policy analysis gave me insights into the assumptions of my own discipline as well as a better understanding of why topics were selected for policy analysis and how the research questions were framed. This kind of understanding can arise from formal study, but, like learning a foreign language, it probably requires continuous immersion to become deeply embedded in one's thinking. Working in an interdisciplinary team provides that immersion.

It is critical that scholars from different disciplines work together from the outset of research rather than coming together with finished products to discuss or to integrate. Regular and repeated face-to-face contact allows a generative process that ultimately goes beyond parallel play. The New Hope Project and the subsequent products of the MacArthur Network would probably not have happened without the assemblage of a critical mass of researchers from different disciplines with different methodological specialties. The frequent meetings provided time to germinate and refine ideas, and the variety of backgrounds and institutional affiliations led to connections with important sources of data. Research teams that met regularly over time could respond as the work evolved, planning the next steps together, often moving back and forth from one method to another. The interactions between the ethnographic and quantitative team members allowed the two methods to inform each other. Unfortunately, mixed methods often do not reach this level of integration; teams go their separate ways, with the ethnographic data used primarily as stories to illustrate quantitative findings.

Funders and employers need to create the institutional structures to make interdisciplinary work possible, particularly because such research often spans institutions. It is significant that the MacArthur Foundation specifically stated that it wanted the network to do some research that would probably be too risky for NIH or NSF. Certainly federal agencies would be unlikely to hand a group of social scientists a check with few restrictions or constraints on the kind of research that would be conducted. Once we had established that New Hope had significant impacts on children, we received NICHD grants for the subsequent waves of data collection, but the MacArthur funds and open approach were critical to initiating the work.

Administrative logistics have to be overcome. MDRC was the lead organization for the initial New Hope study, with subcontracts to the University of Texas, Northwestern University, and the University of California, Los Angeles. The MDRC contract had some wording about the right to review publications that violated the University of Texas rules about open publication. It took some negotiation to work out a compromise based on my assurance that I trusted MDRC not to suppress findings.

People are, of course, the critical components of any research enterprise. The kind of collaboration that I describe here is not for loners. One or two people ultimately left the MacArthur Network because they did not find the collaborative mode compatible. Participants need to "play well with others," respecting the positions and contributions of people with quite different sets of assumptions, knowledge, and background. Being comfortable with one's own competence and points of view is important, so long as one is still able to listen to others.

Trust and mutual respect underlay any successful collaboration. Social scientists are sometimes taught to devalue the methods and approaches in other disciplines. Successful collaboration requires not only overcoming such prejudices (e.g., the value of quantitative vs. qualitative methods) but also appreciating the value added by other approaches. Although there are no formulas for establishing trust, frequent face-to-face contacts provide opportunities to discuss disagreements, confront problems, and know the people one is working with. When communication is infrequent, misunderstandings can mushroom. Even with frequent contacts, however, mistrust can lead to wasted time arguing over relatively minor issues and can divert the enterprise away from the science.

Relationships among investigators matter. Prolonged and intensive work generates relationships that affect the scholarship produced. One unique feature of the MacArthur Network was annual "family meetings." One of the four annual network meetings was held in an attractive venue, and the foundation paid room and board for investigators' families to attend. (Of course, family members played while we worked.) As a result, we got to know each others' spouses and children, and they got to know one another. We watched the children grow over the 8 years of the network's existence, forming relationships with one another that went beyond the purely professional. The foundation's rationale for family meetings was that busy scholars were spending 10 to

12 days a year away from home at network meetings. Including families was not only a "reward" but also a way of acquainting families with the people and activities in the network—giving them a sense of belonging and involvement. It is impossible to know whether these family meetings enhanced the science we produced, but they certainly created bonds that enriched our experience of doing so that, I believe, increased the likelihood that we would continue collaborating after the network ended.

Possessiveness about data can become problematic. Economics and sociology have different traditions than psychology does about ownership of data, probably because they typically use publicly available data (e.g., census, large surveys), whereas we psychologists put time and effort into designing and collecting data. The members of the NICHD SECCYD, for example, assumed at the outset that the data belonged to us to analyze and publish. After the study was launched, however, NICHD came under increasing pressure to make federally funded data available for public use, creating a set of issues about timing of release and protection of the subjects' privacy. Having a clear understanding about ownership, availability, and access to the data from the outset can avoid these problems.

Fluid membership and incorporation of new people as needed characterized each of the successful enterprises I have described. There was never any sense that the MacArthur Network members were an elite group whose prestige had to be protected by excluding others. From the outset, additional senior and junior scholars were involved in individual studies. The network meetings often had invited guests who did presentations and met with ongoing groups, enriching our intellectual experience immensely and occasionally becoming more involved in network activities. Similar fluidity occurred in New Hope, Next Generation, and CAPCA, and it was specifically programmed in the NICHD SECCYD as the children aged when investigators with expertise in middle childhood and adolescence were added.

Training junior scholars is critical to building a cadre of people who will carry interdisciplinary research to its next level of integration. Postdoctoral fellows and graduate students participated in the individual studies spawned by the MacArthur Network, and both the Next Generation Project and CAPCA incorporated them explicitly into the basic structures. The Next Generation meetings in New York included many early career scholars as full members, and relatively junior investigators were the leaders of its three teams. CAPCA takes training one step farther, offering training workshops in statistical methods and mentoring graduate students and young scholars by incorporating them into the meetings and research of the center.

Finally, it is important to have agreements about publication credits, outlets, and opportunities. Playing fair and giving everyone a chance is essential, particularly for young investigators who have to satisfy the requirements of their universities and their professional colleagues. It may be easier for people from different disciplines than for individuals from the same discipline to share publication opportunities because they have different reward structures and different publication outlets. We published New Hope findings in child development, economic, and anthropology outlets.

In the SECCYD, the issue of publication credit arose early because the investigators came from the same discipline, had published on the topic of child care, and had a range of positions on the issues we were investigating. Who would be first author on the initial paper reporting the effects of child care on attachment? How would we deal with the need to have approximately 20 names on the list? The solution was a corporate author, the NICHD Early Child Care Research Network. Although it solved the problems of priority on named author papers, corporate authorship created other difficulties. Several universities refused to give full credit to faculty for the corporate authored papers, and abstracting services were not equipped to deal with a corporate author. Moreover, graduate students and junior investigators were excluded from authorship on network papers, a requirement that significantly reduced their participation at any level except as paid research assistants.

CONCLUDING REMARKS

Research by individual scholars within disciplines can be extremely valuable, but interdisciplinary research has the potential for unique contributions. It is almost required for the big science that appears necessary for solving many social problems. Investigators with different knowledge bases and different types of methodological expertise can bring the tools needed to create new approaches to questions and new means of generating answers. Bringing together the theories, methods, and know-how of scholars from a range of disciplines is essential to accomplishing the goal of contributing knowledge with application to social problems and social policy.

Actualizing the potential of interdisciplinary research can be difficult both because of investigators' training in single disciplines and because the institutional structures in which research occurs are not well designed to facilitate it. I am persuaded that interdisciplinary thinking and collaboration grow slowly through a process of immersion in thinking outside one's discipline, particularly in a context allowing the germination of new research. It requires time and openness to ideas outside one's usual circles. Funding structures that encourage individuals to engage in cross-disciplinary study, like the intrauniversity professorship, are one means to generate such research. Centers, networks, and groups of investigators within or across institutions are another, but funders have to be willing to take a chance by putting people in a common space and giving them latitude to create new ideas and approaches to research problems rather than requiring all of the details of the research before the funding is given.

Finally, relationships matter. Although I did not begin writing this chapter with the intention of discussing relationships, it became clear as I thought about my experiences that interactions, connections, trust, mutual respect, willingness to listen and consider another's point of view, ability to compromise, and willingness to do more than one's share are the grease that make interdisciplinary collaborations work over the long haul. These attributes sound familiar to anyone studying interpersonal relationships. They are not just luxuries that make life more pleasant; they are also essential to making the science as good as it can be.

REFERENCES

Bandura, A. (1977). *Social learning theory*. Englewood Cliffs, NJ: Prentice-Hall.

Berkowitz, L. (1990). On the formation and regulation of anger and aggression: A cognitive-neoassociationistic analysis. *American Psychologist, 45*, 494–503. doi: 10.1037/0003-066X.45.4.494

Bronfenbrenner, U., & Morris, P. A. (1998). The ecology of developmental processes. In W. Damon (Series Ed.) & R. M. Lerner (Volume Ed.), *Handbook of child psychology: Vol. 1. Theoretical models of human development* (5th ed., pp. 993–1028). New York, NY: Wiley.

Cooper, C. R., Garcia Coll, C. G., Bartko, W. T., Davis, H. M., & Chatman, C. M. (Eds.). (2007). *Developmental pathways through middle childhood: Rethinking contexts and diversity as resources*. Mahwah, NJ: Erlbaum.

Duncan, G. J., & Brooks-Gunn, J. (Eds.). (1997). *Consequences of growing up poor*. New York, NY: Russell Sage.

Duncan, G. J., Huston, A. C., & Weisner, T. S. (2007). *Higher ground: New Hope for the working poor and their children*. New York, NY: Russell Sage.

Gennetian, L. A., Magnuson, K., & Morris, P. A. (2008). From statistical associations to causation: What developmentalists can learn from instrumental variables techniques coupled with experimental data. *Developmental Psychology, 44*, 381–394. doi:10.1037/0012-1649.44.2.381

Gibson-Davis, C. M., & Duncan, G. J. (2005). *Qualitative/Quantitative Synergies in a Random-Assignment Program Evaluation*. In T. S. Weisner (Ed.), *Discovering successful pathways in children's development: Mixed methods in the study of childhood and family life* (pp. 283–304). Chicago, IL: University of Chicago Press.

Hauser-Cram, P., Warfield, M. E., Stadler, J., & Sirin, S. R. (2007). School environments and the diverging pathways of students living in poverty. In A. C. Huston

& M. N. Ripke (Eds.), *Developmental contexts in middle childhood: Bridges to adolescence and adulthood* (pp. 198–216). New York, NY: Cambridge University Press.

Huston, A. C. (1983). Sex typing. In P. H. Mussen (Series Ed.) & E. M. Hetherington (Vol. Ed.), *Handbook of child psychology: Vol. 4. Socialization, personality, and social development* (4th ed., pp. 387–467). New York, NY: Wiley.

Huston, A. C. (Ed.). (1991). *Children in poverty: Child development and public policy.* Cambridge, England: Cambridge University Press.

Huston, A. C. (2005). Connecting the science of child development to public policy. *Social Policy Report of the Society for Research in Child Development, 19,* 1–18.

Huston, A. C., Duncan, G. J., Granger, R., Bos, J., McLoyd, V., Mistry, R, . . . Ventura, A. (2001). Work-based antipoverty programs for parents can enhance the school performance and social behavior of children. *Child Development, 72,* 318–336. doi:10.1111/1467-8624.00281

Huston, A. C., & Ripke, M. N. (Eds.). (2006). *Developmental contexts in middle childhood: Bridges to adolescence and adulthood.* New York, NY: Cambridge University Press. doi:10.1017/CBO9780511499760

Karoly, L. A., Kilburn, M. R., & Cannon, J. S. (2005). *Early childhood interventions: Proven results, future promise.* Santa Monica, CA: Rand.

Majchrzak, A. (1984). *Methods for policy research.* Newbury Park, CA: Sage.

Mayer, S. E. (1997). *What money can't buy: Family income and children's life chances.* Cambridge, MA: Harvard University Press.

Mistry, R. S., Lowe, E. D., Benner, A. D., & Chien, N. (2008). Expanding the family economic stress model: Insights from a mixed-methods approach. *Journal of Marriage and Family, 70,* 196–209. doi:10.1111/j.1741-3737.2007.00471.x

Morris, P. A., Gennetian, L. A., Duncan, G. J., & Huston, A. C. (2009). How welfare policies affect child and adolescent school performance: Investigating pathways of influence with experimental data. In J. Ziliak (Ed.), *Welfare reform and its long-term consequences for America's poor* (pp. 255–289). New York, NY: Cambridge University Press.

NICHD Early Child Care Research Network (Ed.). (2005). *Child care and child development: Results from the NICHD Study of Early Child Care and Youth Development.* New York, NY: Guilford Press.

Rossi, P. H., & Lyall, K. C. (1978). An overview evaluation of the NIT experiment. In T. D. Cook, M. L. Del Rosario, K. M. Hennigan, M. M. Mark, & W. M. K. Trochim (Eds.), *Evaluation studies review annual* (Vol. 3, pp. 412–427). Beverly Hills, CA: Sage.

Salkind, N. J., & Haskins, R. (1982). Negative income tax: The impact on children from low-income families. *Journal of Family Issues, 3,* 165–180. doi:10.1177/019251382003002003

Surgeon General's Scientific Advisory Committee on Television and Social Behavior. (1971). *Television and growing up: The impact of televised violence.* Washington, DC: U.S. Department of Health, Education, and Welfare.

Vandell, D. L., Belsky, J., Burchinal, M., Steinberg, L., & Vandergrift, N. (2010). Do effects of early child care extend to age 15 years? Results from the NICHD Study of Early Child Care and Youth Development. *Child Development, 81*, 737–756. doi:10.1111/j.1467-8624.2010.01431.x

Yoshikawa, H., Weisner, T. S., & Lowe, E. D. (Eds.). (2006). *Making it work: Low-wage employment, family life, and child development*. New York, NY: Russell Sage.

12

BACK TO THE FUTURE: RESURRECTING AND VITALIZING THE UNREALIZED CALL FOR INTERDISCIPLINARY RESEARCH ON CLOSE RELATIONSHIPS

TIMOTHY J. LOVING AND TED L. HUSTON

The call in the subtitle of this book for an interdisciplinary integration of close relationships research is hardly a new one (see Chapter 1). The eminent social psychologist Harold Kelley (1983), in the concluding chapter of a book that sought to provide a blueprint for studying intimate relationships, made the case for an interdisciplinary science of relationships almost 30 years ago:

> Having concluded that a science of close relationships is essential, we must finally return to recognition of the interdependence between different levels of knowledge and the mutual interrelatedness among scientific efforts at the individual, close relationship, and societal levels. Close relationship research cannot afford, any more than can individual or social research, to be isolated from the efforts and results in neighboring disciplines. Many of its questions as well as many of its answers must be drawn from these associated areas. (p. 503)

Robert Hinde (1987), a Cambridge University ethologist, fleshed out a case for a transdisciplinary approach to the study of close relationships:

> The nature of an interaction or relationship depends on both participants. At the same time, the behaviour the participants show in each interaction depends on the nature of the relationship: What an individual does on

each occasion depends on his assessment of and expectations about the interaction in which he is involved. . . . Indeed, in the long run, the behaviour an individual *can* show is affected by the relationships he has experienced in the past. At the next level, participants' views of the relationship affect the nature of interactions within it, and the nature of the relationship is determined by its constituent interactions. And at the group level the relationship between A and B is affected by A's relationship with C, and thus the nexus of relationships in which it is embedded. . . . Furthermore, how individuals behave in any interactional context is influenced by the social norms current in the group, and by the rights and duties appropriate to persons in the role they are occupying. (p. 25)

Social psychologist Clyde Hendrick (1989) suggested that the examination of close relationships is central to the work of scholars with a variety of disciplinary concerns:

It seems clear that a new discipline has emerged. It is not a discipline in the usual sense because research interest spans several traditional disciplines, including psychology, sociology, communications, areas of home economics, anthropology, and philosophy. The study of personal relationships appears to be similar to the study of language: It is relevant to the interests of many academic disciplines, but no single discipline can encompass all of the relevant facets. Thus, the study of personal relationships must truly become a multidisciplinary enterprise. (p. 6)

More recently, prominent social scientists have begun take note that the early hope of multidisciplinary unification has not been realized:

Relationship research and theorizing is spread across several academic domains, each with its own assumptions, theories, and preferred methods; such domains include sociology, communication, clinical psychology, sociobiology, and social psychology. This is both the glory and the nemesis of the close relationship area. (Fletcher & Fitness, 1996, p. xii)

Once there is some consensus about the denotation of key terms across originating disciplines, then we can move to . . . truly interdisciplinary work . . . and . . . away from "disciplines at parallel play." (Perlman & Duck, 2006, p. 27)

As the foregoing quotations make abundantly clear, one constant over the past 3 decades is that prominent relationship scientists have continued to reiterate Kelly's call for an interdisciplinary integration of close relationships research. Unfortunately, close relationships researchers would be hard-pressed to find much evidence of significant progress toward achieving that integration. The reasons for this failing are multiple and reflect the broader challenges interdisciplinary research and researchers face across academic disciplines and departments regardless of subject matter (Campbell, 2005; Stokols, Misra,

Moser, Hall, & Taylor, 2008; see also Chapter 11, this volume). In many ways, the purpose of this edited volume is to add to the literary history of these calls in hopes that, one day, the field will finally overcome the disciplinary isolation that undermines a holistic understanding of close relationships.

In these final pages of this volume, we have chosen not to simply reiterate the reasons why such integration is necessary yet apparently elusive (see Campbell, 2005; Fincham, 1995). Instead, we briefly address four specific challenges close relationship scientists, across academic disciplines, must confront before integration is likely. First, we believe it critical that the basic meaning of the term *close relationship* not vary as a function of the disciplinary focus of the investigator. Second, but relatedly, researchers across disciplines must become more aware of the idiosyncratic language neighboring disciplines use to describe similar close relationships phenomenon. Third, and relevant to social psychologists in particular, the limited ability of experimental methods to inform "true" relationship processes must be recognized. Fourth and finally, we close with a few thoughts about what we believe this volume has, and has not, accomplished in regard to achieving an interdisciplinary integration.

WHAT IS A CLOSE RELATIONSHIP?

In order to focus on close relationships, it is essential to get some agreement on what the term encompasses. Otherwise, social scientists may reach discordant conclusions about the possibility of a synthesis not because the data are contradictory but because they are not studying the same kinds of phenomena. That so many social scientists for so long have made the call for synthesis with so little effect is noteworthy. We believe that such calls have gone unheeded in large part because the terms *close* and *personal* have become strongly identified with positive sentiments (e.g., love, affection, attachment, trust, forgiveness) and the intimacy-building behavior associated with them. The fact that the work carried out under the umbrella tends to concentrate on relationships that have a positive valence overall does not mean that negative elements are not given their due attention, of course. But because the relationships examined have a strong "voluntary" element, their hedonic tone is of central importance: Such relationships are largely created by good feelings, and they are often sundered if the climate turns sour and the good feelings are replaced by ambivalence or hostility.

There is reason to believe that framing the field in terms of attraction-based relationships would discourage the interest, for instance, of an anthropologist studying marriages arranged by kin, of a sociologist studying gender patterns in the division of household labor, or of a developmental psychologist interested in how parents inculcate values in their children or help them acquire the knowledge and skills necessary to succeed in adulthood. The phenomena of interest to these investigators are rooted in ongoing, highly interdependent relationships, but from the brief descriptions offered, such researchers are not necessarily interested in the hedonic character of the relationships, and if they were, it would be examined as one feature among a larger panoply of relationship matters. The anthropologist might focus on "culture" as embodied by shared understandings and expectations about the process of mate selection, the sociologist might be interested in gender politics, and the developmentalist might be interested in how kids internalize their parents' ideas of right and wrong.

These investigators pose an interesting dilemma for the "would-be" interdisciplinary field of close relationships. The lives of the partners are tightly wound, and the relationships have substance and importance to the people involved, but the individuals involved do not necessarily think their relationship is purposed by love.

Kelley and his colleagues (1983), more than 25 years ago, concluded that any relationship that has substance and a significant influence on the "partners" should be admitted to the pantheon of "close relationships":

> Close, as we use the term, is virtually synonymous with *influential*. People in close relationships have a great deal of impact on one another. Whether the impact is for good or ill for the individuals involved is a separate issue from classifying the relationship as close or not. So, too, is the question of whether the two people subjectively feel close or verbally report that they are close. There is little doubt that through interaction the individuals involved develop beliefs about their relationships (e.g., whether it is "close" or "superficial, or "happy" or "destructive") and about the partner (e.g., whether he or she is "sincere" or "loving"). The degree of correspondence between the participants' beliefs about the relationship and the investigator's actual description of properties of the actual relationship encompasses a large set of interesting questions. (p. 13)

This definition places emphasis on the impact each person's behavior has on the other—aggregated over time—with each partner's actions both affecting and being affected by the other (see Chapters 2 and 3). This broad definition encourages highly textured, multifaceted characterizations of ongoing relationships, ones that do not inevitably give priority to the kinds of interpersonal events that are particularly likely to reflect and to reinforce intimacy-building in relationships. We are not suggesting here that the development of a sense of "couple identity," a sense of secure bonding, is not important. The analysis of such bonds will always be central to any full-bodied understanding of how close relationships work. Indeed, we believe the study of how couples create and sustain intimacy in a relationship may prove a fertile site for interdisciplinary cross-fertilization; the roster of factors that affect intimacy in married couples cuts across disciplinary boundaries. Married couples' intimacy may be undermined by work schedules (that leave them with little time to be together), gender-related attributes such as stoicism in men, one or the other partner's high need for independence, a lack of common leisure interests that draw them together in enjoyable activity, a difficult temperament in one or both partners, attitudes about the allocation of obligations that encourage specialization in regard to household work (subsequently reducing opportunities to develop a shared sense of responsibility), a deep investment of one or both spouses in their children (or in their extended family), oversensitivity, stress that leads to self-absorption or depression, a lack of love or commitment to the marriage, and so on.

A broad integration of work on close relationships is possible, but only if social scientists embrace a more inclusive definition of *closeness*, one that does not define the term in ways that favor a particular type of close relationship, or does not narrow the focus to some limited feature of such relationships, or is built around models that most accurately describe dynamics in voluntary relationships. Ultimately, we believe a concerted effort by relationship scholars, regardless of disciplinary affiliation, to distinguish between phenomena applicable to close relationships versus a specific type of relationship will pave the way toward a true interdisciplinary integration. Or, as Ellen Berscheid (1995) so eloquently stated:

> These cultural definitions for behavior associated with relationship type are the gargantuan boulders on the relationship beach we are exploring, casting their dark shadows over us as, head stooped and magnifying glass in hand, we examine the pebbles that surround them. (p. 531)

IDIOSYNCRATIC LANGUAGES

The term *close relationship* tends to have different meanings across and within academic disciplines, but the problem does not end there; the lack of a common language is endemic in close relationships science (see Chapters 1 and 11). On a concrete level, such idiosyncratic languages across disciplines can inadvertently create the illusion that a particular research topic is understudied even when a large body of relevant work exists. One such example of how a lack of common language can undermine the genesis of research ideas and theory comes from investigation into the role outsiders have in adult romantic relationships.

Adult romantic relationships researchers have long known that couple members' friends and family have an impact on romantic relationship dynamics and outcomes (Agnew, Loving, & Drigotas, 2001; Huston, 2000; Milardo, Johnson, & Huston, 1983; Parks, Stan, & Eggert, 1983; Sprecher & Felmlee,

1992). We have both published on this topic and, not too long ago, would have claimed with some confidence that we were aware of the vast majority of relevant published research. Imagine our surprise and excitement when, after reading Kobak and Herres's chapter (Chapter 6), we found ourselves in a lengthy discussion about the implication of their work for investigations into the social context of adult romantic relationships.

Briefly, Kobak and Herres provide an excellent overview of their research regarding the strength and purpose of attachment bonds within the parent–child and adolescent peer context. One of the real highlights of their chapter is the developmental context in which they place adolescent maturation and the development of peer relationships. Among other things, their work underscores that the relative role of parents versus peers shifts throughout adolescence and, as such, the relative influence that parents versus peers will have on individuals' lives (and by extension, their romantic relationships) also shifts over time. Although clearly not novel in the developmental literature, few, if any, "adult relationships" researchers have approached the social network context of romantic relationships with such a developmental mindset. As a result, we would argue that much of this extant work by adult relationships researchers has been static, providing only a snapshot of network influences at one instance. It is important that the empirical and theoretical literature that serves as the foundation for Kobak and Herres's chapter has been accessible by common literature search mechanisms for some time. How did we miss it? Put simply: We were not searching with the right terms.

Imagine, for example, that a researcher trained in the social psychological tradition wanted to conduct a study on how friends might have an impact on romantic relationship outcomes. That researcher would most likely, using PsycINFO or a similar database, begin to search for papers via the terms *dating* and *friends* and might expand the search with key terms such as *adult romantic relationships* and *network members*, and so on. Such a search would generally pull up a large number of hits—but they would overwhelmingly represent work by other social psychologists. Moreover, the social psychologist likely would be most drawn to work by those in her or his discipline. In contrast, it is probably safe to say that developmental psychologists, at a minimum, would refer to the same subject matter as *late adolescence* or *emerging adult* romantic relationships, given that the vast majority of the social psychological studies on this topic focus on undergraduate college students (who are typically far younger than the cutoff of 25 years of age for the upper end of the *emerging adulthood* label; Arnett, 2000). Additionally, what social psychologists would call *friends* or *network members* are often described as *peer* relationships in the developmental literature.

These differences in language have important implications. Although a literature search will turn up some useful information, the nondevelopmentalist will uncover little to nothing regarding how and why we would expect different types of network members (e.g., peers and parents) to play different types of roles in romances at various points in life. Additionally, the Kobak and Herres chapter (see also Chapter 5) has the added benefit of highlighting the important effect socioeconomic status has on attachment hierarchies, which has the potential to offer a more holistic explanation for how peers influence "adult" romantic relationships across ethnic groups.

We realize we have provided a simplistic account of the process by which researchers search for relevant work. We do not, however, believe our simplistic account underrepresents reality; pick up any article on the social context of relationships and the cited literature will represent primarily offerings from a specific academic discipline. Granted, part of this phenomenon is driven by the target audience of a given paper. After all, if I expect my work to be read mostly by individuals from a single academic discipline, then why should I care that I have not necessarily cited related work from other disciplines? To this we can only argue that our critique is based on the assumption that the goal of close relationships researchers, regardless of disciplinary affiliation, is, or should be, to capture as accurately as possible the way real relationships function in the real world. This is not to say that all research endeavors have to be everything to everyone. Many very specific questions remain to be answered, and in many cases there is no need to adopt an interdisciplinary approach. But, at a minimum, we think it important that researchers always remain mindful of exactly what questions they have and have not answered and be cautious not to overgeneralize given the very limited contexts in which we often study close relationships phenomena.

CLOSE RELATIONSHIPS EXIST IN CONTEXTS AND OVER TIME

As we noted in the preceding section, one of the many benefits the developmental literature bestows on social psychological studies of close relationships phenomena is that developmentalists have long recognized that close relationships function differently in different contexts (e.g., socioeconomic status, age). Part of the reason we highlighted this specific discipline's contribution to relationship science is because of the limitations inherent in cross-sectional and experimental approaches to the study of close relationships. Whereas the latter are quite useful for studying and teasing apart microlevel processes, they often oversimplify the reality, which is that close relationships exist in much larger sociocultural environments (Berscheid, 1995; Levinger, 1994).

Thus, among the many benefits an inter- or multidisciplinary approach to the study of close relationships offers, we view the increase in the use of longitudinal methods, which are more apt to tap natural developmental shifts in close relationship functioning, as most critical. Further, integration of multiple disciplines' perspectives on close relationships is sure to bring sociocultural contexts to the forefront of theory building and study design (see Berscheid, 1995). We are certain such an expanded focus will make it quickly clear that simply reporting the ethnic composition of study/survey samples does not do justice to the important role that individual backgrounds and social contexts play in close relationship initiation, development, and functioning. Admittedly, such investigations are typically far costlier and time consuming than one-shot surveys or lab studies. But, if close relationship develop "through interaction," then studying these interactions as they occur over time seems not just warranted but also necessary.

CONCLUSION

Much of our focus in this final chapter has been directed at the social psychological approach to the study of relationships. We felt it prudent to cast a critical eye toward our own discipline and lines of research. But, we believe our general argument holds for other disciplines as well. The organization of social science into disciplines and subdisciplines encourages favoring some connections over others. Yet, there are excellent examples in the literature of what can happen when an interdisciplinary or multidisciplinary approach is adopted. Consider the enormous influence attachment theory has had on the field of close relationships. The adoption of, and application of, attachment theory by developmental psychologists, anthropologists, social psychologists, family studies scholars, and sociologists no doubt contributes significantly to the prominent representation of attachment theory in the close relationships literature (and this volume).

One of the strengths of this edited volume is that it brings together, in a single source, a diverse set of chapters on the topic of close relationships. Admittedly, this is a collection written primarily by psychologists. Thus, its "integration," per se, is by way of creating an avenue through which scholars will be exposed to writings they might otherwise never have come across. Without such opportunities, the cross-pollination of ideas remains an uphill battle; it is only through dialogue that ideas will fertilize and different languages will find a common voice.

REFERENCES

Agnew, C. R., Loving, T. J., & Drigotas, S. M. (2001). Substituting the forest for the trees: Social networks and the prediction of romantic relationship state and fate. *Journal of Personality and Social Psychology, 81,* 1042–1057. doi:10.1037/0022-3514.81.6.1042

Arnett, J. J. (2000). Emerging adulthood: A theory of development from the late teens through the twenties. *American Psychologist, 55,* 469–480. doi:10.1037/0003-066X.55.5.469

Berscheid, E. (1995). Help wanted: A grand theorist of interpersonal relationships, sociologist or anthropologist preferred. *Journal of Social and Personal Relationships, 12,* 529–533.

Campbell, D. T. (2005). Ethnocentrism of disciplines and the fish-scale model of omniscience. In S. J. Derry, C. D. Schunn, & M. A. Gernsbacher (Eds.), *Interdisciplinary collaboration: An emerging cognitive science* (pp. 3–21). Mahwah, NJ: Erlbaum.

Fincham, F. D. (1995). From the orthogenic principle to the fish-scale model of omniscience: Advancing understanding of personal relationships. *Journal of Social and Personal Relationships, 12,* 523–527. doi:10.1177/0265407595124004

Fletcher, G. J. O., & Fitness, J. (1996). *Knowledge structures in close relationships: A social psychological approach.* Mahwah, NJ: Erlbaum.

Hendrick, C. (1989). *Close relationships.* Thousand Oaks, CA: Sage.

Hinde, R. A. (1987). *Individuals, relationships and culture: Links between ethology and the social sciences.* New York, NY: Cambridge University Press.

Huston, T. L. (2000). The social ecology of marriage and other intimate unions. *Journal of Marriage and Family, 62,* 298–320. doi:10.1111/j.1741-3737.2000.00298.x

Kelley, H. H. (1983). Epilogue: An essential science. In H. H. Kelley, E. Berscheid, A. Christensen, J. H. Harvey, T. L. Huston, G. Levinger, . . . Peterson, D. R. (Eds.), *Close relationships* (pp. 486–503). New York, NY: Freeman.

Kelley, H. H., Berscheid, E., Christensen, A., Harvey, J. H., Huston, T. L., Levinger, G., & Peterson, D. R. (1983). *Close relationships.* New York, NY: Freeman.

Levinger, G. (1994). Figure versus ground: Micro- and macroperspectives on the social psychology of personal relationships. In R. Erber & R. Gilmour (Eds.), *Theoretical frameworks for personal relationships* (pp. 1–28). Hillsdale, NJ: Erlbaum.

Milardo, R. M., Johnson, M. P., & Huston, T. L. (1983). Developing close relationships: Changing patterns of interaction between pair members and social networks. *Journal of Personality and Social Psychology, 44,* 964–976. doi:10.1037/0022-3514.44.5.964

Parks, M. R., Stan, C. M., & Eggert, L. L. (1983). Romantic involvement and social network involvement. *Social Psychology Quarterly, 46,* 116–131. doi:10.2307/3033848

Perlman, D., & Duck, S. (2006). The seven seas of the study of personal relationships: From "the thousand islands" to interconnected waterways. In A. L. Vangelisti & D. Perlman (Eds.), *The Cambridge handbook of personal relationships* (pp. 11–34). New York, NY: Cambridge University Press. doi:10.1017/CBO9780511606632.002

Sprecher, S., & Felmlee, D. (1992). The influence of parents and friends on the quality and stability of romantic relationships: A three-wave longitudinal investigation. *Journal of Marriage and Family, 54,* 888–900. doi:10.2307/353170

Stokols, D., Misra, S., Moser, R. P., Hall, K. L., & Taylor, B. K. (2008). The ecology of team science: Understanding contextual influences on transdisciplinary collaboration. *American Journal of Preventive Medicine, 35,* S96–S115. doi:10.1016/j.amepre.2008.05.003

INDEX

Individual differences
    in adolescent attachment hierarchies
        and risky behaviors, 146–148
    in approach and avoidance
        motivation, 54–55
    in partner attachment
        representations, 163–164
Industrialization, 229–230, 241–242
Infidelity, 17
Inflammation, 89
Inhibition, 93
Institutional structures, 266–267
Integrated specificity model, 85–86
Intensity, 156
Interdependence
    cultural beliefs about, 120
    in human evolution, 27
    and peer influence, 128
    in relationship maintenance, 42
Interdisciplinary scholarship and
        research, 253–270, 273–280
    and boundaries between academic
        disciplines, 9
    child care in, 263–264
    children in, 255–256
    on close relationships, 4–10,
        273–277
    collaboration processes in, 264–269
    contexts and time in, 279–280
    definitions of, 254
    gender in, 255
    of MacArthur Network, 259–262
    on mate selection, 10–18
    meanings across academic disci-
        plines, 277–279
    on middle childhood, 262–263
    public policy in, 256–259
    television in, 255–256
Intergenerational obligations, 242
International trends, 228–230
Interpersonal processes, 92–95
IPI (Important People Interview), 141

Job stress, 185, 188–189
Joint physical custody, 234
Julien, D., 163
Junior scholars, 268

Kagan, J., 8
Karney, B. R., 185, 189

Kelley, Harold, 4, 273, 274, 276
Kemeny, M. E., 90–91, 94
Kenrick, D. T., 30
Kiecolt-Glaser, J. K., 29
King, K., 29
Kin networks, 144–146
Knobloch, L. K., 17
Knoester, C., 113
Kobak, R., 141, 147, 162, 278, 279
Kohut, H., 39
Kuhl, J., 66
Kulka, R. A., 29

Ladd, G. W., 110
Landis, K. R., 28–29
Language
    of academic disciplines, 7–8, 211,
        212, 277–279
    object, 211, 212
Latency period, 263
Latino families, 121–122, 124–129
Laursen, B., 119
Levels of analysis
    individual vs. social-structural,
        256–257
    in relationship science, 205–206
    in stress effects on marriage,
        181–188
Life span, 3–4, 112–113, 156–158
Literature, 4, 6–7
Longitudinal studies, 264
Lowe, Edward, 263
Lymphocytes, 90

MacArthur Network on Successful
        Pathways Through Middle
        Childhood, 259–263, 266, 268
Madsen, S. D., 163
Maintenance processes, 209–210
Major stressors, 192–193
Maladaptive response patterns, 186
Marital development, 179–197
    implications for public policy,
        195–197
    and marital satisfaction, 179–181
    stress as detrimental to, 191–195
    stress crossover effects on,
        188–191
    two-route model of effects of stress
        on, 181–188

Noonan, K. M., 217
Norsen, L. H., 29

Object languages, 211, 212
Ontogeny, 30
Operant conditioning, 68
Oppenheimer, V. K., 14
Organizational developmental
        perspective, 155–172
    differential predictions in, 171–172
    experience and expression of
            emotion in, 165–171
    relationship representations in,
            158–161
    on relationships across life span,
            156–158
    on romantic relationships, 161–164
Organized action sequences, 157
Origin, 209, 210
Oriña, M. M., 164
Ought-self regulatory focus, 61
Overly controlling parenting, 60
Overton, W. F., 207
Ovulation, 215, 219

Pain, 231–232
Pair-bonding, 214
Paley, B., 164
Paradigm, scientific, 211
Parallel play, 254
Parental influences on peer relations,
        109–129
    demographic variations in, 118–122
    existing theory on, 122–129
    with general parenting practices,
            114–115
    in global relationship processes,
            111–113
    mechanisms of, 113–114
    mediated pathways of, 117–118
    and social competence of children,
            115–117
    theories and frameworks for, 111
Parent–child relationship
    in approach and avoidance
            motivation, 53, 60–65
    in child development, 69–71
    disciplinary practices in, 115, 117
    as relationship template, 112–113
    security of, 71–72

Parenthood
    accelerated transition to, 147–148
    and stress resilience, 194–195
Parenting coordinators, 233
Parenting style
    authoritarian, 120–121
    coercive, 115, 117
    controlling, 60
    power-assertive, 115, 117
    responsive, 61–64
    unresponsive, 62–64
    variations in, with ethnicity,
            118–122
Parke, R. D., 110
Partners, alternative, 17–18
Passivity, 63
Pasupathi, M., 87–88
Payne, C. C., 164
Pearson, J., 164
Peer interactions, 254
Peer pressure, 122, 124–129
Peer relations. *See also* Parental
            influences on peer relations
    in adolescent social network,
            137–138
    attachment bonds of, 139
    and risky behaviors, 146–147
    social competence in, 167
Penton-Voak, I. S., 215
Perceived partner responsiveness, 27–45
    and capitalizing on positive events,
            38–42
    in health and well-being, 28–31
    as organizing principle, 31–35
    and personal well-being, 35–38
    and relationship maintenance,
            42–44
Perceptions, 34
Perlman, D., 274
Personalismo, 121
Personality traits, 6–7
Personal Responsibility and Work
        Opportunity Reconciliation Act,
        238
Personal success, 39
Personal well-being, 35–38
Phylogeny, 30, 209–210
Policy research organizations, 265–266
Porter, L. A., 29
Positive affectivity, 58, 59, 67

Positive events, 38–42
Positive illusions, 43–44
Possessiveness, 268
Poverty. *See also* Economic disadvantage
    and attachment hierarchies,
        143–146
    effects on children, 260–261
    intervention research on, 258
    and public policy, 256–259
    rates of children in, 256, 258–259
Power-assertive parenting, 115, 117
Prakash, K., 62
Predictions
    differential, 171–172
    in organizational perspective,
        156–157
    salient developmental experiences
        in, 158–159
Predispositions
    in approach and avoidance motiva-
        tion, 64–65
    genetic, 55–56, 59–60, 65
Primary caregivers
    affectional bonds with, 137
    attachment bonds with, 142
    early relationships with, 86, 157
    early representations of, 162–163
Primary care physicians, 36–37
Proinflammatory cytokines, 89–91
Prorelationship behaviors
    adaptive responding in, 184–187
    and marital development, 195–196
    stress-buffering model of, 187–188
Prosocial behavior, 42, 118
Proximate causation, 210, 212
PsychINFO database, 278
Psychoanalytic perspective, 112, 128
Publication credits, 268–269
Public policy
    children in, 232–235, 257
    on divorce, 235, 237–238
    external stress implications for,
        195–197
    on families, 228, 241–243
    on marriage, 196, 232, 235, 237
    organizations for research of,
        265–266
    and polarity of language between
        disciplines, 7–8
    and poverty, 256–259

    on psychological consequences of
        divorce, 230–237
    research with implications for,
        257–258

Qualitative data, 136, 261, 263
Quantitative data, 261

Random-assignment studies, 259–261
Reactivity, 185–186
Reciprocity, 110, 115, 119
Reed, G. M., 94
Reframing, 87, 93–94
Reis, H. T., 5, 29, 30, 32–34, 36, 41, 42
Relatedness, 36
Relationship representations
    and behavior in romantic
        relationships, 163–164
    of early attachment experiences, 162
    and early experiences, 158
    and social behavior, 158–161
Relationships. *See also specific headings*
    across lifespan, 4, 112–113, 156–158
    in adolescence, 135
    among research collaborators,
        267–268
    approach and avoidance motivation
        in, 71–72
    attraction-based, 275–276
    emotion in, 165–166
    as emotion regulators, 92–95
    evolutionary perspectives on,
        206–212
    in health and well-being, 84–86
    internal processes of, 180–181
    maintenance of, 42–44
    measures of, 169–170
    in mental health, 29–30
    nonmarital, 17–18
    primacy of family over other, 122
    superficial, 41–42
Relationship science
    central organizing principles for,
        31–33
    close relationships in, 4–6
    evolutionary perspectives in, 208,
        220–221
    levels of analysis in, 205–206
    need for, 273
    organizing principles for, 31–35

ABOUT THE EDITORS

Lorne Campbell earned his PhD in social psychology at Texas A&M University in 2001. He was an assistant professor at Simon Fraser University before joining the faculty at the University of Western Ontario in 2002, where he is currently an associate professor of psychology. From 2008 to 2009, Dr. Campbell was a Harrington Faculty Fellow at the University of Texas at Austin in the Department of Human Development and Family Sciences. Dr. Campbell is a recognized expert in the fields of interpersonal relationships, research design and data analysis, and evolutionary psychology. He is on the editorial board of the *Journal of Personality and Social Psychology* and *Personality and Social Psychology Bulletin* and is the editor of the journal *Personal Relationships*. His research is currently funded by the Social Science and Humanities Research Council of Canada, and his work has been published in the *Journal of Personality and Social Psychology*, *Personality and Social Psychology Bulletin*, *Personal Relationships*, *Personality and Individual Differences*, and the *Journal of Social and Personal Relationships*.

Timothy J. Loving received his PhD in social psychology from Purdue University in 2001. He is currently an associate professor in the University of Texas at

Austin's Department of Human Development and Family Sciences. Prior to arriving at Texas, he received postdoctoral training at the Ohio State University College of Medicine, where he was funded by a National Institutes of Health training grant in psychoneuroimmunology. Dr. Loving's research addresses the mental and physical health impact of relationship transitions, with a particular focus on affectively positive transitions (e.g., falling in love) and the role that network members serve as relationship partners adapt to these transitions. He is an associate editor of *Personal Relationships* and a member of the editorial board for the *Journal of Personality and Social Psychology*. His research is currently funded by a grant from the National Institute of Child Health and Human Development, and his work has been published in the *Journal of Personality and Social Psychology*, *Personal Relationships*, *Psychosomatic Medicine*, *Psychoneuroendocrinology*, and *Archives of General Psychiatry*.